P9-EDU-033

AUGUSTANA UNIVERSITY COLLEGE
LIBRARY

$5.9

OUR PRECARIOUS HABITAT

It isn't ignorance that causes the greatest harm; it's knowin so darned many things that aren't so.

Josh Billings

OUR PRECARIOUS HABITAT

REVISED EDITION

MELVIN A. BENARDE

W · W · NORTON & COMPANY · INC ·
NEW YORK

CAMROSE LUTHERAN COLLEGE
LIBRARY

TD
180
B45 / 13,066

Copyright © 1973, 1970 by W. W. Norton & Company, Inc.

Library of Congress Cataloging in Publication Data
Benarde, Melvin A.
    Our precarious habitat.
    Includes bibliographies.
    1. Pollution. 2. Man—Influence on nature.
3. Man—Influence of environment. I. Title.
TD180.B45 1973   301.31   72–13412
ISBN 0–393–06360–7
ISBN 0–393–09372–7 (pbk)

ALL RIGHTS RESERVED
Published simultaneously in Canada
by George J. McLeod Limited, Toronto
PRINTED IN THE UNITED STATES OF AMERICA

2 3 4 5 6 7 8 9 0

To my father and mother,
Isidor and Belle

Nothing in life is to be feared, it is only to be understood. Now is the time to understand more, so that we may fear less.

Marie Curie

CONTENTS

FOREWORD

Life for all of us is a continuous series of risks in a constantly changing world, where all too often we ourselves generate the forces that are potentially dangerous to us. We must, it seems, continually alter the world around us. We develop synthetic products and we alter the air we breathe, the water we drink, and the food we eat. We build cities, factories, and machines that generate waste, stress, and injury; and we create radioactive devices that can sow the seeds of further harm. As life becomes more congested and technology more advanced, these new factors may in turn become the agents of new diseases. Man's power to manipulate and exploit his world has obscured his appreciation of the damage he inflicts on the environment. We are, for example, only beginning to explore the implications of air and water pollution on the health of communities. Similarly, we actually know little about the effects on community health of ionizing radiation, noise, pesticides, and a host of other environmental pressures.

To cope with the increasing number of actual and potential environmental health problems at the community level requires a well-informed citizenry. My purpose in writing this book will have been achieved if the presentation enables the interested reader to evaluate these problems from a basis of knowledge and understanding, rather than of emotional fervor founded on ignorance, superstition, and prejudice. After considerable reflection, I have come to realize that the scientific community has almost entirely ignored the need of the general public to know how science and technology affect its life. This condition has gone on far too long and is one of the contributing reasons for the large readership of books and magazine articles of the "purple prose" variety.

As a working scientist, I have stood on the sidelines far too long watching this happen. Additionally, some years ago, when I began to instruct non-biologists in environmental health problems, I searched in vain for a suitable single volume that would be of use to students entering this area for the first time. An appropriate book was unavailable. From colleagues around the country I learned of the growing need for a pertinent text in this area, as an increasing number of formal courses in environmental health or environmental sciences were being instituted. The material gathered together herein can serve the needs of either a one- or a two-semester course. Although this is a dynamic, multidisciplinary area in which new findings occur almost daily, experience has shown that this material can provide a sound basis for more advanced training. It is hoped that the interested non-student—the general reader—will also find it helpful in understanding what is happening to this world.

Today, in retrospect, I'm satisfied and comfortable with these ideas from the foreword to the first edition. I'm satisfied that my efforts have brought a degree of reason to problems fraught with confusion and inflammatory rhetoric.

However, I am not so satisfied that I am ready to put down my pen. I am still sufficiently discomfited by the lack of understanding of environmental problems as well as means to attain their solution. Consequently, I feel the need to continue to write.

Happily, this is not solely my personal attitude. I have been encouraged to continue to write. The wide circulation of this book, the number of adoptions and invitations to speak, have indicated that students, teachers, and the general reader prefer substance to rhetoric and polemics. I have tried to continue this approach in this second edition.

The need most frequently mentioned was for a chapter on population. With the addition of Chapter 15, Population and Progress, I hope I have added a significant statement and filled a glaring lacuna. The obverse side of this coin was the removal of the former Chapter 15, Biological and Chemical Warfare. At present, it appears that biological warfare is a dodo bird—able to flap its wings, but getting nowhere for all its flapping. It is now widely accepted that biological warfare offers little more than some psychological effect, and that may not be worth the effort. Chemical warfare, if the Vietnam experience is any guide, is itself highly tenuous. The results obtained were equivocal as far as they went, and it will be some time before the ecological effects can be adequately evaluated. Consequently, the decision to drop this chapter met little resistance.

The title of this book could have been *Our Habitat*. However, after some consideration, I felt the need to insert *Precarious* to describe the *potentially hazardous* condition of our environment, one which there is yet time to repair.

Melvin A. Benarde

PRINCETON, NEW JERSEY
MAY 1972

ACKNOWLEDGMENT

The ideas presented in this book were tested and retested in discussions with many colleagues, who were forced to suffer my continued need to talk, to discuss, to question, and, most necessary, to argue controversial ideas.

The brunt of this testing fell upon one person, whose office—unfortunately for him, but fortunately for me—was always open. Dr. W. Brewster Snow of Rutgers University has that rare quality of being able to suffer a fool gladly; he suffered often. But he could give as good as he got, which meant that I had to back up everything I wrote or chuck it. Consequently, he forced me to refine and sharpen my thinking and writing. If this book is received as a significant contribution, he deserves a large measure of credit.

My gratitude is extended to Dr. Frank Jankowski of the Department of Nuclear Engineering, Rutgers University, for his close reading and detailed comments on Chapter 14, Ionizing Radiation; to Dr. John Lawler of the firm of consulting engineers Quirk, Lawler and Matusky, for his critical comments on Chapters 7 and 8, Sanitary Sewage and Water Pollution. My thanks also go to Mrs. Bernice Marcus, principal of Public School 128, Brooklyn, New York, who waded through each chapter checking for readability, giving each the benefit of her knowledge of the English language.

My gratitude is also extended to Mrs. Marilyn Tobias, who single-handedly prepared the manuscript and did such a remarkably good job without previous experience.

Finally, I must acknowledge the help of my family: my wife, Anita; my son, Scott; and the girls, Andi and Dana, who were short-changed many weekends and holidays, and who were so often told to "be quiet while Daddy works." Perhaps, in time, they'll think it was worth it.

Preparation of the extensive revisions incorporated in this second edition fell to my secretary, Mrs. Virginia Moony. Hers was not an enviable task; I threw material at her in batches—and bits and snatches. But she was up to it.

I am indebted to all those who took time to comment by letter and in person. Those comments were extremely useful in preparing this revised edition. It is with great pleasure that I acknowledge the good works of the many people at W.W. Norton, who took the time and pain to transform the manuscript into an important book.

OUR PRECARIOUS HABITAT

1

THE ENVIRONMENT AS A SYSTEM

> *All things by immortal power*
> > *near or far*
> > *hiddenly*
> *To each other linked are,*
> *That thou canst not stir a flower*
> *Without troubling of a star.*
>
> > *Francis Thompson*

Much has been written about air and water pollution, chemicals in food, noise levels, pesticides, waste disposal, flood control, overpopulation, the concretizing of our countryside, and man's other alterations of his environment. Little, however, has been said about the fact that the health and welfare of man—both as an individual and in society—are rooted not in air, water, food and so on, but in a complex system made up of *all* the facets of his habitat, including man himself, interacting with and on each other. Study of our environment makes no sense if it focuses on one aspect without the others.

The many stresses created by our industrial society impinge upon us all. But does it follow that they are or need be harmful? Much of the popular writing on this subject would have us believe that these stresses are indeed harmful and have brought much of the population to the brink of illness or death. No one would argue that air pollution, radioactive fallout, or chemical insecticides washed into a water supply, to take a few examples, are beneficial; but I would suggest that the physiological effects of these environmental pollutants are not so well understood or established that the purveyors of gloom and doom can write about them as though they were. We must learn to be chary of such dramatic alarms as: "Man is exposing himself to hundreds of new chemicals in the air he breathes, the food he eats, and the water he drinks. As chronic bronchitis, lung cancer, and emphysema grow more prevalent, man seems to be choking to death on his own technology." Such statements abound in pitfalls for the unwary; they do little to help us understand the very dangers they seek to expose. They are as oversimple as is the statement that since the life expectancy of Western man is rising steadily and world population is "exploding," environmental pollution obviously is beneficial to health. The failure of both approaches is the failure to realize that our environment is a vast complex that cannot be understood in terms of any one of its parts. It is impossible to understand and deal with air pollution, for example, without considering its relationship to waste disposal, electric power generation, public transportation, human and animal health, or the chemistry of agriculture, to name just a few parts of an intricate interrelationship. A diagrammatic representation of such an interrelationship is shown in Figure 1.

In 1969 the town of Westport, Connecticut, scored what its more enlightened citizens considered a notable victory for conservation and progressive thinking. Banding into committees and threatening action in the state legislature, they successfully defeated an entrenched electric power company that planned to build an atomic power plant on a scenic island in Long Island Sound off Westport's shore. The citizens' committee that led the battle consisted of the elite of a highly educated and progressive community. These people did not rely entirely on emotional pleas for the preservation of beauty and recreational areas. They were sophisticated enough to call in ecologists who warned of the effects

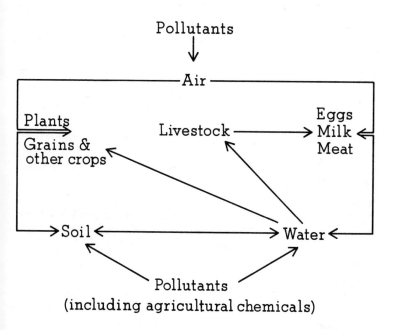

Figure 1. Interrelationships within the environment. (Adopted from L. Goldberg, The Amelioration of Food: The Milroy Lecture. Journal of the Royal College of Physicians, 1 (1967): 385.)

on sea life of warming the waters of the Sound. Their victory was considered a triumph for conservation. But actually how much of a victory was it? As the island in question was one of the very few sites near urban power consumers and on a body of water large enough to supply the cooling needed by atomic power plants, the electric company's defeat forced it to return to coal burning on an ever-increasing scale. The effect this will have on air pollution in an already polluted area is readily foreseeable.

Another example of the results of man's failure to think of his environment as an interacting *system* is the Aswan High Dam on the Nile. It is a dramatic example of man's constant tinkering with an environment he understands only slightly. Although a few

pertinent facts have emerged, the full impact of the dam will undoubtedly remain unknown for years.

The diplomats and engineers responsible for the dam saw it
as the rescuer of Egypt's agriculture, the supplier of needed
power—in short, the savior of her starving poor. They were unaware of its impact on the sardine industry in the eastern Mediterranean Sea. Late in 1966, at a meeting sponsored by UNESCO
in Split, Yugoslavia, scientists from thirteen concerned countries
divulged the facts: the Aswan High Dam had sharply reduced the
sardine population; the annual catch was down by 50 percent.
By the time the dam is fully operative the catch should be reduced
still further, eliminating the sardine industry—a staple of the
Mediterranean economy.

It is well to note that a dam on the upper reaches of the
Nile can alter sardine fishing from Alexandria to Lebanon; comparable indirect consequences must be anticipated from any tampering with the environment. Before the dam was built, with the
flooding of the Nile each year millions of tons of nitrates and
phosphates were carried by the silt into the relatively mineral-
deficient Mediterranean. This yearly dose of fertilizer permitted
the growth of luxuriant blooms of phytoplankton (microscopic
aquatic plants).* The phytoplankton provided zooplankton (microscopic aquatic animals) with a ready source of nutrition that
allowed them to flourish in great numbers. And the sardines that
quickly fattened on the abundant zooplankton filled the nets of the
local fishermen. This cycle had existed longer than recorded history. With the completion of the dam ** the Nile will no longer
carry minerals and fresh water to the Mediterranean; the phytoplankton and zooplankton will drift to more hospitable areas or die
—and with them will go the sardines.

Other effects of the dam have not yet become clear, but the
available evidence indicates that there will be additional far-reaching dislocations. For example, the dam is expected to initiate a
precipitous increase in the incidence of bilharziasis by extending
the range of infected snails into new and hospitable habitats.
Thus, even before its completion, this great engineering achieve-

---

* This would be considered pollution in the streams and rivers of the
United States, where algal blooms are unwanted.
** See Chapter 8, Water Pollution.

ment, another monument to man's technical skill, will have disrupted two ecological relationships, and both will prove inimical to man's best interests.

By 1975 construction is expected to begin on a sea-level canal across the Isthmus of Panama, linking the Atlantic and Pacific Oceans. However, before the first earthmover scoops out a trench of earth, a number of serious allegations of environmental dislocations will be laid to rest.

Although the Atlantic-Pacific Interoceanic Canal Study Commission * devoted only four of the 109 pages of its report to environmental considerations, scientists have sharply differed on the consequences of such a canal. One group claims that the interchange of Atlantic and Pacific species would be detrimental. For example, a number believe (without supporting evidence) that the crown-of-thorns starfish currently responsible for devouring coral reefs in the Pacific would become established in the Caribbean with consequent harm to the reefs there. Other marine biologists, also without supporting evidence, feel there is no basis for such a contention.

Several researchers believe their limited studies on *Pelamis platerus,* the yellow-bellied sea snake native to the Pacific, show that it would quickly become adapted to Atlantic conditions and that natural predators in the Atlantic would soon learn to shy away from it because of its toxic venom. These scientists noted that the psychological shock of large populations of this sea snake around the Caribbean islands would have an appalling effect on tourist trade. Because of the paucity of reliable data, the Canal Commission gave these "beliefs" short shrift, noting that the ecological risk of the proposed canal was "acceptable." Is it? It would be nice to know more before a new canal is dug.

Surely there must be a better way to act than uninformed tinkering. A beginning has been made, but biologists will have to unravel a great many more of the complex interrelationships before "total planning" for a healthy community becomes possible. Whether it is called an ecological community or an ecosystem, this interrelated complex governs biological and physical aspects

* This Commission was first appointed by President Johnson, then reappointed by President Nixon. Chairman of the Commission is Robert B. Anderson, former Secretary of the Treasury.

of man's life. Disease and disorder may be viewed, therefore, as a lack of adequate adjustment by man to factors in the environment. The point is that the social, physical, and biological components function as an integrated system, and any tampering with any part of the system will affect each of the other parts and alter the whole.

An excellent description of the unity of our habitat that still has lessons for us today is the statement of Hippocrates on "Airs, Waters and Places," written some twenty-five hundred years ago. He said:

> Whoever wishes to investigate medicine properly should proceed thus: in the first place to consider the seasons of the year and what effects each of them produces. Then the winds, the hot and the cold, especially such as are common to all countries, and then such as are peculiar to each locality. In the same manner, when one comes into a city to which he is a stranger, he should consider the situation, how it lies as to the winds and the rising of the sun; for its influence is not the same whether it lies to the north or the south, to the rising or to the setting sun. One should consider most attentively the waters which the inhabitants use, whether they be marshy and soft, or hard and running from elevated and rocky situations, and then if saltish and unfit for cooking; and the ground whether it be naked and deficient in water, or wooded and well watered, and whether it lies in a hollow, confined situation, or is elevated and cold; and the mode in which the inhabitants live and what are their pursuits, whether they are fond of drinking and eating to excess, and given to indolence, or are fond of exercise and labor, and not given to excess in eating and drinking. . . . if one knows all these things, or at least the greater part of them, he cannot miss knowing when he comes into a strange city, either the diseases peculiar to the place, or the particular nature of common diseases, or commit mistakes, as is likely to be the case provided one had not previously considered these matters.

Hippocrates did not have all the answers, but surely he pointed to the questions. The deeper the analysis of the web of life is pushed, the more meaningless becomes the word *independence*.

Study of the environment as a system lends itself to the methods developed by systems analysts. One of our predicaments is that we cannot deal with the total system because of its bewildering complexity. A common conceptual framework and methodology enabling scientists from disparate disciplines to work together is wholly lacking. They don't even speak the same language. Ecologists, demographers, chemists, engineers, and physiologists not only have no language in common, they often refuse to talk to one another. This is understandable; each feels insecure in the presence of the others. Unfortunately, understanding this failing does not help solve our predicament.

To attempt to deal with this lack, Dr. Aurelio Peccei, with a group of concerned individuals, formed the Club of Rome. The Club's members selected the method of System Dynamics, developed by Professor Jay W. Forrester of MIT,* a theory of system structure and a set of tools for representing complex systems and analyzing their dynamic behavior, as a means of dealing with the multivariable problems that affect the total environmental system.

With the use of computer simulation techniques, a number of variables can be tested with respect to their effect on one another, as well as the entire system. Figure 2 is a flow diagram or pictorial representation of the assumptions in this specific model. The assumptions deal with the interrelations among world population, economic development, natural resources, pollution, and food production capabilities.

As described by Professor Forrester, "only two types of variables, levels and rates, are necessary to express any relationship in a system."[1] He noted that *levels* represent the variables that characterize the system at any point in time. Population, natural resources, capital investment, agricultural capacity, and pollution are the five levels in the phase one model. In Figure 2, each of the *levels* is represented by a rectangle. Unimportant levels have a cloud attached to the rectangle.

Rates, on the other hand, are the system's action or policy variables, which change the levels. If we are to understand global problems and interrelationships, such factors as birth, death, and

* Professor Forrester's system was originally intended for application to industrial problems.

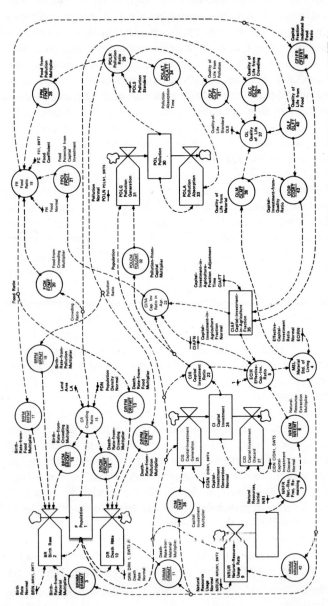

Figure 2. Flow diagram of assumptions in model. (Courtesy of Professor Jay W. Forrester, MIT.)

pollution generation ratios must be known or estimated along with such others as capital investment rate and resource depletion rate. The symbol of a valve represents rates in the figure. Dotted lines indicate influence in the direction shown by the arrows.

In Professor Forrester's system, when a sequence of influences leads back to its own starting point and thus forms a closed circuit, it makes a feedback loop. A pollution-population feedback loop is shown in Figure 3.

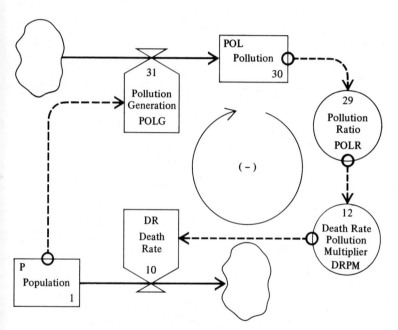

Figure 3. Population-pollution feedback loop. (Courtesy of Professor Jay W. Forrester, MIT.)

When a model is simulated by a computer the printout obtained can be like Figure 4, which shows the effect nine variables have upon one another. After one run, changes are made in the model and their effect on the other factors is observed. The hope is that inserting the best available estimates of *levels* and *rates* will bring out a pattern that acceptably represents reality.

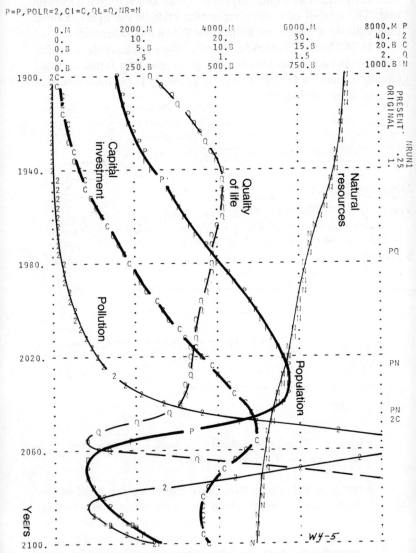

Figure 4. Standard computer run from world model, including period from 1900 to 2100 A.D. (Courtesy of Professor Jay W. Forrester, MIT.)

This type of investigation, while only one of the approaches to complex problems, is a sophisticated procedure that may enable us to get handles on otherwise elusive problems. More on this in Chapter 15, Population and Progress.

Reference

1. Jay W. Forrester, "The Club of Rome—Project on the Predicament of Mankind, Phase One: The Dynamics of Global Equilibrium." Speech delivered on November 6, 1970 at the Massachusetts Institute of Technology, Cambridge.

Suggested Reading

Forrester, Jay W. "Systems Analysis as a Tool for Urban Planning." Paper read at Symposium, The Engineer and the City, National Academy of Engineering, Washington, D.C., October 22–23, 1969.

Kadanoff, Leo P. "From Simulation Model to Public Policy." *American Scientist* 60 (1972): 74.

ECOLOGY OF HEALTH
AND DISEASE

*One of the greatest weaknesses of the human mind consists
in a kind of lazyness, in the urge to find either or solutions
and to explain everything by a single principle instead of
considering the multiplicity of factors in their interrelationship.*

Franz Alexander

Not a day passes without a report by investigators in the
United States or elsewhere around the world on the effect of
some aspect of the environment on human health. One in particular whose possible contribution to chronic disease is being studied
in several countries is water. There has been a spate of reports
tending to correlate water softness with coronary heart disease.
Thus far no cause-effect relationship has been established. Magne-
tism and its effect on human physiological processes, long considered in the realm of quackery, is currently a respectable subject
of investigation at several universities in the United States. In the

Netherlands, scientists are investigating the differing effects of drug therapy when administered at different hours of the day; there are indications that man's physiological processes are affected by the presence or absence of daylight, as are those of lower forms of life. At the University of Pennsylvania, scientists are studying arthritics who claim to be able to predict changes in the weather twenty-four to forty-eight hours in advance. The researchers want to discover how the body receives and uses weather signals.

An ecological view of life may lead to an acceptance of some theory such as holism,* the idea that man is but one unit, a part of a comprehensive system of "dynamic interdependencies" that is more than the sum of its parts. Several formidable examples may serve to illustrate this concept.

An ecological upset that vividly portrayed these dynamic interdependencies and man's place as only one thread in the total tapestry of life was witnessed by the ornithologist Robert Cushman Murphy, who described it several years ago. This disruption occurred along the coast of Peru in 1925.

Each year around Christmas, the dry desert regions along the northern coast are watered by rains brought by currents of warm air. These rains are so regular and so welcome in this otherwise arid land that they have come to be called *El Niño* ("the Christ child"). These rains sustain life through the many months of drought.

Although El Niño's arrival usually means plenty (some of the finest cotton in the world is grown in the northern coastal areas of Peru), it can also mean disaster. Two or three times a century, El Niño makes its way too far south and does not quickly return to its usual area. This change in position disrupts the ecological balance on land and sea so drastically that even man does not escape the consequences.

In 1925, the warm current ranged far south, killing the marine life adapted to the normally cold-water coast. Unable to outrace the warm current, fish in fantastic numbers perished and were cast up on the beaches. To the vast seabird population

* Holism is the term given by Jan Christiaan Smuts to the concept of whole-making or the holistic tendency fundamental in nature, binding the living and nonliving elements of the universe into a unified process.

that frequented the coast, the death of the fish meant starvation. The bodies of countless dead and dying birds literally concealed the beaches and blocked the harbors. The putrefaction was so great that hydrogen sulfide, a product of the microbial degradation of protein, was produced in quantities sufficient to blacken the paint on ships in the harbors. The pollution of the sea with the dead birds, which implies an overabundance of nitrate nitrogen, gave rise to blooms of a microscopic marine protozoan that actually turned the water blood-red.

On land, where rain fell for five months, the barren soil eroded, destroying the huts of the inhabitants. Without their supply of fish, the people began to starve. In the standing pools of water, mosquitos began to breed in large numbers and malaria flourished. Contamination of the water supply with human fecal matter, as a result of seepage into wells, precipitated an outbreak of typhoid fever. The rat population, cut off from its normal food supply, began to die of plague, and, shortly thereafter, so did the natives.

(To the shock of most Peruvians, El Niño changed its pattern again in 1972. Instead of growing cold and dying away in April, as it normally does, it has lingered on the coast. By August, the anchovy schools that make Peru the largest fishmeal producer in the world had not returned. Record flooding has destroyed crops and food prices have soared. Should El Niño continue through September and October, we might see a repetition of the 1925 cycle of disease and destruction.)

This havoc resulted from a slight elevation of the temperature of the seawater. And it clearly shows the links that bind man, animals, and plants so closely together with the physical environment. Such an example shows the necessity to know in advance the effects on water, its flora and fauna, and other forms of life dependent upon it that may be expected from nuclear wastes or toxic chemicals disposed of at sea. And the question arises: If the decision not to dispose at sea is made, what then will be the disposition of the waste? Can wastes be safely tucked away anywhere?

Another example of the intimate weaving of the biological with the physical environment emerged from investigations concerning prevention and control of African or Gambian sleeping sickness.

In Central and East Africa, the agent associated with the clinical symptoms of sleeping sickness is a microscopic protozoan, *Trypanosoma gambiense*. This parasite was early found to be transmitted to the human population by the bite (injection) of the tsetse fly, *Glossina palpalis,* when taking a blood meal.

The natural habitat of *G. palpalis* is restricted to the dense tropical forests that border lakes and rivers. Its usual source of nourishment is the marshbuck, or Situtunga antelope, which is, in turn, the main dietary staple of leopards. Thus there is an ecological relationship between the leopard population and the incidence of human sleeping sickness. In years when leopards abound, the marshbuck population is kept low, and as a consequence the tsetse flies obtain few animal blood meals to sustain them between human blood meals.

Intensive detective-like investigations aimed at controlling sleeping sickness uncovered a unique chain of events in the Rhodesias. Control now depends in large measure upon preventing the tsetse fly—in this instance a different species, *G. morsitans*—from reaching adulthood. To accomplish this, the natives in the area are prevented from burning off the grass in the treeless savannah regions.

It was found—after years of arduous searching—that the grass fires destroyed the ants that fed on the tsetse fly pupa (the developmental stage between larva and adult). The heavy mats of grass aided in increasing soil moisture, which in turn encouraged the growth of the ant population, which kept the tsetse fly population in check, which ultimately meant fewer transmissions of protozoan parasite and fewer cases of sleeping sickness.

From French Polynesia in the east, through New Caledonia, to the Philippines, Thailand, and China, eosinophilic meningitis is a widespread and well-known ailment that manifests itself in agonizing headaches. In January 1967, the final clue uncovering the ecological chain of events leading to the disease appeared to have been discovered.

The headache is caused by a microscopic flatworm that resides in the heart and blood vessels of rats, doing them no harm. These worms are regularly passed out in feces and are present in garden soil and other areas frequented by rats. In turn, the planarian worms are ingested by snails and slugs during their nocturnal maraudings in garden soil.

South Sea Islanders and Thais who eat raw or partially cooked snails and slugs are especially susceptible to the headache of eosinophilic meningitis. When the snails are eaten by the natives, the threadlike worms are liberated in the stomach and begin eating their way to the brain, where they initiate an infection that gives rise to the excruciating headache.

The infection can also be contracted by eating fish and shrimp that have previously eaten worm-infested snails and slugs, or by eating improperly washed strawberries, salad greens, or tomatoes. Once the infection occurs, no medication can alter its course; relief can be effected only by a spinal tap, which reduces pressure on the brain.

Charles Elton, an ecologist, described an illuminating example of the many interrelations within a community that also showed that the balance of nature is not as neat an arrangement as some would have us believe. He stated that:

> In a year of mouse abundance, many animals change their feeding habits to feast royally on mice. Bears and wolverines do this. In 1905 Cabot says that the grazing was so much spoilt by the mice that the caribou left this part of Labrador in a body to seek food elsewhere. In consequence of the absence of caribou, the Indians in the interior were compelled to subsist mainly upon fish, being also greatly handicapped for lack of deer skins from which to manufacture their clothes. In one area the annual crop of crowberries failed in some places, owing to the young shoots having been devoured by mice. According to Hutton, the shortage of empetrum fruit, the usual and almost the only berry food of the Eskimos, gave rise to a pandemic of a pustular skin disease, due apparently to the deficiency of some food factor contained in the crowberries.[1]

An example closer to home may be useful. Lead encephalopathy—lead poisoning—takes its toll of thousands of children in Philadelphia, New York, Chicago, and other cities each year. The cases of lead poisoning begin their annual rise in the spring, reaching peak proportions in July and August. Apparently, after ingestion of a quantity of chips of lead-based paint, the higher temperature, combined with the active (ultraviolet) rays of the sun, stimulates increased intestinal absorption of the lead. Thus the number of cases appears dependent upon the season.

The idea that physical factors exert an influence on health is as old as man himself. The language and traditions of primitive peoples everywhere refer to the ill effects of certain winds, the changing of the seasons, the phases of the moon, and the influence of the sun and stars. While it is currently acknowledged that some such effects exist, much remains in the realm of speculation.

Until the 1860s physicians believed that health and disease were influenced by the external physical environment. During the 1860s, however, Louis Pasteur in France and Robert Koch in Germany were laboring on their investigations of human microbial diseases. The idea that a completely invisible living agent might be the cause of many fatal diseases of men and animals was considered utterly preposterous by most people. How could so small an entity kill a man?

Although it was in 1857 that Pasteur published a paper describing the bacterial fermentation of grape sugar to wine—a historic event because it ascribed to germs what had been regarded as a purely chemical reaction—it was the year 1877 that was truly memorable: then, for the first time, a microbe was shown capable of causing an important human disease. Robert Koch isolated *Bacillus anthracis,* the microbe responsible for anthrax. The "Golden Age of Bacteriology" was swiftly ushered in. For the next seventy years, microorganisms were believed to be responsible for all man's ills; the germ theory of disease had advanced to center stage, relegating the environment to the wings.

With the germ theory of disease, which states that each disease is provoked by a specific microbe with characteristic pathological effects, scientists acquired insight into an important mechanism of death and disease. Many leaders in medicine and public health were convinced that the germ theory explained fully the spectrum of disease and firmly believed that vaccines and antitoxins were the principal means for the protection of the health of the public. Unfortunately, too many still do.

Between 1930 and 1950 several new concepts were introduced into medicine, with far-reaching implications for public health. These were *homeostasis, deprivation,* and *stress.* Essentially, they implied that illness or disease could occur as a result of exposure to sudden or marked changes in the environment, subjecting an individual to more pressures than he can tolerate. Infectious living agents had no place in this scheme.

Beri-beri, pellagra, rickets, iron-deficiency anemia, and hypothyroidism are several dramatic examples of deprivational disorders. However, a young child denied the care and affection of its mother can be seriously affected for the remainder of its life. This too is an example of deprivation and stress.

Stress is a concept that is easier to appreciate than define; it may be considered as any force to which the body responds in order to maintain its equilibrium and/or protect itself against injury. During a lifetime, stressful situations are encountered regularly: entrance to school, adolescence, acceptance into or rejection by college or university, selection of a mate, middle life, working conditions, living conditions, income, availability of food. Each can impose a hazard upon people, and individuals respond in a variety of ways. The increasing number of hospital beds used for mental patients or for patients whose illnesses have a psychosomatic component attests to the severity of many stressful stimuli and the inability to deal with them without becoming ill.

In June 1967, the *New England Journal of Medicine* carried a report by four physicians from Johns Hopkins Hospital. They concluded that family strife could stunt the growth of a child who was emotionally disturbed by constant contact with the marital discord of his parents. They noted that "an adverse environment acting during the early critical years of childhood can be responsible for the growth retardation." They went on to say that when the children they had studied were placed in a convalescent hospital they demonstrated remarkable growth acceleration. In fact, one boy grew seventeen inches after being abandoned by his parents. When the children were released and sent home, they stopped growing again.

Today, illness and disease are increasingly being studied not from the view of a single causative factor, but rather as the result of a multitude of causes. That is, a growing number of investigators now believe that prevention and control of disease may be given increased impetus by breaking one or several of the links in the chain of causation. This chain or web of causation implies that a series of events rather than a single event is necessary for illness to occur. It also suggests that a choice of sites is available for interdiction; if one is not feasible, another may be. In this scheme, control and/or prevention is much more attainable than curing an illness already contracted.

For example, today the attempt to control typhoid fever is not directed solely to a search for a bacterium. Instead, there is concern about such factors as raw milk, inadequate sewage disposal and unprotected water supply systems, poor personal hygiene, low educational levels, inadequate community financial resources, lack of industrialization, and the historical development of the country.

It is not sufficient simply to isolate a microbe and eradicate it. It has been found that in many instances people can harbor a microbe without showing clinical symptoms of illness. Some people are more resistant to the invasion of microbes than others. For example, all people who have tuberculosis are infected with *Mycobacterium tuberculosis,* the organism associated with TB. However, not all people from whom this organism can be recovered have tuberculosis. This is not contradictory. It implies a spectrum of resistance or susceptibility in the population. The microbe is a necessary but not sufficient cause of the disease. Something in addition to the microorganism is needed for the disease to occur. If all the factors predisposing to illness were known, prevention, control, and even eradication might be possible.

Considering the concept of multiple causation, programs to control or prevent lung cancer should consider the contribution of air pollutants, cigarette smoke (and cigarette advertising), entrenched habits, radioactive particles, the tobacco plant, environmental stress, and insecurity. Perhaps other considerations are more important, but we have not yet ascertained what they may be.

Study of the environment as it relates to human health presents great obstacles. Scientists may not yet be ready for such an enormous task. For the most part, their research investigations are based on maintaining all but one factor constant while testing the effect or effects of a single variable on cats, dogs, fish, fowl, or humans. Only in special cases have two variables been investigated. The fact that health depends on the interreactions of a multitude of variables that can be understood only as a whole system, not as separate parts, is a staggering realization to the researcher.

In a democratic society additional difficulties are imposed. For example, the association of cigarette smoking with lung cancer has received significant support from a multitude of different types of competent investigation. The evidence, albeit circumstantial, and the relationship appear highly valid, yet large segments of the population demand absolute direct proof before accepting preventive legislation. The only way to obtain this type of evidence would be to gather together several thousand children about age ten, divide them into two comparable groups of equal size, lock them in a stockade and observe them for several years, then start one group smoking while preventing the others from doing so. Since the effects of smoking are generally seen in the fifth or sixth decade of life, these two groups would be required to be under lock and key for at least forty years, under the scrutiny of scientists recording their every activity. Then, and only then, would absolute direct evidence of a cause-effect relationship be forthcoming. As this experiment is not possible, one can only wonder about the motives of those who clamor for "real" proof.

Currently, the United States and most of the countries of Western Europe are experiencing a major epidemic of two infectious diseases, syphilis and gonorrhea. Gonorrhea was well known in Biblical times, but the bacterium associated with it was not isolated until 1879. The corkscrew-shaped bacterium that causes syphilis, a disease apparently unknown in Europe before the return of Columbus and his crews in 1493,* was described in 1905. Both bacteria are readily rendered impotent by the antibiotic penicillin. Yet we are experiencing more new cases of both diseases than ever before. Knowledge of the microorganism is simply insufficient to control or prevent its incursions. Today, a total

---

* Debate goes on as to whether Columbus and his crew brought syphilis back from the New World to the Old. Thus far, this debate has been "settled" twice in my lifetime. I look for it to be debated and settled at least once again.

Figure 5. Man Struggling with His Environment *by Adolf Gustave Vigeland.*

environmental or ecological offensive is needed. It is necessary to consider the psychology of promiscuity, prostitution, social mores, homosexuality, drug addiction, penicillin, the microbe, educational levels, and family life. Factors such as these are currently being used in the attempt to control the precipitous increase in cases in the fifteen-to-twenty-five age group, where the incidence is highest.

The day of the individual scientist working alone on an infinitesimal part of the whole problem may be passing. It may be replaced by an integrated team effort to understand the cause-effect relationship between man and the world around him. So many different forces or stresses impinge upon us simultaneously during each hour of the day that to understand the contribution of each, or the combined action of several in concert, will require experimental models not yet devised. Thus statements based on single variable studies, isolating some single environmental factor as responsible for human illness, are of doubtful validity.

The investigation of man's interrelationships with his environment entails studying the whole man and studying him as a functioning unit. This will prove difficult, but the challenge is being taken up. New departments of community medicine and community health have been formed and are being formed in medical schools and schools of public health. These are dedicated to the idea that today's physician cannot merely treat the sick patient but must consider him as a member of society as well. He must both restore the patient to health and prepare him to return to his place in the community. This calls for a greater knowledge of the many environmental problems that affect an individual and can influence the genesis, aggravation, and continuance of disease.

Some years ago, Adolf Gustave Vigeland created a statue depicting man's constant struggle with the forces of nature; it is plain that he believed man had not yet overcome—nor would he in the near future—the many forces that impinge upon and affect him. His statue, *Man Struggling with His Environment* (Figure 5), stands today in the city park of Oslo, Norway. It speaks for itself, this chapter, and this book.

Reference

1. Charles Elton, *Animal Ecology* (New York: Macmillan, 1927).

Suggested Reading

Rasmussen, H.; and Rasmussen, A. E. "The Unstable Ecology of Estuaries." *Science Journal,* September 1970, p. 35.

Cassell, E. J. "The Environment as a Social Cause: 1845 and 1970." Paper read at the American Medical Association Air Pollution Medical Research Conference, October 5, 1970, New Orleans, Louisiana. (Copies available from Dr. Cassell, Cornell Medical Center, New York, New York.)

Oglesby, R. T.; Carlson, C. A.; and McCann, A., eds. *River Ecology and Man. Proceedings of an International Symposium on River Ecology and the Impact of Man.* New York: Academic Press, 1972.

BACTERIAL FOOD POISONING

*I find that nonsense, at times,
is singularly refreshing.*

Talleyrand

August 1959 will long be remembered by thousands of people in Indiana. To the 1,216 men, women, and children who became violently ill after eating poisoned food at two picnics that month, the memory will be especially vivid.

On August 15, seventeen hundred employees of a large pharmaceutical plant and their families gathered for a picnic lunch. Food was served beginning at about 11:30 A.M. By 1 P.M., the first cases of food poisoning (gastroenteritis) began to occur. By 4 P.M., over eight hundred people had become ill. The Indiana Department of Health had recorded one thousand victims by 9 P.M.

Since "forewarned is forearmed," planners of a picnic given by an electrical parts manufacturing firm on Saturday, August 22, should have been alerted by the previous week's events. But apparently it was not a learning experience. August 22 was a particularly warm day; 1,813 people turned out for the festivities. Food was served at 4:30 P.M. By 7 P.M. that night, symptoms of severe gastroenteritis were evident in 25 to 30 people. An additional 100 were ill by 10:30 P.M. In all, 216 cases were reported.

Indiana had its August, but other communities in the United States and around the world are not immune. Food poisoning occurs regularly throughout the United States and around the world. The incidence of one form of gastroenteritis has risen from seven hundred cases reported in 1946 to over ten thousand in 1962. As the incidence of food-borne disease is poorly reported in most countries, the number of illnesses reported doubtless represents only a fraction of those actually occurring.

Food poisoning of bacterial origin is primarily a result of improper food sanitation. Food sanitation may mean many things to many people, but L. V. Burton's pithy appraisal that "sanitation is nothing more than a race between men and the lower forms of life to determine who gets the food supply first" admirably epitomizes the subject. Bacterial food poisoning and food sanitation are often facets of the same problem; the absence of the latter may give rise to the former. There is no general method of food protection analogous to pasteurization of milk or chlorination of water supplies. Suitable protection must be achieved through accepted procedures of cleanliness and handling. The number of illnesses that may be transmitted by food is large indeed, but the incidence of individual food-borne illnesses varies considerably throughout the world.

Diseases spread by foods can conveniently be placed in three major groups: foods containing a toxin as an end-product of bacterial metabolism; those containing significant numbers of bacteria that on ingestion release toxins that evoke specific responses; and those containing a more complex form of parasite that can initiate a more involved type of disease. The following list of food-borne infections, though not exhaustive, indicates the wide range of biological forms involved. We will be concerned with only some of these.

I. *Bacterial Toxins*
   Botulism
   Staphylococcal intoxication

II. *Bacterial, Viral, and Rickettsial Infections*
   Typhoid and paratyphoid fevers
   Salmonella food poisoning
   Streptococcal sore throat, scarlet fever, and streptococcal
      food poisoning
   Bacillary dysentery (shigellosis)
   Diphtheria
   Anthrax
   Brucellosis
   Tuberculosis
   Tularemia

III. *Parasitic (Protozoal and Zooparasitic)*
   Amoebiasis (amoebic dysentery)
   Taeniasis (beef tapeworm infestation)
   Trichinosis (pork roundworm infestation)
   Ascariasis
   Hydatidosis

   At this point bacterial food poisoning must be distinguished from food spoilage. Although it is erroneously believed that one is synonymous with the other, they are, in fact, quite dissimilar conditions. In order to understand the difference, it may be helpful to recall that bacteria are unicellular plants that exist in three main forms: as rod-shaped cells, with and without flagella, and as spherical cells called *cocci*. Figure 6 is a typical rod-shaped bacterium with flagella arranged completely around the body. A curved rod (vibrio)—Figure 7a—is typical of the organism associated with cholera, a water- and food-borne disease. Figure 7b shows the chainlike aggregation of streptococci, 7c the grape-like clusters of staphylococci, and 7d pairs of diplococci. The third group, spiral forms, is seen in Figure 7e. They are not involved in any known food-borne disease. Figure 7f shows clostridial forms of the type involved in food spoilage and food poisoning. These cells have a spore stage, shown in Figure 7g, that is instrumental in protecting them against destruction by heat. This characteristic, as we shall see, is particularly significant in food processing and sanitation. It would make a very neat package if I could now say that the cocci or grapelike forms are primarily responsible for food poisoning and the rod-shaped forms for food spoilage. Unfortunately, this is not exactly the case. Although cocci

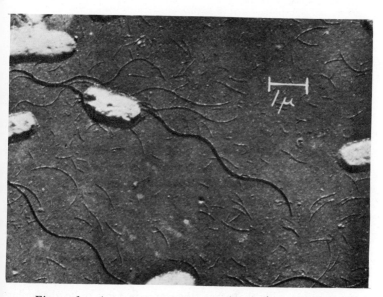

Figure 6. A typical rod-shaped salmonella bacterium. (Courtesy of American Society for Microbiology.)

do cause a form of food poisoning and rods do produce food spoilage, two rod-shaped organisms are responsible for food-borne disease.

The question must now be asked, "When is food fit to eat?" You might reply that food is edible when looking at it and smelling it testify to its edibility. If this is a valid standard, then a food is inedible when your eyes and nose say, "This is not fit to eat." Some people, mainly Europeans, like their game meat "high." Most Americans would call such meat spoiled and not fit to eat. "High" or "gamy" meat usually has a strong odor and taste, both produced by bacterial action. Titmuck, fish buried to allow bacterial fermentation to occur, is eaten by Eskimos as a delicacy. Eskimo dogs, however, refuse to eat this semi-liquid, foul-smelling delight. Most Americans would call it putrid. Yet it is putrefaction that gives Limburger cheese its gourmet qualities! These examples of spoilage are caused by the growth and metabolic activity of microorganisms, but food poisoning is not involved.

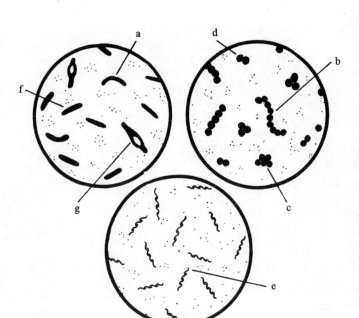

Figure 7. (a) curved rod (vibrio); (b) typical strep-tococci chain; (c) grapelike clusters of staphylococci; (d) pair of diplococci; (e) typical spiral forms; (f) clostridial rods with rounded ends; (g) spore stage.

Food poisoning, also the result of microbial activity, is a subtly insidious process, limited to only a few types of bacteria. In most cases they give no warning of their presence in the form of off-odors or off-tastes; not a hint of suspicion surrounds the food.

Every housewife is familiar with the common signs of food spoilage. Many would consider fruit spoiled and unfit to eat when partially or wholly covered with mold. Aesthetically such fruit may be unattractive, but it is not poisoned. That is, it does not evoke gastroenteritis if eaten. Many people pare away molded areas of fruit to enjoy the winy flavor imparted by the microbial conversion of fruit sugars to alcohol. Cottage cheese and hamburger are two readily perishable products. To some people, they become unfit to eat after two days of refrigeration. Others accept these items after a week or more. The point is that spoilage is a relative thing, associated with offense to the senses, but is not inherently dangerous.

Most foods are subject to some degree of deterioration. Considering the ease of spoilage, foods can be categorized as *nonperishable, semi-perishable,* and *perishable.* The degree of perishability simply refers to the ease with which microbes are able to use a food as a nutriment. Examples of relatively nonperishable foods are dry grains, sugar, flour, and dried beans. Without sufficient moisture, microbes find it difficult to spoil foods. Potatoes and apples are examples of semi-perishable foods containing more available moisture, while meats, fish, poultry, eggs, and milk—the high-protein foods with large amounts of moisture— are highly perishable. Because these foods are desirable sources of nutriment for both humans and microbes, it is easy to see the aptness of L. V. Burton's statement that food sanitation is nothing more than a race between man and animals to see who gets the food supply first.

Foods undergoing bacterial spoilage are usually contaminated with large numbers of rod-shaped organisms called pseudomonads. Pseudomonads of one type or another spoil cottage cheese, poultry, meats, and fish. Pseudomonads have not been found to elaborate toxins capable of initiating human illness. Additionally, ingestion of pseudomonads has not resulted in gastrointestinal upsets. On the other hand, certain clostridial organisms can spoil low-acid canned foods. But the presence of a *specific* clostridium is required to produce the food poisoning known as botulism.

One of the most striking changes in public health over the past twenty-five years has been the enormous increase in the incidence of bacterial food poisoning. Figure 8 shows the steady increase in salmonellosis, one type of food poisoning.

Our knowledge of the multiple factors responsible for bacterial food poisoning has also increased. A recent publication issued by the U.S. Department of Health, Education and Welfare states that "despite the progress which has been achieved, food-borne illness continues to be a major public health problem," and it also notes that "the total amount of food-borne illness in the United States is not known, since reporting is neither complete nor accurate." Estimates of the annual number of cases range

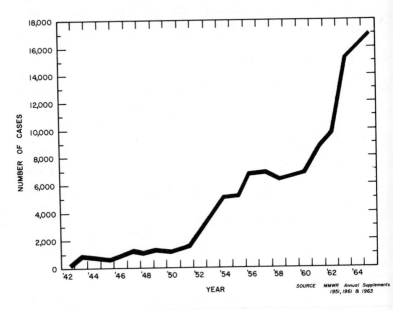

Figure 8.   Yearly increase is salmonellosis, 1942–1965.

from 200,000 to 300,000. Apparently, only a fraction of the number that occur is reported to local, state, or federal agencies.

The magnitude of food poisoning cases caused by improper handling by nonprofessional individuals, as opposed to persons engaged in commercial preparation, is seen in Table 1. This table represents reported illnesses of persons eating in large groups at private homes, schools, picnics, and church gatherings. A similar chart for the contribution of public dining places is unavailable. The lack of such information should not be construed as implying greater safety in restaurants than in private homes, although this has been suggested. A newspaper article recently stated that it is safer to eat in restaurants than in homes or at private functions because health departments receive fewer reports of food poisoning from restaurants than from picnics, private parties, and private homes! Eighty million meals are believed to be served each day in public places in the United States. The difficulty of tracing a

TABLE 1.

Types and incidence of food-borne illness at large private gatherings.

	STAPHYLOCOCCAL FOOD POISONING		SALMONELLOSIS		STREPTOCOCCAL INFECTIONS		SHIGELLOSIS		GASTROENTERITIS, ETIOLOGY UNKNOWN	
	No. of outbreaks	No. of persons affected	No. of outbreaks	No. of persons affected	No. of outbreaks	No. of persons affected	No. of outbreaks	No. of persons affected	No. of outbreaks	No. of persons affected
Poultry	10	340	6	464	1	30	1	50	18	1,188
Other meat	21	519	2	21	0	—	1	3	41	1,496
Custard-filled dessert	10	167	2	23	0	—	0	—	12	186
Salad	2	36	3	105	2	900	1	192	7	456
Other	10	231	7	135	1	100	1	12	12	106
Not determined	5	367	10	859	0	—	7	497	42	2,503
Total	58	1,660	30	1,607	4	1,030	11	754	132	2,935

case of gastroenteritis to a restaurant is formidable indeed. Restaurants may well be less safe than private homes, even though fewer cases of food poisoning are reported.

According to a recent report from the Bureau of Preventable Disease (an aptly named organization) of the New York City Department of Health, most food poisoning in New York City occurs in restaurants. The second most common site is the home —but bear in mind that much of the food eaten at home is prepared elsewhere. One additional point: it has been estimated that currently 55 percent of all food eaten in the United States is eaten away from home.

A second major contributor to explosive outbreaks of especially severe and often fatal food poisoning is inadequately processed canned and packaged low-acid food, from both home and factory. Botulism is undoubtedly the most severe and dramatic of all types of food poisoning, and is being seen more and more as new packaged foods appear.

At this point, two questions are appropriate: Why do we have bacterial food poisoning? And why is it increasing in magnitude?

Curiously enough, the answer to the first question has been known for some time. It has been reasonably well advertised but flagrantly ignored. Disease transmitted by food usually originates with an infected person who inadvertently inoculates the food during handling. Careless food handling practices foster abundant growth of the organism in a highly nutritious medium. The time between preparation and serving to an unsuspecting, happy, and hungry population allows the multiplying bacterial population to produce enough toxin to infect a large number of people. The potent toxin requires the ingestion of only a morsel of food to evoke the characteristic set of symptoms. A review of many food-poisoning experiences (Table 2) shows the effects of various lapses in food sanitation. Food handlers cannot afford to ignore these findings. The category of general insanitation must not be glossed over. We shall treat it at length shortly.

To answer our second question we must look to our changing environment. The rapid substitution of a technological, industrially oriented society for an agricultural one has radically changed our

T A B L E 2.

Ascribed causes and incidence of food poisoning.

Ascribed cause	% of outbreaks
Inadequate refrigeration	41
Disease carriers	18
Infected sores (fingers, arms)	17
General insanitation	12
Cases of disease (sick people)	9
Chemicals in foods	4

way of life. Intricately involved in this change are factors that abet food poisoning.

An affluent industrial society encourages women to join the labor force. In order to purchase desired goods and services, the income of both husband and wife is often necessary. The homemaker of the past is now often a member of the work force. Whatever her job, she is no longer able or willing to spend long hours at home preparing meals. Domestic help, once abundantly available, has also succumbed to the siren call of industry. For those women who do not have to work, free time for pleasurable pursuits is more compelling than kitchen drudgery. As if to punctuate the problem, the smaller homes and apartments of the urban areas have forced grandparents to live away from children. All this makes home cooking less and less common. As a consequence, we now routinely bring home ready-to-eat, precooked, prepackaged foods. We also eat out more often. And to cater to our newly educated tastes, large quantities of specialty foods are imported from places around the world where food sanitation practices are quite often less than adequate. New types of food items are sold in unique types of packaging whose potential for disease transmission is unknown until an illness occurs.

While studying the effects of cooking temperatures on antibiotic residues in breaded and fried crab and oyster cakes, fellow researchers and I noted that heat penetration was slow but sufficient to kill bacterial pathogens. We speculated on the degree of heat penetration into precooked frozen crab cakes and undertook a small-scale study using the following experimental procedure.

Several varieties of frozen crab cakes were obtained from retail stores in our area. Since many housewives often save additional minutes in preparing precooked frozen items by placing them in cold ovens and bringing the oven to the suggested temperature, the samples were split, one half being placed in an oven preheated according to label instructions and the second half in a cold oven. It was noted that different companies recommended different cooking times at the specified temperature. Temperature readings were obtained by inserting 24-gauge copperconstantin thermocouple wires into the approximate center of the cakes and connecting the terminal ends to a Brown portable potentiometer (Model 126W3).

The results obtained, while interesting to us, were of particular concern to frozen food packers, many of whom subsequently changed their label directions. Before the heat penetration determinations were made, the surface and internal temperatures of the frozen cakes were taken. Readings of 32° to 35°F were obtained at the surfaces and 19° to 23°F internally. The suggested cooking time on the wrapper was eight minutes in an oven set at 300°F. After eight minutes in the "cold" oven, the cakes had reached 142°F, approximately the minimum temperature considered necessary to prevent food poisoning. The cakes in the preheated oven reached 175°F, which might seem safe. But there is a risk that it might not provide adequate heat treatment in view of the protective effects of many of the colloidal materials contained in crab cake mix. Another experiment was carried out using larger cakes whose wrapper directions called for twenty minutes of cooking after the oven arrived at 400°F. We found that after twenty minutes in the cold oven, 126°F was recorded at the center of the cakes, while 150°F was attained in the preheated oven. Present wrapper directions for home heating of precooked frozen crab cakes leave much to be desired in providing an adequate heat treatment from a public health standpoint, especially if heating is done in an unpreheated oven.

In 1965 the National Academy of Sciences issued a special report recommending that emphasis be given to research on new foods and packaging, which produce wholly new conditions for microbial growth.

We noted earlier that the great majority of food-poisoning cases fall into three groups. By far the most common is that caused by staphylococci enterotoxin. Not all strains of "staph" elaborate enterotoxin, nor do the toxin-producing strains produce enterotoxin in all foods. Staphylococci are commonly found in the nose and throat, and on the skin in pimples, boils, carbuncles, and whitlows.

Such items as ham, chicken, and egg salad, custard-filled cakes, meat pies, and boiled ham are the most notorious sources of food poisoning. They offer a most nutritious, high-protein diet to the staphylococci, and they are usually prepared in large amounts that are difficult to cool rapidly. Put the same organism on a slice of tomato and no toxin production will occur. When refrigeration is unavailable, inadequate, or simply not used, the microbe, gaining entry from a sore finger or droplet from the food handler's nose, finds the warmth and nourishment needed for growth and toxin production begins. As the hours pass, the unrefrigerated food becomes a potential bomb. At mealtime nothing is suspected. The food has not changed in appearance, odor, or taste.

Two to six hours after eating, the bomb explodes. The first symptoms are usually nausea and vomiting (the body tries to rid itself of the poison as rapidly as possible), abdominal cramps, and diarrhea. In severe cases, blood and mucus may appear in the patient's stool and vomitus as a consequence of violent retching.

Just such conditions caused the events in Indiana in August 1959 that we described at the beginning of this chapter. The explosive outbreak of August 15 was ascribed to boiled ham that had become contaminated during preparation. Toxin in potato salad and ham caused the episode on the following Saturday. This was pinned down by swift laboratory analysis. Both outbreaks could have been prevented by proper refrigeration.

In another series of staphylococcal gastroenteritis cases, refrigeration was not the primary break in the chain of causation. During May and June 1971, a half-dozen people in Colorado, Wisconsin, and Washington became ill with typical symptoms of staphylococcal intoxication three to six hours after eating Genoa salami. Investigation revealed upwards of a million coagulase-positive staphylococci per gram of meat. The number and type of organisms are prima facie evidence of food-poisoning microbes. Under the supervision of the USDA, the Armour Company (which produced the salami in its Minneapolis plant) quickly initiated a total recall order.

The most striking form of food poisoning, botulism, results from ingestion of an enterotoxin elaborated by *Clostridium botulinum* and *para-botulinum*. This sublimely potent toxin is the most deadly natural poison known to man.* Since the clostridia are normal inhabitants of the intestinal tract of animals, they are universally found in agricultural areas in close proximity to crops. It has now been established [1] that these bacteria are also natural inhabitants of marine environments, probably as a result of soil runoff. Consequently, food fish harbor them as part of their natural flora. Unlike the staphylococci, which are introduced as a result of poor personal hygiene on the part of food handlers, clostridia are already present and not adequately removed from the produce when it is washed before canning or packaging. Most cases of botulism can be traced either to ingestion of under-processed home- or factory-canned low- or nonacid foods, or to packaging in containers providing suitable conditions for toxin production.

Recall Figure 7g, in which a spore was shown. Spores are generally considered to be the most heat-resistant forms of life on our planet. It is just this characteristic that food processors must guard against, especially home canners and purveyors of specialty items that receive only light heat treatments. Foods such as stringbeans, corn, beets, asparagus, mushrooms, tuna, chicken pie, and smoked fish, known to be naturally contaminated with spores of *C. botulinum,* must be processed for at least thirty-five minutes at 240°F (115°C) to guarantee safety. Spores of several food-spoilage (but not food-poisoning) clostridia are more heat-resistant than spores of the botulism organism. When heat processing is adequate to destroy the food spoilage forms, food poisoning will not occur. Commercial canned food processors have developed heat treatments for each food and can size, based on the heat resistance of a test organism known to be more heat-resistant

---

* Less than 1×10^{-10} (0.0000000001) grams can kill a mouse.

than most of the spoilage organisms. Interestingly enough, a form of built-in protection also exists. The food "spoilers" produce unbearably putrid end-products as a result of anaerobic metabolism in canned foods. Consequently, if processing has been inadequate the insufferable odors will prevent the food from being eaten, thus protecting the consumer against the botulism toxin present along with the malodorous products.

In most cases of botulism no warning odors are present. The foods are usually eaten at home for dinner, which accounts for the extensive family involvement. The first symptoms appear about twelve to thirty-six hours later. In some cases on record the incriminated food had been eaten more than four days before, but this is unusual. An astounding case was reported by Dr. Dack of the University of Chicago: that of a patient who was active for eight days before hospitalization, even attending the funerals of other victims and testifying at the coroner's inquest! [2] Typically, however, the toxin seeks the central nervous system. Thus, in addition to nausea, vomiting, and diarrhea, the characteristic symptoms are double vision, indicating involvement of the third cranial nerve, and difficulty in swallowing. This is followed by slurred speech. In fatal cases the pharyngeal muscles are paralyzed and death results from respiratory failure. Over 70 percent of cases end in death, primarily because treatment with antitoxin is started too late. For antitoxin to be useful, it should be given before symptoms appear. Unless there is reason to suspect botulism, this is seldom done. In addition, symptoms of botulism are often confused with a half-dozen other nervous-system illnesses, and treatment is often delayed until information is obtained that the patient ate certain foods that are commonly associated with botulism.

The citizens of Indiana had their August of '59, but Americans in fifty states will not soon forget the summer of '71. And the Bon Vivant Soup Company of Newark, New Jersey, will never forget "V-141/USA-71." With the death on the morning of July 1 of sixty-one-year-old Samuel Cochran, Jr. of Bedford Village, New York, households from coast to coast knew fear of botulism as they had never known it before.

Once the Westchester County Health Department understood they had a death from botulism in their jurisdiction, they knew they had to initiate a nationwide alert. Having learned that Mr. and Mrs. Cochran (she is fully recovered) had eaten vichyssoise soup (it had tasted so bad they couldn't finish it), the Health Department realized that every can made from the same batch was a potential killer.

To trace the cans of vichyssoise, it would be necessary to get the code number identifying the lot. This number is embossed on all can lids. Inspectors rushed to the Cochran home and found the lid in the garbage can. Stamped on the lid was "V-141/USA-71," numbers that within hours became known throughout the country: "V" for vichyssoise and "141" for May 21, the 141st day of the year—the day on which this lot was processed.

Six thousand four hundred forty-four cans were in that lot, and they had to be found. To further this effort, all sales of soup with this lot number were embargoed by the FDA. In fact, as the days passed, the FDA embargoed all Bon Vivant products and within a few weeks the 108-year-old company was out of business.

A portion of every can of vichyssoise brought to government laboratories was injected into mice. Of the original 6,444 cans, 5,344 were found. Of these, only four contained toxin.

Before an anxious public could recover from this explosive story, carried far and wide by all the mass media, the Campbell Soup Company issued a recall of chicken vegetable soup canned on July 15 in its Paris, Texas plant. In this instance, the company's own quality control laboratory had found the botulism organism in samples it tests from each day's run. Within a few days it ordered the recall of vegetarian vegetable soup also made in Paris, Texas. The chicken vegetable had been shipped to ten states in the South and West; the vegetarian vegetable had gone to eight states in the same region.

The wide distribution of canned goods in America today, as well as the deadliness of botulism, make it cause for alarm, even though very few cases occur in any year. Considering the billions of cans of food packed and eaten, and the canning industry's good record of freedom from spoilage, what could have gone wrong in these two cases? What are the possible sources of contamination or microbial survival? A number of possibilities have been advanced.

Given an hypothesis, laboratory experiments ought to verify

it and suggest reasonable cause-effect relationships. This was the approach taken by food scientists attempting to ascertain what caused the contamination in these two instances.

At the outset, the cause was believed to be a combination of unusual coincidental factors having to do with ingredients and processing conditions. After some 300 controlled tests, the growth of clostridium and toxin production were duplicated in laboratory trials. For the Campbell soups, the simultaneously occurring events turned out to be above-average viscosity of can contents, over-fill of the cans, and incomplete hydration of the dry ingredients, coupled with a new process recently installed in the Paris, Texas plant. Ironically enough, this process had been designed to produce a better product; it involved a higher than usual rate of product agitation to permit greater heat penetration in a shorter cooking cycle. Thus the factors of fill, head-space, and hydration conspired to reduce the ease and degree by which convection currents permit adequate heat distribution.

On Wednesday, October 27, 1971, Captain William C. Cleveland, Jr., a Marine Flight Instructor at Pensacola Naval Station, sat down with his four-year-old son to a meal that included Stokely-Van Camp's Finest French Style Green Beans. Because, as Captain Cleveland later noted, "the beans tasted like sauerkraut," and because the recent vichyssoise and vegetable soup episodes were still very much on his mind, he took himself and his son to the base hospital to be examined for possible botulism poisoning, even though they both felt perfectly well.

In the chain of events that followed, the Florida Department of Agriculture issued the initial alert, which was followed soon after by the FDA's "urgent warning." Recall orders began fanning out through the United States. Fortunately for the Clevelands there proved to be no botulism toxin in the beans. Medical opinion is that the two mice that died following injection of blood from the four-year-old child were killed by medicine given him for his cold weeks before.

Less than a week after the "urgent warning," Commissioner Edwards of the FDA called a press conference to rescind the warning and recall order. Botulism was not involved and the product was safe. However, in defense of the recall action the Commissioner said, "In dealing with life and death problems such as botulism, there are times when the public interest demands action before the scientific test is complete."

There is an unfortunate aspect to this episode: the harm done to the Stokely-Van Camp name. Unquestionably the wide publicity given the initial incident would not be matched by equal publicity for the retraction. According to a company spokesman, "In the long run the insult to our product could cost us millions." We need to find a point between alarmism and laxity that will adequately protect both the public and the food processors. Additional comment on protection against botulism will be found in Chapter 4.

An instructive case that points up the major problem with home canning of low-acid foods came to light on July 4, 1970. On that day, a housewife in Holmes County, Ohio, noticed that her home-canned corn had spoiled. She mixed the spoiled corn from two quart jars in with food for her hogs. At the same time she emptied two more quart jars in the woods near her home. The next day, a dozen piglets and a sow were found lying on their sides with flaccid paralysis and labored breathing. The sow and one piglet recovered. Some days later, a half dozen chickens were found dead in the woods where the corn was strewn. Two weeks later two more quarts of corn were mixed in with the hog food. Twenty-four hours later, a sow, boar, and pig exhibited symptoms of toxicity. Both the sow and pig died; the boar recovered.

Laboratory examination of the corn revealed type B, clostridium botulinum toxin. And it was learned that the woman had bottled the corn by boiling in water for only thirty minutes! Such inadequate heat treatment could not possibly inactivate the naturally present spores.

There were ten cases of botulism intoxication in 1971, more than in any year since 1965. (Figure 9 shows the number of cases of botulism per year in the United States between 1950 and 1970.) Five were caused by home-canned foods, one by commercially canned soup, two have not been pinned down to a specific food, and two were caused by wound infections. While botulism from commercially processed food receives wide publicity in the mass media, more cases are caused by improperly home-canned food, and unfortunately receive little public attention.

As noted earlier, bacterial food poisoning occurs in two ways:

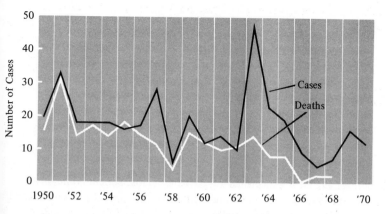

Figure 9. Reported cases of botulism in the United States, 1950–1970. (Source: Department of Health, Education and Welfare.)

eating food containing toxin, and eating food containing large numbers of certain bacteria. Salmonellosis is that form of food poisoning produced by ingesting the rod-shaped bacteria *Salmonella typhimurium* rather than a preformed enterotoxin. Salmonellosis is the sad result of poor personal hygiene in food handlers. It is caused by the contamination of food by human fecal matter. Of all food-borne illnesses, it is the most inexcusable, particularly because of the high level of sanitation attainable in our society. It is estimated that in 1968, two million people, 1 percent of the population, suffered attacks of salmonellosis. Obviously few of these cases come to the public's attention.

Salmonella organisms, the rod-shaped cells shown in Figure 6, are natural inhabitants of the bowel (colon) of man and animals. Thus they are passed out with feces and can be introduced into food from soiled hands. Additional sources of human infection are animal products such as poultry, eggs, and milk; egg products such as noodles and cake mixes; and meat items such as meat pies, brawn, pressed beef, and sausages that have contacted animal excreta. In March 1966, chocolate candy bars were recalled from stores because of salmonella contamination. Usually, the infectious organism is spread by the human excreters, either those with obvious cases of the illness, those convalescing from the illness, or asymptomatic healthy carriers. Healthy carriers are our greatest problem. They don't know they are shedding salmonella organisms and outwardly appear perfectly healthy. Because of the difficulty in detecting carriers who have no symptoms, preventive measures are largely ineffective.

As with the toxin types of food poisoning, the appearance, smell, and taste of food contaminated with salmonellae are unaltered. Similarly, the foods and their preparation methods offer excellent media for bacterial growth. Ten to twenty hours after eating, the first symptoms of gastroenteritis appear. The onset is sudden. Headache, shaking, chills, abdominal pain, elevated temperature, and foul-smelling diarrhea usually appear. Prostration, muscular weakness, and dehydration can be severe, leaving the patient totally debilitated. The severity of the illness depends on the number of organisms ingested and on individual sensitivity. Infants and adults over fifty tend to have severe symptoms, and considerably more fatalities occur in these two groups.

In 1970, 49 outbreaks with a total involvement of 3,852 people were reported. In these, turkey products were most often the vehicle of infection. Pork products, ice cream, chicken, potato salad, lemon tarts, and bread pudding were also found in decreasing order of magnitude.

Food poisoning is not the only illness caused by salmonellae. Unlike other salmonella infections, the only known reservoirs of infection of typhoid fever are human carriers. Typhoid fever, also caused by the ingestion of food or water containing fecal matter from people ill with the disease, is a very different illness from food poisoning. Classical symptoms of typhoid fever include high fever, abdominal tenderness, enlarged spleen, slow pulse, a rose-colored skin rash, headache, cough, and nosebleeds *—quite a different set of symptoms from those seen in salmonella food poisoning.

To the more than five hundred men and women who were hospitalized with typhoid fever in Aberdeen, Scotland in the sum-

---

* Of course, each case does not present all of these symptoms.

mer of 1965, canned corned beef will always recall their narrow escape from death. On May 19, 1965, ambulances brought to the City Hospital in Aberdeen four people ill with high fevers. By midnight the following day the Health Department had identified the suspected microbe, *Salmonella typhi*, from stool and blood cultures. *S. typhi* is the agent of typhoid fever.

Desultory outbreaks of typhoid occur from time to time, but in countries with modern sanitation facilities they are usually of little consequence. However, in Aberdeen, as the days passed, it became all too clear that this was no ordinary episode. By May 30, the number of confirmed cases jumped to 136 and the first death was recorded. The following day a newspaper carried the following account: "The trim streets of Aberdeen were nearly deserted tonight and in some places the air was heavy with the odor of disinfectant as the city fought to stamp out a typhoid epidemic."

By June 27 the epidemic had run its course and Queen Elizabeth sent a message indicating that she would visit the city. Over five hundred people had been hospitalized and five had died. Aberdeen, a major tourist attraction, had also suffered disastrous losses in trade. Thus, the city welcomed the sign that the Queen thought Aberdeen was safe enough for her and for her subjects, safe from the havoc wrought by a can of corned beef.

During the period of the outbreak, a great deal of confusion and misunderstanding regarding the nature of the disease's communicability elicited behavior in many segments of the population more typical of the Middle Ages than the twentieth century. For example, the streets of Aberdeen were sprayed with disinfectant, as though the typhoid bacterium had blanketed the environment and could be picked up and carried about on the soles of shoes. Workers in cities far to the south went so far as to refuse to unload trucks that passed through Aberdeen. Students were told to avoid public transportation, as though the bacillus could be transmitted from person to person much like influenza, a respiratory-tract infection spread by droplet nuclei from a cough or sneeze. To make matters still worse, prophecies of impending national disaster were foretold. That these tragicomic behavior patterns should have occurred in the sixty-sixth year of the twentieth century is cause for concern over our educational processes. I say *our,* for I am quite certain that similar behavior would result in the United States should a major outbreak of typhoid occur.

The cycle of events leading to the epidemic began in a meat-canning plant in Argentina. After a canned food is heated (to reduce * the bacterial population and cook the food), it is placed in cold water to lower its temperature rapidly, which prevents overcooking. Heating causes the seams to expand and offers an entrance to bacteria. The cooling water in this case was drawn from a stream that was polluted with fecal matter containing typhoid bacteria. (Chlorination, which was not used, could easily have sterilized the water and prevented the episode.) Bacteria were thus reintroduced after cooking. By the time the corned beef arrived in Scotland and was used, a significant increase in bacteria had occurred. One of the busier supermarkets on the city's main street opened one of the six-pound tins and sliced the beef on its slicing machine. As other meats were also sliced on that machine, they in turn were inoculated with the typhoid organisms. Several of the employees became infected while handling the meat, and they spread the disease further. But for the expert protective measures instituted by Dr. Ian MacQueen at the onset of the outbreak, additional thousands could have become ill.

Asymptomatic carriers are people who harbor typhoid organisms in the gall bladder, where the bacteria multiply slowly. The organisms leave the gall bladder in bile and are passed out of the body in feces. These people do not appear ill and on medical examination show no signs of typhoid; they are healthy (chronic) carriers who continue for years to shed infectious organisms. These people can be the focus of explosive epidemics if allowed to work in any aspect of food handling. In New York City, for example, 264 healthy carriers are constantly under surveillance to prevent their employment in the food industry.

Late in May 1967, a sizable typhoid outbreak occurred at

---

* Although subjected to temperatures as high as 240°F for thirty-five minutes, canned food is not meant to be sterilized in the strict sense of the term. Temperatures high enough for sterilization (the complete absence of life) would produce food unfit to eat. Consequently, the heat treatment applied to various products is designed to reduce microbial populations to harmless levels.

the Beta Theta Pi fraternity house at Stanford University in Palo Alto, California. Apparently, healthy carriers working in the kitchen were responsible for passing the infection to some eighteen fraternity members. Positive stool cultures were obtained from the cook and two waiters.

The problem of the carrier is particularly troublesome since the bacteria are lodged in the confines of the gall bladder, defying all current forms of medication. Surgical removal of the gall bladder is the only positive means of preventive treatment, but most known carriers will not submit to it.

In the United States, 369 cases of typhoid were reported in 1966. About 3 percent were fatal. Babies and invalids are the most vulnerable.

Table 3 shows the mechanisms of the three major types of food poisoning. In each instance the mechanism reveals the means of prevention. That such preventive measures have been known and widely disseminated for many years testifies to the lack of concern on the part of individuals. Bacterial food poisoning has no place in highly industrialized, affluent societies. That it not only persists but continues to increase indicates community failure to protect itself.

TABLE 3.
*Mechanisms of food poisoning by the
leading infectious microbial agents.*

Clostridium perfringens—Most common source is reheated cooked meat; incubation period 8 to 24 hours; symptoms include diarrhea, abdominal cramps; symptoms usually gone after 8 hours.

Staphylococcus—Most common sources are custard- and cream-filled bakery goods, also ham, tongue, processed meats, cheese, ice cream, potato salad, hollandaise sauce, chicken salad; incubation period 1 to 6 hours; symptoms include severe and sudden abdominal cramps, nausea, vomiting, and diarrhea; recovery usually follows in 6 to 8 hours. Organisms gain entrance via food handlers.

Salmonella—Most common sources are poultry, eggs, and products containing dried eggs, such as cake mixes; incubation period 8 to 24 hours; symptoms include nausea and vomiting followed by chills, high fever; symptoms may persist for two weeks; can be fatal to infants and elderly. Source of infection is fecal matter containing microbes, introduced by food handlers.

Shigella—Most common sources are milk and ice cream, but may include any food contaminated by infected workers in food plant or by insects carrying bacteria; incubation period about 48 hours; symptoms include severe diarrhea, abdominal cramps, mild fever; symptoms usually last several days.

Escherichia coli—Most common sources include shellfish and sewage-contaminated water used in food processing; incubation period 6 to 24 hours; symptoms include cramps, diarrhea, nausea, vomiting; symptoms usually subside in 6 to 8 hours.

Clostridium Botulinum—Found in low-acid canned foods (string beans, corn, beets, tuna, smoked fish). These bacteria are naturally present in soil and marine environments; they gain entrance to containers when food is canned or packaged. Organisms multiply only when conditions are favorable. The organisms produce heat-labile toxin as a by-product of their metabolism. The toxin, ingested with food, acts on the central nervous system and on peripheral nerves. As early as two hours or as late as four days after ingestion, vomiting, diarrhea, and diplopia occur, usually followed by inability to talk and swallow. The disease is frequently fatal as a result of respiratory collapse.

Figure 10 is a pie diagram depicting the major etiologic categories responsible for outbreaks of food poisoning and their relative percents reported to CDC from all sources during 1970. There were a total of 366 outbreaks in 1970 compared to 371 for 1969. Bacterial infections accounted for the majority of all food-borne outbreaks. Parasitic and viral agents were incriminated in less than 4 percent of the outbreaks. In 27.2 percent of outbreaks, no cause could be ascribed. The subcategory "Other" under the "Bacterial" heading includes outbreaks attributed to *Bacillus cereus,* enterococci, *Escherichia coli,* and *Vibrio parahemolyticus.*

Thus far I have not mentioned ptomaine or ptomaine poisoning, and for good reason. There really is no such thing. Ptomaine poisoning is an old concept that is dying hard. Although it has been established beyond question for many years that ptomaines are not involved in bacterial food poisoning, the term persists. The name comes from the Greek *ptoma* ("dead body" or "cadaver"); ptomaines as a class are foul-smelling chemical compounds. For

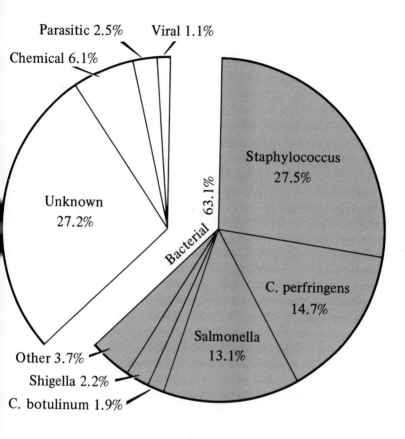

Figure 10. Food-borne disease outbreaks (confirmed and unconfirmed), by causative organism, United States, annual summary, 1970.

those with training in chemistry, it may be useful to note that ptomaines are aliphatic diamines formed from the decomposition of proteins by bacteria. Actually, the ptomaine putrescine is formed by the decarboxylation of the amino acid ornithine, and the ptomaine cadaverine is formed by the removal of CO_2 from lysine. Figure 11 shows the decarboxylation reaction. Neither of

Figure 11. Decarboxylation reaction.

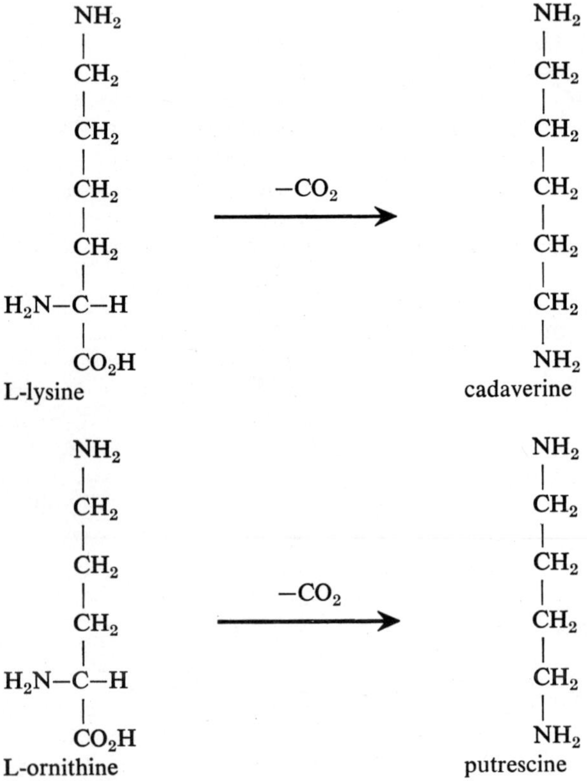

$$
\begin{array}{ccc}
NH_2 & & NH_2 \\
| & & | \\
CH_2 & & CH_2 \\
| & & | \\
CH_2 & & CH_2 \\
| & \xrightarrow{-CO_2} & | \\
CH_2 & & CH_2 \\
| & & | \\
CH_2 & & CH_2 \\
| & & | \\
H_2N-C-H & & NH_2 \\
| & & \\
CO_2H & & \\
\text{L-lysine} & & \text{cadaverine}
\end{array}
$$

$$
\begin{array}{ccc}
NH_2 & & NH_2 \\
| & & | \\
CH_2 & & CH_2 \\
| & & | \\
CH_2 & \xrightarrow{-CO_2} & CH_2 \\
| & & | \\
CH_2 & & CH_2 \\
| & & | \\
H_2N-C-H & & CH_2 \\
| & & | \\
CO_2H & & NH_2 \\
\text{L-ornithine} & & \text{putrescine}
\end{array}
$$

these ptomaines is harmful when taken by mouth. That is, they do not produce symptoms of gastroenteritis. If a large amount were introduced directly into the bloodstream with a hypodermic syringe, illness would occur, but no food poisoning symptoms. Perhaps the less said about ptomaines the better.

Investigations of the causes of bacterial food poisoning invariably turn up evidence of failure to employ basic sanitary practices in preparing and preserving food. As noted earlier, bacterial food poisoning has no place in a modern, affluent society. It is an entirely preventable disease. Prevention requires attention to two broad areas: personal hygiene and temperature control. For example:

1. Hands must be washed with soap before preparing, handling, or serving food following use of toilet facilities. Unwashed hands, particularly those soiled with human or animal waste, can introduce food-poisoning organisms into food.

2. The nose and mouth should be covered with a handkerchief or other effective barrier when a person handling food is sneezing or coughing. After handkerchiefs containing exhaled mucus and sputum are handled, hands should be washed with soap.

3. Fingers should be kept out of glasses and dishes, and off bowls, spoons, fork tines, and knife blades.

4. In commercial food establishments, food handlers should be checked regularly for evidence of open sores, boils, sore throats, colds, and intestinal disorders. An employee who reports to work with any of these signs should not be allowed to handle food.

5. Salads made of meat, poultry, seafood, potatoes, and eggs must be held below 45°F until served. This applies as well to custards and cream-filled cakes. All these items should be eaten on the day prepared.

6. Stuffings, poultry, and stuffed meats should be heated to reach at least 165°F deep in the center of the product.

7. If a food that can be heated must be stored for two to three hours, it should be maintained at about 145°F while stored.

8. If there is any suspicion that a canned food—particularly a home-prepared, low-acid food—is undercooked, poorly sealed, or leaking, the contents should be boiled for a minimum of 15 minutes before being eaten.

Although there is no substitute for proper training in food handling, adherence to these eight rules should prove helpful in preventing outbreaks of bacterial food poisoning.

References

1. E. M. Foster, J. S. Deffner, T. L. Bott, and E. McCoy, "Clostridium Botulinum Food Poisoning," *Journal of Milk and Food Technology* 28 (1965): 86.

2. G. M. Dack, *Food Poisoning,* 3rd ed. rev. (Chicago: University of Chicago Press, 1956).

Suggested Reading

To my mind, the most comprehensive and up-to-date classification of diseases transmitted by foods is Frank L. Bryan's *Diseases Transmitted by Foods.* This 48-page compilation (with 113 references) published in 1970 is a veritable mine of information for those who want an overview of the field. It is available from the Center for Disease Control, Atlanta, Georgia.

Put, H.M.C.; Van Dorn, H.; Warner, W. R.; and Kruiswijk, J. Th. "The Mechanism of Microbiological Leaker Spoilage of Canned Foods: A Review." *The Journal of Applied Bacteriology* 35 (1972): 7.

4

CHEMICALS IN FOOD

To have ideas is to gather flowers; to think,
is to weave them into garlands.

Madame Swetchine

Thanksgiving was less than two weeks away. The cranberry growers around the United States had harvested a bumper crop, the largest of any in the past ten years, and large stocks of cranberry products were on grocers' shelves throughout the country. No one would be without cranberry sauce—or so it was thought.

On November 9, 1959, Arthur Flemming, then Secretary of the Department of Health, Education and Welfare, held his usual Monday press conference. But this was to be no routine conference. The next day, newspapers, radio, and TV were retelling with high drama versions of the distressing affair. The federal government warned the public that some cranberries grown in Washington State and Oregon had been contaminated by a weed-killer—Aminotriazole—that induces cancerous growths in the thyroid of rats.* . . . If housewives were unable to determine where berries

* Aminotriazole, a weedicide with a long history of use in cornfields, blocks formation of chlorophyll (the green pigment of plants), thus prevent-

51

were grown, the government advised them not to buy either in canned or fresh form despite the approach of Thanksgiving. . . . It had not been proved that the weed-killer produced cancer in human beings. Across the country, the commotion started in Washington that Monday caused grocers to remove cranberry products from their shelves and restaurants to drop cranberry sauce from their menus.

That episode, along with the earlier warnings of potential cancer hazard from the black dye used in jellybeans and the chemical diethylstilbestrol used on chickens to produce caponettes, is still reverberating today.

In March 1960, George P. Larrick, commissioner of the Food and Drug Administration, stated that "the general public, confused by the cranberry, caponette, and black jellybean episodes, and by misleading information from various sources, is understandably uncertain over just what the so-called chemicals-in-foods-problem is all about."

Two questions continue to be asked, and rightly so: (1) Is our food supply safe? (2) Is it necessary to add chemicals to food? The answer to both of these questions must be an unqualified yes, but not without extensive evidence and reason.

Between 1900 and 1960, our country more than doubled its population. Between 1960 and 2000, just 28 years from now, we are expected to more than double again. In 1920, the arable land under cultivation fed 106 million people. In 1972, an additional 110 million people will be fed on less arable land, and by 2000 there will be more than two mouths to feed where there was only one 28 years before. The simple fact is that not only must more food be produced on less and less available land, but, perhaps even more important, what is produced must be protected until it can be harvested, bought, and eaten. Crop and livestock pests exact an appalling tribute despite all our efforts to thwart them. Each year the equivalent of eighty-five to ninety million acres of crops is debased by all manner of pests. Added to this are the

---

ing carbohydrate formation and causing the death of the weed. Feeding rats ten to one hundred times the amount of aminotriazole found on cranberries for seventy to one hundred weeks caused the formation of thyroid carcinomas in the animals.

losses suffered in storage, processing, and transportation, equivalent to another thirty million acres of crops. Agricultural economists estimate that 20 to 25 percent of our annual production is lost to predation: either ruined "on the vine" or spoiled after harvest. To prevent additional losses the farmer uses the only effective means thus far available to him—chemical pesticides.* In order to prevent losses of livestock, milk production, meat, and hides by the ravages of microbes, ticks, lice, flies, and worms, chemical control is vital.

In addition to protecting the food supply at its source, chemicals aid in coping with the changes wrought by an industrial society. The complexity of modern life and changes in our eating habits require that in addition to fresh ** or freshly cooked items available in season locally, new methods be found to provide for year-round requirements, in and out of season. In 1920, a few hundred food items were available to consumers. By 1941, some fifteen hundred items could be counted on grocers' shelves. It was quite clear that people wanted variety in their diets; they were not content with the drab, unvaried fare served up day after day. In 1960, we could choose our foods from over six thousand items, and in 1970 over seventy-five hundred were available. Variety the year round is now readily available to the consumer.

A problem related to lack of variety in diet presented itself during World War II. In the early years of the war, Britain was besieged. The problem of feeding a nation that relied so heavily on imports became a matter of acute anxiety. A study was under-

---

* See Chapter 5 for a discussion of pest-control methods presently being investigated.

** The concept of freshness implies a time factor: the interval between harvesting and eating. To a person with a pea, melon, or tomato patch, food eaten directly off the vine is fresh. To a person buying from a typical supermarket that imports from a distance, the word should connote an interval of perhaps several days between picking, packing, shipping, retailing, and eating. The length of time elapsed between harvesting and freezing a ten-ounce package of green peas, for example, is relatively short. That frozen item arrives at the supermarket several days after harvesting, but resembles closely the product picked days before. Freshness then might properly describe the condition of the food at the moment of eating, whenever it left the vine.

taken to determine the nutritional requirements of an adequate diet. It was soon learned that all the nourishment for such a diet could be obtained from a combination of green vegetables, bread, and milk. Using men and women in scrupulous tests, it was found that such simple but tedious fare could easily support vigorous activity. This diet would have drastically reduced the need for imported food. To the consternation of many, it was not adopted because it was considered to be far too monotonous and dull to maintain a highly advanced country for any sustained period. A British scientist, Magnus Pike, commented: "A diet may be perfectly balanced nutritionally, but if it is not sufficiently attractive a workman may not eat enough of it to do his work. If a chemist can enhance the attractiveness of such a diet harmlessly, he is, in fact, contributing to nutritional well-being." [1]

The entrance of large numbers of women into the labor force, coupled with their desire to spend less time preparing meals, has given great impetus to precooked, prepackaged, ready-to-eat foods. In 1971, 55 percent of all meals eaten in the United States were prepared outside the home. To accomplish this, a variety of chemicals are needed.

New discoveries, the result of nutritional investigations during the past forty years, have measurably enhanced our food supply. Most of us are aware of the importance to general health of vitamins, minerals, proteins, fats, and carbohydrates. Many of these chemicals can be manufactured so that foods can be "fortified" or "enriched." Potassium iodide, for example, added to common table salt, can easily eliminate simple goiter. Enrichment of bread with chemicals such as the B-vitamins (thiamin, niacin, and riboflavin) has just about eliminated pellagra from the United States. The minerals, vitamins, and other nutrients so common in many foods today—the list would read like an inventory of a chemist's laboratory—have undoubtedly upgraded the general health of our population. Finally, use of chemicals in foods, combined with other forms of preservation, permits stockpiling to cope with emergencies. Food technologists are in fact modern-day Josephs, evening out the fat and the lean years.

Although some foods keep better than others, all are subject to microbial attack. Because of their low moisture content cereal grains (wheat, barley, rye), nuts, and seeds, for example, require little intervention for their preservation. Such items as potatoes, carrots, flour, dried fruits, and butter, because of their relatively low moisture content, have a fairly long storage life. Foods with high moisture content, such as meats, fish, and poultry, have poor keeping characteristics and thus require effective means of preservation if they are to survive microbial onslaughts. Of the many methods of food preservation—heating, freezing, dehydration, smoking, pickling—chemical methods are assuming increased importance. Certain chemicals are used to color foods; others add flavor; some impart firmness, while others soften; still others thicken, moisten, dry, or acidify, while others retard or hasten chemical reactions. Recall that what are called "foods" are in reality plant and animal tissues composed of proteins, carbohydrates, fats, minerals, water, and a host of other organic and inorganic substances, all of which are chemicals that can enter into many chemical reactions. The browning of sliced apples, peaches, and potatoes is an example of the chemical change that occurs when the oxygen in the air contacts the naturally present chemicals—enzymes released by the cut tissue. To prevent or retard these chemical reactions, such chemicals as sodium bisulphite or ascorbic acid (Vitamin C) are added to processed foods.

Although baking can destroy the spores of molds and most bacteria that are naturally present in flour and other ingredients, baked goods are constantly exposed to spores present in the air and on baking utensils. The mixtures of chemical ingredients we call cake, bread, and pastry are as tempting to bacteria as they are to man. Despite sanitary precautions, molds develop when temperature and moisture conditions are favorable. Flour often contains the spores of a hardy bacterium, *Bacillus mesentericus,* which are able to survive the heat of baking. During storage the bacteria become active and multiply, producing a "ropy" condition that renders the baked product inedible. To retard or prevent this type of spoilage, small quantities of sorbic acid or sodium propionate or other weak organic acid are added to baked goods.

Wheat flour in its natural, freshly milled state has a yellowish tint caused by the presence of small quantities of carotenoid and other natural pigments.* When this flour is stored it slowly

---

* *Carotenoid* means "resembling carotene," a natural pigment found in carrots and other yellow vegetables. The carotenoids are precursors of Vita-

becomes whiter and undergoes an aging process that ultimately yields a dough of enhanced breadmaking quality. Until fifty years ago it was necessary for the miller to age flour so that the baker could produce the type of loaf the public would buy. It was then found that certain chemicals incorporated into flour in small amounts would alter the natural yellow tint and improve the baking quality quickly. This also reduced the storage costs and the losses that inevitably occurred from microbial spoilage and rodent and insect infestation during the long storage periods. Some of the chemicals used, such as benzoyl peroxide and the oxides of nitrogen, only whiten; they do not influence the baking properties. Others, such as chlorine dioxide and nitrogen trichloride, both bleach and affect baking properties. Nitrogen trichloride is known commercially as Agene.*

The maturing of flour is of much greater practical significance than bleaching and is done chiefly because consumers prefer bread with a soft texture.

The flour milled from some wheats requires little chemical treatment (oxidation), while that milled from other species requires a good deal more to produce a flour that makes consistently good commercially baked bread. The maturing and bleaching agents aid in smoothing out the wide variations encountered in wheat and thus enable the miller to produce a uniform product from day to day and year to year.

Bread improvers used by the industry contain such substances as potassium bromate; calcium peroxide; mono-, di- or

---

min A that can be converted to Vitamin A in the human body. Thus one must distinguish between the actual Vitamin A content and the Vitamin A activity of food. The carotenes are thus provitamins. Not all carotenes are effective in this respect, however, and lycopene, the red carotenoid pigment found in tomatoes and other vegetables, is devoid of any Vitamin A effect. The same is true of xanthophyll, a yellow carotenoid found in wheat.

* In 1946 Sir Edward Mellanby reported that when puppies were fed a diet consisting largely of flour heavily treated with Agene, they developed running fits, or canine hysteria. Although Agene has not been found harmful to humans, its use was discontinued.

In 1950, the mechanism of canine hysteria was discovered. Apparently, Agene (nitrogen trichloride) reacted with methionine, an amino acid naturally present in flour protein, to form methionine sulphoximine, a compound toxic in puppies.

tricalcium phosphates; and ammonium chloride. They serve as food for the yeast cells, helping to assure vigorous and even fermentation (gas production, for the most part) of the dough and produce loaves of uniform quality.

Fatty or oily foods that have become rancid have characteristic odors. To prevent or retard rancidity, which may be caused either by bacterial attack on the food or by the reaction between naturally occurring chemicals in the food and air or minerals, chemical antioxidants such as butylated hydroxyanisole (BHA), butylated hydroxytoluene (BHT), or propyl gallate are added in small amounts.

Foods are among the most difficult products to package successfully. Such considerations as protection from microbial invasion, penetration by atmospheric oxygen, loss of volatile substances through evaporation, and choice of a container that will not itself adversely affect the food are important if the item is to come to the consumer in an edible state the year round. Chemicals help make this possible.

In the past eight years aerosol dispensers of food have come onto the scene and added a new dimension to both diversity and chemistry. In 1964 some 110 million cans of aerosol-dispensed whipped topping and cheese were sold. By 1972, it is estimated that 625 million cans will be sold. A major problem is how to get rid of all those cans.

In order to propel the food from the pressurized can, a gas—Freon C-318, octafluorocyclobutane—has been approved by the Food and Drug Administration as harmless and suitable for human consumption. But can a chemical with so obviously ominous a name, barely pronounceable, really be safe for human consumption? The fact is that the recital of unfamiliar technical names and scientific terms or the mere statement that a large number of strange-sounding substances are used in foods is singularly uninformative to consumers who are not chemists. Many people object to these chemicals mainly because they are unfamiliar. It would be less frightening if everyone knew what these chemicals are, the extent to which they are used, and the reasons for their use; but unless we all become chemists this is impossible.

Synthetic or man-made chemicals may be incorporated into a food item during its growth or during its storage and processing.

For convenience such substances are described as *additives*. It is generally understood that an additive is any substance used in food, directly or indirectly, that affects its characteristics. It usually becomes a component of the food. When introduced to preserve or improve the quality of a product it is known as an *intentional* additive because it is purposely added to serve a specific purpose. Such materials as artificial coloring, synthetic flavors, sweeteners, vitamins, microbial inhibitors, antioxidants, emulsifiers, and minerals are all intentional additives. All are added to the food product in carefully controlled amounts during preparation. Common table salt, sodium chloride, is one of the oldest intentional additives known; octafluorocyclobutane, Freon C-318, is one of the newest; and cyclopentanoperhydrophenanthrene,* used to enhance the nutritive quality of milk or bread, is simply the chemist's name for Vitamin D! Chemicals in foods are not new; what is new is the means of adding the correctly measured chemical in pure form, which results in a uniform product.

When primitive man first learned to preserve a portion of his food supply by smoking it in his fire, he was utilizing chemicals unknowingly. It was (and still is) the production of formaldehyde, phenol, and related compounds, coupled with the drying action of heat, that retarded microbial spoilage. Chemicals in the wood smoke also impart unique organoleptic properties.

Diethylstilbestrol (DES), a white, odorless, crystalline powder, is a non-steroidal synthetic chemical, exhibiting female sex hormone (estrogenic) activity. It was used for a time in the poultry industry to produce caponettes. (A capon is a male bird that has been castrated to fatten it. This was usually done surgically. Castration by chemical means produces a caponette.) Although the Food and Drug Administration authorized the use of DES in 1947, safety evaluation tests on laboratory animals later showed the chemical to be toxic for them and thus potentially hazardous for human consumption. As a result, it was withdrawn and is no longer used in poultry.

However, DES is still certified as an allowable additive for

---

* Cyclopentanoperhydrophenanthrene is actually the skeletal framework for a group of compounds such as steroids, hormones, natural pigments, and vitamins. Each of these differs by specific additions of carbon and hydrogen atoms to the basic skeleton.

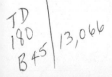
TD
180
B45 | 13,066

CAMROSE LUTHERAN COLLEGE
LIBRARY

cattle and sheep. Here, too, it is used to achieve rapid growth. An animal fed DES can often gain as much as 300 to 400 pounds in a matter of months; far more weight, and in less time, than when fed standard fodder without DES. Today, the battle rages over its continued use in cattle. It is now well established that DES is rapidly excreted by cattle and sheep. And it is excreted in the feces—unchanged chemically, which means that it does not remain in the tissue as residue, nor does it become metabolized to other chemically reactive substances. In addition, certification for its use is granted to feeders by the FDA on the condition that it not be fed for at least seven days prior to slaughter.

Current indications are that the high doses used for poultry —some 40 times those used in cattle given the proportionate sizes of the animals—probably overloaded the chickens' excretory mechanism and resulted in large residues in poultry meat. Nevertheless, opposition to the use of DES, a hangover from the poultry experience twenty years ago, continues today. The most frequent objection is that DES is carcinogenic.*

In a study completed in 1970, a team of physicians from the Cancer Control Bureau of the New York State Department of Health found five cases of vaginal adenocarcinoma between 1950 and 1970 in young women whose mothers had received large amounts of DES in a regimen of synthetic estrogen therapy to prevent threatened abortion.** However, these appear to be the only documented cancer cases attributed to DES, and they are related to intensive drug therapy, not food.

---

* On August 2, 1972, the FDA summarily banned manufacture and use of liquid and dry mixed forms of DES. Implanted pellets were not affected by the ban. Although the order became immediately effective, continued use of DES in feeds was to be permitted until January 1, 1973, "because," as the Commissioner noted, "there isn't any evidence of a public health hazard" and "there isn't any justification for abrupt disruption of the production of the nation's meat supply."

In tests with six steers it was found that up to one part per billion of DES could persist in beef livers even when it was withdrawn seven days prior to slaughter. While this finding precipitated FDA's ban, Dr. Edwards made it clear that "human harm hasn't been demonstrated in over seventeen years of use."

** The mothers had received large amounts of DES. Beginning with 5 mg per day, doses were increased to 100 mg and more.

In addition to intentional additives, other chemicals may be present in food at the time of consumption. These are usually called *incidental* or unintentional additives and get into the food in a variety of ways. A chemical insecticide or weedicide such as Aminotriazole may be applied to a crop prior to harvesting and can be carried over into the processed food as a result of insufficient washing. A grazing steer may eat a plant that has a chemical residue on it. The chemical could survive the metabolic gyrations intact and appear in the meat of the steer. Packaging material such as a wrapper may contain an oil-soluble chemical that may migrate into an oil-based food, such as butter or lard. Or the ink on a wrapper or carton may migrate. Radioactive particles, the result of fallout from testing fission or fusion weapons, are another example of an unintentional additive. These particles can settle on foods such as vegetable crops. In essence, these are all chance contaminants, and as a consequence of inadequate washing they may be ingested with food.

A second category of intentional additives could more properly be termed *malicious*. In this category are chemicals added by dealers who want to peddle spoiled or nearly spoiled food. This group includes processors who label a food as "the fresh natural product" when in fact it is a mixture prepared by them.

Several years ago a fish dealer in Philadelphia wanted to vend a batch of spoiled fish. In order to do so, it was necessary to mask the "off" odor and color to make the fish seem fresh. Accordingly, he liberally dosed the fish with sodium nitrate. Sodium nitrate, or Chile saltpeter, is one of the most abundant naturally occurring nitrates. When used properly, it is a rather innocuous substance. During the late Middle Ages it was discovered that the color of meat became fixed when nitrate was added. It has been used for this purpose ever since. It is also well known that nitrates in sufficient quantity can cause a rapid drop in blood pressure through vasodilation—enlargement of the blood vessels.

In this instance, the fish was freely dosed with the nitrate and shipped out to markets along the Atlantic coast. Within a short time 150 people became ill with nitrate poisoning; many were hospitalized and a three-year-old child died.

Recently, much publicity has been given to nitrate and nitrite as potentially hazardous substances capable of inducing methemoglobinemia in infants and children. A good deal of newspaper space has been devoted to elevated levels of nitrates in infant foods and drinking water.

What is methemoglobinemia, how is it induced, and is it actually the hazard it is reported to be? Methemoglobinemia is a condition of the blood in which the hemoglobin, the oxygen-carrying pigment, is converted to methemoglobin. In this form, its oxygen-binding capacity is sharply reduced. As part of its molecular configuration, hemoglobin contains iron in the ferrous form. Any number of substances, including the chemical of bee stings, can oxidize ferrous iron to ferric; nitrite is one of these oxidizing agents. Usually, the nitrite is formed from nitrate (most often sodium nitrate) by microbial action.

Recently, W. E. J. Phillips of the Food and Drug Directorate of the Department of National Health and Welfare, Ottawa, Canada, reported on nitrates and nitrite in foods in relation to infant methemoglobinemia. Dr. Phillips found no evidence that the nitrate content of commercially prepared foods constitutes a hazard to human health. He did find that when fresh, naturally nitrate-rich, unprocessed spinach was held under refrigeration for several days, conversion of nitrate to nitrite occurred in quantities capable of inducing methemoglobinemia. He recommended that home-cooked spinach not be stored for subsequent feeding to infants. He further noted that "it would be regrettable if the practice of feeding leafy vegetables to infants were discredited, for these plants are extremely important dietary sources of vitamins and trace elements." [2]

Recent studies by D. N. Maynard and A. V. Barker of the University of Massachusetts have confirmed these findings; they show that increased use of nitrate fertilizers in this century has not materially increased the nitrate content of common food plants. Reporting their findings at a recent meeting of the American Society for Horticultural Science, they showed not only that tests of the nitrate level of fresh vegetables for 1907, 1964, and 1970 from Chicago, Washington, D.C., and Amherst, Mass. respectively reflected no substantial changes, but that in all cases nitrate levels were far below toxic levels.

In 1971, Dr. John R. Goldsmith told an audience gathered in Minneapolis for the ninety-ninth annual meeting of the American Public Health Association that in the twenty-five years since 1945 an estimated 1,500–2,000 cases of methemoglobinemia have occurred throughout the world. He also reported that virtually all cases reported in the United States "were from rural households with well water supplies of questionable sanitary construction. This suggests that heavy bacterial contamination might also have been present."

Dr. Goldsmith, Head of the Environmental Epidemiology Division of the California State Department of Health, concluded his remarks by stating that "compared to the effects of age and state of health in elevation of the methemoglobin level, the effect of ingesting nitrate-nitrite-nitrogen from community water supplies studied is difficult to detect."

At this point, it seems proper to raise four questions. (1) Is there a difference between naturally occurring chemicals and the synthetic or man-made variety? (2) Are chemicals inherently poisonous? (3) How is the safety of a chemical additive evaluated? and finally, (4) Is our food supply safe?

There is a notion in some quarters that anything produced from the soil—naturally—is safe to eat, while changes produced or chemicals added by man are harmful. In fact there is no difference between a chemical made in a high school or college chemistry laboratory and a flower or plant. Sucrose ($C_{12}H_{22}O_{11}$), the ordinary sugar used for sweetening purposes, is the same whether obtained from the sugar beet, sugar cane, or the dabbling of a freshman in an organic chemistry class. The "bite" in horseradish is the result of small amounts of allyl isothiocyanate, the same allyl isothiocyanate that can be manufactured and placed in bottled horseradish to increase its "bite" for those who like it hot. The only fundamental difference between a hamburger, a fish patty, Swiss cheese, vitamins, mold inhibitors, and non-nutritive sweeteners is the way their molecules are strung together; they are nothing but complex arrangements of a number of chemical elements. Foods, as we noted earlier, are much more complex arrangements of molecules than food additives, whose exact chemical formulas are known. As yet, nobody can write the chemical formula of a T-bone steak, crêpes Suzette, or a western omelette. Nevertheless, they are nothing more than proteins, carbohydrates, minerals, fats, and a number of other compounds laced together in unique fashion.

Obviously some chemicals and some additives may be injurious, and as they become known they should be omitted from our diets. But chemicals as a whole cannot be condemned out of hand, without adequate testing. On the other hand, some of the most pernicious substances known are produced by natural processes. Ergot, a plant alkaloid produced when rye and other grains become infected with the fungus *Claviceps purpurea,* has long been a notorious killer. The beautiful mushroom *Amanita phalloides* contains amanitine ($C_{40}H_{56}N_{10}O_{13}S$), which is about as virulent as a substance can be, with the possible exception of the toxin produced by the bacterium *Clostridium botulinum,* the deadliest substance known.

Toxic weeds are a well-known source of congenital birth defects for range animals. Lupine, locoweed [*Oxytropis* (white) and *Astragalus* (blue)], and *Veratrum* (cow cabbage) can produce dwarfism, cleft palate, and Cyclops eye when eaten in small amounts by pregnant animals; when consumed in large amounts they are fatal. Naturally occurring toxicants result in about a 3 to 5 percent death rate for grazing range animals each year. The sheep in Utah that were recently thought to have been killed by esoteric nerve gases probably died from an overdose of halogeton weed. For years, ranchers believed that defective animals resulted from poor hereditary traits and often killed the ram or bull that sired the defective. Now they know better.

A booklet, *Toxicants Occurring Naturally in Foods,* published by the National Research Council, reviews a number of chemicals found in plant crops capable of producing goiter, tumors, paralysis, and death. Being "natural" is no guarantee of safety; neither is a synthetic chemical harmful *per se.*

As one of the 102 elements naturally present in the earth's crust, lead, not surprisingly, has a habit of straying into our food. Its use in pipes and pewter over a thousand years has left a legacy of harm.

Lead can enter food in a most curious way: as a result of storing food or drink in earthenware containers. For hundreds of years lead oxide and lead chromate, two compounds of lead, have been important ingredients in many glazes applied to ceramic ware. Lead glazes * are known to impart brilliance and enhance the colors of the pigments used to decorate the pieces. If the glaze is properly applied and adequately fired, the lead compounds are firmly sealed and cannot be leached out by the food that contacts the ceramic surface. If not properly sealed, the lead is readily withdrawn, particularly by acidic foods: tomato juice, apple cider, orange juice, wine, pickles, sauerkraut, and salad dressings containing vinegar, to name a few. Lead poisoning of this type can occur over a period of a few weeks or a few years, depending upon the amount of lead leached and ingested.

Two young boys, a two-year-old and his four-year-old brother, were brought to a hospital emergency room with nausea and vomiting over a three-week period. Because these symptoms are common to a variety of illnesses, rest and fluids were advised. Unfortunately, the fluids were from the same ceramic vessel that caused the condition and only aggravated it. Both boys were hospitalized when lethargy, anorexia (loss of appetite), and hyperirritability became evident. A urinary lead level of 138 mg/liter (.02–.08 is normal) was found in the youngest; 60 mg/liter was found in the four-year-old. Despite vigorous therapy, the two-year-old died. Five months after treatment the older boy's blood and urine lead levels were near normal.

In another incident, a physician was hospitalized with lead poisoning after ingesting 3.2 mg of lead per night for two years. He had been using a ceramic mug made by his son in his university ceramics class.

To be sure you are purchasing a safe ceramic vessel, ask the dealer to show you evidence that the item has been adequately tested. Amateur potters can obtain a test kit with which to check out their creations. For information on these kits, contact a local FDA office.

We have mentioned cyclopentanoperhydropenanthrene as the chemical designation for Vitamin D and Vitamin D-like compounds. Whether prepared in the laboratory (as it can be by any good senior university student) or extracted from fish oil, it is identical. The naturally occurring and synthetic substances pro-

---

* A glaze is the thin layer of glass fused onto the surface of clay wares.

duce the same effect when fed to humans and animals and cannot be distinguished by standard analytical procedures.

When Swiss cheese is chemically analyzed, one of the naturally occurring products found is sodium propionate. This is the same chemical used in bread baking to inhibit mold.

Coumarin is a naturally occurring chemical that imparts a unique bouquet to sweet clover, tonka bean, and certain common grasses. It can also be synthesized in the laboratory from acetic anhydride, salicylaldehyde, and sodium acetate. Natural or synthetic, it has proved harmful to laboratory animals and was removed from the list of approved additives after some years of use as a vanilla substitute.

Many people who eat fish, tomatoes, or acidic fruits erupt with hives. Their bodies are responding adversely to natural chemicals. Although called *allergy* and at times considered fashionable, this reaction is nevertheless an injury evoked by a natural product. Unfortunately, "natural" or "naturally occurring" is no guarantee of safety; similarly, "synthetic" or "man-made" is not prima facie evidence of hazard.

Whether a chemical additive is natural, synthetic, intentional, or incidental, the question invariably asked is: Is it poisonous? Before a reliable answer can be given, it is necessary to know what a poison is. The ancient adage, "One man's poison is another man's porridge," reminds us that a poison—a chemical—has variable consequences depending upon the individual involved. This should perhaps suggest that the unavoidable question, "Is it poisonous?" is not readily answered by yes or no. Recall the spoiled fish sprinkled with sodium nitrate; when this substance is used in properly prescribed amounts, no problems arise. When greater than prescribed doses are administered, some adults become mildly ill, others so ill as to require hospitalization, and others may not even be uncomfortable. On the other hand, babies often die. Thus any definition of a poison must consider who is to use it and how much is to be given. In addition, such factors as age, sex, nutritional condition, and general state of health exert much influence on the type and degree of response. Accordingly, everything and nothing can be poisonous depending upon a constellation of factors. Good examples of this concept are aspirin and penicillin, which have a long history of successful use to alleviate pain and infection, respectively. However, overdoses of aspirin are responsible for hundreds of deaths among men and women each year. Aspirin consumption is also the leading cause of accidental poisoning among children aged one to five. Although penicillin, the first broad-spectrum antibiotic, has performed well since its introduction some twenty years ago, a number of severe allergic reactions to its presence in the body (analphylatic shock) are reported each year.

Common table salt is essential to life; yet an "overdose" would probably kill a man if taken over a short time. Many metals such as copper, manganese, zinc, and cobalt are essential to health in trace amounts but can become toxic in larger quantities. Both Vitamins A and D, when taken in doses larger than prescribed, are known to cause severe damage to the human system. Thus, to answer the original question, a poison can be any substance that may cause death or illness when taken in sufficient quantity. This was well known to the Romans, who coined the expression, "*Dosis sola facit veneum*"—"what makes a poison is dose."

A further distinction that must be made is that between *hazard* and *toxicity*. While these terms are used synonymously and interchangeably, in reality they connote totally different ideas. Toxicity is the capacity of a substance to produce injury. Hazard, on the other hand, is the probability that injury will result from the use of the substance, if continued in the manner and amount proposed. Whereas toxicity implies a known fact, hazard is a presumption based upon the statistical likelihood derived from a number of previous events or experiences. In short, it is speculative.

Although we are still quite unaware of the causes of cancer, the fear of it is widespread in our society. This is an understandable reaction to the unknown; it is not surprising that there is clamor to prohibit the use in food of any substance not absolutely guaranteed to be noncarcinogenic. Many people, when told that a chemical is hazardous—that it has produced cancer in laboratory rats or running fits in puppies—will shy away from it.

Although this may seem a reasonable reaction, the situation is not as simple or straightforward as it may appear. Such basic nutrients as glucose (dextrose) and sodium chloride have produced cancer in laboratory animals when injected in 20-percent and 15-percent solutions, respectively; yet both are needed for survival.

René Dubos noted that "according to a recent report, even hens' eggs contain a carcinogenic substance. Chickens and mice fed a diet made up of wheat bran and eggs grew faster and became sexually more mature earlier, but developed cancer of the ovary." He went on to say that "it is unreasonable to insist on zero concentrations of a given substance in food merely because administration of massive doses of it has increased the incidence of tumors in the experimental animals. . . . It is far from simple to evaluate whether the consequences of complete prohibition of a food additive are beneficial to society on balance."

For some years EDTA, ethylenediaminetetracetate, has been used as a chelating or sequestering agent in a number of foods. This means that it is an intentional additive that prevents discoloration by binding trace quantities of metallic ions (copper, iron, chromium). However, a new role for EDTA may just be over the horizon. If the recent botulism outbreaks can be considered a guide, EDTA may be a welcome addition to the food technologist's arsenal.

Chapter 3 presented the problem of clostridial food poisoning. We saw that the bacteria producing toxins A, B, and E, of primary concern as producers of human botulism, will not grow in low-acid foods (with a pH below 4.5). Additionally, a fair number of foods can be given a high heat treatment that will remove the culpable bacterial spores. Nevertheless, such items as cured hams and smoked fish cannot be subjected to severe heat treatments. For this reason, refrigeration or bacterial inhibitors must be depended upon to prevent bacterial growth and subsequent toxin production.

The search for chemical inhibitors has been going on for years. Recent laboratory experiments have shown that low concentrations of EDTA can completely inhibit both growth and toxin formation in a number of foods. Should this discovery be borne out in field trials with low acid canned and packaged items, botulism may be a thing of the past—but EDTA will require re-certification for use for a new purpose. Will it receive public acceptance? Or will it be frowned upon as just one more synthetic chemical in the pot?

To protect the public from potentially hazardous chemicals, Public Law 85–929 was enacted. Also known as the Food Additives Amendment of 1958, it contains the Delaney Clause, which states that "no additive shall be deemed safe if it is found, after tests which are appropriate for the evaluation of safety of food additives, to induce cancer in man or animal." Clearly, any law that proscribes the use in food of any chemical producing cancer in animals must be called into question. Too many fundamental nutrients can be shown to be carcinogenic by devising the proper laboratory experiment.

On the other hand, the Delaney Clause clearly enunciates ". . . after tests which *are appropriate* for the evaluation of safety. . . ." Unfortunately, and for reasons not readily comprehensible, a number of animal studies have clearly violated this requirement. The recent controversies surrounding cyclamates and MSG are excellent examples of this.*

Concerning these two food additives, the joint FAO/WHO Expert Committee on Food Additives had this to say: "The Committee discussed the production of tumors of the urinary bladder following implantation of cholesterol pellets containing cyclamate. It held that these results were not in themselves definitive for the assessment of a toxic effect, since ingestion of the substance is the only route of administration of food additives." About MSG they said, "Much of the recent work on the effects of glutamate is concerned with high doses which produce acute pharmacological reactions, but there is little in this data to suggest long-term toxic hazard."

The current concept of protection of public health via food consumption requires that certain additives such as pesticides or other suspected carcinogens be present in zero quantity. What is the meaning of zero tolerance? As analytical techniques become more accurate and precise, what was not measurable today may well be measurable tomorrow. Thus, zero one day can be a positive finite number another. In reality, nothing has changed except the ability to detect and measure smaller quantities. The concentration of an additive in a food has not changed. As a consequence, the concept of a zero changing from month to month loses its

---

* On September 1, 1970, cyclamates were banned for all human consumption in the United States.

original meaning and, in fact, has no meaning. As the methods for the detection of additives in biological systems become more sensitive, the investigator needs to become more critical in his interpretation of the significance of these trace levels.

Magnus Pike, writing on "Food Facts and Fallacies" in the *Royal Society of Health Journal* for April 1967, said:

> It is now recognized that to demand what the United States authorities describe as "zero tolerance" is a philosophical impossibility. For a number of years, however, there was a legal demand for officially approved foods to contain zero amounts of certain chemical compounds. Chemical analysis, however, is science not magic. Analytical determinations demand that at the end one drop of reagent shall cause the color to change, to take a simple example. This one drop can represent 1 part per million and allow the analyst to say that this amount is or is not present. Should he develop a method ten times as sensitive, he can say that one-tenth part of a substance under investigation is or is not there. But he can say nothing about less, and no analyst can ever say that the amount of allegedly toxic agent is zero. In order to avoid cross-examination by a lawyer prosecuting on behalf of the public authorities, the best a food manufacturer could do was make sure that his product has not been analyzed at all!

Dr. Pike went on to illustrate the absurdity of this position by noting that

> the difficulty of distinguishing wisdom from fallacy when presented with the problem of where to draw the line has been grotesquely high-lighted by an argument about fish flour. This is a product composed of fat-extracted, dried and powdered fish. Incorporated in an impoverished diet, it could contribute protein. The United States Food and Drug Authority hesitated to approve it as fit for human consumption, not because anybody has ever been harmed by eating it, but because since it contains the viscera of fish and their contents as well as fish muscle, it was classified as "filthy." By a historical anomaly . . . oysters, clams, cockles and mussels, all of which are offered as human food with their digestive parts in them, are accepted as wholesome.[3]

It appears that in a society altered by huge population increases, by women in large numbers going into the labor force and having little time for kitchen chores, and by the great bulk of the population insisting upon a wide selection of foods all the year round, chemicals are a necessary part of our lives. This does not sanction or even suggest the use of any and all chemicals in foods. It does suggest that as reasonable people we understand the need for their use and we also understand that certain chemicals, after proper testing and proper surveillance, can increase, improve, and preserve our food supply.

It is generally recognized that all chemicals are toxic to man and animals if large enough amounts are ingested. Even such seemingly innocuous substances as salt, pepper, vinegar, sugar, and mustard—chemicals all—may induce untoward effects when taken in excessive amounts. Consequently, a limit on the daily intake of a substance is essential for protection of health. The World Health Organization's Expert Committee has set up levels of acceptable daily intakes—ADIs—for chemicals to be used as food additives.

An *unconditional* ADI is given only to those substances for which the available data include results of adequate short- and long-term toxicological studies or information on the biochemistry and metabolic fate of the chemical, or both. A *conditional* ADI is given in cases arising from special dietary requirements. A *temporary* ADI is issued when the available data are not considered adequate to establish the safety of the compound; WHO requires that additional evidence be provided within a stated time. If the requested data are not forthcoming within this period, the temporary ADI is withdrawn. Finally, an ADI can be withheld if evidence of safety is lacking or inadequate. For example, the Committee concluded that MSG could be given an unconditional ADI of 0–120 mg/kg applicable to the general population except infants under one year of age. On the other hand, it withheld an ADI for brominated vegetable oil previously used to adjust the density of essential oils in soft drinks when evidence was presented that high doses caused degenerative cardiac lesions in experimental animals. The fact is that the books are never closed on any additive: new data obtained by different methods are scrutinized periodically to ascertain the need for re-evaluation.

It may be helpful to review the criteria used in establishing efficacy and safety of any chemical. The Food Protection Committee * of the National Academy of Sciences–National Research Council, a private, nonprofit organization of scientists dedicated to furthering science and its use for the general welfare, has also undertaken to study the procedures for investigating and evaluating the safety of chemicals used in foods.

Studies of the biological effects on experimental animals of chemicals that may be introduced into food have as a major objective the prediction of possible hazard to man. One of the foremost difficulties in animal studies is the interpretation and prediction of safe levels in man. Generally, toxicity experiments aim to obtain estimates of maximum daily intakes that would be safe for all segments of the population.

The report that large doses of MSG produced brain lesions in newborn animals is a formidable example of the difficulty that currently exists in extrapolating the data to man. Any attempt to interpret this finding runs into two problems: the unusually high levels used in the animal feeding studies vis-à-vis the low levels normally found in food, and the problem of how far developmental stages in animals parallel man. The question that remains to be answered is: are animals and man equally vulnerable at similar developmental periods of growth? As yet no one knows, but studies are in progress to attempt to shed more light on this sticky problem.

To judge the safety of an additive, several factors must be considered. First, the most suitable animal species must be chosen, as no one species can be said to be *the* satisfactory substitute for man. Another factor is information on the expected amounts and patterns of consumption of the food containing the additive; this is particularly germane and highly variable. An important prac-

* The Food Protection Committee operates under the Food and Nutrition Board, but is independently financed by grants from food, chemical, and packaging companies, commercial laboratories, and individuals. The Food and Nutrition Board was established in 1940 under the Division of Biology and Agriculture of the NAS-NRC. It serves as an advisory body in the field of food and nutrition, promotes research, and helps interpret nutritional science in the interests of the public welfare. The members of the Board are appointed from among leaders in the food and nutrition sciences on the basis of experience and judgment.

tical objective is to select animals with short lifespans. This is not a difficult criterion to satisfy, as the only species that are available in large numbers and convenient to house are all rodents: the rat, mouse, hamster, and guinea pig. Both the rat and mouse have been shown to be susceptible to the carcinogenic action of a large variety of chemicals; in fact, most of the current data on the carcinogenic action of chemicals are rodent data.

Because of the difficulties of extrapolating from rodent to man, a non-rodent is often used as a second test type. Although the dog, monkey, and pig have relatively long lives, they are often used. Two animal species are still far from equaling the human system, but taken together the data become highly suggestive. Figures 12 and 13 show types of procedures employed in animal feeding studies.

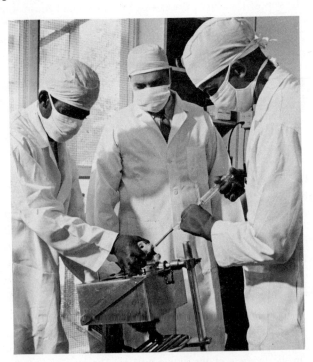

Figure 12. Insertion of a chemical additive. The monkey is in a restraining cage. (FDA photo.)

*Figure 13. Testing of food additive in an albino rat.
(FDA photo.)*

Toxicity is usually determined on both a short-term and a
long-term basis. An estimate of the acute toxicity of a chemical
may be obtained relatively rapidly—within a few days to a few
weeks—by determining how much of the chemical in a single dose
is necessary to kill 50 percent of the test animals—the LD_{50}. The
purpose of the acute toxicity test is to obtain a first approximation
of the inherent pharmacological character of the compound. If
the proposed level of use of the substance approximates the lethal
dose, the tests can be concluded and the chemical quickly disap-
proved.

Experiments to estimate the effects analogous to lifetime
ingestion can be carried out over a period of ninety days. These
subacute toxicity tests can serve as guides for selecting feeding
levels for the chronic toxicity studies.

Long-term feeding (chronic toxicity) studies are carried out on the premise that the effects of lifetime ingestion of an additive by man cannot be predicted from experiments less rigorous than the total lifespan of a short-lived animal (two to three years).

In chronic toxicity studies, the chemical is generally fed to three or four groups of 20–30 animals per group. Each group is given a varying amount of additive. A control group receiving the same diet minus the additive is always included. Feeding is started as soon as possible after weaning and is continued for at least two years. During the two years of the tests a host of qualitative and quantitative observations are made; these include total food consumption, growth, weight, mortality, chemical analysis of blood and urine, behavior, and reproductive capacity.

An unusually instructive example of the way researchers develop information on a potentially harmful additive is exemplified in the recent report of Löfroth and Gejvall.[4] Their experiments showed that Diethyl Pyrocarbamate (DEP), Baycovia, an antimicrobial food additive used primarily in beer, wine, and citrus juices, itself a non-toxic substance, can on interaction with ammonia (normally present in a number of foods as a result of the natural conversion of amino acids) produce ethyl carbamate (urethan), a known carcinogen.

A most interesting feature of this work is its bringing to light of new data on a substance that had previously been tested without finding the potentially carcinogenic by-product. It is particularly noteworthy that the new findings had to await the advancement of our technical capability. The unusually sensitive isotope dilution technique used by Löfroth and Gejvall had not yet been developed for use in this area when the substance was first tested. From studies such as this one, recommendations can be made on the amounts of DEP that can safely be used in foods.

The decision as to whether a proposed chemical is safe for human consumption can be arrived at only after evaluation of several factors: the maximum dietary level that produced no untoward response in both test species; experience with other chemicals of similar structure; and estimation of the potential human consumption of all foods containing the additive.

Recently, even the most common foods have come under question. The Food, Drug and Cosmetic Act defines a GRAS (for

Generally Recognized As Safe) substance as one "generally recognized, among experts qualified by scientific training and experience to evaluate its safety, as having been adequately shown through scientific procedures . . . to be safe under the conditions of its intended use." GRAS substances are not considered food additives and, therefore, are exempt from the regulations established by the Food Additives Amendment of 1958. The current GRAS list contains some 700 substances.* In his consumer-protection message to Congress on October 30, 1969, President Nixon directed the Food and Drug Administration to review and re-evaluate the safety of all food chemicals generally recognized as safe. Ordinary household items such as salt, pepper, vinegar, sugar, and spices, as well as hundreds of others that have been eaten for hundred of years, are now to be tested. At the request of the FDA, FASEB, the Federation of American Societies for Experimental Biology, will evaluate the vast published literature on each substance on the GRAS list. Its recommendations will go to FDA for final action.

In its recent publication, *Evaluating the Safety of Food Chemicals,* the National Academy of Science defined safety as "the practical certainty that injury will not result from the substance when used in the quantity and in the manner proposed for its use." It will at once be seen that absolute certainty of no risk is not a part of this definition. And it cannot be. Absolute guarantees of safety cannot be made by men for men.

By its very nature, the study of chemicals in food encompasses a broad spectrum of topics. Among them must be the natural forms of incorporation of chemicals by plants and animals. Of exceptional instructional value (bearing out the Red Queen's observation to Alice that "That is a well known fact, so well known that it may not be true at all") are "organic" farming as a means of obtaining crop plants of enhanced nutritional (chemical) quality, and mercury uptake by a variety of fish and its effect on health.

Organic farming has an ancient heritage. Well before the advent of the agricultural sciences and experiment stations, farmers believed that feeding soils a variety of organic materials (fish,

---

* The actual number and name of all substances on the GRAS list can be found in the *CFR,* the Code of Federal Regulations, Parts 120–121. This should be available in most libraries.

blood, manure, crop residues, bonemeal, etc.) resulted in increased plant growth. While the results may have justified the use in a number of instances, the concept was fallacious. Without knowing it, the farmers were only adding minerals, minerals that may have been lacking or in short supply in the soil. Simply stated, plants cannot take up organic material (molecules). But this is not a new discovery. In 1699, John Woodward sent his *Thoughts and Experiments on Vegetation* to the Royal Society of London. From his experiments on growing plants in rain, river, and muddy water he found that plants grew far better in muddy water. By 1840 this observation could be explained: Justus von Liebig, a German chemist, showed by careful analysis of soils and plants that it was the minerals in soils (and muddy water) that were responsible for adequate plant growth. For over a hundred years, it has been demonstrated at experiment stations around the world that plant roots take up only minerals; the application of fertilizer in the form of animal manures, composts, crop residues, animal blood, bonemeal, fish, or other organic matter contributes nothing but the unique combination and quantity of minerals present in the organic fertilizer used.

In Figure 14 the process is graphically set forth. Organic fertilizers contribute their supply of minerals only after soil microorganisms have metabolized the fertilizer releasing the minerals to the soil. Synthetic or man-made fertilizers, the so-called chemical fertilizers, do not require microbial decomposition as they are already in usable form. Once in the soil, minerals move in moisture to plant roots and up into the plants.

Meanwhile, the process of photosynthesis is taking place in plant leaves. This process produces the organic energy-containing compounds in the plant. Together, the minerals taken up via the root system and the sugars, amino acids, starches, etc. manufactured in leaf cells account for plant growth.

Organic farmers and cultists continue to repress these well-known facts of plant physiology and nutrition. Many refuse to acknowledge what has been demonstrated time and again—that organic fertilizers are often deficient in a number of minerals particularly nitrogen and phosphorus. They will not admit that organic material used as fertilizer never reaches the plant—it cannot. It is from inanimate chemicals in soil and from photosyn-

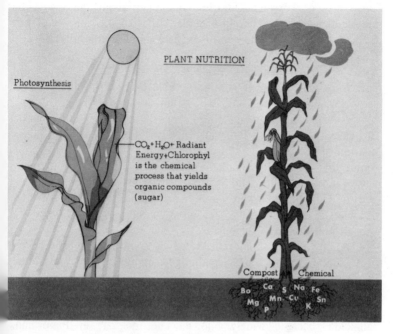

PLANT NUTRITION

Photosynthesis

CO_2 + H_2O + Radiant Energy + Chlorophyl is the chemical process that yields organic compounds (sugar)

Compost   Chemical

Bo Ca S Na Fe
Mg Mn Cu Sn
P K

Figure 14.   The cycles of plant nutrition.

thetic processes in leaves that the living crops we call food are produced. And it has yet to be shown that plants grown in organic residues yield more nutritious food. In fact, all evidence is to the contrary.

It is an inescapable fact that all foods, all things, are nothing but chemicals strung together in different ways. Grapefruit is different from carrots, which are different from steak and potatoes, only as a consequence of proteins, carbohydrates, fats, minerals, water (all chemicals), and a variety of other chemical compounds put together in unique order. To deny chemicals is to deny ourselves.

The case of mercury uptake by fish and seafood and its relationship to human health recalls not only the Red Queen's observation to Alice, but also the story of Chicken Little. Is the sky really falling?

In March 1970, Norvold Fimreite, a graduate student at the

University of Western Ontario, concerned about the increasing industrial use of mercury in Canada, collected 42 samples of fish from Lake St. Clair. He sent these fish samples to a laboratory in California for mercury analysis. The results he received indicated levels of methylmercury chloride far above the arbitrarily pegged guidelines of 0.5 ppm in the raw, edible parts of fin and shellfish set in 1969 by the Food and Drug Administration.

Advised by Canadian officials of the mercury contamination in Lake St. Clair, the FDA's Detroit district office began an investigation of the level and source of mercury pollution. It was soon found that two chlorine-alkali plants were discharging mercury wastes into the Detroit and St. Clair Rivers. By April, both Canada and the United States were banning and embargoing all freshwater fish caught in these lakes. The great mercury scare of 1970–71 was off and running—furiously.

At this point, as if orchestrated by some master hand, magazine and newspaper articles dredged up every mercury-related incident. Minamata disease * became a household word. The Iraqi accident reported ten years earlier, in which flour was mixed with wheat seed that had been treated with a mercury-containing fungicide, became widely known. The incident in Panorama, Guatemala, in which Guatemalan Indians ate wheat seeds treated with Panogen (1.5% methylmercury dicyandiamide) rather than starve before crops would be available, although reported in a relatively obscure journal in 1966, was given wide circulation in the press.

To top the list of horror stories making the rounds, the tragedy of the Huckleby family in Arizona could be found in a dozen magazine articles. Berton Roueché's account, "Insufficient Evidence," in the *New Yorker*'s "Annals of Medicine," was undoubtedly the best of the lot. Here too, Panogen-treated grain was the culprit. Hogs had been fed floor sweepings containing the grain. Exhaustive investigation revealed that all but two of the nine members of the family had eaten pork from the slaughtered hogs. Four of the children showed evidence of complete central nervous system involvement and may never fully recover. The two sisters,

* Characteristically, Minamata disease, named for the Japanese village in which the illness was first diagnosed, affects the peripheral nervous system and the cerebellum. Loss of hearing, vision, and balance are not uncommon.

aged 8 and 21 (1969), had hair mercury levels far in excess of any ever reported in the medical literature—1,397 and 2,436 ppm. These accounts were served up again and again as though the tuna and swordfish that were summarily banished from food markets in the United States were in any way related. Did anyone care? Was anyone listening? What was important—getting the tuna and swordfish off the market or really protecting the health of the American people? The outcry on the mercury problem by the press produced a state of alarm approaching hysteria. Was it necessary to raise the anxiety of the population further? I think not.

Figure 15 shows the world's major tuna fishing grounds. These hardly relate to Lake St. Clair, Arizona, or Guatemala. Banning walleye pike and perch taken from the industrially polluted waters of Detroit and Ontario makes sense, but hardly the extension to tuna and swordfish. It is also difficult to understand why U.S. officials had to banish all canned tuna and frozen swordfish so spectacularly when Canada, Great Britain, and Sweden, all major fish-eating nations, did not believe it necessary to do so. In fact, Sweden, where more research on mercury has been done than anywhere else, has a 1.0 ppm allowable level of mercury in fish—twice ours.

Considering the shortcomings in the techniques of mercury analysis of which all scientists at work on the problem are aware, it has been demonstrated that over the past 30 to 40 years mercury levels in fish have not changed substantially. As to levels in humans, a recent study shows it to be decreasing. A team of pathologists headed by Dr. Jack Kevorkian of Saratoga General Hospital, Detroit, examined preserved human tissues taken at autopsy as far back as 1913. Comparing these with tissue of Michigan residents who had died of causes unrelated to mercury poisoning, they found an extraordinary decline in mercury content in almost all the organs studied. Dr. Kevorkian remarked, "There is no increasing health threat from mercury. The body content appears to be decreasing." He went on to say that there was no scientific data to support the 0.5 ppm standard. The facts indicate a "gratifying cleansing of the environment." [5]

In a recent publication in the *New England Journal of Medicine,* Dr. Thomas B. Eyl of St. Clair, Michigan reported on the

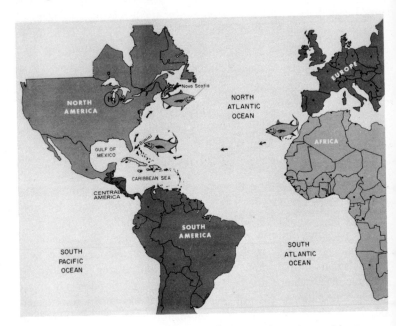

Figure 15. Major tuna fishing areas of the world.

International Conference on Environmental Mercury Contamination held in the fall of 1970. Dr. Eyl stated that

> an even more serious source of almost certain error in our calculations to date is that most current tests measure only total mercury levels. Since fish usually contain 100 per cent methylmercury, we have mistakenly jumped to several conclusions: that most or all of the total mercury found in food, blood, hair, etc. is organically bound (i.e., alkylmercury); that any other form of mercury in these samples is as dangerous as alkylmercury; and that the desirable level of mercury (alkyl- or total) for health and well-being of plants, animals and man is nil.[6]

Blood tests on people who have been "heavy eaters"—up to four times a week—of Lake St. Clair fish have shown total mercury blood levels of up to 70 parts per billion, with an average of 29 ppb, well below the 100 ppb established as safe by an international panel.

In a recent article, "Mercury in the Environment," Dr. Leonard J. Goldwater of Duke University stated that "it would be foolish to declare an all-out war against mercury. The evolutionary evidence suggests that too little mercury in the environment might be as disastrous as too much." [7] He also called for detailed investigation of how mercury is being redistributed and concentrated in the environment by man's activities.

As if to directly answer this call, Weiss, Koide, and Goldberg of the Naval Undersea Research Center and Scripps Institution of Oceanography reported on "Mercury in a Greenland Ice Sheet: Evidence of Recent Input by Man." After calculating the amount of mercury produced throughout the world in 1968 and the amount displaced by degassing of the earth's crust, they concluded that "the recently measured concentrations in such pelagic fish as tuna and swordfish are probably not far removed from the norm. The input of twice as much mercury to surface waters of the ocean in recent times can only increase the amount of mercury in the lower trophic levels by, at best, a factor of 2." [8]

Further reinforcement of the view that for thousands of years natural mercury levels in fish have been as high or higher than the 0.5 mg/kg (ppm) arbitrarily set by the FDA, was supplied by the recent studies of Dr. Edwin Wilmsen. Dr. Wilmsen, Curator of the University of Michigan's Museum of Anthropology, sampled specimens of fish (drum, tuna, cat, anchovy) preserved in the Museum's collection. These fish ranged in age from 300–2000 years and contained levels of mercury up to 9.5 parts per million.

Putting these pieces together, it appears that there is little evidence to support the precipitous removal of tuna and swordfish from markets. I must call the mercury scare of 1970 an unconscionable act perpetrated upon an already anxiety-ridden public. At this point, I return to Chicken Little and the Red Queen. No, the sky is not falling; and there is much about mercury in food that is not at all true.

"How can I get the facts, or know if what I read is true?" This question is obviously one every consumer should ask, and is being asked with greater frequency. Unfortunately, it is not easily answered. The following example highlights this predicament we all face.

On February 1, 1972, the *New York Times* reported an interview with Bess Myerson, Commissioner of the Department of Consumer Affairs, New York City. The article quoted Miss Myerson as saying that a number of chemicals used in frankfurters have never been tested. The article noted that a typical all-meat frankfurter contains beef, pork, corn syrup, dextrose, flavoring, erythorbic acid, sodium nitrate, sodium nitrite, salt, and water.

Because I believed this statement to be erroneous, I wrote Miss Myerson on February 1, asking which ingredients have never been tested. Having had no response by March 2, I wrote again. On March 14, Miss Myerson's office replied. Her representative wrote that the *Times* article was misleading. Miss Myerson, the letter noted, was speaking generally and referred not to frankfurters but to all food additives; and furthermore, the FDA could substantiate the fact that fully half of all food additives have never been tested.

On March 20, I wrote a letter to the editor of the *New York Times* indicating the discrepancy between their article and the Commissioner's office. On March 21, I wrote a letter to Dr. Virgil O. Wodicka, Director, Bureau of Foods, FDA, asking if he could substantiate the report that fully half of all food additives had never been tested.

The *Times* responded first. Their letter of March 29 questioned the idea that there was anything "misleading" about their article. On May 5, Dr. Wodicka responded. He suspected that by suggesting that half of all food additives had never been tested, Miss Myerson was referring to substances on the GRAS list. In the frankfurters, this would mean pork fat, corn syrup, salt, and any other ingredient deemed safe and in use prior to January 1, 1958. The statement could not have referred to any regulated additive. This was indeed a different kettle of fish.

Plainly everyone cannot indulge in this letter-writing game (a few phone calls were also required). How else, then, can people find this type of information? The answer I must give is not satisfactory. First of all, question the source; all those writing and speaking on environmental subjects are not equally competent. Write letters, even though they go unanswered for long periods.

Dr. Wodicka made a point of telling me that a large volume of mail is received by the FDA and that for the most part it is answered—even if it takes three or four months.

Finally, contact professors at nearby universities, but don't be satisfied with an unsupported opinion. At best, with all the communications media, we are shortchanged on reliable information. To attempt to deal with this issue, I recently wrote a decalogue for consumers. If followed, these ten commandments could provide consumers, the public, with the type of aid and support needed.[9]

References

1. Magnus Pike, "Food Facts and Fallacies," *Journal of the Royal Society of Health* 82 (1967): 10.

2. W. E. J. Phillips, "Naturally Occurring Nitrate and Nitrite in Foods in Relation to Infant Methaemoglobinaemia," *Food and Cosmetics Toxicology* 9 (1971): 219.

3. Pike, "Food Facts," p. 10.

4. Göran Löfroth and T. Gejvall, "Diethyl Pyrocarbamate: Formation of Urethan in Treated Beverages," *Science* 174 (1971): 1248.

5. J. Kevorkian et al., "Mercury Content of Human Tissues During the Twentieth Century," *American Journal of Public Health* 62 (1972): 504.

6. T. B. Eyl, "Organic-Mercury Food Poisoning," *New England Journal of Medicine* 284 (1971): 706.

7. L. J. Goldwater, "Mercury in the Environment," *Scientific American* 224 (1971): 15.

8. H. V. Weiss et al., "Mercury in a Greenland Ice Sheet: Evidence of Recent Input by Man," *Science* 174 (1971): 692.

9. M. A. Benarde and N. W. Jerome, "Food Quality and the Consumer: A Decalogue," *American Journal of Public Health* 62 (1972): 1199.

Suggested Reading

Winarno, F. G.; Stumbo, C. K.; and Hayes, K. M. "Effect of EDTA on the Generation of and Outgrowth from Spores of *Clostridium Botulinum* 62-A." *Journal of Food Science* 36 (1971): 781.

Evaluating the Safety of Food Chemicals. Washington: National Academy of Sciences, 1970.

Evaluation of Food Additives: Fourteenth Report of the Joint FAO/ WHO Expert Committee on Food Additives. Geneva: WHO Tech. Rept. Ser. 462, 1971.

CHAPTER

5

PESTICIDES

There are occasions when the general belief of the people, even though it be groundless, works its effect as sure as truth itself.

Schiller

A million men, women, and children, fatigued from working round the clock, are plucking the leaf worm and its cocoon and eggs from the cotton leaves in a struggle to save Egypt's cotton crop. At least a quarter of the national crop is believed to have been destroyed already. The final figure is likely to be much higher. A sense of crisis pulses across the cotton-growing lands flanking the River Nile. This week is likely to be crucial in the effort to save the vital crop on which the country's hard-pressed economy so closely depends.

This dispatch from Cairo in 1966 dramatized the fact that insects have not yet succumbed to man's attempt to protect his crops from their depredations.* The leaf worm and the boll weevil

* On June 26, 1967, Cairo radio announced that the cotton-leaf worm

are so resistant to chemical insecticides that the only sure method of destroying them is by hand-picking.

Insects pose a real threat to our food, fiber, health, and comfort, and must be contained. Unfortunately, nature does not go out of her way to favor man. We live as one of the many species inhabiting this planet and must struggle as best we can with nature's laws.

Fortunately for us, however, we are endowed with the intelligence to regulate our environment to our advantage. However, our handling of the enormous problem of insect pests may suggest how intelligent we really are. Of course, the insects start with a great advantage; they have evolved over some 250 million years, compared to our one million years. This seniority has led to some remarkable survival characteristics that have attuned them almost perfectly to their ecological niche. Their ability to adapt to a hostile environment was seen in the resistance they displayed to chemical agents they had never before encountered. How resourceful we humans will be, remains to be seen.

Insects and other arthropods * are all around us: they live in our houses, puncture our skin, and consume our food and clothing. There is scarcely a place on the planet that is not home to at least one insect. They have been found in deep underground caves, and termites have been trapped at altitudes of twenty thousand

---

was ravaging the cotton crop. This time, little if any insecticide was available. Thousands of children were ordered into the fields to pick the worms by hand from the cotton plants.

* When we speak of insects and arthropods, we refer to specific forms. True insects differ in several major characteristics from other arthropods. True insects have three body parts: head, thorax, and abdomen; three pairs of legs; usually two pairs of wings; and one pair of antennae. Ticks and mites, on the other hand, have a sac-like body with no segmentation, four pairs of legs, and no antennae. They are not true insects. All arthropods (*arthros*=joint-legged) are classified as follows:

PHYLUM ARTHROPODA

Class Crustacea:	crabs, shrimps, barnacles
Insects:	ants, bees, flies, mosquitoes, beetles, wasps, lice, roaches, aphids, moths, fleas, termites, and locusts (to note a few)
Arachnida:	spiders, scorpions, ticks, mites
Myriapoda:	centipedes, millipedes

feet. Some forty varieties live in the Antarctic region; mosquitoes and other biting insects penetrate the polar regions as far as the warm-blooded animals on which they feed. Insects are abundant in desert areas and in rushing waters. Different species are adapted for life in the air, on land, in soil, and in fresh water, brackish water (1 percent salt), or salt water (3 percent salt). Wherever they live, they seem to be indestructible. Man has never eradicated a single insect pest from the earth. In fact, a number exhibit increased resistance to chemical agents designed specifically for their destruction. Insects have been frozen solid at −35°C and have still lived. Others inhabit hot springs where temperatures reach 50°C (120° to 125°F). Petroleum flies spend part of their lives in pools of crude oil around well heads. Many insects can endure long periods without water; they possess fuel reserves and can get the water they require by metabolizing carbohydrates to carbon dioxide and water.

Insects have an enormous size range—probably greater than any other major animal group. The smallest, approximately 250 microns, are smaller than some single-celled protozoa; the largest are larger than mice. The Atlas moth of India measures twelve inches from wing tip to wing tip.

Why are insects so successful? As a group their success seems to be due to at least six major assets:

1. *Adaptability*: As previously noted, they can live within a wide range of environmental conditions. They can eat anything—corks, mummies, tobacco, cotton, paper, etc.

2. *External skeleton:* * Their cylindrical shape offers the strongest possible construction for a given amount of material. Being wax-coated, it is resistant to drying from inside and outside.

3. *Small size*: As a consequence of their usually small size, their food and water needs are comparatively quite small.

4. *Ability to fly*: Wings allow wide distribution and thus greater choice of food and environment and escape from predators.

5. *Metamorphosis*: This is the gradual change in form or structure that occurs during the insect's developmental period.

---

* The exoskeleton or cuticle contains a polysaccharide, chitin, which is made up of a series of glucosamine units, joined by beta-linkages, which imparts structural integrity.

Three types of insects are recognized. Some, such as flies, mosquitoes, and moths, undergo complete metamorphosis, consisting of four stages—egg, larva, pupa, and adult. In those insects that undergo incomplete metamorphosis, with egg, nymph, and adult, several nymphal stages can occur in which the insect simply grows larger. Cockroaches, grasshoppers, and body lice are examples of this type. The third type exhibits no metamorphic development. The young possess all the features of the adult; they simply increase in size. The silverfish, a primitive type of insect, is an example of this type of development. These various types of metamorphosis confer enormous survival value, as each stage is often spent in a different environment. Thus the insect is not dependent upon a single food supply or on one set of environmental conditions. (While these types of metamorphosis serve the insects, they also permit a variety of methods for controlling insect populations.)

6. *Specialized system of reproduction*: After mating, the female can often delay fertilization until the proper food supply and environmental conditions are located. When mating occurs, the sperm from the male is stored in a special sac; when conditions are favorable, the sperm is released for fertilization. This mechanism has extraordinary survival value.

Thus it can be seen that after 250 million years insects have evolved their own bag of tricks to frustrate our attempts at preventing them from taking our food supply or making us ill.

Although the number of insect species is between 670,000 and 1,250,000, the number of insect pests * is relatively small; fewer than 900 types attack humans, animals, and plants. Of the 900, by far the largest number are agricultural pests. It has been estimated that the yearly loss of food crops to insects in the United States approximates three billion dollars. Until the advent of chemical pesticides, it was evident that the battle for the food supply between man and insects was being won by the insects. Crops, like humans, are susceptible to disease and injury, which either destroy them completely or reduce their food-yielding capacity. In 1963, the corn borer was responsible for reducing the available corn supply by 120,648,000 bushes. Because plants cannot as yet

---

* Bear in mind that an insect becomes a "pest" only as we call it so. It is a pest when it annoys us in some way.

be vaccinated against disease (this may be a possibility by 1978), the next best thing to do is to spray them with chemicals to keep them healthy and edible or productive. Figures 16 and 17 show examples of the depredations on foods by insects. Figure 16 shows Khapra beetle larvae in powdered milk, while Figure 17 shows them in lima beans.

Trees and plants are susceptible to over fifteen hundred diseases. Together, the loss in food crops and trees is placed at ten to fifteen billion dollars annually. In addition, carpet beetles, silverfish, and moths destroy another two hundred million dollars' worth of property. The losses from termite destruction are far higher.

Before chemical insecticides were introduced, millions of people in the world died each year from a host of insect-borne diseases. Table 4 lists examples of plant and human diseases trans-

Figure 16. Khapra beetle larvae feeding on powdered milk. Note caking.

Figure 17.   Khapra beetles feeding on lima beans.

mitted by insects and ticks. Before the availability of chemical insecticides, malaria alone killed millions each year. For example, the case rate in 1955 was estimated to be 250 million. By 1962, it had dropped to 140 million, and by 1967 there were less than 100 million cases. Figure 18 indicates the dramatic effectiveness of DDT against typhus, a disease of rats transmitted to man by the bite of the rat flea. It is clearly seen how the application of this chemical precipitously reduced the number of cases of typhus. Similar charts could be presented for relapsing fever, yellow fever, smallpox, cholera, and bubonic plague.

Figure 19 shows the direct application of DDT to a child in a village in Afghanistan, in order to prevent typhus and malaria. Figure 20 shows the use of DDT on the walls of a home in Mexico. This type of treatment leaves a residue on the wall that remains effective for up to three months. Mosquitoes that seek a blood meal indoors alight on the DDT-treated walls and pick up the

TABLE 4.

Examples of diseases transmitted by insects and ticks.

	Disease	Transmitting Arthropod (Vector)	Pathogenic Agent
Plant	Dutch elm	Bark beetle	Fungus
	Cucumber wilt	Cucumber beetle	Bacterium
	Curly top of sugar beet	Beet leaf hopper	Virus
Animal	Yellow fever	Mosquito	Virus
	Bubonic plague	Flea	Bacterium
	Malaria	Mosquito	Protozoan
	Typhus	Louse and flea	Rickettsia
	Tularemia	Fly and tick	Bacterium
	Encephalitis	Mosquito	Virus
	Filariasis	Mosquito	Nematode worm
	Rocky Mountain spotted fever	Tick	Rickettsia
	Texas cattle fever	Tick	Protozoan
	Chagas disease (South American sleeping sickness)	Giant bedbug	Protozoan
	Dog tapeworm	Louse and flea	Worm

chemical on their legs. In the process of cleaning their legs with their mouth parts, they swallow the insecticide, which acts as a stomach poison.

It has been suggested that the prosperity of a country is inversely proportional to the time and effort required to produce the necessities of life. In 1913, for example, it took about 135 to 140 man-hours to produce one hundred bushels of corn. Today, one hundred bushels can be obtained in 15 hours. Approximately 8 percent of our labor force produces our food needs, leaving 92 percent to work elsewhere. Time-consuming manual methods of weed control, requiring the labor of many people, have been eliminated through the application of chemical weed-killers by tractor-drawn sprayers. It is also important to bear in mind that by the year 2000, just 27 years from now, the population of this

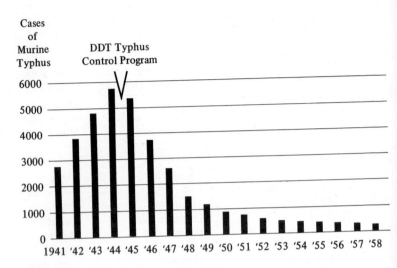

Figure 18. Effect of DDT on the incidence of typhus.

country will be between 350 and 450 million, which will mean two mouths to feed for every one in 1960. It must be done on less and less arable land each year. It has been well established that chemical insecticides and herbicides not only increase yield per acre, but also increase grade or quality.

Barnyard grass, a weed that bears a striking similarity to rice, is easily killed by most herbicides; but so is the rice. The presence of one barnyard grass plant per square foot will reduce the yield of rice by one thousand pounds per acre. A new chemical, Propa-nil, applied within eight days after barnyard grass germinates, essentially eliminates it. In the three years since its introduction the national rice yield has increased from three thousand pounds per acre to over four thousand.

If we are to eat, remain relatively disease-free, and prosper, the insects' freedom must be curtailed. At this point in our technological development, chemical pesticides are the only significant means at our disposal.

Five classes of chemical pesticides are generally recognized:

1. *Naturally occurring (plant) products:* For years extracts, dusts, and smoke from the dried heads of the chrysanthemum

Figure 19. Direct application of DDT in a village in Afghanistan.

Figure 20.   Application of DDT to the walls of a hut in a Mexican village. Residual concentrations on walls remain effective against malarial mosquitoes for up to three months.

have been used as insecticides. Pyrethrin I and II are the active agents in these formulations. Rotenone and nicotine are examples of other natural products.

2. *Inorganics:* These are preparations containing such metals as lead, copper, zinc, arsenic, and mercury as the insecticidal ingredient. In the early 1870s Paris green, an arsenical (copper aceto-arsenite), was used to control the codling moth in apple and pear orchards. Bordeaux mixture, a compound containing copper, was first used in 1882, as a fruit spray. Currently inorganic, metal-based insecticides are not widely used, having been superseded by the organic compounds. However, in cases where resistance to organics has arisen, the inorganics may again be of value.

3. *Chlorinated organics:* The best known and most widely

used of the synthetic organic insecticides is DDT (dichlorodi-phenyltrichloroethane). Although it was first prepared in 1879, its insecticidal value was not discovered until 1937. The modern era of chemical control began with the commercial introduction of DDT in 1946; it had first been used on a large scale in World War II to combat typhus in military and civilian populations. Some other members of this group of insecticides are benzene hexachloride (BHC), methoxychlor, dieldrin, chlordane, and heptachlor. All are barely soluble in water and several are more potent than DDT.

4. *Organophosphorus compounds:* This new group of in-secticides was originated during World War II by Gerhard Schrader, a German chemist who was searching for more potent agents of chemical warfare. Such compounds as parathion, malathion, and diazinon are highly toxic to insects. All of these are poorly soluble in water but readily so in aromatic hydro-carbons and vegetable oils. They are highly effective in extremely small quantities against a wide variety of insects.

5. *Petroleum oil fractions:* These oils are generally used alone or in combination with one of the other classes of insecti-cides. They have proven most useful as mosquito larvicides. The oils are applied as a thin film on the surface of water of mosquito breeding sites. The larvae coming to the surface to feed or breathe contact the oil film, which penetrates the breathing tube (trachea) and kills by suffocation or poisoning.

This brings us to the fact that insecticides do not all act in the same way, and for good reason: insects do not all feed in the same way, nor do they attack the same parts of plants, and their habits are markedly different. For these reasons, insecticides must be de-veloped to perform a specific function. Thus, the five groups of insecticides are also categorized by the way they get into the insect's body cavity. Stomach poisons must be swallowed or ab-sorbed through the gut; this restricts their use to insects whose mouth parts are suitable for biting, sucking, or lapping food. Contact poisons enter through the cuticle or skin, and thus must be fat soluble, while fumigants enter the respiratory system through the spiracles, the external openings of the trachea.

Although insecticides have been categorized as to what types of substances they contain and how they enter the insect's body, neither of these categories should be confused with the mechanism by which the insecticide kills or stuns. For example, pyrethrin penetrates through the cuticle, but it causes paralysis by blocking nerve impulses in the insect's central nervous system. Rotenone appears to cause paralysis of the breathing mechanism. Paris green, a stomach poison, is considered a general protoplasmic poison that disrupts several enzyme systems. Lindane, a chlorinated organic, is a fumigant, entering via the spiracles, while DDT is classed as a contact insecticide; both appear to affect the peripheral nervous system and muscle tissue of insects. The organophosphorus compounds are powerful contact insecticides that inhibit the action of cholinesterase, thereby preventing the normal mechanism of nerve-impulse transmission.

In 1962, 194 million acres of land were treated with three-quarters of a billion to one billion pounds of a host of insecticides. Nearly one acre in ten has been treated with an average of about four pounds per acre. By 1966, the outlay for insecticides and herbicides in the United States had reached one billion dollars.

There is no doubt that the question of the use and accumulation of pesticides dangerous to health is an important one. I think it is necessary to accept one important fact: safety is a negative condition; that is, it is the absence of hazard. Actually, no amount of research or study will ever provide absolute assurance of safety. It is possible, however, to assure practical certainty of safety. People vary over wide ranges in their sensitivity to chemicals. Some people are hypersensitive to aspirin, others to penicillin. This does not prevent the beneficial use of these drugs by millions of others who are not sensitive.

Care should be exercised in using pesticides. Their chemical and physiological characteristics must be studied and understood so that they can be employed in the smallest quantity that will achieve the desired effect. It is estimated that the annual death rate from all types of pesticides is about 150 persons per year. This is primarily due to acute poisoning. One-half to three-quarters of these deaths are in young children who, playing in kitchens or garages where pesticides may be stored, manage to open and eat these chemicals. An occupational hazard appears to exist for spray pilots, greenhouse workers, and those working directly in the production of insecticides. On the other hand, chronic or long-term, low-level contact is decidedly more complicated. For example, it has been well publicized that DDT has an affinity for fatty tissue and that hardly anyone is free of DDT. This has been cited as evidence that we are being "poisoned" by the accumulation of pesticides in the environment. The fact is that the U.S. Public Health Service has made it quite clear that "there is no well described case of fatal uncomplicated DDT poisoning" resulting from proper use. Cases do exist of people who died after swallowing DDT solutions, but that must be considered akin to placing one's head inside an oven and turning on the gas. Figure 21 indicates the death rate per 100,000 people for a half-dozen non-infectious diseases, and their relationship to DDT. The slope of the curves suggests that leukemia was on the rise long before DDT was introduced; it continued to rise at the same rate after DDT's introduction. Thus, one would not tend to implicate DDT as a factor in leukemia. Hodgkin's disease and agranulocytosis show a similar lack of correlation. For purpura and aplastic anemia there is too little data collected before 1948 to yield meaningful interpretation.

As with air pollution and ionizing radiation, many believe that the accumulation of pesticides in the environment causes actual and potential harm in the form of residues ingested in food and water or inhaled with each breath; others maintain that the effects of long-term low-level exposure are unknown. At this stage of our knowledge, both views must be considered. The most reasonable course balances benefit against risk. By determining the amount of pollutant (whatever it may be) that a given population can be expected to contact, an estimation of the risk of injury may be made. By estimating dividends accruing to the community from the use of pesticides, ionizing radiation, or any of the processes that release polluting effluents, benefit can be calculated. When both are known, perhaps an acceptable accord between benefit and risk can be established.

A more concrete problem that can be readily corrected is the inefficient and wasteful application of pesticides. The White House Conference on Environmental Pollution [1] pointed out that only 10 to 20 percent of insecticides applied as dusts and 25 to 50 percent applied as sprays are deposited on plant surfaces where they can be effective against pests. Under the best conditions, the report noted, present methods waste 50 to 75 percent of the insecticide, which drifts away to become an undesirable environmental contaminant. Much research is needed to prevent this inadvertent

DEATH RATE PER 100,000 POPULATION

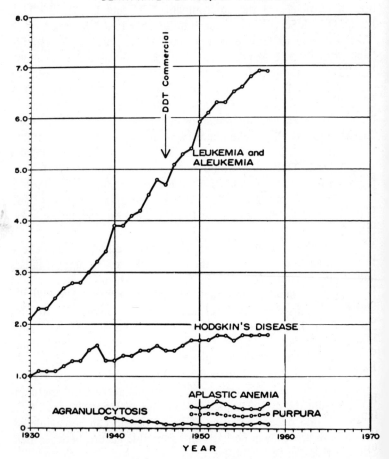

Figure 21. Effect of the commercial introduction of DDT on several non-infectious illnesses. (Source: Vital Statistics of the United States.)

contamination. A second requirement is the development of pesticides with molecular structures that can be degraded by microorganisms. Too many commercially available pesticides persist in soil and water because bacteria and fungi cannot use them as a source of nutrition; the chemical structure of the pesticide does not offer the bacteria a "handle." Chemists must develop chemicals that microbes can digest.

These considerations have given impetus to the development of methods of biological control based on the fixed behavior of insect pests and on the fact that certain insect species are natural enemies of others. Chemicals are not used and consequently environmental contamination does not occur.

Many insects locate their food supplies, mating partners, and favorable sites to lay eggs by built-in automatic responses to chemicals emanating from these sources. The three types of chemical stimuli are known as food attractants, sex attractants, and oviposition lures.

Food attractants utilize the fact that certain insect species feed only on a specific plant or animal host. For example, the boll weevil feeds almost exclusively on the cotton plant. It has recently been found that volatile substances released into the atmosphere by the cotton plant enable the weevil to find the plant, its food supply. Attempts are currently being made to isolate and identify these substances. Their use to lead insects to capture and death would be a major step forward. Once the insect is led to the food supply by the food lure, other chemical components of the food source may stimulate the insect to begin feeding. Recently a synthetic feeding lure, methyl eugenol, which attracts only male flies, was used in combination with an insecticide to eradicate the oriental fruit fly from the island of Rota in the Pacific.

Pheromones * or sex attractants, the second type of bait or lure, are chemicals emitted by one of the sexes, most often the female,** to excite or attract the males for mating. The potency of these compounds is so great that sexual partners may be lured upwind over distances as long as two miles. Often, trace amounts

---

* In 1959, Karlson and Luescher defined pheromones as "substances which are secreted to the outside by an individual and received by a second individual of the same species, in which they release a specific action, for example, a definite behavior or development process." They coined the term from the Greek *pherein*, to transfer and *hormon*, to excite. (P. Karlson and M. Luescher, "Pheromones, a New Term for a Class of Biologically Active Substances," *Nature* 183 (1959): 55.)

** Grandlure, the sexual pheromone obtained from the boll weevil, attracts only females. Pellets containing synthetic attractant are placed in traps covered with sticky coating.

are sufficient to bring a pair together. A sex lure isolated from the male cockroach (*Periplanata americana*) is so powerful that females respond to it when it is diluted to a concentration of 10–14 micrograms—some thirty molecules of the substance! Pheromones are also highly specific; insects of one species do not respond to the attractants of even closely related species.

After great effort, employing the most sophisticated analytic techniques and often thousands of insects, the chemistry of some twenty attractants has been elucidated. Before trans-10, cis-12-hexadecadien-l-al could be identified as the sex attractant of the silkworm (*Bombyx mori*) and duplicated for use in the field, it required 500,000 female silkworms from which a total of 12 milligrams of attractant could be obtained for analysis.

One of the most serious defoliators of hardwood trees is *Porthetria dispar,* the Gypsy moth. It has been ravaging forests from New England through the Carolinas for at least 75 years. Figure 22 shows officials of the USDA examining a forest on Cape Cod, Massachusetts that has been denuded by Gypsy moth caterpillars. The state of New Jersey had five acres defoliated in 1967. By 1969, with the discontinuance of DDT, 40,000 acres were ruined. The figure had risen to over 200,000 acres in the summer of 1971. Across the country over $100 million has been spent on Gypsy moth eradication and control programs with little to show for it. The answer may be cis-7, 8-epoxy-2-methyloctadecane-"Disparlure," an attractant developed at the USDA's Agricultural Research Service by Dr. Morton Beroza and coworkers. In field trials Disparlure, in amounts of one microgram, has been shown to be enormously more effective in capturing males than the natural extract from 10 female abdomen tips.

In addition to attracting males to sticky traps, another as yet untried approach would be to permeate the air with sex odor and so confuse the males that they become exhausted or insensitive. The obvious question is whether placing the lures, which are synthetic chemicals, in the air would pose additional problems for man. Two answers seem appropriate. Toxicological tests have been conducted by the Environmental Protection Agency (EPA). They found that Disparlure administered orally, placed on intact and abraded skin, placed directly in the eyes, and fed intravenously, produced no toxic symptoms in test animals and human subjects. Second, insects have been emitting these chemicals for as

Figure 22.   Two officials of the U.S. Department of Agriculture are shown August 3, 1970 examining a forest in Cape Cod, Massachusetts, which has been denuded by gypsy moth caterpillars. (USDA photo by Larry Rana.)

long as they have been on earth. If they are harmful, we have yet to discover it.

Oviposition lures, a third type of pheromone, induce egg-laying females to oviposit on the chemically impregnated materials serving as food for the larvae. The idea is that once they begin to feed, the larvae will not make it to adulthood.

Knowledge of chemical attractants suggests ways in which an insect's responses may be used against it. Used in traps, the attractants can be employed to detect and estimate insect populations; to delineate areas of infestation; to ascertain when insecticide applications should begin and end; and to detect accidental introduction of foreign pests via international transportation, such as recently occurred in El Salvador. San Salvador, the capital of El Salvador, had been free of yellow fever since 1959. In 1965, *Aedes aegypti,* the mosquito carrying the virus of yellow fever, was detected in the city. The mosquito's eggs were apparently reintroduced in used tires imported from abroad. Rainwater trapped in the hollow tires formed the breeding pools for the mosquito. *Aedes aegypti* is a fast-breeding type of mosquito, and in several months it had infested all of San Salvador plus about twenty-five localities ringing it.

Attractants could be used to lure harmful insects to limited and selected areas where they would be deprived of their natural food supply or subjected to insecticides or chemosterilants. Feeding stimulants might be incorporated into insecticides or chemosterilant preparations to induce insects to feed on these harmful substances. Oviposition lures might be used to induce egg-laying in non-nutrient materials where the developing young would starve.

Another, quite different approach to insect control is based on the use of chemosterilants—physical or chemical techniques that produce sexually sterile insects. Ideally, a chemosterilant should have no effect on the insect other than to prevent the hatching of eggs; that is, it should cause the insect to produce infertile eggs. Use of chemosterilants eliminated the screwworm fly (*Cochliomyia hominovorax*) from Texas, Florida, and Curacao.

The adult female screwworm fly lays a mass of two hundred to three hundred eggs in the wounds of cattle, sheep, goats, or horses. Any wound, accidental or surgical, a tick bite, or the navel of a newborn animal can be an egg-laying site. From twelve to twenty-four hours later, maggots (larvae) hatch and begin to feed in the wound site. The feeding causes an additional bloody discharge whose odor attracts more flies for additional egg-laying. Death of the animal is inevitable unless it is found and treated. Even though treatment can save the animal, the hide will have holes and blemishes that reduce its value, and the irritation caused to cattle in particular reduces milk production. Before the elimination of screwworm flies from the Southwest in 1959, the economic loss amounted to about $25 million annually. In this elimination program male screwworm flies were sterilized by gamma irradiation from a cobalt-60 source.

With the sterilization procedure, thousands to millions of fly eggs are collected on screens or in troughs. The eggs are placed on an artificial food until the larvae emerge. The larvae are reared through pupation. The pupae, in plastic containers, are placed in a gamma cell to be exposed to radiation from a cobalt-60 source. The radiation is sufficient to sterilize them without greatly reducing their activity. After sterilization the pupae are placed in paper bags, in which they develop into adult flies. These bags of flies are placed in dispersing tubes aboard an airplane. A tube can handle one bag every two to three seconds and thus is capable of dispersing millions of flies over a wide area. Air, streaming through the dispersing tube, whips the bag out of the tube. As it leaves the tube, the bag is slashed by a hinged knife; the bag sticks on a hook for a moment and the flies are scattered.

The sterile-male technique * has three important advantages over the conventional application of chemical pesticides. In the first place, it is highly selective, involving only a specific insect while leaving all other forms (insects, worms, birds, plants, etc.) undisturbed. In addition, the target species cannot acquire immunity to sterile mating, as it too often does to chemicals. Finally, chemical agents often become less efficient as the population against which they are being used declines. As a consequence, the few survivors can begin to rebuild their decimated ranks. On the other hand, the sterile-male procedure becomes even more efficient as the population dwindles.

This technique, a modification of that used to eradicate the screwworm fly in 1959, is now being used in an attempt to eradicate another insect pest, the Mediterranean fruit fly (*Ceratitis capitata*). The "Med" fly lays its eggs in the peel of fruit, and the maggots (larvae) penetrate to the meat. Even where the eggs do not develop, the hole caused by the fly's sting leads to decay. Some countries prohibit imports from areas infected by the fly.

In 1955, the Mediterranean fruit fly appeared in Costa Rica. It spread from there to El Salvador, Guatemala, Honduras, Nica-

* Although this is called the sterile-male technique, in fact both sexes are sterilized and released; the cost of separating the sexes in mass-reared species is prohibitive.

ragua, and Panama, despite all attempts to contain it. It is feared that unless it is brought under control, the annual loss in fruit crop could exceed eighty million dollars. Over the past four years, small-scale experiments involving up to 25 square miles and releases of up to a billion flies have proven the method suitable as well as feasible. A plan to eradicate the Med fly from all of Nicaragua was recently put forward. It will involve 1500 square miles, some $6 million, and at least four years of persistent effort.

Another potentially useful aspect of natural control is the use of one species to reduce or control the population of another. The state of New Jersey recently entered into a cooperative agreement with the federal government. Under the terms of their contract, the New Jersey Division of Plant Industry will raise predaceous insects for distribution in all states that need them. Here too, the Gypsy moth provides instruction. Although New Jersey and the New England states have been the hardest hit by the moth's voracious eating habits, it is now establishing itself in Alabama, Tennessee, Ohio, Michigan, and Wisconsin. The Gypsy moth is an excellent example of an insect removed from its ecological niche, where it was kept in check by natural predation. Once it escaped the niche, available food supply (trees), combined with its high order of fecundity, produced explosive population growth.

This moth was brought to the United States from Europe in 1869 to start a silk-producing industry in New England. As is often the case, some moths escaped. By 1890, with no enemies to control its growth, the Gypsy moth had become a menace, and has remained so ever since. Current efforts seek to establish its natural enemies (biological pressure) as a means of control. For natural predation, attempts are being made to raise some insects that can attack the egg, some that prefer to attack the larvae, and others that prefer the pupal stage. Among the parasitic predators being reared are three tachinid flies; one from Yugoslavia (*Exorista larvarum*), one from India (*Exorista rossica*) and one from Spain (*Exorista segregata*). All three attack the moth's larval stage. Figure 23 shows such a fly at work. Although two of these have already been released for field testing, there is no evidence that they have become established. We can expect thousands of defoliated acres of trees and a great deal of hard work on the part of scientists before the Gypsy moth is brought under control by "natural," nonchemical means. Consider too that to eliminate

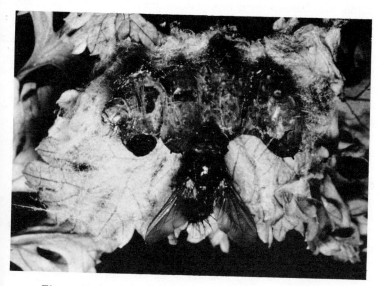

Figure 23. A fly is obtaining a meal at the expense of a caterpillar. (Photo courtesy of Ciba-Geigy Journal.)

or control the many insects that prey on man, animals, and plants, specific natural enemies must be found. Who will do it, and who will pay for this major undertaking?

As I go around the country talking with students, I find a growing aversion to science and careers as scientists. It is curious that the people most concerned lest the land be contaminated with synthetic chemicals such as DDT and other chlorinated hydrocarbons give little thought to how or by whom natural prevention will be achieved. They appear to want to banish from their minds the fact that it takes well-trained scientists to do this work.

The study of natural control of pest populations is the part of ecology that attempts to undersand how potential population increase is limited and more or less stabilized by environmental factors. Natural control can be defined as the maintenance of a certain population density of an organism—within certain definable upper and lower limits—over a period of time by the actions of abiotic or biotic environmental factors. The upper and lower limits will change appreciably only if the actions of the regulatory factors are changed, or if certain ones are eliminated or new ones added. Natural control is therefore an essentially permanent condition, as opposed to chemical control, which reduces populations only temporarily unless indefinitely repeated. Darwin's term "struggle for existence" is what we now call natural control. Biological control, a phase of natural control, is the action of parasites, predators, or pathogens in maintaining another organism's population density at a lower level than would otherwise occur.

The fact that an organism achieves and maintains pest status makes it obvious that climatic and other ecological factors favor it—biological pressure is low. Thus it reasonably follows that to curtail or depress its density, a modification in environment or ecological relationship is needed. Natural enemies are one such means.

Natural control via biological pressure is not new. The Arabs of Yemen, for example, have for hundreds of years used predaceous ants to protect date palms from other harmful ants. Each year the date growers of Yemen bring colonies of the beneficial ants down from the mountains and place them in palm trees, where they eat the ants that feed on the palms.

Snails, fish, amphibians, birds, and mammals have been used from time to time to control economic pests. Insects that prey on other insects (entomophagous species) and microbes that initiate infection and disease have also been used. In 1965, as an experiment, the state of Florida imported several sea cows (manatees) to check the growth of aquatic plants that had made navigation all but impossible in Florida's inland waterways. Both chemical and physical treatments had proven useless. The manatees were reported to do such a good job of weed control that several more were imported. However this can only be considered a stop-gap measure. Manatees reproduce far too slowly to keep up with weed growth.

Currently, activity in natural control efforts centers on microbial agents. In particular, bacterial infections appear to offer hope for a commercially feasible product.

A bacterium, *Bacillus thuringiensis,* originally isolated from a diseased flour moth in Thuringen, Germany in 1911, appears to be pathogenic to 110 species of moths and 8 species of flies. It is currently recommended for the widespread control of the cabbage looper, the alfalfa caterpillar, and the tobacco hornworm. This bacterium produces a diamond-shaped proteinaceous crystal that destroys the gut lining of many insects. It was selected for commercial use because of its ability to grow readily in large numbers on artificial sources of food. It can be prepared as either a dust or a spray which the insect must ingest, and which acts as a stomach poison that eventually produces paralysis and death. Over the past five years, the potency of Thuricide, the commercial designation for the bacterial insecticide, has increased about eightfold as a result of technical advances. Since the first product was marketed, a wettable powder, two dusts, a bait, and a home and garden spray have become available. Not only has Thuricide proven successful, but it appears to have great growth potential—well beyond its original conception.

Thuricide must be eaten by the insect to be effective. Once it is ingested, Gypsy moth larvae and inchworms, for example, will stop feeding within one-half to 2 hours, depending on the dose. Death usually follows in 3–5 days, without further feeding. In Thuricide's favor is the fact that birds, bees, and wildlife are generally unaffected, and results of human toxicity studies have thus far shown it to be nontoxic in both acute and chronic studies.

The most outstanding example of pest control by a microbial pathogen is milky disease of the Japanese beetle (*Popillia japonicum*), which generally infests and destroys vegetables and fruit. The beetle grub (larva) ingests *Bacillus popilliae*,[2] and the bacterium multiplies in the insect's gut. The blood of the infected grub becomes milky-white, and it ceases activity and dies.

In the commercial preparation, spores of *Bacillus popilliae* are mixed with powder to be broadcast over soil. The larvae of beetles or other susceptible insects ingest the spores and are destroyed within two weeks by milky disease. Applied to turf in the eastern part of the United States, the preparation has provided excellent control of the Japanese beetle. The spores of *Bacillus popilliae* persist for long periods in soil and achieve long-term control of the beetles.

Natural methods of control have intrigued the public for many years. Some mistakenly believe this type of control can entirely supersede chemical insecticides and thereby put an end to such concerns as insect resistance, chemical residues in food, and harm to wildlife. But it is in the order of life that nature provides for the survival of both beneficial and destructive insects. The destructive insect is actually a creation of man, who provides the environmental conditions necessary for an insect to become a pest. There is also no guarantee that a predator introduced to check a pest population will not itself become a pest; and as has been so dramatically demonstrated in Australia, a pest can develop immunity to a microbe. The myxoma virus was introduced into Australia from England in the 1950s to eradicate the rabbit population, which had become a severe economic threat. In the first year of the virus' dissemination, rabbits fell ill and died in great numbers. By the third year it became evident that the rabbit population had developed an immunity to the disease, myxomatosis, and was rebuilding its decimated ranks. With the disease now endemic, there is a cyclic rise and fall in the rabbit population.

In June 1967, the World Health Organization and the Pan-American Health Organization met in Washington, D. C. to review the state of insecticides.

It was noted that although the sterile-male technique had proven so successful with the screwworm fly and the Mediterranean fruit fly, it had little success with mosquitoes. Apparently gamma-irradiated sterile male mosquitoes did not compete as well for the female as did their non-sterile counterparts. Consequently, enough fertile unions occur to maintain significant population levels. However, a new technique was reported that may yet eradicate certain species of mosquito on a local level. Field trials of the new technique were successfully held in Rangoon, Burma. Each day scientists released five thousand male mosquitoes obtained from Fresno, California. Although they were the same species as the Rangoon mosquito, *Culex pipiens fatigans*, there were sufficient genetic differences between the two to prevent normal conception; fertilization produced no living progeny. In twelve weeks, the Rangoon species was eliminated from the area.

Dr. Rajindar Pal of the World Health Organization suggested that this species difference would probably be found for other forms and could result in the control of insect carriers of many important diseases.

At this meeting, Dr. George B. Craig of the University of Notre Dame proposed yet another approach to controlling insect pests. His method, thus far still a laboratory experiment, calls for the breeding of insect strains that have an abnormally in creased genetic tendency to produce male offspring. Certain mosquitoes are known to produce ninety-five males for each one hundred fertilized eggs. Because of the precipitous shortage of females, these insects breed themselves into extinction within a few generations.

Although natural control offers many advantages, we cannot look for an early end to the use of synthetic chemicals; our knowledge of the pests is not yet great enough. The phrase "use of synthetic chemicals" will make a number of readers uncomfortable. Realizing this, a few thoughts on attitudes about chemicals may be in order.

One cannot be alive today and not be aware of the raging controversy between those who are certain that synthetic chemical pesticides are a proven health hazard and those who hold an opposing view, that there is little evidence to support such a claim. The difficulties, peculiarities, and vagaries of scientific research, as well as the demand in the popular press for news of scientific activities, make such controversy inevitable.

After much give-and-take on the subject, I have come to believe the general public is not interested in anything but black and white. Shades of gray occupy no place in its thinking. "Is it or isn't it harmful?" is the question. As scientific study cannot deal with absolute issues, and all scientific studies are not equally reliable or comparable, the public cannot help but be confused. They know neither whom nor what to believe. This is a disgraceful and indefensible state of affairs. Unfortunately, few, if any, magazines, newspaper articles, TV or radio personalities are prepared to discuss why reports of pesticide hazards appear contradictory.

But are they really contradictory? Differences can arise because one investigator uses mice while others use dogs, chickens, guinea pigs, or goldfish. Some researchers may use too few animals to draw valid statistical inferences, while others may include only male animals or only females in their tests, or only animals of one age group. Some researchers may keep an experiment going for three months, while others feel that suitable data can only be collected after a minimum of a year. Differences may also arise because a pesticide was administered in different concentrations or in a different manner. Was it painted on the exposed skin of the animal's belly? Or was it placed in the eye? Or was it inoculated into the muscle or directly into the blood stream? Or was it surgically implanted into the bladder? Further, most important, and all too often lacking in many studies that rush into public print, is use of controls, untreated as well as treated animals. Were the controls properly selected and maintained, and are they comparable to the treated group?

Many investigators forget or are unmindful of these factors, and most writers on science are not aware of them. Why shouldn't the public be confused, and why shouldn't two (or more) sides be at odds? To complicate the problem further, politics enters the issue too. It has become "good politics" to take sides on these "big" issues. And one doesn't have to look far for an example.

Report on 2,4,5-T: A Report of the Panel on Herbicides of the President's Science Advisory Committee, raised a ruckus of charge and countercharge from which the dust remains unsettled. As the psychoanalyst Robert Waelder remarked, "Strongly held opinions often determine what kind of facts people are able or willing to perceive." It was differences and opinions such as those noted that forced Dr. Jesse Steinfeld, Surgeon General of the United States, to testify before Congress that he had no reliable evidence that the herbicide 2,4-D was hazardous to health. Of course, at the time it was widely believed (and it still is) that 2,4-D was toxic. How could the Surgeon General not know this? Everyone else seemed to.

The *New York Times* reported Dr. Steinfeld's remarks in a few lines, then moved quickly to discuss in two full colums an article in the *New Yorker* magazine purporting to show 2,4-D to be hazardous. This is typical of the current state of affairs: the *Times* prefers its personal opinion to that of the Surgeon General and the available evidence.

Similar confusion exists with respect to pesticide residues in our food supply. Here too, sides have been taken, again primarily on the basis of what people prefer to believe.

The fact that the FAO/WHO joint committee on pesticide residues in food [3] found that in countries where measurements have been made, amounts of pesticide residues are usually well within the limits of safety, will probably be ignored in preference to the more comforting belief that our food supply is full of hazards to health.

The fact that the National Academy of Sciences recently

agreed to conduct a comprehensive study and investigation to determine (a) the ecological dangers inherent in the use of herbicides and (b) the ecological and physiological effects of the defoliation program carried out by the Department of Defense in South Vietnam, suggests that the answers to such questions are not as clear as some would prefer to believe.

From a recent gathering of scientists from around the world, we have another pertinent piece of information. The WHO Regional Office for Europe held a conference on "Modern trends in the prevention of pesticide intoxications" in Kiev, USSR, in June 1971. The members believed that with all the concern for pesticides as an environmental pollutant, little thought had been given to those who daily worked in pesticide industries.

They found that "deplorably little has been done to ascertain whether the materials commonly selected for gloves, aprons, boots and other articles of clothing constitute an effective barrier to pesticides." They indicated areas of research that needed study but after evaluating data from around the world came up with three impressions:

(a) Pesticide poisoning constitutes no more than a small proportion of poisoning as a whole;

(b) Many of the more severe cases are attributable to deliberate self-poisoning with pesticides and not to occupational or incidental exposure;

(c) Cases of poisoning by organochlorines are rare compared with poisoning by organophosphorus. Because organochlorines are being phased out in preference to other pesticides with higher mammalian toxicity, more cases should be seen in the future.

I suspect, too, that there is an additional factor involved in the confusion of the public. This is the miserable job scientists of every stripe have done in community education. Scientists, who ought to know better, have been content to work in their laboratories among their test tubes and animals and ignore the public, for whom they are supposed to be working. This situation will have to change.

In addition to his by now well-known remarks on the need for DDT, Dr. Norman Borlaug, speaking on improvement of crop foods, quoted the following from Gulliver's Voyage to Brobding-nag:

> And he gave it for his opinion, that whoever could make two ears of corn or two blades of grass grow upon a spot of ground where only one would grow before, would deserve better of mankind, and do more essential service to his country, than the whole race of politicians put together.

References

1. President's Science Advisory Committee, Environmental Pollution Panel, *Restoring the Quality of Our Environment* (Washington: Government Printing Office, 1965).

2. K. H. Steinkraus, "Studies on the Milky Disease Organisms, II: Saprophytic Growth of Bacillus Popilliae," *Journal of Bacteriology* 74 (1957): 625.

3. *Report of the 1970 Joint FAO/WHO Meeting, Pesticide Residues in Foods* (Geneva: WHO Tech. Rept. Ser. no. 474, 1971).

Suggested Reading

Sterile-Male Technique for Eradication or Control of Harmful Insects. Proceedings of a Panel. Vienna: International Atomic Energy Agency, 1969.

Durham, W. F.; Fla, P.; Wolfe, H. R.; and Elliott, J. W. "Absorption and Excretion of Parathion by Spraymen." *Archives of Environmental Health* 24 (1972): 381.

Report on 2, 4, 5-T: A Report of the Panel on Herbicides of the President's Science Advisory Committee. Washington: Government Printing Office, 1971.

"Use of 2, 4, 5-T." Letters to the Editor. *Science* 174 (1971): 545.

Laws, E. R., Jr. "Evidence of Antitumorigenic Effects of DDT." *Archives of Environmental Health* 23 (1971): 181.

Laws, E. R., Jr.; Curley, A.; and Biros, F. J. "Men with Intensive Occupational Exposure to DDT: A Clinical and Chemical Study." *Archives of Environmental Health* 15 (1967): 766.

Jukes, T. H. "DDT Stands Trial Again." *Bioscience* 22 (1972): 670.

6

ZOONOSES

Felix qui potuit rerum cognoscere causas.
(*"Happy is he who can grasp the causes of things."*)

Anon.

Yetlington is a tiny farming village in the north of England and not the most likely place for history to be made. But Bob Brewis lived in Yetlington, and he made history in December 1966, when foot-and-mouth disease ravaged the area.

Although foot-and-mouth disease is one of the most contagious infections of cattle, sheep, goats, and pigs, world attention would not have focused so sharply on Yetlington had not Brewis become involved.

During the height of the epizootic,* Bob became ill. He reportedly told his physician that he felt groggy and thought he was getting the flu. On examination, the blisters characteristic of foot-and-mouth disease were found in his mouth. Laboratory examination of the blister fluid confirmed the presence of the virus. Bob

---

* An epizootic is a disease of epidemic proportions among animals.

113

Brewis had foot-and-mouth disease, the first case ever reported in a human. To make matters worse, he had to be quarantined to prevent his infecting the remaining healthy animals in Yetlington.

Animals and man have lived in close association for thousands of years. Man has used animals for food, clothing, and shelter, and has taken animals into his home to warn him of danger, control rodents, and serve as companions for his family. The friendship of men with animals, especially dogs and horses, has been immortalized in the songs and stories of many lands. The breeding and selling of domestic animals and the commercial processing of animal products are fundamental to the economy of many countries.

In these close associations between man and animals, man has exposed himself to their diseases. When animals are brought into living quarters, exposure becomes even more thorough. Members of the household play with, hug, kiss, and occasionally share food and bed with domestic animals. As increased leisure time permits more people to camp out, more contact with wild animals is made, and as we push our communities farther into sylvan areas, additional new contacts are made. Living in such close proximity, it is not surprising that man contracts illnesses from the many animals around him. The animal world must be considered a constant reservoir of various infections that can be transmitted to man either directly, or through the agency of biting insects, or by the consumption of food derived from infected animals.

Veterinarians and other public health scientists call diseases of animals transmissible to man *zoonoses:* some one hundred are known. (The reverse is also true: man can transmit certain infections to animals.) Table 5 lists some of the more common zoonoses.

Not only has man's welfare been endangered by epidemics of animal diseases, but colonization of many areas has been restricted by man's inability to control certain zoonoses. A dramatic example of this can be seen in Central Africa, where African sleeping sickness (Gambian fever) has prevented the use of hundreds of thousands of acres of arable land, this is the tsetse fly belt.

During World War II, the pressing need for South American rubber galvanized efforts to clean out the hitherto uninhabitable yellow fever mosquito areas, in order to plant and cultivate additional rubber trees. Cost was not a consideration. In other cir-

TABLE 5.
Some major zoonoses.

Viral
Rabies
Encephalitis
Cat-scratch fever
Ornithosis-psittacosis

Rickettsial
Q-fever
Spotted fever
Typhus
Rickettsial pox

Protozoal
Toxoplasmosis
American leishmaniasis (Chiclero ulcer, espundia)
Trypanosomiasis (Chagas' disease)

Helminthic
Hydatidosis
Taeniasis (beef tapeworm)
Trichinosis (pork tapeworm)
Hookworm

Bacterial
Anthrax (wool sorter's disease)
Brucellosis (undulant fever)
Leptospirosis
Tularemia (rabbit fever)
Tuberculosis
Diphtheria
Salmonellosis
Listeriosis

Fungal
Ringworm
    tinea corporis—body
    tinea capitis—scalp
    tinea pedis—foot
Histoplasmosis
Coccidioidomycosis (San Joaquin fever)

Arthropods
Mites (scabies—the itch)
Lice (pediculosis)

---

cumstances, the cost might well have been considered prohibitive, and the effort would not have been made.

This interaction is not without its benefits. The fact that certain illnesses are shared by animals and man makes it possible to use animals in experimental biochemical research and to produce vaccines used to immunize both animals and man against a host of communicable diseases.

Even as our society moves inexorably from an agricultural to a technological environment, the health of animals and the health and well-being of man remain closely linked. This may be seen in the numbers of domestic animals that play an intricate part in our lives. Table 6 indicates the number and type of household pets in the United States. Table 7 indicates the number of domestic animals, including an estimate of dogs and cats, both pet and stray.

T A B L E   6 .
Household pets in the United States.

Dogs Cats Parakeets Canaries Finches Turtles Monkeys Skunks	75,000,000

T A B L E   7 .
Domestic animals in the United States.

Cattle	22,100,000
Hogs	100,000,000
Sheep	57,000,000
Goats	31,500,000
Horses Mules	4,020,000
Dogs	3,100,000
Cats	24,135,000

It is obvious that there are far more domestic animals than people. If to these are added the great number and variety of wild animals, such as opossum, rats, foxes, raccoons, wolves, deer, rabbits, and bats, it becomes clear that animals far outnumber people and that they must play a significant role in our lives.*

Zoonoses do not occur with equal frequency around the country. Of the hundred known, forty-nine are known to occur in

---

* See Chapter 9, Solid-Waste Disposal, for a discussion of the problem of water pollution via animal excrement.

the southern states, forty-six in Texas alone. Although brucellosis (undulant fever) occurs chiefly in Illinois, Iowa, Nebraska, and Kansas, where raw milk and dairy products abound and large numbers of carcasses are handled, it is not restricted to rural areas; 41 percent of reported cases occurred in urban areas. On the other hand, tularemia (although often called rabbit fever, it occurs in a wide variety of lagomorphs and rodents) is found primarily in the rural areas of Missouri, Arkansas, and the Gulf Coast states, where squirrels, rabbits, and other rodents are hunted and trapped. The virus of rabies, once thought to be transmitted solely by the bite of rabid dogs, is now known to be disseminated by bats, foxes, skunks, and raccoons. These four species are concentrated from the East Coast westward to the central states.

Of particular importance for those concerned with the prevention and control of zoonoses is the observation that many exhibit marked seasonal fluctuations. For example, the several types of arthropod-borne encephalitis (St. Louis encephalitis, Western equine encephalitis, Eastern equine encephalitis) principally occur from July to October, whereas the incidence of brucellosis climbs sharply between April and August. Leptospirosis appears to begin its rise in May, peaks in July, and fades as fall approaches. This pattern is unique in the United States; the disease has a different pattern in Vietnam, for example, where the conditions promoting its survival and passage are distinctive.

For convenience, zoonoses are divided into two major categories: those occupationally induced (see also Chapter 13, Occupational Health) and those transmitted to the general public in a variety of ways. Of course microbes, being rather perverse creatures, don't read books and consequently are not aware of what is expected of them: thus there are overlaps in which a disease agent normally of occupational origin infects an individual having nothing to do with that industry or occupation.

Leptospirosis is a disease that overlaps. For the most part, it occurs in sewage-plant operators, miners, and agricultural laborers raising such crops as rice and sugar cane by irrigation. But children may become infected when swimming in stagnant or slow-moving ponds, usually in farm areas. The infecting bacterium is passed into water via cattle, rodent, or dog urine. The microbe, a corkscrew-shaped organism, enters the human body either through breaks in the skin or by penetrating the mucous membranes lining the nose and eyes. Nine cases occurred in one family as a consequence of infection by the family dog. Figure 24 shows the six major sources of infection by leptospires. The precipitous rise of leptospirosis in May and June corresponds to the period of use of the "old swimming hole" in which animals have passed urine. A high incidence of leptospirosis has occurred among American troops in Vietnam. Soldiers spend a good deal of time wading waist-deep in stagnant rivers and streams polluted by infected cattle and rodent urine. Although the disease has a low mortality rate, it is severe enough to require hospitalization, thus making soldiers who are infected inactive for ten days to two weeks.

Toxoplasmosis, a highly infectious protozoal disease of infants, is also a more common cause of abortion and stillbirth than is generally appreciated. In the newborn, toxoplasmosis can be extremely grave, killing some of its victims and blinding, crippling, or producing deafness or mental retardation in others.

Apparently this exotic-sounding illness is widely distributed in our population on a subclinical level; that is, blood samples

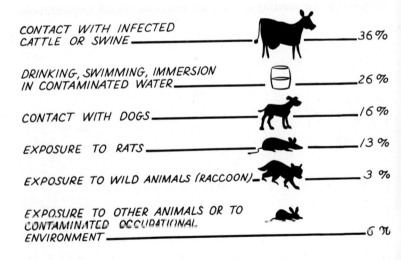

CONTACT WITH INFECTED
CATTLE OR SWINE —————————————— 36%

DRINKING, SWIMMING, IMMERSION
IN CONTAMINATED WATER—————————— 26%

CONTACT WITH DOGS————————————— 16%

EXPOSURE TO RATS—————————————— 13%

EXPOSURE TO WILD ANIMALS (RACCOON)———— 3%

EXPOSURE TO OTHER ANIMALS OR TO
CONTAMINATED OCCUPATIONAL
ENVIRONMENT——————————————————— 6%

Figure 24. Major sources of infection by leptospires.
(*Source:* Vital Statistics of the United States.)

from 20 to 50 percent of adult Americans and almost 100 percent of residents of Central America over age forty exhibit antibodies even though clinical symptoms are not evident.

The protozoan parasite that infects man, *Toxoplasma gondii,* obtains its name from the gondi, a rat-like rodent found in North Africa. Since being isolated from the gondi, the parasite has been found in rabbits, rats, mice, swine, dogs, cats, chickens, and birds, all the way from the Arctic to the Antarctic.

Clinical cases of toxoplasmosis have been reported in Japan, New Zealand, Tahiti, the United States, Sweden, and Holland. Women appear to be the chief transmitters of the parasite to new-born infants. Recent studies have demonstrated that the infectious organism passes via the placenta to the fetus. Although it is believed that the mother picks up the parasite from close association with some animal reservoir, the mechanism has not been definitely established. Because the symptoms are variable, the condition can easily be missed on examination. The lack of a good diagnostic test has been a serious impediment to treatment.

Early in June 1967, Dr. Jack S. Remington of the Stanford University School of Medicine described a new and highly promising test to the meeting of the Pan-American Health Organization. The test is based on the detection of a specific antibody that does not pass to the fetus from the mother's circulatory system. The presence of the antibody shows that the newborn baby has contracted toxoplasmosis while still in the womb. This identification allows immediate institution of therapeutic measures to prevent or control further harm.

Although epidemiologists believe that millions of people around the world have had contact with *Toxoplasma gondii,* relatively few cases have actually been reported. Until November 1968, no epidemics of toxoplasmosis had ever been recorded. In that month, five students at New York's Cornell Medical College became ill with fever, muscular aches and pains, rash, and severe pain around the eyes. On investigation, it was learned that two weeks earlier, all five had eaten hamburgers at the dormitory lunch counter and that in the rush to serve all the people who wanted a snack before going to hear a famous surgeon from South Africa, the beef was undercooked and was little more than raw. Dr. B. H. Kean, the physician who attended these students, believes this outbreak to be the first evidence of transmission via beef. If this is proven, the question of how *T. gondii* got into the beef will remain to raise the specter of another food-borne disease that must be guarded against.

Trichinosis is commonly considered to be of little importance as a public-health problem. Most people believe that it is only the rare individual who suffers from trichinosis during sudden outbreaks and requires immediate hospitalization. Unfortunately, this is not the case. Most recent estimates of the national prevalence of trichinosis range from 16 to 36 percent of the population, with an average of 20 percent. This would imply that approximately forty million people—men, women, and children—have unsuspected, subclinical infections. Hence, trichinosis must be regarded as a widespread rather than a limited condition, with a potential of infecting all people who eat insufficiently cooked pork and pork products (see Chapter 9, Solid-Waste Disposal). In trichinosis, larval roundworms encyst in muscle tissue, frequently causing nothing more than sporadic but elusive symptoms often mistaken for a half-dozen non-specific abdominal and chest pains. The larval worms travel through the blood vessels, entering the muscles of the diaphragm, ribs, tongue, and eyes. In the muscles, they continue to increase in size to a maximum of approximately one-eighth of an inch. They curl up in the muscles and are walled off by the host as a response to their presence. In severe cases the pain can be intense, and death is not uncommon.

Strangely enough, with all the publicity given trichinosis over the past twenty years, people still eat rare pork. Pork is one meat that must not be eaten rare. Up to 10 percent of the pork sausage in large city markets has been found to be infested with trichinella worms. One of the reasons so few obvious cases are seen each year is that many people harbor only a few larval worms in their systems. However, each year three hundred to four hundred new cases are reported, despite the fact that most states do not require that trichinosis be reported. In 1961, two Canadian scientists reported a high rate of trichinosis among the Eskimos of Cape Dorset, who eat rare or raw bear and walrus meat, both of which are known to harbor the parasite.

Authorities agree that trichinosis is a serious public health problem. No specific treatment is available but the means of prevention is absolutely clear: pork must be cooked at a minimum of 140°F for at least thirty minutes per pound to insure the complete destruction of any parasitic worms that may be present.

Encephalitis is an inflammation of the brain. Several types of arthropod-borne encephalitides are of current interest. In the summer of 1964, Houston, Texas, experienced a severe epidemic of St. Louis encephalitis.* Some five hundred adults and children were stricken with the disease. Mental retardation, paralysis, and brain damage with accompanying deformities are some of the conditions that resulted. Areas of New Jersey and Pennsylvania had similar but milder outbreaks that summer. Florida had had a major outbreak two years before. All four outbreaks were arthropod-borne; that is, the virus gained entrance to the human host by the bite of mosquitoes. On puncture, the virus particles contained in mosquito saliva are transferred. Actually, man becomes infected accidentally (Figure 25). Although many types of wild birds are natural reservoirs of the virus, they do not appear to be affected. Female mosquitoes in the vicinity obtain a blood meal from these birds, at which time they pick up the virus. If a man or a horse should wander into the mosquito-bird environment, or if man allows or encourages bird flocks and mosquitoes to flourish in his environment, as is the case in many cities today, the mosquitoes will prefer to obtain their blood meals from men or horses. As the bite is made and blood is drawn up, saliva and virus are delivered into the wound; the saliva contains an enzyme that prevents the blood from clotting too rapidly, thus allowing the mosquito to imbibe at its leisure. Regular, planned control of bird and mosquito populations is essential to prevent the spread of encephalitis to man.

During July and August of 1971, an explosive epidemic of Venezuelan equine encephalitis (VEE) swept through the Mexican state of Tamaulipas, just across the border from Brownsville, Texas. By the time Mexican President Luis Echeverria ordered the army out to man roadblocks in an attempt to localize the disease, 12 people had died and between 500 and 1,000 had be-

* As the virus of this disease was first isolated in St. Louis in 1933, it bears this name even though it has not appeared in St. Louis for many years.

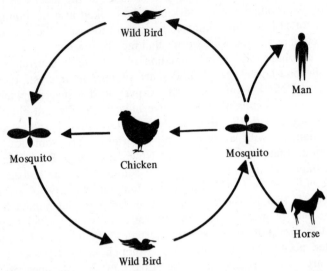

Figure 25. Cycle of transmission of St. Louis encephalitis.

come ill with this disease, which resembles sleeping sickness. In addition, some 20,000 horses had died and the virus was on its way across the border.

Hospital reports from Brownsville indicated that at least 34 people in the lower Rio Grande Valley had exhibited typical symptoms: nausea, chills, headache, fever. By October 1971, 84 confirmed cases had been reported from the Southwest. In both Texas and California, hundreds of thoroughbred horses died before sufficient supplies of vaccine were made available.

Another disease whose incidence is on the rise today is rabies. Although rabies has been well known throughout recorded history, it is only within the past twenty-five years that reservoirs of rabies other than the dog have become apparent. Rabies as a community health problem was considered well controlled as long as dogs were the only reservoir of infection. Now that it has been established that wild animals such as the fox, raccoon, skunk, and bat are additional natural reservoirs, a serious public health problem has developed.

A few years ago it was believed that the vampire bat was solely responsible for human and cattle rabies in Mexico and South America. More recently, insect-eating and fruit bats have been found to harbor rabies virus. As a consequence of this widespread natural infection, control becomes almost impossible. In 1953, a young boy was attacked by a rabid yellow bat in Tampa, Florida. A woman was similarly attacked in Pennsylvania. Attacks by bats have now been reported from a dozen states. Apparently, the bats pass the infection among themselves in their rookeries in caves. Every so often a rabid bat becomes maddened by the effects of the disease on the nervous system, and attacks people. However, the bite of a skunk is now known to be the worst of all animals; 100 to 1,000 times more virus is present in the saliva of rabid sunks than in any other animal. Consequently, when a skunk bites, there is no question about the prompt need for rabies vaccine.

In 1963, some four thousand cases of rabies from all sources were reported in the United States. Many midwestern states report increasing rabies among campers who are bitten while sleeping. Approximately five hundred thousand cases were reported to the World Health Organization from sixty-three countries in 1963.

Ever since Louis Pasteur successfully used rabies vaccine on Joseph Meister on July 6, 1885, it has popularly been thought that the treatment for rabies should be avoided if at all possible. This aversion has been engendered by two factors: (1) some people are hypersensitive to the proteinaceous material of the vaccine, and (2) the treatment involves fourteen injections. Although fears of the procedure are unwarranted, they persist. The fact is that allergic reactions to brain-tissue vaccine used to occur in perhaps one in two thousand individuals, but the duck-embryo vaccine used over the past five years has all but eliminated such reactions. The inoculations themselves, although still fourteen in number, are made with short needles just under the skin of the arm, leg, or abdomen, and are no more unpleasant than a flu shot.

Vaccine is given to prevent the appearance of symptoms. When clinical signs do appear, the outcome has never been in doubt; death ensues. From the medical viewpoint, therefore, the fact that seven-year-old Matthew Winkler of Willshire, Ohio, bitten by a rabid bat, survived clear neurological signs including a week-long coma, is a significant first. By January 1972, five months after being bitten, Matthew was completely well and back in school. Unusual or "miracle" drugs were not used. After the course of duck vaccine injections failed and clinical signs appeared, his attending physicians placed him in an intensive care unit and treated his condition as they would other neurological diseases—for convulsions, respiratory distress, and tissue oxygen deficiency (hypoxia). This may herald a new direction in rabies management.

Recently, a vaccine to be used before being bitten was made available for experimental field trials. The vaccine will be given to people in high-risk jobs, such as mailmen and policemen. If successful, it could mean the end of the series of vaccinations now given after an individual is bitten.

For the past five years, there has been increasing discussion of the possibility of eradicating * such diseases as rabies, malaria, and yellow fever, among others. Although such a prospect is attractive, when some of the practical realities are fully considered the eradication of rabies, for example, seems highly unlikely.

Rabies can infect almost any warm-blooded animal. The virus leaves the animal only in its saliva, so that biting is the normal route of transmission and puncture wounds of the skin the usual portal of entry. So long as canines were the sole source of infection, eradication had possibilities. Local outbreaks of rabies in the United States can usually be controlled by elimination of stray dogs and vaccination of all registered dogs. When, however, it was learned that bats, skunks, squirrels, and a wide assortment of wild animals harbor the virus and can transmit it to man, hope of eradication vanished. The bat reservoir alone is far too inaccessible.

In addition to the biological problems, religious considerations are involved. In Arab and Asian countries, dogs are considered unclean. Accordingly, few Moslems are willing to handle them for the routine vaccination procedures. In those countries of Southeast Asia where Buddhism is the dominant religion, stray dogs are considered an integral part of the cycle of life and must not be

* Eradication is an all-or-nothing concept. It is similar to sterilization in that neither can be done partially.

killed. Thus, cultural practices impede prevention and control measures (see Chapter 2, Ecology of Health and Disease).

Brucellosis, or undulant fever, as it is often called (suggesting the cyclic, wave-like rise and fall of fever during a seizure) is a chronic illness of long duration with periods of fever and pain between periods of apparent health. Most cases have come from drinking raw milk from infected cows or goats. Packinghouse and slaughterhouse workers and veterinarians become ill after handling infected carcasses and hides. Recently an Iowa swine slaughtering plant reported 110 cases of brucellosis that appeared to be due to inhalation of airborne brucella, the bacterium responsible for the infection. Apparently during the slaughtering bacteria, in the form of an aerosol, were released into the air and dispersed in a wide area; the organisms were of sufficiently small particle size to penetrate into the alveoli of the lungs (see Chapter 10).

Transmission of brucellosis to humans can be prevented if all milk is pasteurized or, barring that, is from inspected, disease-free herds. Control of brucellosis, like tuberculosis, is under the federal government, through its Brucellosis Eradication Program. Between 1954, when only 24 percent of cattle were under control, and 1959, when 55 percent were controlled, the incidence of brucellosis in man dropped from over eighteen hundred new cases in 1954 to less than five hundred in 1959. By 1970, only 200 cases were reported.

Anthrax, an acute infectious disease of cattle, horses, sheep, and goats, is an admirable example of occupational exposure inducing infection in man. Two forms of the disease occur: one type is external, involving the skin and subcutaneous tissues; the other is systemic, and often mimics pneumonia or meningitis. The cutaneous form is seen most often and, fortunately, yields readily to antibiotic therapy. The systemic lesion, exemplified by wool sorter's disease, can be rapidly fatal. In this instance, workers inhale airborne spores of *Bacillus anthracis* from hair, hides, wool, bristles, or other animal products.

In anthrax we also see the intimate ecological interrelationships between man, animals, and the inanimate physical environment. In the summer of 1971, an outbreak of anthrax occurred in Ascension Parish, Louisiana. The epizootic appears to have been precipitated by a prolonged period of semi-drought followed by heavy rains that promoted extensive growth of the bacillus in the soil. Between June and September, 460 head of cattle, 28 horses, and 17 other animals died of anthrax.

During this period, two veterinarians reported typical cutaneous pustular lesions of the hand shortly after having necropsied cows that died of anthrax. In both cases, treatment with penicillin for ten days resulted in complete recovery.

Of particular concern to public health scientists are the varied diseases associated with household pets. One of the newest problem areas concerns a well-known disease, salmonellosis, a typhoid-like illness. Turtles are among the many animals that normally harbor the salmonella bacterium in their intestines. These organisms are regularly passed out in fecal matter and contaminate whatever they contact.

The state department of health in Minnesota recently reported that pet turtles infected twenty-two children under six years of age. This meant that the children had swallowed turtle feces. When it was discovered that a two-year-old had placed some of the brightly colored pebbles from the aquarium in her mouth, the source of infection became readily apparent.

Maryland's State Department of Health has a reputation for keeping good records of illness within the state. By December 1971, the Health Department had logged 2,000 cases of salmonellosis. Of these, 95 percent are believed to be caused by pet turtles. In response to his five-year-old son's agonizing bout with this gastrointestinal illness, Allen Kurtz of Silver Springs waged a one-man battle to outlaw the sale of turtles. Today, Maryland has joined Pennsylvania as the second state to make the sale a misdemeanor. The state of Washington has legislation requiring turtles to be certified as safe. Unfortunately this is misguided legislation; a turtle can be certified free of the infection, but its offspring can carry the bacteria. What is needed is a federal law prohibiting interstate shipment of turtles. But this will not happen until numbers of irate citizens light fires under a few key Senators and Congressmen.

California has begun implementing a new law aimed at protecting the public from zoonotic illness by imposing quarantines of up to 90 days on wild animals brought into the state. The law covers 145 species of animals including a wide variety of primates, such as spider monkeys, and wildcats, such as ocelots. The law is expected to improve the chances of a customer buying a disease-free monkey or wildcat. It is also expected to provide a mechanism for ascertaining the incidence of disease in imported animals. The California law springs from a warning issued by the National Academy of Sciences, which noted that imported primates "should be viewed as possible vectors of a number of diseases transmissible to man, such as tuberculosis, the dysenteries (salmonellosis, shigellosis, amebiasis), yellow fever, and infectious hepatitis."

One of the most interesting examples of the interrelatedness of human and animal health is the relationship of influenza virus to both man and animal. It is well known that a wide range of viruses of Group A influenza occur not only in man and pigs but in birds and horses as well. Recent studies have shown that human influenza A_2 (Asian) can cause natural, inapparent infections in horses and swine. It has also been found that swine may act as a reservoir of the human strain. In fact, swine influenza and human influenza are considered to be the same infection; the great pandemic of 1918 was responsible for the epizootic in swine that followed shortly thereafter. Recent laboratory findings suggest a rather disturbing possibility concerning the human and avian (bird) influenza viruses. It has been discovered that an avian and a human strain could be hybridized. It is thus conceivable that a strain could emerge with the virulence of fowl plague (not normally pathogenic for humans) and the host specificity of a human strain. Fowl plague has a mortality rate of nearly 100 percent within a few hours of onset. While this unique combination of traits may be unlikely in nature, the possibility of the emergence of entirely new strains as a result of interbreeding remains a threat that cannot be disregarded, even though at the moment such hybridization is little more than a laboratory showpiece.

However, microbes from animals can protect man against illness. Swine influenza, noted above, is a case in point. A virus for a vaccine to protect man against human influenza has been found in the snouts of pigs from Taiwan. The virus appears to be a weakened version of A_2, which originated in Hong Kong in 1968 and continues to evoke "flu" in a number of countries.

When susceptible volunteers were injected with samples of the Taiwan virus, antibodies against the Hong Kong virus appeared in their blood, but no colds occurred. The importance of this discovery is that the Chinese swine flu virus seems to have crossed the "species barrier" between man and other animals. It is therefore highly likely that other pigs and even birds are presently incubating the viruses suitable for use in preparing human vaccines at an early stage of future outbreaks. A search for these ready-made vaccines has already started among animals in the Far East since so many pandemics appear to originate there.

Animals and humans are in reality so kindred that knowledge of a certain disease in one can often be applied to the other. This area of research is known as comparative medicine. Cardiovascular, degenerative, nervous, and rheumatic diseases occur in animals as well as man. Because domestic animals are slaughtered for food or other useful products, they seldom live on to old age. In recent years, several universities have established research centers in which animals are studied as they live out their full potential of years.

Atherosclerosis occurs in primates (including man), swine, chickens, turkeys, and pigeons. Cerebrovascular symptoms appear to be common in aging pigs. Viral leukemia is well established in chickens and mice and may also occur in dogs, cats, and cattle. Since this virus can infect a large number of animal species, all researchers are wondering whether man can be infected from the animals around him. As yet, the viral etiology of human cancer is controversial. Much more research is needed before it can be pinned down.

The existence of degenerative diseases among animals raises the possibility that animal research studies could be as helpful in understanding and controlling chronic degenerative human ailments as they were in understanding communicable diseases. One of the most beneficial aspects of the animal relationship is the far shorter life-span of most animals, which conveniently compresses into a few years events that are spread over a half-century in man.

As we continue to obtain information about our environment, it becomes increasingly evident that man's health is intimately associated with that of the many animals occupying his habitat. Thus, real comprehension of many community health problems must encompass knowledge of both animal and human disease.

Suggested Reading

Steele, James H. "Zoonoses of Domestic Animals." In *Critical Reviews in Environmental Control,* vol. 2, issue 2, edited by R. G. Bond and C. P. Straub, pp. 243–292. Cleveland: CRC Press, 1971.

Baker, E. F.; Anderson, H. W.; and Allard, J. "Epidemiological Aspects of Turtle-Associated Salmonellosis." *Archives of Environmental Health* 24 (1971): 1.

CHAPTER
7

SANITARY SEWAGE

*An individual cannot achieve renewal if he does not believe
in the possibility of it. Nor can society.*

John W. Gardner

"Thou shalt have a place also without the camp, whither
thou shalt go forth abroad: and thou shalt have a paddle upon
thy weapon; and it shall be, when thou wilt ease thyself abroad,
thou shalt dig therewith and shalt turn back and cover that which
cometh from thee" (Deut. 23:12–13).

Although the Israelites did not have the benefits of waste
disposal by water carriage,* they seemed well aware that human
excreta could be a vehicle of disease transmission. It was not un-

* The water-carriage system of waste removal is simply a supply of
water under pressure that removes excretal waste from dwellings. Its introduction in the 1840s involved engineering problems of considerable magnitude. However, it only shifted the problem to a point away from the dwellings. At some point on the outskirts of the city the combined discharges of
the whole community had to be cared for. The introduction of sewage-
treatment plants was a logical extension of the waste-removal system.

til several thousand years later, however, in the filthy, sewage-laden industrial cities of London, Boston, Cologne, Edinburgh, and New York, that social pressures forced the introduction of the water-carriage system of waste disposal.

After a rainfall in the city of London, Jonathan Swift wrote the following lines; they could apply to any community circa 1740:

> Now from all parts of the swelling kennels flow and bear their trophies with them as they go; filth of all hues and odors seems to tell what street they sailed from by the sight and smell, sweeping from the butchers' stalls, dung, guts and blood, drowned puppies, stinking sprats, all drowned in mud; dead cats and turniptop come tumbling down the flood.

Descriptions of conditions in streets of European and American cities in the eighteenth and nineteenth centuries * clearly show the appalling filth (by our standards) in which the people lived. One traveler wrote: "In the tenements of Glasgow dung was left lying in the courtyards as there were no lavatories in houses. This lack of lavatories led to the habit of house dwellers filling chamber pots with excreta and after some days, when completely full, and with a shout of, beware slops, emptying the contents out of the window into the street below." This practice quickly led to the pollution of wells and to the infestation of cities with rats; both gave rise to diseases of epidemic proportions, which regularly took a great toll in human lives.

Not until the latter part of the nineteenth century was disease transmission via human waste actually demonstrated. The fact is that modern society as we know it today could not have emerged without the benefits of clean water and the removal of sewage literally from its doorsteps.

While the object of sewage disposal is to get rid of sewage, a more important objective if community health is to be maintained is to collect, treat, and dispose of domestic waste (often called sanitary waste) in a manner calculated to protect health, preserve natural resources, and prevent nuisance conditions.

* Travelers to India today are shocked by similar scenes that fortunately represent distinct improvements over eighteenth- and nineteenth-century London or Paris.

With the aggregation of millions of people in large city centers, there is an unprecedented volume of human waste to be treated. In this treatment, the pathogenic microbes (bacteria, viruses, protozoa, fungi, spirochetes, and helminths) must be removed or reduced to harmless levels. It is well known that in any community, at any time, there are always small numbers of people who are either manifestly ill, in some stage of illness but not demonstratively so, or healthy carriers of disease. Together, they constitute a community's normal background or reservoir of pathogenic microorganisms whose elimination in feces means they will be found in sewage. As a result, sewage can be a threat to health, particularly to those who come in contact with water drawn from sewage-contaminated sources. Thus disposal of sewage implies two entirely different propositions: (1) the removal of energy-laden organic matter from liquid waste and its conversion to an innocuous form in order to prevent or control pollution of lakes, streams, and rivers; and (2) the prevention of water-borne disease.

The term *sewage* usually connotes the liquid wastes from homes, schools, commercial buildings, hotels, hospitals, and industrial plants. In addition to human excretal material, it generally contains industrial wastes such as those from meat-packing operations, breweries, milk and food plants, and chemical processing plants. Domestic sewage is generally limited to household wastes from residential areas and contains wastes from water closets and wash water from baths and kitchens. Curiously enough, in the United States domestic sewage varies little in composition and strength from community to community across the country. Although we like to think we are a heterogeneous people, in actual fact we have become remarkably similar. This is due in part to the nationwide storage and transportation facilities that permit extensive distribution of similar food products and to the quite similar eating habits and patterns of living of our population. Figure 26 shows the hourly volume of sewage flow resulting from this national pattern of behavior.

Sewage or liquid waste has the appearance of spent dishwater. It usually contains paper, organic material from feces and urine, soap, and such exotic items as dead animals, fruit skins,

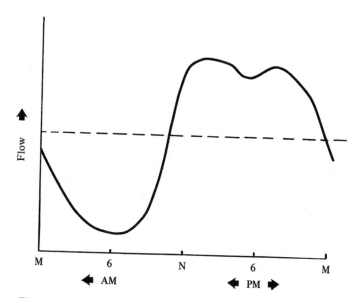

Figure 26. Nationwide pattern of sewage flow. (From Microbiology for Sanitary Engineers by Ross E. McKinney. Copyright 1962 by McGraw-Hill Book Company. Used by permission of McGraw-Hill Book Company.)

old shoes, collar buttons, and anything else that finds its way into the sanitary sewer.

A useful measure of the strength of sewage is the proportion of suspended solids it contains. The suspended solids of interest to the chemist are not the dead animals, shoes, or fruit skins, but organic particles of carbohydrates, fats, and proteins. Generally, sewage consists of 99.9 percent water and .02 to .04 percent solids. Although the amount of suspended solids is small when evaluated on a percentage basis, the total daily amount from a large city can be considerable. For example, in the sewage of a city the size of Washington, D.C., solids amount to approximately 150 tons per day. Of this, 40 to 50 percent is protein, another 40 to 50 percent consists of carbohydrates (sugars, starches, and cellulose), and the remaining 5 to 10 percent is fat. Discharging 150 tons per day of carbohydrates, fats, and proteins would provide more sumptuous meals for the microbes in lakes, streams, and rivers in and around Washington than they could properly digest. The result would undoubtedly be pollution of a magnitude as yet unknown in that area. Although such a discharge is only in the realm of conjecture, it does indicate the degree of treatment necessary.

Before embarking on a discussion of sewage treatment, it may be helpful to delineate the path taken by sewage as it flows from home to treatment plant to final outfall in a watercourse. Treatment of sewage from homes with septic tanks, cesspools, or seepage pits will be discussed separately.

Let us suppose that while you are washing your hands a ring slips off your finger, and before it can be retrieved it has gone down the drain. Figure 27 is a diagrammatic summary of the path the ring takes as it moves along with the liquid waste. At top left, house and street are seen in cross-section. Each of the

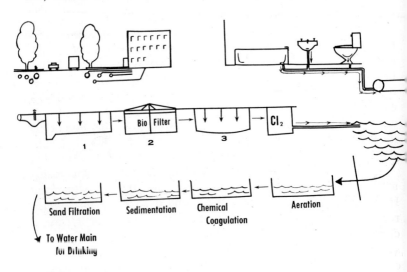

Sand Filtration   Sedimentation   Chemical Coagulation   Aeration

To Water Main for Drinking

Figure 27. Diagrammatic representation of the route taken by domestic waste from an urban dwelling to its final outfall in a river.

various utilities—gas, electricity, water, and sanitary sewers—leads from the street to the house. The largest of the conduits found under the street is the main or lateral branch of the sewage system that collects domestic waste from many houses on the street. A cross-section of the inside of the house is depicted at top right. Connections and flow from sink, tub, and flush toilet are seen leading to the street sewer.

The street sewer joins large trunk sewers from other neighborhoods, through which the waste flows directly to a treatment facility.* The unit at far left in the middle row represents the trunk line arriving at the treatment plant. Wherever practical, sewers are built to allow sewage to flow by gravity; when this is not possible, pumping stations are strategically placed to pump sewage through pressure conduits to points where they can discharge into a gravity sewer.

As the sewage flows along through the many miles of piping, biological activity engendered by the extensive microbial flora naturally present in human waste (together with additional microbial forms from soil, street washings, dead animals, fruit skins, and whatever else falls into sewers, progresses at an ever-increasing rate. The longer the sewage remains in the system, the greater will be the activity. If the sewers are extensive and the rate of flow is low, the biological activity will be so advanced that the waste can be considered as having received partial treatment before it reaches the plant. The key points here, and as the waste continues on, are biological activity and treatment. Both are concerned with rendering this highly putrescible organic material innocuous; that is, preventing water pollution, odors, and unsightly conditions.

At this point, a digression may be in order. Most piping used to transport liquid waste is relatively inexpensive concrete. However, improperly ventilated sewers can undergo severe corrosion as a consequence of microbial activity. Under anaerobic conditions (poor ventilation with insufficient oxygen) hydrogen sulfide (H_2S) is produced. The sulfur-oxidizing bacteria present in the waste can, under proper conditions, convert the H_2S

* Many cities have combined sewers in which both sewage and water runoff from street washing and rain are collected and flow together to the treatment plant.

to sulfuric acid, which in turn reacts with the lime in concrete to form calcium sulfate. Calcium sulfate, having little structural strength, crumbles. To avoid this, more expensive, acid-resistant, vitrified clay pipes must be employed if adequate ventilation cannot be achieved.

At the treatment plant, sewage generally flows through a series of coarse and fine screens to remove large floating objects; the lost ring would most likely pass through the coarse screen, and possibly through the fine screen. From the screens the waste passes through a comminutor, which shreds the remaining solids to a size calculated to prevent clogging at points farther along in the plant.

After sewage has been screened, the next step is removal of the easily settled suspended matter, such as sand, gravel, and ashes, in grit chambers. When a sewage system collects both liquid waste and storm-water runoff, grit chambers are usually provided at the treatment plant to remove these coarse materials, which can cause clogging of moving parts (sludge-collector mechanisms and pumps), pipes, and drains.

From the grit chamber the liquid waste passes to the primary settling or sedimentation tanks (Figure 27) at low velocity. This method is widely used as either preliminary treatment or, as is too often the case, as the sole treatment of sewage before it is emptied into a stream or river. In such cases, raw sewage is placed in the watercourse with the hope that its dilution with large volumes of water will prevent pollution or nuisance conditions. All too often, this hope is unjustified.

The velocity of flow through the primary settling tanks is adjusted to achieve a thirty- to ninety-minute detention time, depending on the strength of the sewage and on whether any additional treatment is to be given. The purpose of primary settling is removal of a minor portion of the suspended solids—the carbohydrates, fats, and proteins that are the major contributors to the pollution-nuisance complex. It is quite likely that the ring originally lost down the bathroom sink will settle out in the primary tanks as a result of the decreased velocity and gravitational effects, and will finally be lost in the accumulated sludge.

During the course of flow thus far, the potentially putrescible organic compounds in sewage have been relatively unaltered. If the waste were dumped into a stream or river without additional treatment, the ability of the stream to purify itself would be seriously impaired, if not completely destroyed. To prevent this, secondary treatment of sewage is designed into the process to deal specifically with the organic compounds. Often, secondary treatment can remove up to 90 percent of the suspended organic compounds. This degree of stabilization can prevent most rivers from becoming polluted.

At this point, depending upon the type of secondary treatment to be given, the sewage will pass to either a trickling filter (biofilter) or an activated sludge aeration tank. Both are based upon the stabilization or neutralization of organic waste by biological action. That is, a host of biological species ranging in size from bacteria to snails and flies take part in the process that eventually produces an inoffensive effluent. It is in either the trickling filter or the aeration tank that the business of removing or physiochemically altering the remaining suspended matter occurs. From either the trickling filter or the aeration tank, the stabilized and clarified liquid flows or is pumped to a secondary settling tank for an additional short holding period.

Up to this point the second of the two major functions of waste treatment, the prevention of disease transmission by virus, bacteria, and protozoa, has been given only cursory attention. Although pathogenic microorganisms are partially removed in the settling process and others are mechanically removed by filtration and aeration, it is the process of chlorination that destroys the great majority of organisms. In addition, chlorine abets the stabilization of the remaining organic matter by its highly oxidizing character. After contact with chlorine for approximately thirty minutes, the clarified disinfected liquid is discharged into a watercourse.

This is a generalized description of the trip sewage takes from home to stream or river. It is at this point of sewage outfall in some watercourse that water pollution can begin, and it is at the point of water intake farther downstream that many of the problems of drinking water begin. Figure 27 also indicates the general path followed by water from point of intake downstream of a sewage outfall, through treatment, and back to the consumer.

The question that remains to be answered is: "If all sewage

follows the path outlined, why do we have polluted rivers and streams?" As has been pointed out, the treatment of domestic and industrial wastes usually depends at some stage in the process upon the metabolic activity of microorganisms and some larger species. Microorganisms use the organic matter and minerals of sewage as a source of nutrients for growth and reproduction. The treatment system described effectively removes the available energy of the waste and neutralizes or stabilizes it. When the stabilized organic waste reaches a watercourse, it is no longer a source of nutriment for the many biological forms in the stream or river.

When microbes metabolize food, in this case sewage solids, oxygen is consumed. The more food available, the more oxygen used up; the more oxygen used, the less available for fish and other stream biota. Pollution or "fouling" occurs as a consequence of the removal of oxygen from the stream. Without an adequate supply of oxygen, life in the stream dies or is driven farther downstream.

A sewage-treatment plant that employs secondary treatment employs a form of biological treatment. Where biofilters are used, the liquid from the primary settling tank flows to the filter or percolation bed. Here, large rotary distributor arms spray the clarified liquid over a bed of stones. Figure 28 shows the entire unit;

Figure 28. Trickling filter in operation outside Paris.

Figure 29. Close-up view of a section of a distributor arm of a trickling filter.

Figure 29 is a close-up view of the liquid falling upon the bed. As the liquid trickles over and between the stones, bacteria, protozoa, worms, snails, spiders, and flies utilize its protein, carbohydrates, and fats to make additional bacteria, protozoa, worms, etc. The waste is thus transformed into energy-free particles that do not need the oxygen dissolved in the stream; with little or no oxygen demand, pollution cannot occur. Thus, the main purpose of secondary treatment (or even tertiary treatment, if it is used) is to reduce the amount of dissolved oxygen withdrawn from the stream. Since many waterways *are* being polluted by sewage, it is clear that stabilized waste is not the only type of waste entering the water. It is well known that many communities pipe their effluents directly from primary settling tanks to a river or stream. Still others permit raw untreated sewage to be emptied into their local rivers and streams. This waste is loaded with energy-rich nutrients that provide food for aquatic microbes. In metabolizing these nutrients, the microbes utilize large quantities of dissolved oxygen, which is then no longer available for fish, aquatic invertebrates, and plants. As oxygen is depleted, the flora and fauna die or move away. The stream becomes anaerobic and offensive to the senses; in short, it is polluted.

Pollution can also occur in another way. Modern technology has produced chemicals that often defy microbial attempts at their degradation in the secondary treatment processes of the sewage plant. Thus they pass unaltered into the river. Many of these chemicals are toxic to fish and other species. When dumped into a watercourse, they bring about pollution by killing the biological species that aid in the purification process. Additionally, toxic industrial chemicals, when combined with sewage wastes at the treatment plant, can kill the microbes in a trickling filter or aeration tank, thereby destroying the filter's stabilization capacity. Thus, again energy-rich waste with a large oxygen demand passes through the treatment plant virtually unchanged and, with its great potential for pollution, gains access to streams.

One of the newest low-cost methods for stabilizing the sewage emanating from small communities is the oxidation pond or lagoon, known in Europe as the oxidation ditch. Like the other methods described, it is based on biological degradation. The sewage, which is not subjected to any preliminary treatment, is pumped directly from a collecting point to the pond, which is essentially a shallow ditch two to six feet deep. The area of the pond is usually dictated by the available land.

The name *oxidation pond* indicates that the process is aerobic—it makes large amounts of oxygen available to the microbes. As the raw liquid waste enters the pond, the heavy particles settle out, leaving the suspended organic matter to be attacked by bacteria, algae, and protozoa. After a rather long retention period, thirty to forty days, the stabilized effluent is released into a nearby waterway. From time to time the accumulated sludge must be removed in order to keep the lagoon in operation.

Such industries as dairies, food canneries, and breweries are turning to oxidation ponds to handle their high-oxygen-demand wastes economically and to prevent overloading of already overburdened municipal treatment plants.

Another means of sewage disposal widely used in the United States, one which often contributes to pollution of streams and drinking water, is the septic tank. This is an individual system used where water is available to carry waste from a home not served by municipal sewer lines. The system is composed of three simple elements: the septic tank, a distribution box, and a disposal field.

Liquid waste is conveyed by pipe from a dwelling to a waterproof concrete or metal container. Figure 30 shows the general plan of the system and a cross-section of the primary container. The tank usually contains two baffles to prevent the heavier solids and the buoyant scum from passing out with the effluent to the distribution box and into the disposal field.

During the retention period in a properly operating system,

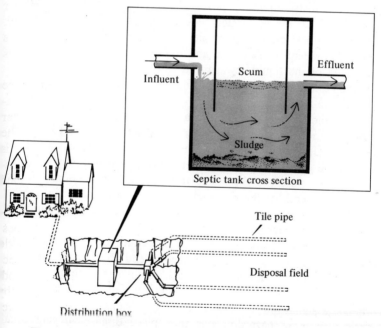

Figure 30. Schematic view of a septic-tank system. (Courtesy of John E. Kiker, Jr., University of Florida.)

from 50 to 70 percent of the suspended solids are removed by sedimentation, which forms a sludge that must be removed periodically. Failure to remove the accumulated solids often results in discharge of solids in the absorption field, with resultant clogging and ponding.

The principle is relatively simple. Because this is a closed system with little ventilation, anaerobic conditions prevail. This implies that the bacterial metabolism will be carried out by anaerobic species. The process is one of digestion, in which both floating scum and the settled solids are reduced in volume and transformed into liquids, gas, and an irreducible minimum of biologically inert solids. The gas diffuses into the atmosphere and the liquids containing organic acids pass into the fields and percolate through the soil, where aerobic bacterial species complete the stabilization.

The distribution box provides a means for even dispersion of the liquids to the perforated tiles. An integral part of the system is the disposal or absorption field, which should be carefully designed. Inadequate field size and too compact a soil prevent percolation of the liquid sewage and result in ponding. As a result, nuisances occur. In areas with sandy soil, contamination of ground water can result.

Although septic tanks are a direct descendant of cesspools, they are not the same. Cesspools have been described as wells in reverse. Untreated domestic waste is allowed to run into a hole or pit in the ground from which seepage or leaching through soil occurs. This stabilizes the waste through bacterial action. All too often the depth of the cesspool places the raw sewage in contact with the water table, with the result that gross contamination of the drinking-water source occurs.

The lack of any disinfection procedure in either the septic tank or the cesspool does not recommend them from the community health standpoint. Although some of the pathogenic microbes are removed during sedimentation and digestion in septic tanks, a significant number do enter the disposal fields. Cesspools are even more hazardous, as they place disease-carrying organisms in close proximity to wells and ground-water aquifers. Public health agencies are quite correct in attempting to eliminate their use.

Although farmers and rural populations generally have used

septic tanks since their development around the turn of the century, it is the rapid expansion of residential areas into formerly rural communities in recent years that has greatly accelerated the number of private sewage-disposal systems.

Of our 200 million people, some two-thirds, or 132 million, are served by municipal sewers. The remainder use septic tanks. Of those 132 million using city sewer lines, about 10 percent live in communities that discharge untreated sewage directly into streams. Another 25 percent live in communities where raw sewage is discharged after a short retention in primary settling basins. Recall that primary treatment includes screens to remove large floating objects, a comminutor for shredding, a grit chamber, and a sedimentation basin for settling of the heavier solids. Little stabilization occurs up to this point.

It has been estimated that the sewage discharges from communities that give primary treatment or none at all correspond to the raw waste of almost fifty million people. Figures published in 1966 reveal that among the 11,420 communities in this country that had sewer systems, 2,139 still discharged untreated waste. Many treatment plants are old, inefficient, and overloaded, so that a substantial portion of the sewage is only partially stabilized. Thus, it is easy to see why water is polluted by domestic and industrial wastes.

It was noted earlier that many of the new industrial wastes are not fully metabolized by the organisms of the secondary treatment facilities and that some of these chemicals coming into the treatment plants in high concentration prove toxic to the stabilization organisms. The saga of synthetic detergents (syndets) is a good example of the dislocations created by new products. Bear in mind that sewage-treatment plants were originally designed to treat human excretal waste, not industrial chemicals.

Both soap and syndets have detergent properties—the ability to clean by emulsification of particles of dirt. Syndets, however, have the added advantage of being able to accomplish this in both hard and acid waters, where soaps precipitate and require large amounts to achieve little if any cleaning. Syndets are molecularly different from soap, and their molecular configuration does not allow bacteria to "eat" them, whereas soap is easily metabolized by bacteria.

Since bacteria in streams and rivers cannot metabolize syndets, little if any oxygen is used up by the presence of syndets and contamination of waterways by syndets is not accompanied by oxygen depletion. The pollution in this case consists of the inordinate amount of foam produced and the fact that the syndets appear in drinking water after passing intact through sewage treatment plants, often disrupting the efficiency of the trickling filters.

One interesting form of sewage treatment makes use of the many nutrients in sewage to increase food supply. Although the need for protein supplements to diet is greater in Asia, Africa, and South America than in the industrialized nations of Western Europe, the huge sewage system in Munich, Germany utilizes fish ponds both to purify sewage effluent and to increase the supply of fish. Instead of being discharged into a river, the effluent is sprayed into a pond stocked with rainbow trout or carp. The fish rapidly increase in weight on the luxurious diet and at the same time purify the waste, which is then discharged into the Yser River; the fish are sold for a smart profit.

Closer to home, we are beginning to give serious consideration to land disposal of municipal sewage and waste water effluents. Land disposal is really nothing more than employment of the soil as a huge filter. Planners envision the discharge of treated effluents (secondary treatment plus chlorination) for crop irrigation, fertilization of gardens, public lawns, golf courses, and other grounds, as well as the creation of artificial lakes similar to the five now in operation at Santee, California. This would free rivers and streams of a major organic burden, return nutrients to the land, restore ground water, and reduce or eliminate the need to add chemical fertilizers to crops. With so many compelling benefits, it would be difficult not to consider it. One drawback currently under discussion is the potential health hazard in broadcasting fecal matter far and wide. However, though an aesthetic hurdle may need to be overcome, little real health hazard is foreseen.

After the introduction of the water-carriage method of waste disposal in the 1850s and the widespread introduction of sewerage systems shortly thereafter, little additional progress in waste disposal was made until the introduction by Corbett in 1893 o large-scale trickling filters in Lancashire, England. This was followed by the introduction of septic tanks in 1905 by Cameron in Exeter, England. Just prior to World War I, Avdern and Lockett, two English scientists, published accounts of their work on the oxidation of sewage, thereby laying the basis for the activated sludge process of sewage stabilization.

The fact is that although modifications in sewage treatment systems have occurred from time to time, they have been concerned with increasing the loading rather than with new approaches. But loading has about reached its limit. Completely new methods for treating sewage have not been produced for over fifty years. And while engineers attempt to design more efficient waste-treatment facilities and units to receive greater and greater hydraulic loadings, the biological basis for stabilization remains virtually unknown. Thus, although advanced waste-treatment procedures such as electrodialysis, reverse osmosis, solvent extraction, eutectic freezing, and distillation are being inves-

Figure 31. Battery of rotating disks for cleaning waste water. (Photo courtesy of Dr. Joel Kaplovsky, Rutgers University.)

tigated by scientists in industry, government, and the universities, there has been little interdisciplinary effort to achieve a much-needed breakthrough. The time is ripe for development of completely new ways of treating human waste.

Such a project is well on its way toward completion and success at Rutgers University. The Department of Environmental Sciences has developed a biological process for removing organic matter from liquid waste that appears to be more efficient than any method previously known.[1] Not only does it remove BOD, but may offer an additional benefit, a by-product in the form of an algal ration for cattle. In this method waste water moves through rotating disks (Figure 31), which provide tremendous surface area for the growth of algae, which, in turn, metabolize the organic matter in the water. Figure 32 is a close-up of the biological disks.

Three ingredients are needed for this type of progress: capable professionals, financial backing, and time.

Figure 32. Close-up of biological disk. (Photo courtesy of Dr. Joel Kaplovsky, Rutgers University.)

Reference

1. W. N. Torpey, H. Heukelekian, A. J. Kaplovsky, and R. Epstein, "Rotating Disks with Biological Growths Prepare Waste Water for Disposal or Reuse," *Journal of the Water Pollution Control Federation* 45 (1971): 2181.

8

WATER POLLUTION

What I tell you three times is true.
Lewis Carroll,
The Hunting of the Snark

"Water, water everywhere,/ Nor any drop to drink." Although this was the plight and plaint of Coleridge's Ancient Mariner, some would have us believe our water supply today fits this description. Though this is surely an overstatement, the pollution of a number of watercourses from which supplies are drawn must in fact be stopped. But what exactly is water pollution, and what can be done about it? Even more pertinent, what *is* being done about it?

Water pollution is a subject that invites wide discussion—and heated discussion at that! As a result, more heat than light is often generated. With all that has been written about pollution, few of the writers bother to define it, mention how it is measured, or suggest how much may be tolerated. Pollution is not an all-or-none concept; degrees of pollution must be accepted and it may be well to recall that there is no such thing as naturally "pure" water. Bodies of water such as rivers, streams, and lakes are natural habitats for a wide variety of aquatic animals, from viruses and bacteria all the way to fish and frogs, and as many varieties of plants. These are all living things, and when they die the organic chemicals that constitute their bodies become an integral part of the water. Natural runoff from land (as a result of rain or flood) and leaf fall at certain times of the year add more organic matter. Accordingly, natural bodies of water cannot be thought of as "pure" in either a biological or chemical sense. All have degrees of impurity. The question is how much is tolerable.

Microbiologists and sanitary engineers consider water pollution as a problem of oxygen deficit; the greater the pollution, the lower the dissolved oxygen present. However, the general public often takes a broader view. To some, water pollution is equated with the coliform index, a measure of the presence of a specific type of bacterium normally present in the human gut. Other opinion holds that any substance added to water as a result of human activity is a pollutant. This concept is unrelated to the operational definition of water pollution in terms of oxygen used by scientists in this field. Nevertheless, such an approach is being taken by the U.S. Senate's Committee on Public Works in S.2770, the Senate bill (some call it the Muskie Bill) likely to become law. Thus empty food cans, soda bottles, automobile tires, old shoes, orange crates, and the rest of the trash that slovenly members of our society dispose of, are considered pollutants. Figure 33 typifies this view. These things are unsightly and aesthetically unappealing, but they have little or no effect on the dissolved oxygen in the water. To a smaller, but highly vocal segment of the population, pollution refers to anything other than chemically pure water, which, of course, has never existed on this planet.

If pollution is taken to mean the depletion of oxygen with consequent septic conditions such as offensive odors, floating masses of sludge, and death of fish and other aquatic life, then pollution is undoubtedly older than recorded history. As man cleared the land and cultivated it, surface water runoff increased and brought with it large amounts of organic material, causing depletions of oxygen. As soon as settlements arose in river valleys, human wastes began to be emptied into streams. The course

Figure 33. *"It's pollution all right, but it's pollution of rather a high order." (Drawing by Stevenson; © 1965 The New Yorker Magazine, Inc.)*

of history leads directly from the Stone Age tanner who scraped his furs into a stream to the river-polluting oil refinery, tannery, or plating plant of the twentieth century. There is, however, an important difference. As recently as a century and a half ago, next to nothing was known of the consequences of dumping human and industrial wastes into rivers. Today, our knowledge of causes, types, and the mechanism of pollution, leaves us no excuse.

When a river receives organic matter, it tends to purify itself; that is, it can overcome or adequately handle the organic load in time. "Running water purifies itself" is an old adage that had much truth to it, but one that may no longer be true. The magnitude and types of waste presently being discharged frequently overwhelm the recuperative capacities of the stream and thus stall recovery. Self-purification, which leads to the stabilization of the added organic matter, depends primarily upon the biochemical activities of bacteria, which, when given sufficient dissolved oxygen, utilize the organic matter as food and break down (metabolize, neutralize, stabilize, digest) compounds to innocuous end-products.

The cycle of self-purification requires an adequate concentration of dissolved oxygen for the microorganisms responsible for the ultimate reduction and transformation of organic matter to carbon dioxide and minerals. It also requires a substantial growth of aquatic vegetation whose photosynthetic processes return oxygen to the water.

This cycle is interrupted by deficient dissolved oxygen levels: turbidity can limit light penetration, which in turn limits photosynthesis. Should self-purification of a watercourse become impossible, metabolism of organic matter proceeds via the anaerobic route, characterized by the production of foul-smelling by-products and incomplete stabilization of the organic load.

Some waterways undergo self-purification in fairly short distances from point of sewage outfall, while others require twenty-five, fifty, or more miles in which to accomplish this. The process is complex, and each stream or river is a unique ecosystem with its own specific capacity for purification and recovery. If oxygen is removed faster than it can be replaced by natural aeration or by photosynthesis, conditions worsen and pollution of virtually an entire river may result.

The balance is readily upset by discharging into waterways quantities of organic waste greater than the available oxygen can cope with. A large amount of waste discharged continuously into a small stream could produce anaerobic conditions for many miles. The same quantity discharged into a river might easily be degraded in a short distance without any ill effects. The function of sewage treatment, therefore, is removal of enough organic matter to produce an acceptable effluent—one that can meet approved standards.

This is the context in which scientists view water pollution; but societal pressure is apparently demanding a broader view. Although too broad a definition can hamper control and prevention activities by blurring the dimensions and direction of control measures, a definition beyond oxygen debt may well be called for. Accordingly, we might consider waterways polluted when as a result of human activity the physical, chemical, and/or biological characteristics of the waterway are altered. Here a cautionary note is in order. It may not be wise to prevent all change in a waterway's characteristics. Some changes may well be beneficial. We will have to decide what alterations we will or will not accept. Of course, this will immediately call forth varying opinions of what is and what is not a tolerable change. Achieving general agreement on this point will need wide discussion.

Water pollution, the availability of acceptable drinking water, and sewage disposal are inextricably bound together. The realization that waste disposal and water use are parts of a cyclical process should aid in the planning a community or region does when considering its own needs and the needs of the neighboring downstream communities.

A city not uncommonly locates its water pumping stations upstream on a river and discharges its sewage effluent downstream into the same river. The next city downstream repeats the process, as do the next and the next. Distances between discharges of sewage effluents and of intakes of raw water are being squeezed closer and closer together because of the outward expansion of communities as a result of increased population. Figure 34 indicates the progressive intake-outlet reuse condition that prevails on many rivers today.

Today's communities and modern industry are both elephantine users of water. The average city-dwelling family of four uses about six hundred gallons of water each day. Industry requires some five gallons of water to produce a gallon of gasoline, ten gallons to produce each can of vegetables, twenty-five thousand gallons to process one ton of steel, and fifty thousand to produce one ton of paper. After use, the spent water, loaded with organic waste, is often dumped directly into a stream or river with the generally mistaken idea that dilution with fresh water will prevent pollution locally or farther downstream. Unfortunately, however, the available water resources are unevenly distributed; many sections of the country are forced to reuse the available supply long before the river from which they draw it has had a chance to purify itself. It has been estimated, for example, that the thirteen-hundred-mile Ohio River is used from three to eight times before it joins the Mississippi at Cairo, Illinois.

The present state of our technical capability requires that we accept a certain degree of pollution. We are still far from develop-

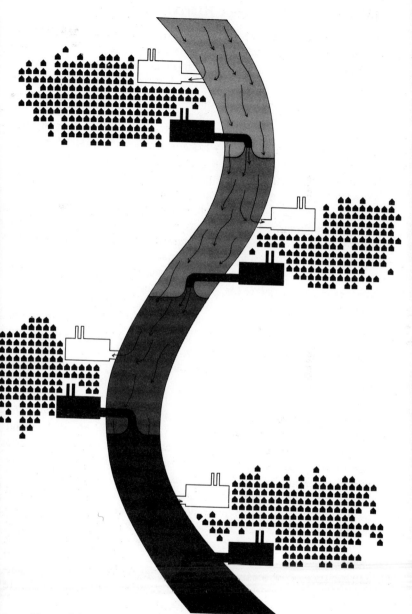

Figure 34. Schematic representation of water reuse by four cities.

ing alternative methods of liquid-waste disposal; consequently, the use of rivers for the disposal of waste is essential. The fact is that industry and residential communities alike would be forced to shut down if unified public opinion demanded pollution-free waterways under the broad definition of pollution. It is, therefore, in the best interests of the community to support research investigations aimed at discovering the degree of waste a stream can tolerate. Decisions as to what constitutes a tolerable degree of pollution must be guided by considerations of the water's natural purification capacity and the purpose for which it is to be used.

Those concerned with water pollution have categorized pollutants as chemical, physical, biological, and physiological. The chemical pollutants include both inorganic and organic compounds, such as dairy, textile, cannery, brewery, and paper-mill wastes, ensilage, laundry wastes, manure, and slaughterhouse wastes. These essentially contain proteins, carbohydrates, fats, oils, resins, tars, and soaps. If these pollutants are not excessive, they will be stabilized by the self-purification process. If they are excessive, death of fish and offensive odors can result. In addition, such mineral nutrients as phosphates, nitrates, and potassium, released in the stabilization process, encourage growth of aquatic plants. As the plants decay, further depletion of oxygen occurs. Metals and cyanides, mainly from engineering industries, can be toxic to fish and inhibit the biological waste stabilization process by killing the necessary microflora.

Biological pollutants include the many types of microscopic animal and plant forms, such as bacteria, protozoa, and viruses, that are associated with disease transmission. These come from domestic sewage, farms, and tanneries.

Physiological pollution manifests itself as objectionable tastes and odors. These may be imparted to the flesh of fish, making it inedible; or water itself may become unfit to drink owing to odors and tastes caused by the presence of inorganic chemicals, such as hydrogen sulfide, or the extensive growth of certain species of algae. Some impart musty odors to the water, while others give it fishy, pigpen, spicy, or chemical tastes.

Various physical effects, such as foam, color, turbidity, and increased temperature are also considered forms of pollution. Water from a nearby stream or river is often pumped into a plant to cool a machine or process that normally generates heat. The transfer of heat to the cooling water raises its temperature several degrees. When this heated water is discharged back into the stream or river, it may disrupt ecological relationships. A rise in temperature of only a few degrees may be lethal to a variety of aquatic plants and animals that, like most living things, are sustained only within a narrow temperature range. The death of certain species removes the food supply of the species that prey on them; without food they in turn will die or be forced to move downstream. Furthermore, the warmer the water, the less oxygen it will contain. At elevated temperatures all chemical and biological activity proceeds at a more rapid rate. This depletes the sensitive oxygen balance of the stream, as well as adversely affecting respiration and metabolism of a wide variety of animals. This series of events can destroy a stream's capacity for self-purification by altering or eliminating vital links of the stream's ecosystem.

Recently, the Ohio Department of Natural Resources reported the first case of an industrial firm being fined for thermal pollution (also called calefaction). The Ohio Sugar Company of Freemont was required to pay the state approximately $3,200 for loss of fish caused by discharges of hot water from its plant. Perhaps this laudable precedent will help discourage similar industrial pollution.

Thermal pollution requires additional comment. Each aquatic species adapts to the seasonal variations in water temperature of its particular habitat. Species cannot, however, adapt to abrupt thermal shocks. Because of the growth of industrial cooling requirements, ecologists fear that discharge of heated effluents will grossly upset the balance of nature. As a result, heat has been added to the list of potential pollutants.

The magnitude of the problem may be interpreted from a few numbers. By 2000 A.D., it is anticipated that nuclear power plants will be generating some 1½ million megawatts of electric power. The total output for all types of generating plants will be in the neighborhood of 2 million megawatts. Obviously, to channel all the waste heat from this power level to waterways is unthinkable. To manage this problem, cooling towers and artificial cooling lakes are being tried. In fact, a number are beyond the experimental stage. On the Green River in Kentucky, the Tennesseee Valley Authority has built three cooling towers (437 feet high, 320 feet in diameter, with a capacity of 280,000 gallons per minute) that will enable the world's largest coal-fueled electric plant to discharge its waste water harmlessly. Fortunately, the addition of heat to water can readily be corrected. Would that other pollutants could be so easily handled.

One of the most widely used measures of the concentration of biologically oxidizable matter in a river or stream is the biochemical oxygen demand, the BOD. Although used as a chemical test, it is in fact a biological procedure, depending for its activity on the microorganisms in the sewage. The BOD test is a quantitative measure of the oxygen used up by a sample of sewage effluent or river water during a five-day incubation period at 20°C. The sample is diluted with fully oxygenated water and the initial amount of oxygen determined. After five days in the dark, the oxygen content is determined again; from the difference between the initial value and the five-day value, the BOD or strength of the original sample can be calculated. Several state health departments have set their water conservation policies by limiting the BOD to a stipulated maximum, while others attempt to control added pollution by limiting the BOD of effluents. In a word, the purpose of sewage treatment is to consume most of the BOD before the effluent is discharged.

Several random BOD values may be helpful: the BOD of the sewage of a residential community generally varies between 150 and 250 milligrams per liter (mg/l). (The BOD of the sewage produced in the five boroughs of New York City averages about 100 to 200.) Milk processing and cannery waste range from 5,000 to 6,000 mg/l, while the liquid discharged from pulping operations, which contains large amounts of wood sugar, casein, and starches, often has a five-day BOD of 10,000 to 15,000 mg/l. Among the strongest wastes going into rivers and streams are those from the wool scouring industry; its waste can have a BOD above 20,000 mg/l.

Another useful indicator of the overall condition of a river or stream is its content of dissolved oxygen (DO). This value, more than any other, determines whether self-purification is likely to proceed satisfactorily and whether the stream community or ecosystem is adequately balanced. University, government, and industrial laboratories are currently pressing research investigations dealing with induced re-aeration by mechanical aerators and flow augmentation schemes as a means of maintaining DO contents compatible with a clean waterway. A pertinent example is the Japanese government's recent announcement that large quantities of oxygen will be pumped into the Taito River. Some 400 tons of presently foul-smelling river water will be drawn out each hour and returned after the addition of liquid oxygen. Similar treatment has been suggested in the United States on a number of occasions, but has either been left lying or rejected as unsuitable or too expensive. It will be instructive to see the outcome of the Japanese experiment.

Theoretically, under conditions of standard temperature and pressure (20°C, 760 mm Hg) 9 mg of oxygen can be dissolved in a liter of water; this is said to be the saturation concentration for this particular temperature. Healthy streams and rivers generally yield DOs of 5 to 7 mg/l. Values consistently below 4 mg/l tend to indicate organic overloading, developing sepsis, and migration of fish species downstream.

One aspect of all these chemical tests seems a bit perverse. Chemical effluents notwithstanding, water pollution is essentially a biological phenomenon. But biological indicators of adverse effects of organic (and inorganic) loading are rarely employed. Yet it is change in or destruction of the fauna and flora of the stream or river that is central to the problem.

For over 150 years, limnologists the world over have developed biological pollution assessment methods based on the presence or absence of certain characteristic species in rivers and streams. One of the most widely known of these methods is that developed by Dr. Ruth Patrick of The Philadelphia Academy of Natural Sciences. Dr. Patrick classifies animals and plants in seven groups. On the basis of their occurrence (or absence) she divides watercourses into zones:

Healthy: abundance of species from all seven groups;
Semi-healthy: species from several groups overabundant, others reduced in number;
Polluted: worms particularly abundant and great reduction in fish and insects;
Very polluted: most groups eliminated;
Septic: biologically dead.

While a number of variations on this system have been proposed, essentially they all deal with the alteration of biota. In effect, each stream and river can be "fingerprinted" by its unique pattern.

Thus, the toxicity of chemicals emptied into a stream and moving along can quickly be shown by analyzing samples of water. A wipeout of expected species quickly indicates the presence of a hazardous substance. For reasons that are difficult to discern, these biological indicators are rarely used even though they are more reliable and more economical measures than chemical tests.

None of the tests mentioned thus far indicates the presence or degree of human fecal matter in a river, stream, or bathing area. The typical aquatic microflora and the bacteria that decompose the organic constituents of sewage have no sanitary or public health significance. That is, they are not found in the intestinal tracts of either human or animal species, nor are they pathogenic agents. Since most streams and rivers used as sources of drinking water have been contaminated by sewage effluent, the presence of fecal matter must be considered a distinct possibility; as a consequence, the presence of agents of infectious disease is not unlikely.

Because contamination by sewage effluent is only an assumption, but one to be ignored at our peril, water for domestic use must be subjected to regular and continuous bacteriological examination. The tests involved are not employed simply to determine the numbers and types of bacteria present; rather, they are specific for organisms whose natural habitat is the human bowel. As epidemiological evidence has established beyond reasonable doubt a cause-effect relationship between water-borne illnesses and certain microbes of intestinal origin, the importance of these bacteriological examinations to evaluate the safety of the water supply has been solidly substantiated. Certainly no bacteriological test is performed more frequently than that for the determination of water quality.

The tests for water quality seek primarily to verify the presence or absence of recent fecal contamination. If intestinal discharges have contaminated the water, large numbers of coliform bacteria are certain to be present. These organisms are benign types, living a saprophytic existence as part of the natural flora of the large intestine (the colon). They incite no illness and are always present in feces; thus their presence in water testifies to the fact of fecal discharge. As natural inhabitants of the human bowel, they do not find environmental conditions in natural waters suitable for multiplication and begin to die off rapidly. Their presence in water samples therefore indicates recent contamination.

If fecal matter is of recent origin it can be assumed that, along with the harmless coliforms, there may also be pathogenic organisms such as *Salmonella typhosa,* the organism associated with typhoid fever; *Shigella dysenteriae,* the organism associated with bacterial dysentery; *Vibrio comma,* the cholera organism; and *Entamoeba histolytica,* a protozoan associated with amoebic dysentery. Pathogens such as these, if present in water supplies, are usually few in number and exceedingly difficult to detect. Accordingly, no effort is made to test for them during routine examinations; instead, an indicator organism is used.

The concept of an indicator organism is well established among public health microbiologists and engineers. It must be an organism whose biochemical reactions and growth characteristics have been extensively studied. In addition, its numbers usually vary with the degree of fecal pollution. Its absence indicates that intestinal discharges are not present and that the water is presumably free of pathogens. The indicator is also hardier than most pathogens: its presence in a sample of water indicates the potential hazard of the supply. Here again mature, professional judgment, combined with standardized criteria, are needed to determine when a water supply is unfit to drink or bathe in. Such decisions cannot be made lightly or be based on political expediency. Nonetheless, public opinion does allocate priorities which may have little to do with the prevalence of disease.

Although several groups of bacteria have served as indicators, no group is as well established as the coliforms. The routine test for determination of coliform density requires that samples of water be inoculated into a series of tubes containing a medium specific for coliform growth, followed by incubation at 35°C ± 0.5°C for 48 ± 3 hours. Gas production, in the form of bubbles of CO_2 rising in the tubes of liquid, is positive evidence of the presence of coliform organisms. A coliform index, or a count of the most probable number of organisms present in the original water sample, can be made on the basis of the amount of sample inoculated into a stated number of tubes. Criteria for the acceptance or rejection of a water supply are based on a long record of correlation of this parameter with the occurrence of waterborne disease outbreaks.

Often, after prolonged or torrential rains, the coliform counts of water samples rise precipitously. Does this reflect the fact that human fecal matter has been washed into waterways as surface runoff? In the United States or Western Europe, this could hardly be the case. How then can this rise in coliforms be interpreted?

By definition, coliforms include all rod-shaped, non-sporeforming Gram-negative bacteria that can ferment lactose with gas production within forty-eight hours at 35°C. Unfortunately, this encompasses organisms that are non-fecal in origin. That is, although they are called coliforms, some of them do not live in the colon of human or animal species. This group is widely distributed in nature, being found in grasses, in soil, and on plants. Accordingly, since these organisms are carried into water sources that are intended for drinking or bathing, and since they are not indicators of fecal contamination or the possible presence of pathogens, a means of distinguishing between fecal and non-fecal coliforms is necessary.

To distinguish *Escherichia coli,* a major fecal coliform species, from *Aerobacter aerogenes,* a major representative of the non-fecal coliforms, simple, straightforward, but accurate biochemical procedures have been developed. If members of the genus *Escherichia,* particularly *E. coli,* are present, then gas production is a positive indication of fecal contamination, with all its attendant implications; if organisms belonging to the genus *Aerobacter,* particularly, *A. aerogenes,* are producing the gas, then fecal contamination can be ruled out.

Two additional points are worthy of note. The Atlantic Ocean is the "old swimming hole" for most of New York City's residents. It has a salt content of approximately 3.5 percent. This is not conducive to the survival of disease-transmitting pathogens, which are among the most fragile and sensitive of all microbes. Furthermore, the ocean has never been incriminated as a vehicle for any waterborne disease. French scientists studying the problem of waterborne poliomyelitis found that the prevalence of clinically manifest paralytic poliomyelitis was not higher in bathers who swam regularly in the Mediterranean Sea near Marseilles, France, than in non-bathers. Speaking at a symposium, "Transmissions of Viruses by the Water Route," Dr. Joseph Melnick of Baylor University Medical School noted that small doses of virus in water supplies may serve to immunize against rather than produce disease. He noted that sewage workers had the lowest rate of absenteeism among all occupational groups studied. "It appeared that sewage workers were regularly immunized by their exposure to small amounts of infected material," he said.[1]

Historically, the primary reason for water-pollution control was prevention of waterborne disease. If public health authorities in the United States and Western Europe were asked to point to their single greatest accomplishment, it would undoubtedly be eradication of the classical waterborne diseases. Nevertheless, many infectious waterborne diseases remain endemic in other areas of the world, particularly the non-industrialized nations of Asia, Africa, and Latin America.

In addition to cholera, typhoid, and dysentery, the developing countries contend with bilharziasis, commonly contracted when bathing in fecal- and urine-polluted streams and canals; urban filariasis, transmitted by the bite of an insect vector that breeds in polluted water; and infectious hepatitis, which was responsible for a recent major epidemic that included approximately thirty thousand cases in New Delhi, India.

Because of the rapidity of human migration from endemic areas, coupled with the possibility that certain disease agents may adapt to new habitats in new environments, constant surveillance of water supplies must be maintained. It is necessary, however, to keep a sense of proportion and to bear in mind that present microbial hazards of pollution are trivial in the United States, Canada, England, and Western Europe.

Figure 35 shows that proper treatment of raw water can substantially reduce illness resulting from the ingestion of water contaminated with pathogenic microorganisms. In Philadelphia, there were from six thousand to ten thousand typhoid cases each year between 1890 and 1907. With the introduction in 1907

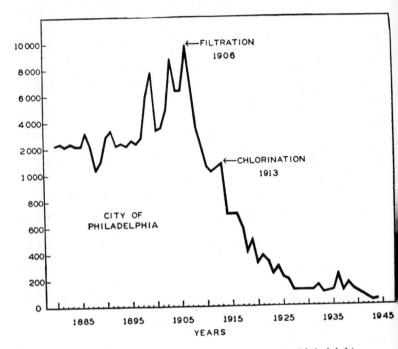

Figure 35.   Reduction of typhoid fever in Philadelphia following treatment of the water supply. (Adapted with permission of The Macmillan Company from Preventive Medicine and Public Health, *3rd ed. by W. G. Smillie and E. D. Kilbourne, © The Macmillan Company, 1962.)*

of so simple a device as sand filtration of drinking water, a precipitous reduction in illness was achieved. Six years later, the introduction of chlorination, over the strident protests of those opposed to the addition of synthetic chemicals to water, caused another abrupt drop in typhoid cases. Clearly, mechanical and chemical treatment could control waterborne disease. As if to remind us that we cannot wear our laurels lightly, and that vigilance cannot be relaxed, an epidemic of waterborne typhoid involving some eighteen thousand people occurred in Riverside, California in 1966. As yet, conclusive evidence as to the mechanism of its entry and transmission has not been obtained.

Three years earlier, a classical explosive outbreak of typhoid occurred at one of the most affluent playgrounds of Europe: 437 cases and three deaths occurred in Zermatt, Switzerland. Months after the epidemic had passed, a leakage of sewage into the chlorination tank was found. Because of the additional burden of organic matter, the chlorine concentration and hence its disinfecting action was precipitously reduced.

Despite these outbreaks, progress in the United States has been gratifying. Figure 36 indicates the pattern of typhoid fever for the entire United States during the past thirty years. Similar patterns can be drawn for a large number of infectious diseases.

Another example of water's ability to convey infectious

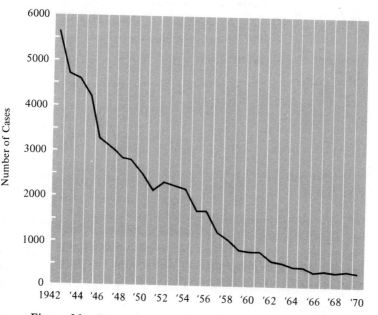

Figure 36. Reported cases of typhoid fever in the United States, 1942 1970. (Reprinted from Morbidity and Mortality Report, *Center for Disease Control, PHS, Department of Health, Education and Welfare.)*

material is bilharziasis,* also known as schistosomiasis or snail fever. This is considered to be the world's most prevalent disease; estimates of the number infected range between 120 and 250 million. It is primarily a disease of tropical and subtropical areas, but because of the ease and rapidity of world travel, it is also found in other regions. For example, New York City has an estimated forty thousand cases imported from Puerto Rico and Cuba. There is little danger that the disease will spread in the United States, as it is not directly communicable and our ecological conditions hinder its establishment in a new habitat.

Bilharziasis, while seldom directly fatal, is debilitating and eventually contributes to the death of its victims. While the afflicted endure the illness for years, their ability to work is severely restricted. The economic loss to a country such as Egypt, with 47 percent of its population (fourteen million people) infected, has been calculated as approximately $560 million per year.

Over a hundred years passed from Bilharz's discovery of the flatworm in the blood of a patient to the complete untangling of the complex life cycle of the human illness, which includes a snail, three growth stages in the development of the minuscule worm, and man.

A crop of eggs laid by the worms gains entrance to irrigation canals and streams via urine or feces. The eggs hatch out as pear-shaped, ciliated miracidia which must find a snail host within twenty-four hours or die. Those that locate a suitable snail host burrow into it and undergo a two-month period of incubation. During this period the miracidia are transformed. They become fork-tailed cercariae that leave the snail and seek another host, usually a warm-blooded one, human or animal. In countries where streams, canals, ponds, or any other watery area such as rice paddies serve as latrines, laundries, and recreational areas, it is the rare cercaria that cannot locate a human host. Thus, the cycle is completed—and often repeated.

These free-swimming cercariae appear to fasten themselves to human skin by a sticky secretion, then penetrate with the aid

---

* In 1851 Theodor Bilharz discovered the parasite in the blood of victims. The disease is often called bilharziasis in his honor. Schistosomiasis, another name for the disease, refers to the type of parasite that causes the disease, a schistosome or flatworm.

of proteolytic enzymes, which dissolve a path for them. Upon reaching a blood vessel they pass to their ultimate sites, the veins of the upper and lower intestinal tract, or the veins of the bladder and rectum. After several months the cercariae develop into adult schistosome worms. At the height of the disease hundreds of worms can be found in a victim; each lays as many as three thousand eggs per day. The number and size (approximately two centimeters) of the adult worms causes mechanical blocking of hepatic circulation, which produces the fluid-filled, swollen abdomen characteristic of bilharziasis. After three to six weeks, an explosive onset of fever occurs, along with generalized aches, diarrhea, and extreme weakness. During the chronic stage the victim grows emaciated and steadily weaker. Thus far, treatment has been worse than the disease. Because drug therapy has proved unsuccessful, attempts have been made to rid canals and streams of the host snail by chemical molluscicides such as copper sulfate and sodium pentachlorophenate. Unfortunately, this too has been unsuccessful.

Although snail fever was first described in a four-thousand-year-old Egyptian papyrus, it has been given added impetus by man in the name of progress. The construction of huge irrigation projects in the underdeveloped countries of the world has spread the disease into areas where it was previously unknown. The construction of the Aswan High Dam,* for example, will now control the annual silt-laden floods that in the past reduced the snail populations in Egypt. Cautious estimates suggest that 55 to 70 percent of the population in the reclaimed areas can be expected to become infected as the water backing up behind the dam spreads the snails and worms over greater and greater areas. If only 55 percent of the population becomes infected, an additional 2,650,000 new cases are anticipated after the completion of the dam. This will bring the total number of cases in Egypt alone to over 17 million. While the Aswan project will make new

---

* After eleven years of construction, the dam was officially opened on January 15, 1971, President Nasser's birthday. Between the time of its inception and completion Egypt's population rose from 26 to 34 million, in itself negating much of the gain accrued in cropland. In addition, one of every two Egyptians now has bilharziasis, and one of every ten deaths is attributed to it.

land available for cultivation, the medical costs may offset the agricultural gains.

As was noted above, although there are some forty thousand known cases in New York City and some additional cases spread around the country by returning servicemen and tourists, bilharziasis is not expected to establish itself here. However, two of our native snails, both of the genus *Pomatiopsis,* are potential hosts of the fluke. One is limited to Louisiana; the other is more widespread—its range is from the Great Lakes to Kentucky and from Iowa eastward to the coast. Public health authorities appear fully convinced that our system of sewage disposal and our personal hygiene habits do not offer the necessary ecological conditions for the infection to become established. Again, vigilance and regular surveillance are expensive but necessary precautions.

It is of interest to note that cercarial dermatitis, also known as swimmer's itch and clam digger's dermatitis, is the result of an infection by an avian form of schistosome worm. The eggs reach the water in bird droppings, and the miracidia locate suitable host snails in which to develop into fork-tailed cercariae. The cercariae invade human skin, producing pustules that itch intensely. The itch is well known in such diverse states as Michigan, Minnesota, New York, Rhode Island, Florida, and California.

A type of water pollution that affects man only indirectly is entirely man-made. This is the menace of poisoning in grazing ducks who eat lead shot.

Many water birds, particularly ducks, feed by harvesting a varied fare from the bottom of lakes, marshes, and ponds. In areas that are heavily hunted, waste lead shot accumulates in large amounts at the bottom of these waters. The feeding birds pick up the shot, which resembles seeds, only to have it lodge in their gizzards. The grinding action of the gizzard on the shot, coupled with the action of acidic digestive juice, erodes the lead from the surface of the pellets. The soluble lead salts pass into the digestive tract and initiate a complex of symptoms. The first manifestation of toxicity is a reduction of food intake resulting from a paralyzed gizzard. This leads to starvation and ultimate death. Large numbers of birds have been known to ingest such large quantities of waste shot pellets that death resulted from a highly acute form of lead poisoning. In 1966, the Bureau of Sport Fisheries and Wildlife estimated that each year tens of thousands of ducks and geese fall victim to spent shot. Fortunately, the lead, toxic to the birds, does not appear to affect people who unknowingly eat the meat.

To the credit of the arms industry, major American and Canadian producers of sporting firearms have financed a ten-thousand-dollar study at the Illinois Institute of Technology to investigate the possibilities of developing a substitute for lead shot or so modifying it that it will not pose a threat to water birds. Thus far, no substitute that possesses lead's ballistic characteristics has been found.

Perhaps it is too much to expect that the tragic experiences of one country, still within memory, will not be repeated by another. Unfortunately, it appears that the Soviet State Timber Industry Committee has not heard of "Albany beef."

At the turn of the century, the Hudson River supported a thriving caviar industry. The fish-roe delicacy obtained from the giant sea sturgeon that frequented the clear waters of the Hudson River was exported to Russia by the barrelful. Sturgeon meat, another high-priced appetizer, was often called "Albany beef." Unfortunately, commercial sturgeon fishing in the Hudson River lives only in the memory of old men and in newspapers yellowed with age. The large volume of sewage and industrial wastes discharged into the Hudson has profoundly altered life in the river.

Lake Baikal in Soviet Siberia, its southern tip just a few miles from the Mongolian border, may be headed for a fate similar to that of the Hudson River. By any limnological standards the Hudson River and Lake Baikal are hardly comparable. Baikal is the largest freshwater lake in the world. With a volume of 5,520 cubic miles and a maximum depth of 5,314 feet, it is twice the size of Lake Superior and five times as deep. It also has the distinction of being the oldest lake in the world, roughly twenty-five million years old.

According to recent reports,[2] Baikal is being polluted by the waste from a huge new pulp mill. To limnologists—scientists who study freshwater lakes—this is a disaster because of the lake's purity and its diversity of biological species. Over one thousand varieties of plant and animal forms are found only in Baikal. Over millions of years many of them have evolved unique physiological processes permitting them to thrive in its peculiarly cold, mineral-free water.

It is feared that the large volume of high-oxygen-demand pulp waste will remove a great part of the existing biota, while the thermal pollution will raise the temperature of the normally frigid water high enough to permit predators, heretofore barred by the extremely cold water, to invade and annihilate other forms.

At present, the lake supplies 35 percent of Siberia's edible fish supply, including trout, perch, pike, and sturgeon. Because Baikal is over a mile deep in places and 395 miles long, water flowing into the lake remains there for about four hundred years. Although this implies that pollutants may accumulate, it also implies that a good deal of time will pass before the input equals the output. This does not mean that the Soviet government has time to do nothing. If it fails to heed the warning signals, an irreplaceable natural resource could be headed for extinction. That productivity rather than conservation is all-important to the Soviets was seen in the announcement made in April 1971 of a second wood-pulp mill to be built at Selenginsk, a hundred miles northeast of the first plant.

When the American-owned tanker *Torrey Canyon,* bound for Britain with 117,000 tons of crude oil in her tanks, foundered off the southwest coast of England in March 1967, a grave national crisis developed: at stake were the beaches that line the Cornish coast as well as the abundant flocks of sea birds and marine animals that could be lost by suffocation and drowning from the oil slick that would blanket everything.

The incident of the *Torrey Canyon,* while grim, had great instructional value. With the initial shock came all manner of "scientific" suggestions about how best to deal with the threat. Because the Royal Navy had built up a backlog of experience dealing with oil spills in harbors, its advice was sought. The Navy suggested that detergents were the answer. Accordingly, 2.5 million gallons were sprayed on beaches and at sea. This proved to be more toxic and damaging to the aquatic flora and fauna than the oil. The greatest toll was exacted from among the many species of diving birds that breed in this area; a total of twenty-five thousand dead birds was reported. Fortunately, because northerly winds blew for two months after the ship discharged its oil at a time when winds usually blow from the southwest, less than half the anticipated amount of oil ended up on the beaches.

For us, the important lesson was the lack of adequate knowledge about the effects of chemical pollutants on marine life. As if in response to a recent statement that technology exemplified by the lunar landing contrasts sharply with the scattered hay used to control oil pollution on international beaches, many sophisticated techniques for the detection and identification of such pollutants have been developed during the past few years.

One of the most intriguing is a method of "fingerprinting" oil. Between 5 and 10 million tons of oil are released each year into the world's oceans as a consequence of off-shore oil well activity, collisions, groundings, splitting or cracking of ships, or just simple leaking. This does not include the intentional discharge of oily bilge water as well as wash water from ships' tanks. When an oil spill occurs, it has been nearly impossible to ascertain the ship it came from. Oil is oil, we say; but is it? Oil chemists now tell us that oils from different areas are distinctive, as a consequence of the unique geological formations. Not only is oil from Kuwait chemically different from oil from West Texas, but West Texas oil is significantly different from East Texas oil.

Now, thanks to advances in scientific theory and its practical application, such procedures as neutron activation analysis, infrared spectroscopy, gas chromatography, and mass spectroscopy, oil can be "fingerprinted," as shown in Figure 37. These fingerprints are, in fact, tracings of the boiling points of various constituents of the oil. Although every student taking a first course in organic chemistry runs a boiling point experiment in which he learns that all substances have a characteristic point at which they change their state, oil is such a complex substance that it has had to await development of unusually sensitive equipment to study it.

Another technique focuses on the metals oils contain in trace amounts. Neutron activation analysis, one of the newest analytical tools in the chemist's arsenal, zeros in on the trace metal. A beam of neutrons is fired at an oil sample. As a result of energy transformations, the trace metals emit characteristic radiation patterns that can also be used to tell one oil from another. It won't be too long before tankers and oil companies, realizing they

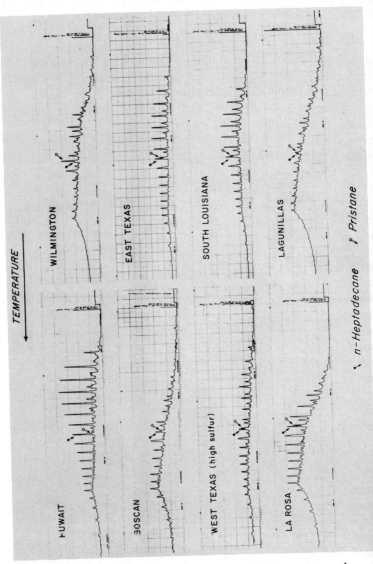

Figure 37. "Fingerprinting" of oil. (*Photo courtesy of Woods Hole Oceanographic Institute, Woods Hole, Massachusetts.*)

can be detected and fined, will think twice before discharging oil at sea.

Another tool that may be applicable for pollution control is remote sensing, or imaging techniques.[3] Less technically, this is actually aerial reconnaissance or photography—color photography, ultraviolet, thermal infrared, or radar. And indeed, these techniques are not limited to oil spills. Color and infrared photographs can by their tones show areas of a river or stream with low dissolved oxygen. They can even "show" foul odors. An infrared photograph of a trickling filter bed in good condition is black, while one with a serious odor problem photographs red. Although these techniques are in the experimental stage, they seem to be moving rapidly into practical use.

Another example of modern technology's ability to control or prevent environmental pollution comes from the paper industry. Since the invention of paper by the Chinese some nineteen hundred years ago, the process had remained virtually unchanged. With it, pollution of waterways usually occurred wherever paper pulping plants were located. Recall that these are high-BOD wastes. A dry papermaking process has long been dreamed of. Recently Karl Kroyer of Denmark discovered an entirely new dry process for assembling cellulose fibers. His process resembles the setting of women's hair. Each hair (fiber) is positioned where it is needed and the whole is finally sprayed to set it more or less permanently in position. Because fibers can be positioned as desired, many types of paper can be prepared. But, most important, the waste emanating from paper manufacture can be drastically reduced.

Another form of paper has stirred a national environmental controversy. This is toilet paper, specifically the colored variety. Although no one seems to know or is willing to admit how it got started, it is known that the *Missouri Conservationist,* a magazine issued by the Missouri State Conservation Commission, urged people to use only white toilet tissue as an anti-water-pollution measure. The admonition to avoid colored paper towels, facial tissue, and toilet paper presumably had its genesis with someone who believed the dyes used to color these papers were not biodegradable and consequently polluted streams. The fact is that microorganisms have long been known to be able to metabolize dyes. A number of "pollution survival kits" no longer carry colored tissue papers on their warning lists.

Pollution and deterioration of waterways are not always irreversible processes. This is seen in two recent examples.

By 1960 Lake Washington, an eighteen-mile-long body of fresh water in the Seattle area, had deteriorated to a foul-smelling, fish-killing state. Interestingly enough, this damage was done by regular and continued dumping of treated effluents from ten newly constructed waste treatment plants. Obviously, even low-BOD waste over long periods can deplete oxygen levels in sensitive lakes. To restore one lake, the State of Washington built an integrated waste disposal system that carried the waste of all towns surrounding the lake out into Puget Sound. By 1970, the odors had left Lake Washington, the water was clear, and the fish had returned.

A similar future is predicted for the Hudson River. Although some people have declared the Hudson dead, New York's Commissioner of Water Resources believes it is only "a little sick." Cleaning the Hudson depends on the cooperation of a number of towns and cities in New York and New Jersey, and a large sum of money; perhaps a half-billion dollars.

Lake Washington's steady and progressive deterioration as a result of effluents carrying an organic load—even a modest one—illustrates the need for additional or different treatment of sewage waste. A proposal being given wide study is land disposal of sewage effluents. Essentially, this means re-use of treated waste water (usually given secondary treatment plus chlorination) for such purposes as crop irrigation, public lawn and garden watering, forest fire protection, and creation of artificial lakes for public recreation. Not only would this method of treatment add nutrient to soil, but the soil itself would become a huge filter, straining out microorganisms to the extent that the water percolating through the soil would be renovated almost to the level of acceptable drinking water. This is not a new idea. Semi-arid regions of the United States have practiced sewage reuse for years. As noted in Chapter 9, because of the low level of infectious disease in the United States, this practice is not likely to be a health hazard to communities adopting it.

Piecemeal attempts to abate and control water pollution

are doomed to failure. In fact, they waste a community's limited financial resources. Ecological or regional schemes are more reasonable and offer some certainty of success. They include planning for adequate sewage treatment throughout a watershed and the course of a river, and planning for land use, agricultural and industrial requirements and their by-products, and recreational needs. Of course, this implies some loss of local authority, which is never palatable to local business interests and politicians. More will be said about this problem in Chapter 16.

In considering the future of water pollution on an international basis, however, the World Health Organization is not very optimistic. It notes that "population growth in seventy-five developing countries was 40 percent greater than the average for the world as a whole, which probably means that it is at least double that in some of the older industrial countries. Water supply and pollution problems may, therefore, double or more than double every ten years for some decades." It also notes that the increasing population is seen largely in the urban areas and predicts that "the world rate of urban growth is 2½ times greater than the rate of rural growth. Since it is urban growth that causes the most intense pollution problems, it would appear that a doubling of the problem every ten years may well be a gross understatement of the problem."

WHO is less than optimistic about the ability of individual nations to implement policies that will result in unpolluted water internationally, but this does not mean that the United States cannot initiate and pursue a vigorous antipollution program. In fact, it has already begun to do so. By enacting Public Law 91–190, the National Environmental Policy Act, Congress declared its determination to assure all Americans "safe, healthful, productive, and esthetically and culturally pleasing surrroundings." Details of the National Environment Policy Act will be found in Chapter 16, The Politics of Pollution.

References

1. Gerald Berg, ed., *Transmission of Viruses by the Water Route* (New York: Interscience Publishers, 1967).

2. Oleg Volkov, "Pollution in Lake Baikal," *Literaturnaya Gazeta*,

January 29, 1966. Translated in *Current Digest of the Soviet Press,* February 1966, p. 14.

3. F. J. Wobber, "Imaging Techniques for Oil Pollution Survey Purposes," *Photographic Applications in Science, Technology and Medicine,* July 1971, p. 16.

Suggested Reading

Sykes, G.; and Skinner, F. A., eds. *Microbial Aspects of Pollution.* Published for the Society of Applied Bacteriology. London: Academic Press, 1971.

Eutrophication: Causes, Consequences, Corrections. Washington: NAS-NRC, 1969.

Holt, R. F.; Timmons, D. R.; and Latterell, J. J. "Accumulation of Phosphates in Water." *Journal of Agricultural and Food Chemistry* 18 (1970): 781.

Clark, John R. "Thermal Pollution and Aquatic Life." *Scientific American* 220 (1969): 19.

Fjerdingstad, E. "Microbial Criteria of Environment Qualities." *Annual Review of Microbiology* 25 (1971): 563.

Feasibility of Alternative Means of Cooling for Thermal Power Plants Near Lake Michigan. Washington: U.S. Department of the Interior, Federal Water Quality Administration, 1970.

Cleary, E. J. "Evolution of Social Altitudes and Action on Water Pollution Control." *Journal of the Water Pollution Control Federation* 44 (1972): 1301.

Krishnaswami, S. K. "Health Aspects of Land Disposal of Municipal Waste Water Effluents." *Canadian Journal of Public Health* (1971): 36.

Physical and Ecological Effects of Waste Heat on Lake Michigan. Washington: U.S. Department of the Interior Fish and Wildlife Service, 1970. (Among the 75 references quoted here are several reviews which together cover over 1200 articles on this subject.)

Wilson, C. W.; and Beckett, F. E., eds. *Municipal Sewage Effluent for Irrigation.* (Symposium, Louisiana Polytechnic Institute, Ruston, La.) Published by The Louisiana Tech. Alumni Foundation, 1969.

Bartha, R.; and Atlas, R. M. "Biodegradation of Polluting Oil." *Naval Research Reviews* 25 (1972): 17. (Highly recommended.)

SOLID-WASTE DISPOSAL

The Public Interest requires doing today those things that men of intelligence and good will wish, five or ten years hence, had been done.

Edmund Burke

For the ten thousand citizens of Wilton, Connecticut, 1967 began much too dramatically. The town simply ran out of space in which to dispose of its garbage. The nightmare of many city officials around the country had come true for Wilton. By the time Dr. Henry Appelbaum, Wilton's health officer, declared a health emergency, many residents had gone almost ten days without garbage and refuse collection.

Until January 1, 1967, Wilton's refuse was dumped in an open pit provided by the neighboring town of Weston. A ruling by the Connecticut General Assembly stopped this offensive practice because of the unsanitary conditions it created. Wilton responded by purchasing seventy acres of land to use as a sanitary landfill. Residents of the area around these seventy acres went to court to prevent use of the land for this purpose; they won their case. However, Wilton was granted use of the land until May 15, 1967. After that date, they would either have to find another solution or try to have the court decision reversed. Later in 1967, I learned from Dr. Appelbaum that the use of the disposal site would be permitted until a decision was handed down by the State Supreme Court. Almost a year later, in what would surely become a precedent-setting ruling, the State Supreme Court held that because of the potential medical emergency confronting Wilton, the injunction would be set aside, permitting free use of the seventy acres as a sanitary landfill. The judges concurred that with the formation of megalopoli, many communities will sooner or later be confronted with the same dilemma. Accordingly, they gave precedence to life over property. Small towns and big cities alike are confronted with the problem of finding space for their wastes. In many cases, the crisis point is near.

On October 22, 1966, the world read of tragedy in Aberfan, Wales. For almost a hundred years, slag—made up of shale and the other inert residue from the processing of coal—had been dumped on the side of a mountain. On Thursday, October 21, the 400-foot-high pile began to slide. As it slid, it picked up momentum, until a sea of slag came crashing into the village. Engulfed beneath the two million tons of coal waste were a schoolhouse, a farm, and a dozen miners' cottages. One hundred forty-four people died that day. Aberfan's catastrophe shows another side of a common problem: what to do with the solid waste produced by home and industry.

Ever since people began living in communities, there has been the problem of waste disposal: the removal of garbage, rubbish, and litter from their living areas. Moreover, disposal had to be conducted in a manner that did not generate unsavory conditions. As cities have grown, so has the problem. There was a time when people or communities could easily find a place to discard their trash. This is no longer possible. Suitable surrounding areas have been or are rapidly becoming urbanized. In addition, both the quantity and the variety of solid wastes generated by today's urban and rural communites are cause for immediate and pressing concern.

The typical city dweller discards four to five pounds of solid waste daily. This is double the amount of trash discarded by his parents. But, more important, the type of waste has changed considerably. The shift has been toward materials whose disposal is much more difficult, more costly, and perhaps more hazardous to health. Today, our large cities have astronomical quantities of trash to dispose of. In New York City, for example, whose more than eight million inhabitants are augmented each year by millions of visitors, and whose commerce and industry generate all manner of solid waste, approximately three million tons of garbage and refuse are collected yearly. To compound the problem, the amount of refuse is increasing at about 3 percent per year, largely because of the increase in throw-away bottles, cans, and plastic containers.

⌐ Throughout the United States, each year, we must dispose of forty-nine billion cans, thirty-six billion bottles and jars, and sixty-five billion metal and plastic caps. Add to this millions of junked automobiles, 100 million tires, refrigerators, bedsprings, bathtubs, and a myriad of miscellaneous objects totaling some 135 million tons per year and you begin to perceive the dimensions of the problem.* Figure 38 is a less than exhaustive list of the variety of plastic items and metallic cans we have come to accept as part of our throw-away type of living. ⌐

Table 8 shows the steadily increasing number of abandoned cars towed away in New York City in the past ten years. A similar set of data tells the same story in Philadelphia, Boston, Detroit, and Chicago. The bill for collecting and processing this waste is now in excess of three billion dollars annually. And only a small portion of the waste is salvaged for reuse. The unsalvaged remainder has vast potential for pollution, accidents, and illness.

We have used several different terms in talking about solid waste: *rubbish, refuse, garbage,* and others. Strictly speaking, the terms are not synonymous. According to the classification developed by the American Public Works Association, each term refers to a specific type of material. For example, *rubbish* includes two groups: combustible items, such as cartons, boxes, paper, grass,

---

* The demographically and statistically minded may be interested to learn that an estimated 1400 pounds of solid waste are generated by each person per year, and that on a national basis we amass some eight hundred million pounds of waste per day.

Plastic Disposables:
    Food wraps
    Plates
    Tableware
    Glasses
    Patent medicine containers
    Shampoo bottles
    Hand lotion containers
    Containers for suntan oils,
       creams, lotions

Cans:
    Beverages
    Soup
    Vegetables
    Fruits
    Meats
    Puddings
    Juices
    Hair spray
    Deodorants, anti-perspirants
    Perfume
    Paint
    Shoe coloring
    Whipped cream
    Cheese
    Car wax and polish
    Furniture polish
    Shaving cream

Figure 38. Types of disposable products contributing to increasing quantity of solid waste.

TABLE 8.

*Cars abandoned in
New York City, 1961–1970.*

Year	Number of Cars
1961	5,117
1962	6,299
1963	13,579
1964	23,386
1965	21,943
1966	23,795
1967	25,842
1968	31,578
1969	57,742
1970	72,961

plastics, bedding, and clothing; and non-combustibles, such as ashes, cans, crockery, metal furniture, glass, and bathtubs, to name a few.

Garbage is classified as waste resulting from growing, preparing, cooking, and serving food. Included in this category are market wastes. Garbage accounts for approximately 10 percent of the volume of solid waste collected.

A third class is *dead animals,* such as the cats and dogs found on roads and streets, victims of encounters with automobiles. This group also includes rabbits, skunks, porcupines, cows, horses, and deer, whose dead and decaying carcasses are a potential health hazard.

Demolition waste includes some of the most persistent substances, such as bricks, masonry, piping, and lumber (Figure 39).

Sewage-treatment residue, such as septic-tank sludge and solids from the coarse screening of domestic sewage, is another category of solid waste.

The term *refuse* has no official or quasi-official definition. It is a more pleasant word than *garbage* and has been used to denote all types of waste. But no matter what it is called, the critical problem of garbage disposal remains.

More than four billion tons of solid waste were produced in the United States in 1969. Let us ask two questions about it. What makes solid waste? And what are the major contributing sources?

Table 9 lists the major types of solid waste. It is clear that although we are a highly industrialized society, the largest single source of solid waste is agriculture—livestock and slaughterhouse wastes, residues from harvested crops, vineyards, orchards, and greenhouses. Curiously enough, in our industrialized society animal waste disposal is a growing, not a lessening problem, because the demand for animal manure as a soil conditioner is declining.

Of the 110 million tons of industrial waste produced in 1969, the generation of electric power provided over 30 million tons of fly ash, a by product of burning bituminous coal and lignite. It is worth noting that in England, almost 100 percent of the 13 million tons of fly ash produced annually is recycled; 40 percent is sold to the building and engineering industries, while the remaining 60 percent finds its way to the land in reclamation and other

Figure 39. Solid waste in the making. For the concrete, bricks, plaster, wood, steel beams, and wire, very little but burial can be expected in the way of disposal. Note the air-polluting effects of demolition and the inability of the stream of water to prevent them.

projects. For the English, what was once waste is now a valuable by-product. As a result of their experience, we can hardly hide behind a wall of ignorance. More about this further on.

The 1.7 billion tons of mineral waste produced in 1969 represent about 40 percent of total waste production. Of the 80 mineral industries generating waste, 10 percent (or only eight) are responsible for the lion's share. For example, the copper

TABLE 9.

Solid waste production in the United States, 1969.

	Tons (millions)
Residential, commercial, and institutional wastes *municipal*	
Collected	250
Uncollected	(190)
Industrial wastes	(90)
Mineral wastes	110
Agricultural wastes	1,700
	2,280
Total	4,240

(Source: Bureau of Solid Waste, Department of Health, Education and Welfare.)

industry contributes most to the slag heaps and mill tailings that remain after the processing operations. Iron, steel, coal, lead, zinc, and one or two others are among the major contributors.

Often geographical location dictates or suggests a means of waste disposal. For coastal cities, dumping at sea solved the problem for many years. In 1933, however, the state of New Jersey sought relief in court from the nuisance created by New York City's garbage, some of which washed ashore on her beach property. The Supreme Court's decision in favor of New Jersey has virtually eliminated barging and dumping at sea.

But it didn't rule out dumping on land. Open dumps are nothing but areas where community wastes of all types are indiscriminately collected. Certainly this is an easy means of waste disposal for city fathers who want a cheap answer to a nagging problem. Dumping requires little planning, little maintenance, and unskilled personnel—all particularly appealing to budget-minded administrators.

Open dumping is an unsanitary practice that should be discontinued. It allows raw garbage to pile up without treatment. Figure 40 is a close-up view of a hill of refuse and garbage. Dumps offer excellent harborages for disease-carrying rats and highly favorable breeding conditions for flies and mosquitoes,

Figure 40. A refuse dump near San Francisco.

both potential carriers of diseases of public-health significance. When exposed waste is dumped in coastal areas near airports, the thousands of seagulls that come to dine are a hazard to aircraft. In the summer months, spontaneous fires are common occurrences in open dumps, and the surrounding communities must live with the smoke and odor. During 1965–66, fires in old, half-buried dumping areas of the New Jersey marshes near Newark Airport burned for weeks. The inaccessibility of the refuse defied all attempts to extinguish these fires, and the surrounding area was blanketed under a pall of low-lying smoke, with its accompanying noxious odors, for days at a time.

In order to conserve dumping space, open dumps are deliberately set afire periodically. Burning will reduce the amount of refuse, but the smoke increases the load of particulate matter and volatile chemicals in the already overburdened air and thus contributes significantly to air pollution. Burning dumps are a major factor in air pollution in many large cities.

For too long, the attitude toward solid waste has been to dump it, burn it, or bury it. Burying waste can be a satisfactory solution as long as public land is available, and as long as the waste does not leach out and contaminate water supplies. An outgrowth of the open dump is the sanitary landfill. Unlike the open dump, it is a planned and supervised procedure requiring trained personnel. Offensive effects are at a minimum and rodents are practically nonexistent.

Sanitary landfills can be classified according to the shape and location of the space filled. Three methods are employed: area, trench, and ramp methods. With the area method refuse is deposited in horizontal layers on relatively flat ground, compacted, and covered over, sides and top, with soil or another inert material, layer-cake fashion. With the trench method land is excavated in the shape of a trench to a depth, length, and width determined by the particular characteristics of the tract. Depths of ten to fifteen feet and widths up to twenty feet are widely employed. Refuse is deposited in the trench and compacted by bulldozer; then the trench is filled in with earth. In both the area and trench procedures, the compaction of refuse and depth of the soil covering act as a barrier to prevent fly eggs from hatching and rats from boring. Another important feature is that the separation of refuse by walls of soil, as shown in Figure 41, keeps fires from spreading beyond a single cell. The soil cover, from eighteen to twenty-four inches thick, virtually eliminates odors.

Both these procedures usually require about one acre per ten thousand people per year. Therefore, a community must set aside large tracts of land for them. In the face of the increasing demand for living space, the two needs come into conflict. A solution is the ramp method of filling land, which usually employs existing ravines or quarries in which refuse is deposited on an angle, against the side of the ravine or quarry. As with the area and trench methods, inert cover is placed on the sides and top at regular intervals.

When refuse is buried and covered, chemical changes take place as a result of microbial activity. Refuse arriving at a fill site ordinarily contains a lively flora of saprophytes and, at times,

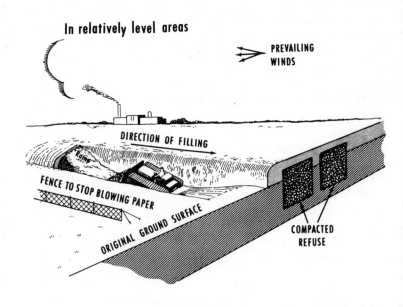

In relatively level areas

PREVAILING WINDS

DIRECTION OF FILLING

FENCE TO STOP BLOWING PAPER

ORIGINAL GROUND SURFACE

COMPACTED REFUSE

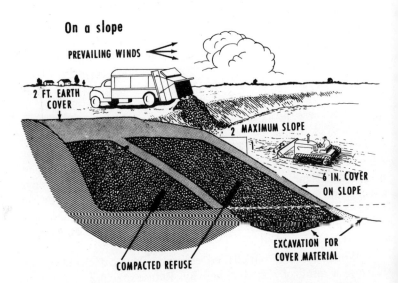

On a slope

PREVAILING WINDS

2 FT. EARTH COVER

2 MAXIMUM SLOPE

6 IN. COVER ON SLOPE

EXCAVATION FOR COVER MATERIAL

COMPACTED REFUSE

Figure 41. Schematic representation of a well-planned sanitary landfill.

pathogenic bacteria, viruses, yeasts, and fungi, which are a potential source of disease to the community. In a controlled, properly designed landfill, the energy released by the chemical changes taking place is so great that there is a precipitous rise in internal temperature. Recordings after seven to ten days have been as high as 150° to 160°F, well above the temperature needed to kill the heat-sensitive pathogens. This offers a fair degree of assurance that the fill is not a health hazard.

Microbial activity in a newly filled area is primarily that of aerobic bacteria, and it will continue until the residual oxygen contained in crevices of the refuse is exhausted. At this point, anaerobic organisms continue the degradation. The generalized expressions of these two reactions are:

(1) organic matter + oxygen + organisms $\longrightarrow$
$$CO_2, H_2O, NH_3 + energy$$
(2) organic matter + organisms $\longrightarrow$
$$CH_4 + H_2S + CO_2 + H_2O + energy$$

A more specific example linked with the production of heat energy is seen in the degradation of the amino acid leucine, present in the protein of many foods:

$$(CH_3)_2 - CH - CH_2 - \overset{\displaystyle \overset{H}{|}}{\underset{\displaystyle \underset{NH_2}{|}}{C}} - COOH + 150 \longrightarrow$$

$$6CO_2 + 5H_2O + NH_3 + 755 \text{ Cal.}$$

The greater the amount of organic matter present in refuse, the higher will be the temperature reached. (See Table 10 for an analysis of typical municipal refuse.) When the anaerobic organisms enter the scheme, their metabolic reactions yield different end products. Such gases as hydrogen sulfide (H_2S) and methane (CH_4) are produced. These can have an effect we will shortly discuss.

In 1961, researchers reported their findings on the relationship of sanitary landfills to water pollution. They noted that rain and snow percolating through landfills can leach out chemicals from the refuse and thereby contaminate ground-water aquifers and nearby wells. This problem deserves increased technical and scientific study in order to elucidate any health hazard and perhaps to modify or control leaching. If this were accomplished, sanitary landfills could become a wholly acceptable method of waste disposal.

Leaching and subsequent seepage of runoff of water-soluble chemicals are a real possibility. When Dr. William Westlin, mayor of Chatham Township, New Jersey, ordered all dumping of garbage on the town dump stopped, he was guided by the news that seepage from the dump had been shown to be a potential hazard to the wildlife of the nearby Great Swamp National Wildlife Refuge Wilderness. Mayor Westlin's order was based on the data recently collected by the U.S. Fish and Wildlife Service. One wonders how many other mayors would have had the courage to act as Mayor Westlin did.

While chemical tests of a water supply for chemical pollutants are standard procedure, biological tests can be more sensitive and more revealing. For example, a day after a chemical is released into a stream or river it will frequently be carried away or so diluted that it will be virtually undetectable. On the other hand, had the biological "fingerprints" (see Chapter 8) of the watercourse been catalogued—that is, if the many species of fish, aquatic insects, and microscopic flora and fauna had been recorded—and if some of these known species had been killed by a chemical passing through, their absence would be detectable for many days or even weeks. The absence of marker species would signal the recent presence of a toxic substance.

This was the case in Chatham. Biologists of the Fish and Wildlife Service, examining samples of water from the Great Swamp, found marker species missing in one area but not in another. "Direct observations revealed that there was a paucity of small organisms within the area influenced by the dump, as contrasted with identical areas of aquatic environment not subject to that influence."

Another case in point, from which a different lesson may be drawn, occurred in Philadelphia. Recently, the city fathers believed they had found the way to dispose of the tons of refuse collected each day: it would be shredded, packed, and shipped upstate for burial in abandoned strip-mining coal pits. It seemed like the ideal solution to a vexing problem. However, almost as soon as the operation got underway, it was vetoed by a state authority as having the potential to cause water pollution through leaching. Unfortunately the issue in this instance, as lofty as it may seem, was surrounded by hints and suspicion of skullduggery. Charges of personal, political, and financial gain have been hurled back and forth. It remains to be seen how this challenging contemporary problem will be solved.

Landfills were usually publicly owned and sufficiently isolated from town or city to prevent the erection of buildings on them. With the growth of urban areas and the mass migrations to the suburbs, however, filled land has been developed by private interests for home sites. Two problems have resulted.

In too many instances, the settling of fill has caused houses to develop large cracks. A sad example of the consequences of erecting homes on fill occurred in New York City in 1966. In 1959, twelve three-story row houses were erected on filled land in the East Bronx. Six months after occupancy, cracks developed in the walls. By 1965, the floors were severely tilted and large cracks had opened along the length of the brick walls. In December 1966, Housing Commissioner Charles Moerdler ordered the houses demolished as unsafe and hazardous. The twelve owners lost their homes and investments.

In 1966, First, Viles, and Levin [1] reported on the danger of toxic gases and explosive hazards in buildings erected on landfills. From our discussion of bacterial activity, you will recall that a half-dozen gases can be produced by both aerobic and anaerobic metabolism of refuse. Dr. First and his group at Harvard found that the principal hazard associated with erecting homes on filled land arose from anaerobic production of methane. They also noted the impossibility of creating gas-tight structures because of the continuing production of gas. In addition, they found unsafe levels of gas in many buildings. The possibility of explosions was great unless suitable venting and aerating were employed.

Perhaps a better solution would be to set filled land aside for much-needed parks and playgrounds.

One of the major uses of landfill is the reclamation of otherwise unusable land, particularly marsh. However, marsh areas may serve as recreational sites and are often ecologically vital for a large number of organisms, many of which are of economic importance—for example, shellfish. Therefore, filling in marsh-land may not be at all desirable. The report of a recent White House Conference on Environmental Pollution noted that the "filling in of marshes to make real-estate must be recognized as the most threatening danger to marshes." In Long Island, New York, between 1954 and 1959, over 13 percent of the wetlands were destroyed by landfill projects.

At the present rate of utilization, New York City will have used up its major sanitary landfill area at Fresh Kill, on Staten Island, by 1975, which is just three years away. Then the city will have to find other disposal sites. Are any available? A look at a map quickly shows that New York, without available land, is facing a real problem.

The planners responsible for such decisions think they have a solution—to fill in Jamaica Bay. If, they say, some four to five thousand of Jamaica Bay's nine thousand acres can be filled in with solid waste, New York City will have solved its waste-disposal problems for the next sixty years. Is this the answer to the problem? And when Jamaica Bay has been filled, under what new rugs will the wastes be swept? This type of piecemeal, crisis-to-crisis solution is not the answer. This is a dilemma of staggering proportions that will require the creative imagination of our best scientific and technical people to solve.

A method of waste disposal particularly suitable for urban areas is incineration. It may also be the solution for suburban areas that have no available sites for burying their waste. Incineration is the reduction to ashes of combustible material by controlled burning at high temperature. Incinerators generally offer the most efficient, hygienic means of disposing of all types of combustible waste. As a result, they can be located closer to communities than landfills. This lowers haulage costs and permits nearby industry to utilize the steam by-product, which also aids in lowering the cost of operation.

Incinerators usually operate at temperatures between 1,600° and 1,900°F. Temperatures in this range produce only inert ashes and smaller particles that leave as stack effluent. The ash must be hauled away for burial, usually to landfill operations. The stack effluents can increase the load of particulate matter in the air. But

90 percent removal of particulate matter is commonly obtained in European installations.

One of the major needs of incineration is new design criteria. Too few engineers are engaged in this type of research. Incinerator design must be based on knowledge of the type and quantity of material to be burned. In our affluent communities today, we throw away more than ever before, and the kind of waste has changed considerably since many of the present incinerators were designed and constructed twenty-five years ago. A city that produces waste of which more than 50 percent is noncombustible has completely different requirements than a city producing refuse of which 10 to 30 percent is noncombustible. Tables 10 and 11 indicate the composition of typical municipal waste and the ranges to be found. Design criteria must be developed for each city; this has been done in only a fraction of our cities, and yet new incinerators and combustion equipment are being built without this needed data.

More and more communities are turning to incineration to solve their solid-waste disposal problems. A recent study by the New York State Office of Local Government revealed the following relationship between population and method of disposal:

Sanitary landfills:	900,000 people, 60+ communities.
Incinerators:	12,200,000 people, 66 communities.
Open dumps and private disposal:	3,659,000 people, 1420 communities.

T A B L E 1 0 .

Chemical composition of typical municipal waste.

		Range
Moisture	21.	0–65
Carbon	28.	16–77
Total hydrogen	3.5	2.4–10.35
Oxygen	22.35	4–45
Nitrogen	0.33	0.05–10.0
Sulfur	0.16	0.01–2.0
Non-combustible	24.93	1–72.30
C:H ratio	39.4	9.1–131
BTU/lb.	9,000.	7000–16,000

TABLE 11.
Organic analysis of typical waste.

	%
Moisture	21.
Cellulose, sugar, starch	46.6
Lipids (fats, oils, waxes)	4.5
Protein, 6.25N	2.0
Other organics (plastics)	1.15
Ash, metal, glass, etc.	24.93

Although this study demonstrates that larger municipalities tend to utilize incineration, the disappearance of available fill land fairly well dictates that smaller communities will have to choose incineration too. Figure 42 shows the type of disposal employed for the 250 million tons of residential, commercial, and institutional solid wastes produced in the United States in 1969.

A highly controversial but potentially desirable disposal method for residential solid waste is composting. It has three advantages: it is a way to handle many types of refuse, it can dispose of sewage sludge, and the end-product can be used as a soil conditioner to enrich depleted soil.

Composting is the controlled microbial degradation of organic materials to a sanitary, nuisance-free, humus-like material. The breakdown of refuse by microorganisms is probably the oldest biological waste treatment method. People have been burying unwanted waste for centuries, and our allies the microbes have split the complex organic compounds into simpler substances, which are then taken up by plants and converted back to complex organic matter. Refuse disposal by microbial action occurs both in the sanitary landfill and in composting. Although composting is not new, only within recent years have major improvements in the process been made that allow its use for large-scale disposal. Basically, the production of compost results from the breakdown of organic matter by bacteria and fungi under aerobic conditions.

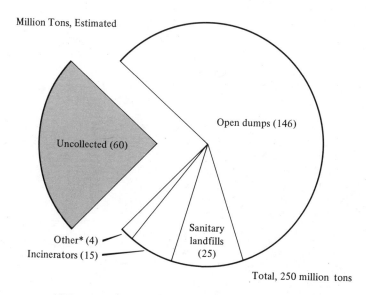

Million Tons, Estimated

Open dumps (146)

Uncollected (60)

Sanitary landfills (25)

Other* (4)

Incinerators (15)

Total, 250 million tons

*Salvaged from collected materials; composted; dumped at sea

Figure 42. Disposal of residential, commercial, and institutional solid wastes, 1969. (Sources: Bureau of Solid Waste Management, HEW.)

Sanitary landfills, you will recall, degrade waste via aerobic and anaerobic metabolism. For rapid aerobic metabolism to occur, it is necessary only to ensure an optimum balance between available air and moisture. This can be enhanced by grinding the refuse for a landfill site to a size that will create optimum surface area for the organisms.

A primary requisite for proper functioning of a composting operation is the removal of such non-compostibles as glassware, metals, and ceramic items. Oxygen needs are provided by tumbling or aerating the compost. Figure 43 is a schematic representation of a typical composting apparatus. The moisture requirement of not less than 30 percent can be provided by sewage sludge, thus disposing of the sludge as well. Temperatures within the compost range above 150°F, which is sufficient to destroy patho-

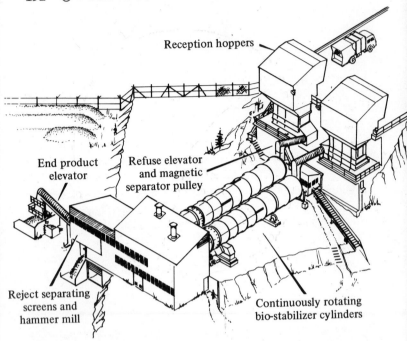

Figure 43. Schematic diagram of a compost plant.

genic bacteria such as the streptococci, *Mycobacterium tuberculosis,* fly larvae, and parasitic worms often found in human waste and garbage. Some dozen composting methods are available, each offering some unique modification. In spite of this, however, every attempt to compost municipal refuse on a large scale in the United States has failed. Apparently, one of the important reasons for failure has been the inability of the compost producer to dispose of his product. Another reason may be the inability of the producer to operate the plant profitably. The large volume of non-compostible material is also difficult to dispose of, and it increases the cost of the operation. Future research in this field may provide a viable method of waste disposal. With the increasing demand for food and with decreasing soil fertility, the use of compost to improve agricultural production could become critically important. The nutrients and humus obtained from composting of waste can be conserved for agricultural use, while at the same time sanitary disposal and protection of the environment are accomplished. Curiously enough, although composting has not taken hold in the larger cities of the United States, European cities make good use of it. One of the largest composting plants in the world, with a capacity of six hundred tons of refuse per day, is in successful operation in Rome. Similar plants (employing Dano Biostabilizer Composting Units) operate profitably in such cities as Ghent, Belgium; Leicester, England; and Jerusalem. Figure 44 shows a Biostabilizer Unit in operation in Auckland, New Zealand. Figure 45 is a cutaway sketch of the Tollemache Composting System in operation in Southern Rhodesia.

Another major means of disposing of certain types of refuse, particularly garbage, is feeding to hogs. Hog farming is an attempt at conservation in which food waste is converted into food. Feeding garbage to hogs is of some economic importance in a few areas of the United States: one thousand pounds of garbage

Figure 44. Biostabilizer unit in operation in Auckland, New Zealand. (Photo courtesy of Dano, Copenhagen.)

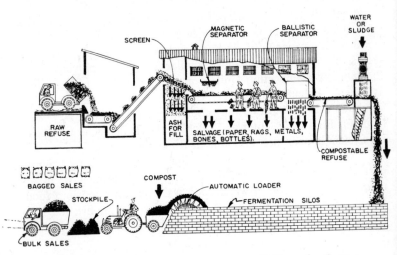

Figure 45. Schematic diagram of a Tollemache System in operation in Rhodesia. (Courtesy of Solid Wastes Program, PHS.)

produce fifty pounds of pork! The economics may be sweet, but the public-health aspects are often foul. Feeding uncooked garbage to swine can be an important means of transmitting trichinosis to those who eat the infected meat. The farms are often so unsanitary that they become major harborages for rats and breeding areas for flies and mosquitoes. The odors in communities surrounding hog farms can be appalling.

Between 1953 and 1955 a virus disease of swine, vesicular exanthema, prompted the U.S. Public Health Service and many state departments of health to develop legislation requiring the pasteurization of garbage (exposure to a temperature of 212°F for thirty minutes) before it could be fed to hogs. The cost of this additional treatment and the increased cost of garbage collection have made hog farming only marginally profitable. As a consequence, fewer farms operate each year. Despite this, the feeding of garbage to hogs is currently a significant method of disposal; it takes care of about 25 percent of the total garbage produced in the United States. Since garbage must be collected separately from other wastes or separated after collection, additional costs are involved. As municipalities shift to single collections, hog feeding may be reduced even further.

An important but little-considered type of waste is that generated by farm and domestic animals—manure. It has been estimated that the farm animal population in the United States is three times the human population. The wastes from swine, chicken, and cattle alone are equivalent to ten times the wastes from the human population. It has been calculated that seven to ten chickens produce as much waste as one person. Thus, a chicken farm with one hundred thousand birds produces as much waste as a town of fifteen thousand people. Additional studies have shown that one hog produces as much waste as two people, and one cow as much as ten people. The biggest technical problem facing livestock producers and, indirectly, the rest of the population, is manure management. The encroachment of urban areas on previously rural areas, the scarcity of land for disposal, and the characteristics of manure make for some particularly difficult problems ahead. An additional worry is the problem of how to dispose of thirty million dead chickens each year.

No discussion of animal waste can be considered complete without noting Professor E. Paul Taiganides' "challenge of the next age in sciences and technology: the age of coprology." Coprology (Professor Taiganides coined the term from the Greek to mean "science of waste") is based on the premise that "there is no such thing as waste. Wastes are things we decided to call economically worthless . . . because we were too obsessed with the production of things for our affluent society." He goes on to remark that wastes are "resources out of place . . . [and] nature must eventually or somewhere assimilate everything that is produced, both product and by-product. Engineers, nutritionists, physicians . . . must help nature assimilate man's wastes. This effort is ushering in the Age of Coprology." Although we are imminently stepping into the Age of Coprology, it may be well to recall, as the professor reminds us, that the Era of Coprophilia was born "when man first discovered the value of manure as a soil amendment and a good source of plant nutrients."

Speaking on Agricultural Waste Management at the 3rd International Congress of Food Science and Technology (Washington, D.C., August 9–14, 1970), Professor Taiganides reminded the audience that "feeding and clothing the average citizen for a year with agriculturally produced food and natural fibers generates 10 tons of animal carcasses, manure, crop residues and logging debris. . . ." Not calculated to ingratiate him with several industries was another pertinent thought: "The food and fiber industry claims to be number one in America in terms of its contribution to the gross national product (GNP). Although the transport industry might quarrel with this statement, there can be no question as to who is number one in the gross national by-product (GNBP) indicator. Food and fiber production generates far more waste." [2] This idea leads us to consider some conflicting opinions as to the cause of our present environmental dilemma. If food and animal fiber production are the prime contributors to waste, would clean (non-waste-producing), synthetic foods and fibers alleviate the problem? At first glance the answer would seem to be yes—most certainly so. On reflection, however, we run up against the synthetic, non-degradable fibers that Dr. Barry Commoner has been calling our most intractable problem. And as if that issue were not difficult enough, consider what the thought of synthetic foods would do to those already dismayed by the present state of chemicals in foods.

If they do nothing else, these thoughts may emphasize the complex nature of our national problems and, perhaps, stimulate new attacks while calming those who demand quick solutions.

It is difficult to believe that concerted research efforts by government, industry, and the academic community in the United States, such as those initiated at a half-dozen British universities by the Central Electric Generating Board in the 1950s, would not solve a number of these problems. Of course such research would help. But funds must be made available.

A National Conference on Solid Waste Disposal was recently held in Chicago to bring together people from many diverse fields to evaluate the state of technology and to discuss future needs. One of the major conclusions that emerged from the conference was that we need to realize the importance of engineers and scientists concerned with this aspect of environmental health. This means that we must attract the best brains to a field that has not had its share. Little status is attached to sewage and waste-disposal research. A second conclusion was that completely new ways of handling our waste must be developed.

On October 20, 1965, President Johnson signed into law the Solid Waste Disposal Act. Public Law 89–272 empowered and authorized the Department of Health, Education, and Welfare to invest over $92 million between 1966 and 1969 for solid-waste research and development activities, demonstration projects, surveys, and technical and financial aid to state, local, and regional agencies for the purpose of promoting interest in solid-waste disposal programs. Let us hope this will be the spark that ignites the much-needed interest in some of our top scientists and engineers to conduct investigations in this sorely neglected area.

Before mentioning examples of new directions being taken by scientists and engineers imbued with new interest in researching the solid-waste problem, a few examples of what British scientists have done with millions of tons of waste fly ash may be instructive.

Fly ash consists of minute glass spheres, with some crystalline matter and carbon. After chemical analysis, a number of agricultural and engineering uses were explored and eventually adopted in Britain. For example, at London's Heathrow Airport hangars were constructed with roof structures made of a new lightweight concrete containing pellets of sintered fly ash. In the Stithians Dam in Cornwall, ash replaced over 25 percent of the cement and concrete normally used. This saved a good deal of the cost and built in improved structural quality. In Winchester Cathedral, presently undergoing restoration, fly ash was used in an improved grout to strengthen the stonework. Agricultural studies showed that cash crops such as wheat can be increased when ash is mixed with soil, manure, or domestic refuse. Note that these uses for waste were found only after researchers at a number of British universities were encouraged by their government to get involved in this important work.

In Poland, engineers have recently found that particulate matter from factory smoke can be converted into a cement-like substance that is ideal for slabs and panels in apartment houses. A factory is being built to mass-produce these slabs and panels.

Sanyo Electric Company, a Japanese electronics company, has discovered that gasoline and kerosene can be produced from discarded plastic. Approximately 95 percent of the polyethylene in a product can be recycled. Another Japanese firm, Tezuka Kozan, developed a compressing machine that uses high pressure to produce stone-like blocks from all manner of waste, from potato peels to refrigerators. This machine scoops up the waste and spews forth solid blocks, a fifth of the volume of the original waste. Tests have shown that these blocks withstand decomposition. A machine capable of handling a thousand tons of waste per day has been constructed.

Dr. David Dinius, a scientist at the USDA's Agricultural Research Institute, Beltsville, Maryland, has found that newspapers and magazines can make tasty meals for cows. He found that a cow can devour the equivalent of several 80-page journals a day when the paper is mixed with molasses, meal, and vitamins. A cow can reach market weight in seventy days on rations of one part ground newspaper to nine parts of the other ingredients. The savings in animal food, as well as alleviation of the waste disposal problem, are the advantages of this discovery.

A unique and interesting kind of recycling has been going on for years with medical and dental X-ray plates. The volume of X-rays taken each year by radiologists and dentists is truly enormous. Usually X-rays are checked and discarded after five years. But disposal in an incinerator or landfill could add to the chemical burden of the soil or air. Instead, X-rays are chemically treated to recover the silver they contain. At $1.50 an ounce for the silver, this becomes a profitable arrangement. Perhaps the profit motive is the secret of large-scale recycling.

The possibilities sophisticated scientific research may hold for alleviating the solid waste problem are exemplified by the Fusion Torch. Recently, two physicists with the Atomic Energy Commission, Bernard J. Eastland and William C. Gough, suggested using the plasma from a thermonuclear fusion reactor to reduce wastes to their constituent chemical elements. This type of system would not exhaust the air or release pollutants into it, nor would its residues or by-products require burial. It would provide valuable raw materials that could be used again and again.

In the heat of a fusion torch (the heat of plasma), some 50 million degrees centigrade, an automobile, for example, would completely vaporize, leaving the elemental iron, tin, zinc, lead, and other substances from which it was originally made. Since natural materials are composed of some 93 elements, there would be no more than 93 (and often far fewer) substances that would need separation from almost any combination of solid wastes.

Unfortunately, although the theory behind the Fusion Torch is good, the engineering problems for a device that can handle garbage practically are many years off. And there is some comfort, however cold at the moment, in the fact that good minds are beginning to think about garbage.

For years, waste has been buried underneath us. Recently, thought has been given to burying it above us. In fact, "Mount Junk," or, as it is officially named, Teufelsberg (Devil's Mountain), rises 380 feet, making it one of Berlin's highest elevations. Mount Junk (Figure 46) is not just a pile of garbage sitting on the edge of the Grünewald Forest. It is an artificial hill built of wartime rubble, covered with soil and planted with grass, trees,

Figure 46. Two views of Mount Junk. A sense of its height can be gained from the size of the people at the pool. In addition, the use of a pool so close by shows that Berliners have accepted their mountain of garbage. (Photos courtesy of the German Information Center.)

shrubs, and vineyards. In addition, it provides a new winter recreation center with its ski and toboggan runs. Most interesting of all is the favorable reception given it by the Berliners.

When the idea of a 2,500-foot-high mountain of compacted and sanitized refuse was suggested by Sanford Garelik, President of the New York City Council, as a way of dealing with New York's horrendous waste problem, it was greeted by a storm of protest. On the other hand, city officials in Chicago are not treating the idea of a 1,000-foot refuse mountain with either the hilarity or outrage "Mount Garelik" received. Frank E. Dalton, Assistant Chief Engineer of the Metropolitan Sanitary District of Greater Chicago, believes that their proposed mountain will eventually spread over five square miles and take twenty-five years to peak. Here again, comfort can be drawn from the fact that all city officials are not always opposed to new ideas, however high they may be.

References

1. Melvin W. First, F. J. Viles, and Samuel Levin, "Control of Toxic and Explosive Hazards in Buildings Erected on Landfills," *Public Health Reports* 81 (1966): 419.

2. E. P. Taiganides, "Agricultural Waste Management." (Paper delivered at the Third International Congress of Food Science and Technology, Washington, D.C., August 9–14, 1970). Reprints available from Dr. Taiganides, Department of Agricultural Engineering, The Ohio State University, Columbus.

Suggested Reading

Taiganides, E. P.; and Strashine, R. L. "Impact of Farm Animal Production and Processing on the Total Environment." Paper read at the International Symposium on Livestock Waste Management and Pollution Abatement, The Ohio State Center for Tomorrow, Columbus, Ohio, April 19–22, 1971.

Elliott, L. F.; McCalla, T. M.; Mielke, L. N.; and Travis, T. A. "Ammonium Nitrate and Total Nitrogen in the Soil Water of Feedlot and Field Soil Profiles." *Applied Microbiology* 23 (1972): 810.

Animal Wastes Profile. The Economics of Clean Water, vol. 2. Washington: U.S. Department of the Interior, FWPCA, 1970.

Srinivasan, V. R. "Biodegradation of Waste Plastics." *Technology Review,* May 1972, p. 45.

Taiganides, E. P. "There Is No More Away and Systems for Automatic Treatment and Recycle of Wastes." Keynote address, 26th Annual Meeting, Pacific Northwest Region, American Society of Agricultural Engineers, Portland, Oregon, October 7–8, 1971.

CHAPTER
10

AIR POLLUTION

The birth of an idea is the happy moment in which everything appears possible and reality has not yet entered into the problem.

Rudolph Diesel

A young gentleman who had inked himself by accident, addressed me from the pavement, and said, 'I am from Kenge and Carboy's, miss, of Lincoln's Inn.'

'If you please, sir,' said I.

He was very obliging; and as he handed me into a fly, after superintending the removal of my boxes, I asked him whether there was a great fire anywhere? For the streets were so full of dense, brown smoke that scarcely anything was to be seen.

'O dear no, miss,' he said. 'This is a London particular. A fog, miss,' said the young gentleman.

'O indeed,' said I.

Although this dialogue from Charles Dickens' *Bleak House* makes it clear that mid-nineteenth-century London was enveloped in the grime of air pollution, it was as long ago as 1273 A.D. that a law was passed to prevent or control pollution of the atmosphere by the burning of soft coal. Complaints against such pollution were frequent in thirteenth- and fourteenth-century England and in 1306 a proclamation was issued by Parliament, requiring the burning of wood rather than coal by the artisans and manufacturers of London during sessions of Parliament. Shortly thereafter, a man was executed for violating this early smog ordinance.

A landmark in the history of this subject was the pamphlet entitled *Fumifugium,* addressed by John Evelyn to Charles II in 1661. Evelyn described the "Evil" as "epidemicall: indeangering as well the Health of Your Subjects, as it sullies the Glory of this Your Imperial Seat." Evelyn suggested that factories using coal be moved farther down the Thames valley and that a green belt of trees and flowers be put around the heart of the city. "But I hear it now objected by some," Evelyn wrote, "that in publishing this Invective against the smoake of London, I hazard the engaging of a whole Faculty against me, and particularly, that the College of Physicians esteem it rather a Preservation against Infections, than otherwise any cause of the sad effects which I have enumerated." The famous seventeenth-century physician Thomas Sydenham, however, had no doubt about the ill effects of London mists containing "the fumes that arise from the several trades managed here, but especially sulphur and fumes of sea coals with which the air is polluted, and these, being sucked into our lungs and insinuating into the blood itself, give occasion for a cough."

Yet three hundred years later there is still uncertainty about the precise effect the fouling of the atmosphere has on health. This lack of understanding is chiefly due to the complexity of the problem. Anyone who has experienced the dense yellow fog that used to be known as the "London particular" will not be surprised by the suggestion that it is bad for the lungs. But a doctor faced with a patient from an area where air pollution has long been severe may find it difficult to determine the extent to which the patient's health has been affected by it. A man with chronic bronchitis may be a heavy smoker, a worker in heavy industry, live in a crowded home, or have had repeated attacks of pneumonia. It is thus difficult to assess any additional effects that exposure to polluted air in his surroundings may have had on his health. But this does not mean air pollution should be allowed to go unabated.

On December 17, 1963, President Johnson signed into law the first Clean Air Act; Public Law 88-206 was a historic milestone in the control of community air pollution. It provided for federal disposition and for the establishment of a program to meet the steadily growing demands for cleaner air. With the signing on October 20, 1965, of Public Law 89-272, an amendment to the Clean Air Act, President Johnson indicated that the federal government would assume an even greater role in guiding and planning for pollution prevention and control in the air over our cities. On signing, the President remarked, "We have now reached the point where our factories, our automobiles, our furnaces, and our municipal dumps are spewing out more than 150 million tons of pollutants annually into the air we breathe—almost one-half million tons a day."

In December 1966, Dr. William Steward, Surgeon General of the United States Public Health Service, sponsored the first National Convention on Air Pollution in Washington, D.C., to focus greater public attention on the need to control air pollution. The battle was joined.

Continuing to fire its broadsides, Congress enacted the Clean Air Act of 1970. This required all states to submit to the Environmental Protection Agency by January 31, 1972, a plan to achieve the act's ambient air quality standards. It also provided a unique twist; a state could elect to adopt air quality standards more stringent than the federal government's. But then, Montana and Arizona had done so years before. Clearly, the federal and state governments were flexing their muscle and emerging as formidable protagonists.

Stretching from the surface of the earth toward outer space is a relatively thin layer of air. This troposphere, some five to eleven miles deep, contains the air we breathe and the air we foul. From the day we are born we contaminate the air around us with every breath, cough, and sneeze. As the years roll by, we add the by-products of cigarette, cigar, and pipe smoking, cooking; driving our cars; and heating our homes.

While man has only himself to blame for the quantity of pollutants present in the air, a truly unpolluted atmosphere never existed. The restless molecules of air carry with them many particles and gases flung up by the forces of nature. Decaying anima carcasses, ozone, bacteria, soil dust, nitrogen dioxide, salts, pollens, volcanic dust (including sulfur dioxide, hydrogen sulfide, and hydrogen fluoride), and the smoke and gases of forest fires would pollute the atmosphere even if man had never appeared on the scene. However, man lost little time in aggravating the problem. With his first technological advance, the discovery of fire for cooking and warmth, man-made atmospheric pollution began. Current estimates of the annual amount of garbage poured into the air above our cities are between 125 and 150 million tons, a greater tonnage than our annual steel production.

Air pollution is the presence in the air of substances in amounts great enough to interfere directly or indirectly with our comfort, safety, and health, or with our enjoyment of property. Public and governmental concern with air pollution is generally considered to spring from the fact that the average person inhales approximately half a liter of air with each breath. As most of us breathe some twenty-two thousand times every twenty-four hours, we inhale about two thousand gallons of air per day. Each liter (approximately one quart) of air in our urban centers has been estimated to contain several million particles of foreign matter. Thus, in a day a city dweller can inhale some twenty billion particles of . . . what? These particles, it is claimed, must certainly impair human health. After all, we can clearly see the ill effects on ornamental plants and crops, as well as the corrosion of buildings and building materials. How can human tissue withstand the onslaught? Does it? Let us defer discussion of the effects of air pollution on health until the total problem has been more fully discussed.

To supply vast numbers of people with electricity to light their homes and offices, schools and businesses, and to power television sets, radios, washing machines, air conditioners, toasters, vacuum cleaners, and the host of other devices that have become an integral part of our daily lives, huge amounts of fuel must be burned. It is this burning of fuel that constitutes one of the primary sources of waste products discharged into the air.

The effluent or exhaust from millions of automobiles, trucks, and buses needed for commercial and private transportation is another major chemical pollutant. The evaporation of solvents and the burning of mountains of paper and other solid wastes add still more to the overburdened air.

Air pollutants may be gases mixed in the air or small solid or liquid particles dispersed in the air (aerosols). The most widely recognized pollutants are the familiar products of combustion: carbon monoxide, oxides of sulfur and nitrogen, hydrocarbons, and particulates. However, many other pollutants are of significance, including pesticides, metal dust, fluorides, asbestos, and radioactive materials. The United States National Air Pollution Control Administration (NAPCA) is currently measuring 24 types of atmospheric pollutants (Table 12). Estimates of the total tonnage of the most important pollutants emitted in the United States during 1968 are given in Table 13. A glance at

TABLE 12.

Atmospheric pollutants currently being measured by NAPCA.

Elements	*Radicals*
Antimony	Ammonium
Arsenic	Fluoride
Barium	Nitrate
Beryllium	Sulfate
Bismuth	
Boron	*Others*
Cadmium	Aeroallergens
Chromium	Asbestos
Cobalt	β-radioactivity
Copper	Benzene-soluble organic
Iron	compounds
Lead	Benzo[*a*]pyrene
Manganese	Pesticides
Mercury	Respirable particulates
Molybdenum	Total suspended particulates
Nickel	
Selenium	*Gases*
Tin	Carbon monoxide
Titanium	Methane
Vanadium	Nitric oxide
Zinc	Nitrogen dioxide
	Reactive hydrocarbons
	Sulfur dioxide
	Total hydrocarbons
	Total oxidants

TABLE 13.

Estimated emissions of principal pollutants in the United States: 1968. (Data in millions of metric tons.)

Source	Partic-ulates	Sulfur oxides (SO_2)	Nitrogen oxides (NO_2)	Carbon monoxide	Hydro-carbons
Stationary fuel combustion	8.1	22.1	9.1	1.7	0.6
Mobile fuel combustion	1.1	0.7	7.3	57.9	15.1
Combustion of refuse	0.9	0.1	0.5	7.1	1.5
Industrial processes	6.8	6.6	0.2	8.8	4.2
Solvent evaporation					3.9
TOTAL	16.9	29.5	17.1	75.5	25.3

the five columns of figures readily shows that particulates, sulfur oxides, and nitrogen oxides are all generated by burning fuel for home and office heating. On the other hand, carbon monoxide and hydrocarbons are the result of operating automobiles and trucks. It is easy to see where preventive and control measures need to be applied.

The number of suspended particles in urban areas is subject to daily, weekly, and seasonal variations, associated with the rhythm of human activities; consequently, it is particularly dependent on the population of a community.

Surveillance of air pollution is an integral part of the total effort to control air pollution. The data derived from atmospheric monitoring and emission measurements are required throughout the various stages of the abatement effort. Surveillance identifies the pollutants emitted to the air, establishes their concentrations, and records their trends and patterns. After air quality and emission standards have been established by legislation (Table 14), surveillance systems may be used to evaluate the progress being made in meeting standards and to facilitate direct enforcement activities, including emergency control procedures during periods of high air pollution.

It is not just industries and municipalities that contribute to air pollution. Few individuals stop to consider that in the course

T A B L E 1 4 .

*National air quality standards for automobile
or related pollutants.*

Pollutant	Standard
Carbon monoxide (CO)	9 ppm for 8 hours*
	35 ppm for 1 hour
Hydrocarbons (non-methane)	0.24 ppm for 3 hours (6–9 A.M.)
Nitrogen dioxide (N_2O_2)	0.05 ppm (annual arithmetic mean)
Oxidant	0.08 ppm for 1 hour

*Not to exceed more than once a year.

of their daily activities they too are polluters. How many people burn leaves in their backyards, blanketing the neighborhood in smoke? How many burn trash and refuse in inefficient home incinerators? And how many leave their car motors running while they do errands? When these activities are brought to people's attention, they are shrugged off as hardly worth noting. To the polluter, there can be no great harm in his bit of pollution. Affluence contributes to pollution in still other ways. In hot climates we build our homes without the large roof overhang that would decrease the amount of air conditioning needed to make the house cool. In northern areas, we build houses with enormous picture windows, thereby increasing the amount of fuel needed for heating. In short, individuals and industry are the culprits together, and, apparently, our way of life is far too comfortable to give up. Table 15 shows the magnitude of the pollution load in New York City from all measurable sources for one day. Will we consider making changes in established habits and patterns of life as a price for cleaner air? I wonder. There is good reason why such countries as India, Venezuela, and Ethiopia, and many of the countries of Africa and South America, for example, still have clean air. They have not as yet reached our state of affluence. When they do, if they fail to profit from our experience, air pollution will be their lot also. Unfortunately, this is already happen-

TABLE 15.

*Air pollution in New York City
on an average heating day (tons per day).*

Space heating	21
Vehicular exhaust	695
Refuse combustion	120
Miscellaneous losses	
AUTOMOTIVE EVAPORATION	120
SOLVENT EVAPORATION	
DRY CLEANING	24
SURFACE COATING	350
ALL OTHERS	176
Miscellaneous, other	74
Overall total (rounded)	1550

(SOURCE: *Air Pollution in New York City,* Council of the City of New York, Report M-970, June 22, 1965.)

ing in some of the developing countries, as they rush to gain the benefits of industrialization without concern for a number of its unwholesome by-products.

We have noted two major sources of air pollution: fuel for heating and electricity, and fuel for automotive transportation. These two fuels produce dissimilar types of air pollutants and, depending upon prevailing geographical and meteorological conditions, produce two dissimilar types of air pollution. The Los Angeles or smog type of pollution is a characteristic of automotive effluents acting in concert with the location of the city. The New York or London type of air pollution, on the other hand, results from burning huge quantities of fossil fuels—coal and oil. Since the effects of both types of air pollution are notably worse during the meteorological mixup called an inversion, it may be appropriate to describe this condition before discussing the pollutants themselves.

Pilots and mountain climbers are quite aware of the reduction in temperature that occurs the higher they climb. With each thousand-foot rise, the temperature drops about 5.5°F (1.8°C). When this normal condition is reversed—that is, when there is a temperature *increase* with increasing height—the condition is called an inversion. Inversions occur most often in the autumn and winter months and during the early morning hours. On a clear, calm night, the surface of the earth cools quickly. In response to this surface cooling, the air in contact with the earth's surface is also cooled. During the hours between evening and morning, this air has cooled considerably, while the air in the upper atmosphere has remained relatively unchanged. The result is a layer of warm air sandwiched between two cold layers—an inversion.

The feature that all inversions have in common is the damping action of the warm layer on the cool bottom layer. This damping action acts like a lid on a pot. It prevents or severely reduces the air's natural upward movement. With such a condition prevailing, the air over a community, city, or region is literally trapped. If the air is trapped over a large industrial or urban area, pollutants emitted from smokestacks or tailpipe exhausts cannot be blown away (diluted), but remain fixed in the area, to pile up to higher and higher levels—sometimes to dangerous levels. Figure 47 shows the increases in pollution levels of four by-products of fossil fuel and gasoline which actually occurred in New York City in 1962.* Figure 48 depicts an inversion and a normal pattern.

The Los Angeles Basin is an area of about four hundred square miles, with the Pacific Ocean to the west and hills on the other three sides. This geography inhibits horizontal air movements. Thus, air masses have little opportunity to escape from the basin. In addition, temperature inversions, prohibiting vertical air movement, occur 260 to 270 days a year. During prolonged inversions, pollutant concentrations increase precipitously as the air mass shifts back and forth—from the city to the ocean during the night, when land breezes prevail, and back over the city in the morning, when sea breezes prevail. The predominantly sunny weather of Los Angeles adds to the problem. In the presence of nitrogen oxides and the sun's energy (in the form of ultraviolet irradiation), organic chemicals undergo a photochemical reaction that can produce entirely new compounds, reduces visibility, and produces eye irritation, crop damage, and characteristic

---

* Unfortunately, the interpretation of this data with respect to human health remains uncertain.

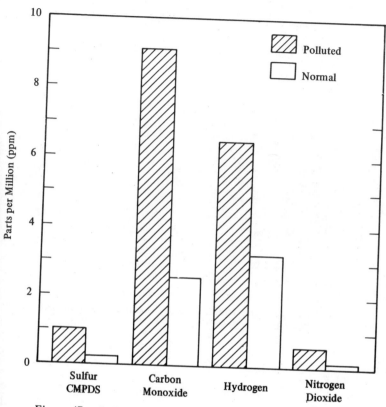

Figure 47. Polluted air levels and normal levels, New York City, 1962.

noxious odors. This peculiar reaction was first noticed in Los Angeles and is, therefore, referred to as Los Angeles or photochemical smog. An important part of the photochemical problem is our transportation system's almost total dependence on gasoline and on the internal combustion engine, which is the principal source of the hydrocarbons (some 130 have already been identified), carbon monoxide, and oxides of nitrogen present in the atmosphere. The concentrations of these compounds emitted by an individual car seem insignificant. However, when multiplied by millions of cars in city traffic, the emissions can be measured

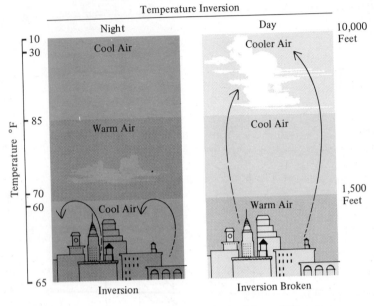

Figure 48. *Inversion and normal condition.*

TABLE 16.
Estimated weekly amounts of pollutants emitted in New Jersey.

Pollutant	Tons per week *
Carbon monoxide	64,800
Hydrocarbons	6,480
Oxides of nitrogen	2,160
Aldehydes	108
Sulfur compounds	162
Organic acids	43
Ammonia	13
Other solids	6.5

* Note that tonnage may not be as important as concentration.

in tons. Even these large amounts are not hazardous until the air masses over a community stagnate as they do during an inversion. Table 16 indicates the estimated amounts of a series of pollutants emitted during one week in New Jersey. The figures for California, with over 8.5 million registered automobiles, more than three times the number registered in New Jersey, would be considerably larger.

Besides its engine, the automobile has two additional emission sources: evaporation from the fuel tank and the carburetor. It has been estimated that for every thousand gallons of gasoline put into gas tanks, five leave unburned, two leave the crankcase ventilation pipe, and one is lost through evaporation. These evaporative losses are hydrocarbons. Neither carbon monoxide nor oxides of nitrogen are involved.

In a vigorous attempt to deal with the internal combustion engine's contribution to air pollution, the state of New Jersey has recently written into its air pollution code a chapter that specifically adds automotive exhaust effluent testing to the required annual inspection by the Division of Motor Vehicles. This rule should serve as a model for other states, and makes New Jersey the first state whose pollution regulations affect vehicles of all ages.

The new code states that any car, truck, or motorcycle will fail inspection if it emits visible smoke from either its exhaust or its crankcase. By limiting the quantities of hydrocarbons, the products of unburned gasoline, the new standards are expected to reduce photochemical smog significantly over the state. Figures 49 and 50 show the type of equipment to be installed at New Jersey's forty inspection stations.

To reduce or eliminate the automobile's contribution to atmospheric pollution, electric cars are being reinvented. Although electrically powered vehicles do not produce hydrocarbons, carbon monoxide, sulfur compounds, or aldehydes, they can produce ozone. Curiously enough, few reports on electric cars have called attention to this or calculated the degree of concentration of ozone in urban atmospheres that might be expected as a result of the operation of millions of electrically driven vehicles. However, with advances in switching design, motor and control

Figure 49. Thirty-second test. A New Jersey motor vehicle inspection attendant demonstrates how a probe is placed in the exhaust pipe of a car to measure exhaust as the engine idles. This is part of the newly enacted inspection routine in New Jersey. A sample is fed into a gas analytical system (in background), which automatically measures carbon monoxide and hydrocarbons (unburned fuel). When a car fails the test, a basic engine tuneup will usually correct the problem. (Photo courtesy of the New Jersey Department of Environmental Protection.)

design, and transistorized switching circuits, an electric car suitable for moderate-speed urban use would be feasible.

Impetus for the eventual mass production of electric cars was provided by a cross-country race that began on August 26, 1968. Two great schools agreed to race the products of their engineering skills: California Institute of Technology used a vehicle containing a lead-acid battery and the Massachusetts Institute of Technology used a "racer" powered by a nickel-cadmium

Figure 50. Close-up view of the exhaust emission tester. (Photo courtesy of the New Jersey Department of Environmental Protection.)

battery. The MIT entry crossed the finish line first, but since it had to be towed across, CIT was declared the nominal winner. Although the race did indicate that an electric car was feasible, it also indicated that mass production of a high-speed, battery-powered electric car is a long way off—at least twenty-five years, if not longer.

It also highlighted the fact that while universities and some few industrial firms are trying with limited financial backing to develop energy sources to power the kind of automobile the public will accept, the utility companies, who stand to profit the most from such developments, have done nothing to advance these expensive investigations. As an electric car will have to be recharged each night by plugging it into a 110-volt, 15 amp outlet, use of electricity in homes and factories will rise precipitously. It would be a welcome change if these huge corporations invested in the community by diverting a portion of their substantial profits into research—or the support of research—that would aid in the control of air pollution. The utilities' campaigns to save energy as a pollution control measure, on the other hand, seem as useful as a wet rag when we consider the wide variety of readily available electric appliances and the public's eagerness to snap them up. The following list, which is by no means exhaustive, suggests the contradiction between the clamor for pollution control and the desire for the "better things of life."

Some common electric appliances include:

frying pans
coffeepots
food mixers
blenders
pencil sharpeners
can openers
refrigerators
dishwashers
clothes dryers
hair dryers
hot combs
carving knives
radios
televisions
clocks
dictaphones
typewriters
shavers
ovens
hair curlers
rechargeable flash equipment
lawn mowers
grills

computers
air conditioners
heaters
toothbrushes
humidifiers
steam irons
hedge clippers
cosmetic mirrors
electric bars
food dispensers
vacuum cleaners
electric blankets
record players
tape recorders
elevators
escalators
shoe polishers
neon signs
telephones
lamps
toasters
motion picture projectors
slide projectors

Pollution-free vehicles are being developed by private individuals and major industrial corporations as well as universities. Sundancer, shown in Figure 51, is the product of ESB, Inc. It is a streamlined two-passenger fiberglass electric car whose lead-acid * batteries can drive it at over 60 mph for up to two hours. Figure 52, by way of comparison, is a photograph taken

* The positive substance in the cell is lead oxide, the negative substance is lead metal, and the electrolyte is sulfuric acid.

Figure 51. The Sundancer. (Photo courtesy of E. S. B., Yardley, Pa.)

Figure 52. One of the earliest battery-powered automobiles. (Photo courtesy of E. S. B., Yardley, Pa.)

in 1910 of an electric car powered by a storage battery. Thomas Edison, its developer, is standing at the front fender.

Although little has been heard of the Minto engine for the past few years, Wallace L. Minto of Sarasota, Florida, had developed a steam engine powered by gas under high pressure. Apparently, the gas was produced by heating Freon (or related fluorocarbon), which rotated helical gears connected to the drive shaft. A condenser returned the gas to its liquid form for recycling.

Recently, E.I. duPont de Nemours & Co. announced that one of its engineers had invented an engine that could lead to the development of a practical steam engine. Dr. William A. Doerner, its inventor, claims that its uniqueness lies in its rotating cylindrical boiler and air condenser, a unit that rotates at 2,500 rpm. Hot vapor from the unit drives a turbine in the opposite direction at 27,500 rpm to supply the energy required to turn automobile wheels. A cutaway drawing of the engine is shown in Figure 53.

Still to be heard from is William P. Lear's steam turbine engine, which is supposed to be in the road-testing stage.

The Clean Air Car Race, which appears to have become an annual event, will see a field of some two dozen entries competing for prizes in 1973. Let us hope that benefits from these races will begin to accrue to the population generally.

Among more recent technological developments to reduce air pollution from urban transportation are automated "personal rapid transit" systems intended to provide nonstop departure-to-selected-destination service for individuals and small groups in areas of high population density. Figure 54 shows a system developed by Transportation Technology, Inc. that uses air-cushion vehicles and linear-induction motors over fixed guideways. Figure 55 depicts a system by Monocab, Inc. that uses suspended monorail vehicles with bypass tracks for loading and unloading. Both systems are unusually clean, quiet, and safe.

Modification of engine design is only one of several means currently being used to abate air pollution. As emissions of waste gases and particulates are also a contribution of industrial processes, methods for their reduction are being moved forward apace.

The removal of particulate matter that contributes to the visible portion of air pollution requires that a force be applied to

Figure 53. DuPont's Rankine cycle engine. Boiler, nozzle ring, and condenser are an integral unit, rotated by external electric motor (not shown) at 2,500 rpm. The expanding gas rotates the turbine in the opposite direction at 27,500 rpm.

External burner (A) boils fluid in annular chamber where liquid (B) is held on outer surface by centrifugal force. Hot vapor travels through tubes (C) to nozzle ring (D), expands through ring and drives turbine wheel (E). Engine power from turbine shaft drives external load (not shown). Vapor goes into condenser tubes (F). Condensed fluid flows back to channel (G). Centrifugal action forces liquid from channel through tubes (H) back to boiler (B). Cooling air is pulled into hollow center of condenser cylinder (I), then between condenser fins (J) by viscous drag of rotating fin assembly.

the particles to move them out of the stream bearing them. Among the types of equipment being used with greater frequency is the mechanical cyclone, a dry collector. It makes use of the

Figure 54. The TTI system, an advanced concept in public transportation. (Photo courtesy of the Department of Transportation.)

inertia of the particle to move it out of the gas stream. Fabric filters trap dust by allowing the gas stream but not the particles to pass through. Wet scrubbers produce their effects by forcing dust particles into drops of water, which are then removed. Electrostatic precipitators bring to bear on a particle an electric charge that drives it out of the gas field.

The first three procedures are mechanical and have the disadvantage of requiring large amounts of energy to effect removal; the fourth, an electrical method, does not require as much energy. However, all methods end up with tons of particulates that must be disposed of by burying or recycling (see Chapter 9).

The electrostatic precipitator, which originated in the early 1900s, appears to offer the greatest benefits and widest range of applications. It can be used not only to collect fly ash from coal-fired boilers, but to recover dust in pulp and paper mills, open hearth furnaces in the iron and steel industry, the cement and petroleum industries, and municipal incinerators.

Though many types of precipitators are available, all consist essentially of a chamber containing wires that act as one electrode, while the surrounding wall usually acts as a second electrode. Figure 56 is a simple diagram of the process. In Figure

Figure 55. The Monocab suspended-monorail rapid transit system. (Photo courtesy of the Department of Transportation.)

57, a "hot" fly ash electrostatic precipitator installation, the Duke Power Company's Lee Steam Station, is shown in operation. The two units on the left control the left stack; the stack on the right will have its fly ash collected once the precipitators are installed. The size of the units can be inferred from the size of the man on the platform in the center foreground.

When fuel is burned inefficiently, large amounts of particulates can easily be found in air samples. Figure 58 is a photo-

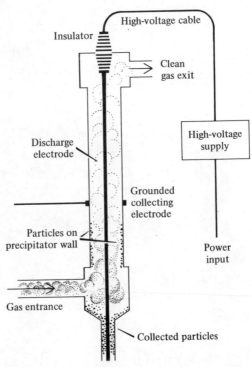

Figure 56.   This simplified diagram illustrates the structure of a vertical gas flow, cylindrical precipitator. The charging electrode wire suspended in the center of the pipe-like outer shell acts as the grounded collecting electrode.

micrograph of a smoke aggregate typical of the particles in air. Obviously, fewer of these particles are found in areas where fuel is efficiently burned or where equipment prevents particles from leaving the stacks.

Earlier, we mentioned that our national air pollution monitoring network was measuring some 40 pollutants. Although this number is but a small fraction of the total, this in itself is a tremendous effort, for thousands of air samples of each pollutant must be taken at any one site if a complete picture is to be ob-

Figure 57. The electronic precipitator on Duke Power Company's Lee Steam Station Unit No. 1 makes a big difference in the amount of visible particulate escaping from its two stacks. The precipitators, which are 99 percent efficient in removing fly ash, take about eight months to install. (Photo courtesy of Duke Power Company.)

tained. In addition to fixed stations, mobile laboratories are being used. Figure 59 shows the Air Quality Monitoring Laboratory developed by General Motors. A number of State Departments of Health have similar units that move about the state collecting air samples. The GM mobile laboratory goes all over the country. Figure 60 shows the internal workings. The long white pipe shown in Figure 59 is the air intake, which conveys the air sample to SO_2CO, hydrocarbons, NO_x and other analyzers.

No discussion of measures for prevention and control of air pollution can omit the effects of public outcry and pressure to forbid activities that, in the public mind, are seen as potentially polluting. However, public pressure is a two-edged sword. An excellent example of its workings was the recent public furor over the SST, the American supersonic transport, an airplane capable

Figure 58. Smoke aggregate magnified 320,000 times.
(Photo courtesy of Medical Research Council, London.)

of carrying 300 passengers at least 1800 miles per hour at altitudes of 60,000 feet (12 miles).

It is well-nigh impossible to recall an issue so fraught with heat and so lacking in light on the subject. The country was divided into two opposing camps, each professing certain knowledge that the SSTs would or would not pollute the atmosphere. And one could easily find scientists to support either side. Whether one approves or disapproves of the SST's *raison d'être*—the need to reduce flying time between New York and London by three hours—an unresolved question remains. What do we actually know, as opposed to what we prefer to believe, about the SST's effect on pollution or climate? *

It is clear that a well-organized national campaign against

* Curiously enough, no one in the controversy has said the predicted climatic change would be good or bad.

Figure 59. General Motors' mobile air-monitoring laboratory. (Photo courtesy of General Motors Research Laboratory.)

the SST was launched by a highly vocal segment of our population. These people were certain that the available evidence patently showed the SST to be a menace. The anti-SST group, flexing its political muscle, found it was as effective a lobby as any of the well-oiled professional promoters. These crusaders blitzed Congress into voting their way—against development of the SST. And they won. Was theirs a Pyrrhic victory? Did anyone really win? I believe we all lost.

The National Oceanic and Atmospheric Administration (NOAA), created within the Department of Commerce to provide a single federal agency to improve our knowledge, under-

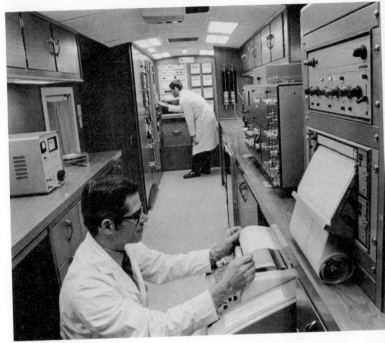

*Figure 60. An inner view of the air-monitoring laboratory.
(Photo courtesy of General Motors Research Laboratory.)*

standing, and use of the physical environment, is the parent organization of GFDL, the Geophysical Fluid Dynamics Laboratory. Working at Princeton University's Forrestal Campus, GFDL's scientists are using computers to develop numerical models that simulate the physical behavior of atmosphere and oceans. A mathematical model * of the atmosphere is a structure of physical laws stated in mathematical language that attempts to describe the behavior of the earth's atmosphere. The physical laws are most often expressed as a partial differential equation describing the change of some variable with time. To simulate a single day of normal weather, the equations must account for changes in temperature, wind, pressure, humidity, and differences

* These are, of course, abstractions and as such have no physical body as, say, a "model" airplane has.

in the moisture available to the atmosphere over sea, land, and desert. In addition, information must be obtained on the various effects of clouds in trapping or reflecting radiation from the sun.

When these pieces of information are obtained, an equation or set of equations is set up for each significant factor in the atmosphere. But (and this is fundamental) the equations must define the interrelationships of all these factors. Even the largest computers will have difficulty managing this. Consider for a moment that climate is a statistical average condition of weather. Put the other way, average weather is climate. Consequently, a single temperature or wind velocity value is simply not good enough. Data on the half-dozen variables noted is required from some 100,000 points around the globe and up to an altitude of 100,000 feet, if predictions of long-range changes in the earth's climate are to be made.

To develop equations for all this information is not just staggering to contemplate, it is mind-blowing. Without computers, this work could not be done. With computers, it has taken fifteen years for some of the country's best minds, working with the most advanced instruments at GFDL, to develop a reasonable model of the normal atmosphere. Scientists at GFDL have also been able in this time to simulate the monsoon over India. They are now planning to investigate prediction of atmospheric behavior in the presence of pollutants. Given the thousands of pollutants discharged into the atmosphere each day, such a study will have to run for fifteen to twenty years to obtain sufficient data for predictions.

At this point, we can return to the question of the SST; a full-scale model is shown in Figure 61. As the lines of battle drew up for the final skirmish in the Senate, leading senatorial antagonists of the SST sought council from the GFDL, which told them that effects on climate of water vapor spewed out by high-flying SSTs would take at least ten to fifteen years to obtain. And there was no guarantee that the findings would be against the SST.

Given the preceding statements, how could the momentous decision to halt the SST program be made? Little, if any, substantive data was available to anyone. Obviously, the decision to terminate was a political expedient. It is not a decision one can point to with pride. In retrospect, it has all the earmarks of vigi-

Figure 61. A full-scale model of the SST. Its 298-foot length and overall dimensions can best be appreciated by comparison with the people around it. (Photo courtesy of Boeing Company, Seattle, Washington.)

lante action—a group got what it wanted, no matter the price. To our collective misfortune, air pollution control has become politically rewarding. Surely we are capable of seeking solutions in more appropriate spheres.

Our Weather Bureau (NOAA) and the Cold War between the United States and the Soviet Union may have saved us from an earlier attempt at climate alteration. Some fifteen years ago, a Russian engineer, Pyotr Midnailovich Borisov, proposed the damming of the Bering Sea between Alaska and Siberia to enable the Gulf Stream to flow north from the Greenland-Labrador area. Borisov believed, with little to back him up, that the warm waters would meet the Arctic ice and turn Alaska and Siberia into a garden. Of course, his predictions didn't include changes as far south as California. Fortunately for everyone, scientists at the Weather Bureau dampened his ardor by suggesting that such a plan could be approved only after extensive study. Fortunately too, fifteen years ago politicians had not yet seen votes in these areas.

The Bering Sea's continued fascination for scientists is seen in the latest proposal to throw a bridge across it. Recently Professor T. Y. Lin of the University of California (Berkeley) organized an International Peace Bridge Corporation, through which he hopes to bring long-lasting peace to the world. The bridge he envisions would span the fifty-mile gap between the United States and the Soviet Union, and would link the Eastern and Western Hemispheres. Although Professor Lin's aspirations are lofty indeed, I would hope that before the first pilings are sunk adequate data are obtained and pressure groups are politely but firmly invited to take their good intentions elsewhere.

In the New York and London type of air pollution, which is the type of atmospheric contamination most often found in large industrialized communities, vertical inversions are not as frequent as in the Los Angeles type, nor is horizontal air passage usually impeded. Dispersal of pollutants is thus not generally restricted. Although vertical inversions do occur, they are relatively infrequent. Restrictive terrain, however, is not a necessary condition for extreme pollution levels if contaminants are being discharged into the atmosphere at a sufficiently high rate. New York City, for example, is not hemmed in by hills at any of its borders, but nevertheless was blanketed by a mass of stagnant warm air above a layer of cool air for several days during the Thanksgiving weekend of November 1966. The effects on human health of the pileup of sulfur dioxide and particulates are still being studied.

Much of the available knowledge of the effects of air pollution on human health has come from acute exposures during prolonged inversional episodes or pollution accidents. Two of these acute episodes occurred in areas where large amounts of fossil fuels were used and where heavy industry also contributed its special pollutants. These two areas were further handicapped by restrictive topographical characteristics. A third acute episode occurred in a large city with no restriction on air flow. Only under the extreme conditions in these three episodes, described below, have fairly strong causal links between air pollution and acute upper respiratory illness been established.

The Meuse Valley of Belgium, scene of some of the bloodiest battles of World War I, is a heavily industrialized area. Blast furnaces, glass factories, lime furnaces, and sulfuric acid and artificial fertilizer plants spew a variety of contaminant chemicals into the atmosphere. During the first week of December 1930, a thick fog blanketed most of Belgium. The air was especially stagnant in the river valleys, particularly along a fifteen-mile stretch of the

Meuse. Three days after this abnormal weather condition began, residents began to report shortness of breath, coughing, and nausea. Thousands became ill; the exact number was never ascertained. About sixty people died. Again, deaths were primarily among the elderly and those with chronic illnesses of the heart and lungs. Once the fog lifted, no new cases occurred.

Because this was the first notable acute air pollution episode of the twentieth century, public health scientists were unprepared. A study of the area after the incident suggested that the effects on health had been caused by a mixture of the sulfur oxides, sulfur dioxide gas, and an aerosol of sulfur trioxide. This has never been fully substantiated, and such an episode has not recurred in the Meuse Valley.

The episode in Donora, Pennsylvania took place during the last week of October 1948. Donora is located some thirty miles south of Pittsburgh in a highly industrialized valley along the Monongahela River. On the morning of October 27 the air over Donora became very still and fog enveloped the city. The air over the city was trapped, and it remained so for four days. In addition to sulfur dioxide, nitrogen dioxide, and hydrocarbon from the burning of coal for heating and electricity, the air contained the effluents from a large steel mill and a large zinc reduction plant, where ores of high sulfur content were roasted. During the period of the inversion these pollutants piled up. As they did severe respiratory-tract infections began to occur in the older members of the population. Eye, nose, and throat irritations were common. Twenty people died in a period for which the normal death rate would have been two. Autopsies of many of those who died showed chronic cardiovascular disease. This finding confirmed the opinion that preexisting heart disease increased the chances of serious illness and death during an air pollution episode. Before the weather changed and broke the inversion, 5,910 of the 12,000 inhabitants of Donora had become ill. This episode has never recurred in Donora.

The highly inefficient burning of soft coal in open grates by the citizens of London was primarily responsible for the fog that blotted out their capital on December 5, 1952. The city, located on a gently sloping plain, is not hemmed in by hills, as are Donora and the Meuse Valley communities. The flow of air over London is not impeded by topographical barriers. But for five days strong inversion and fog enveloped the city to such a degree that the "ceiling" was some 150 feet high. Within twelve hours after the fog had settled over London, residents began complaining of respiratory ailments. By the time the inversion lifted on December 9, four thousand deaths in excess of the normal rate for a four-day period had been recorded in the Greater London area. Some striking differences between this episode and earlier ones were noted. The increase in mortality was not confined to the very old. Although the highest increment was among those over forty-five, deaths occurred in all age groups. Another difference was in the rapid onset of illness: twelve hours, as compared to forty-eight and seventy-two in the earlier episodes. A third difference was the increased death rate in London compared with Donora and the Meuse Valley. Perhaps Londoners were more susceptible.

London experienced a second episode in 1956 that was responsible for the deaths of one thousand people, and a third episode in 1962 that caused seven hundred deaths. The reductions in mortality are believed to be due to the preparations made after the 1952 experience. Sulfur dioxide from the burning of coal was implicated as the irritant mainly responsible for illnesses and deaths.

As I noted earlier, accidents can also yield valuable information. In November 1950, the Mexican village of Poza Rica was subjected to an unusual pollution experience. Tanks of waste hydrogen sulfide accidentally released their contents and blanketed the entire village in a yellow haze. People of all ages were hospitalized, and twenty-two died.

It becomes increasingly clear that air pollution is an extremely complicated process: the degree and type are influenced by climate, weather, industry, traffic density, heating practices, and topography. Yet there is another, perhaps more critical, problem that requires elucidation.

I noted earlier that these acute episodes and accidents have strengthened the hypothesis of a causal relationship between air pollution and illness. It is reasonable to say that acute air pollution can be lethal. As a result of these dramatic periods of abnormal pollution, it has become mandatory to investigate whether higher death and illness rates occur during periods of less intense pollution, that is, in the long-term, low-level, "normal" pollution conditions to which urban dwellers are often subjected. This returns us to a question posed earlier: Can air be lethal when contaminated with a host of chemicals at high concentrations, yet be benign when exposure is of long duration but concentrations are low? This question is at the heart of the present agitation for control or prevention of air pollution. Current research investigations, whether with animals or man, are seeking evidence of the effects of repeated exposure to low concentrations of air pollutants over an extended period.

Another question being studied stems from a similar concern. We have seen that most deaths during the acute episodes were among persons with preexisting illnesses. Thus it is of prime importance to learn whether the effect of certain pollutants or combinations of pollutants during "normal" periods initiates new lesions or aggravates old ones, or both. It is also important to know which pollutants of the myriad present in the air are the culprits and at what levels they produce their effects.

Before discussing current research and what has been learned, a brief digression may be in order. Recall that in most acute episodes only a small fraction of the population succumbs. The great majority do not become ill. This implies that those who do are more susceptible or that their defenses were overwhelmed. In either case, the evidence suggests the presence of some physiological defense mechanism. Although most writers concerned with air pollution either do not know of its existence or choose to ignore it, there is an efficient natural defense mechanism that combats this environmental stress.

Recall that in the course of a day we inhale some two thousand gallons of air—and if we are urban dwellers, this air contains billions of foreign particles. Each breath consists of about half a liter of air,* 20 percent of which is molecular oxygen. The air swirls briefly through a maze of branching ducts leading to tiny sacs (alveoli), a gas-exchange apparatus in which some of the gaseous oxygen is dissolved in the bloodstream. I am, of course, describing the lungs. Do the billions of foreign particles actually enter the alveoli? What protects the lungs and the air ducts leading to them from contamination?

As a prelude to examining the body's defenses, a glance a

---

* Half a liter is approximately a pint.

the respiratory system may be helpful. Figure 62 is a cross-section of the respiratory tract. The nose can be compared to an air-conditioning unit because it controls the temperature and humidity of the air entering the lungs and filters out foreign particles. External respiration begins and ends with the nose. It filters, warms, and moistens the air. The interior of the nose is divided by a wall of bone and cartilage, the septum. On both sides of the septum are a series of scroll-like bones, the turbinates or conchae. The purpose of the turbinates is to increase the amount of tissue surface so that inhaled air will be further conditioned before continuing towards the lungs. The surface of the turbinates is covered with a mucous membrane secreting a continual supply of mucus, which drains slowly into the throat. The mucus gives up heat and moisture to incoming air. It also helps dilute any irritating substances contained in the inhaled air. The mucous membrane is coated with cilia—hairlike filaments that wave back and forth approximately twelve times per second. These millions of cilia help clean the inhaled air. The inhaled air passes through the nasal cavity into the pharynx (a common passage for both air and food), which leads to the esophagus (the food tube) and the larynx (the voice box or Adam's apple). When food is swallowed, a flap of cartilage, the epiglottis, folds over the opening; at the same time, the larynx moves up to help seal the opening. On the side of the pharynx are the tonsils, an additional filtering device that guards primarily against microbes entering the body through the mouth and nose. The larynx is at the top of the trachea, the column that passes the air to the lungs. The trachea continues down the neck into the chest and branches into the right and left bronchi. This is the end of the upper respiratory tract.

Each bronchus divides and subdivides; between twenty and twenty-two bronchial subdivisions have been counted. The smallest bronchi in the depths of the lung are called bronchioles. They end in some three hundred million air sacs, called the alveoli, which are seventy-five to three hundred microns * in diameter. The alveoli are balloon-like structures that give the lungs their spongy quality.

In the upper respiratory tract the hairs in the nose block

* The micron, μ, a unit of the metric system, is 0.001 mm, or 1/25,400 of an inch. A three-quarter-inch-long firefly is to the 1,472-foot Empire State Building as one micron is to an inch—twenty-five thousand times smaller.

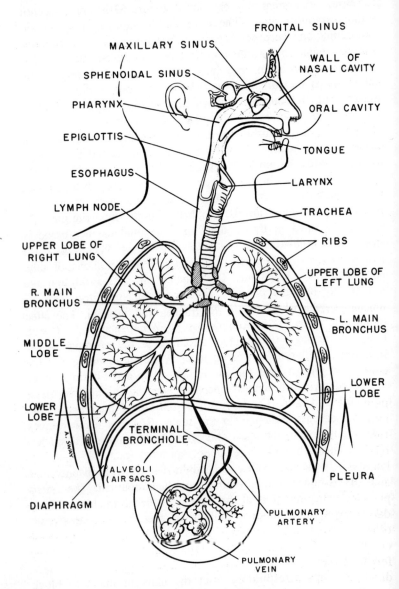

Figure 62. The respiratory system.

the passage of large particles. Beyond the hairs, the involuted contours of the turbinates force the air to move in many narrow streams, so that suspended particles tend to come into contact with the mucous surfaces. The filter system of the nose almost completely removes particles larger than 10 μ in diameter. Particles from 2 to 10 μ usually settle on the walls of the trachea, bronchi, and bronchioles. Only particles between 0.3 and 2.0 μ are likely to reach the alveoli. Particles smaller than 0.3 μ, if not taken up by the blood, are likely to remain in suspension as aerosols to be blown out of the lungs with exhaled air. Foreign matter that settles on the walls of the nose, pharynx, trachea, bronchi, and bronchioles may also be expelled by the explosive blast of air generated by a sneeze or cough; more often it is removed by ciliary action. In action, each cilium makes a fast, forceful forward stroke, followed by a slower, less forceful return stroke that brings it into starting position again. The strokes of a row of cilia are precisely coordinated so that the hairs move together as a wave. The cilia of the human respiratory tract do not beat in the open air; they operate within a protective sheet of mucus secreted by glands in the trachea and bronchi. The effect of their wave-like motion is to move the entire sheet, and anything trapped on it, up through the tract to the pharynx, where it can be expectorated or swallowed. This ciliary escalator is in constant operation.

In spite of all these preventive measures, inhaled particles, particularly those suspended in fluid droplets, manage to pass into the alveoli. However, in the deep tissues the lymphocytes (amoeba-like white blood cells) and the macrophages (closely related forms) engulf and digest these foreign particles. The lymphocytes and macrophages surround particles in the air ducts and ride the muco-ciliary escalator up to the nasopharynx. Some particles do remain permanently attached to lung tissue, as the darkened lungs of coal miners and city dwellers demonstrate. Many of these particles are essentially harmless; others, such as particles of silica, asbestos, and beryllium, for example, can result in the formation of tough, fibrous tissue that causes serious pulmonary disease (see Chapter 13).

Thus the filtration mechanism of the upper tract has several important functions. It is responsible for the interception and removal of foreign particles. It can remove bacteria suspended in the air and also dispose of bacteria, viruses, and even irritant or carcinogenic gases when they are absorbed onto larger particles. Unless the filter system becomes overloaded, it keeps the alveoli practically sterile.

This is not the only protection the lungs possess. Among the reflex responses to chemical or mechanical irritation of the nose are cessation of breathing, closure of the larynx, constriction of the bronchi, and even slowing of the heart. These responses are aimed at preventing potentially harmful gases from reaching the alveoli and, through the alveoli, the pulmonary circulation.

When specific chemical irritants penetrate beyond the larynx, the reflex response is usually a cough, combined with bronchial constriction. This reflex is less active in old people—this is why they are more likely to draw foreign bodies into their lungs and why they are usually the first to become ill and even die as a result of an acute air pollution episode.

Exposure to pollutants that produce severe bronchial constriction can result in excessive secretion of mucus, reduction in ciliary activity, obstruction of the fine air paths, and in some cases cell damage.

Heavy smokers often exhibit depressed ciliary activity as a consequence of prolonged contact with tobacco smoke. As a result, their defense against air pollutants is markedly decreased. These circumstances enable bacteria to penetrate to the alveoli and remain there long enough to initiate infectious lung ailments. They are probably also one factor in the development of such tracheobronchial diseases as chronic bronchitis and lung cancer.

One of the most difficult facts to uncover about the many chemicals released into the air has been which, or how many, are associated with or directly responsible for a specific illness or disease. At the present time it is believed (but is by no means firmly established) that air pollutants contribute to or aggravate such acute and chronic respiratory diseases as bronchial asthma, sinusitis, chronic generalized emphysema,* chronic coughing, eye

---

* Emphysema is by far the most common chronic disease of the lungs. It is the enlargement of a portion of or the whole lung due to loss of elasticity. The main elastic system of the lungs is contained in the bronchi, bronchioles, alveolar ducts, and blood vessels. It is now a matter of record that more than 90 percent of emphysema patients are heavy smokers.

irritation, chronic bronchitis,* the common cold, and skin roughening.

Air pollution is strongly suspected of aggravating cardiac and circulatory ailments. In addition, some medical scientists believe that long-term, low-level exposure reduces resistance to other diseases. Certain experiments have shown that the susceptibility of white mice and golden hamsters to the bacteria related to pneumonia can apparently be increased by exposing these animals to pollutants before, during, and after exposure to the bacteria. Another experiment showed that mice exposed to ozonized gasoline developed large lung abscesses and pneumonia. Examination of lung tissue revealed the presence of a specific microbe. Since no deaths occurred among the untreated control animals, it was concluded that the ozonized gasoline had activated a dormant infection. That is, the microbe had been present in a quiescent condition until mice were exposed to the gasoline.

In 1965, Pearson and Skye reported [1] that lichens (plants consisting of an alga and a fungus in a mutually beneficial relationship) grown in atmospheres of sulfur dioxide of from 100 to 100,00 ppm ** showed abnormalities similar to abnormalities of lichen in Swedish industrial centers. They suggested that certain lichens may be absent from cities because of the presence of sulfur dioxide. When one considers the average sulfur dioxide level around the United States—0.06 ppm, with a range of from 0.01 to 0.38 ppm—one can only wonder why these investigators did not use concentrations more closely approximating existing conditions. What conclusions can be drawn from these data?

A more reasonable approach to the subject of chemical damage to agricultural crops can be found in the report of Weinstein and McCune on the effects of fluoride levels on plants. They

---

* Chronic bronchitis is characterized by excessive mucus secretion in the bronchial tree. It is commonly seen as a recurrent cough with sputum. The Surgeon General's Report, *Smoking and Health,* indicates that cigarette smoking is the most important cause of chronic bronchitis in the United States.

** Most people have no conception of what constitutes one part per million (ppm). A few examples may help:
One inch is one part per million in 16 miles.
One minute is one part per million in two years.
A postage stamp is one part per million of the weight of a person.

say that except for a few instances we do not know what effects fluorides have on agriculture. Where effects have been proved, they have been so severe or evident as to require little expertise for recognition. They go on to say that "although we can find certain effects experimentally, there is considerable uncertainty in predicting whether the effect will occur in the field." [2] Unfortunately too many investigators never go beyond the test-tube stage, but are content to predict danger and harm for man, animals, and plants on the basis of inappropriate testing procedures.

In March 1966, Myrvik and Evans reported to the Conference on Air Pollution sponsored by the American Medical Association that nitrogen dioxide could immobilize macrophages obtained from rabbit lungs.[3] However, at this meeting Corn and Burton of the University of Pittsburgh noted that no substance is present in air in sufficient concentrations as a community air pollutant to produce the classical picture of human tissue inflammation. They added that present sampling procedures do not allow prediction of the irritating capacity of air pollutants.[4] Dr. S. W. Tromp of the Biometeorology Research Center in Leiden, The Netherlands, rejected current views that relate air pollution to bronchial asthma. He maintained that the rapid onset of cold weather was the critical factor.[5]

Between 1959 and 1961, Dr. Warren Winkelstein and his group at the Medical School of the State University of New York at Buffalo carried out a statistical study of the effects of air pollution on men age fifty to sixty-nine in Erie County, New York. One of the most striking observations was the lack of association between air pollution and deaths from cancer of the trachea, bronchus, and lung. Although the study also found a lack of association between air pollution and deaths from cancer of the large intestine and rectum, an association was found between air pollution and deaths from cancer of the prostate, esophagus, and stomach.[6]

Addressing the Eighteenth Annual Meeting of the California Branch of the American Cancer Society in October 1964, Dr. E. Cuyler Hammond, Director of Statistical Research for the Society, noted that his four-year study in three smog-ridden counties of California failed to yield evidence that air pollution seriously affected illness or death rates. He found that coughs, loss of appetite, and nausea were almost as common outside the smog areas as in it. Furthermore, death rates for men were almost identical in smog and non-smog areas. Strangely enough, the death rates for women were lower in the smog areas. It is curious indeed that many of the same people who eagerly accepted Dr. Hammond's statistical studies correlating cigarette smoking with lung cancer received his air pollution report with studied coolness.

In a particularly cogent report, Anderson and Ferris noted that "we have failed to show any increased risk of disease for a twofold increase in dustfall and a threefold increase in SO_2 across three residential areas at Berlin, New Hampshire, and for a sixfold difference in dustfall and a tenfold difference in sulfation rate between Chilliwack, British Columbia, and Berlin, New Hampshire." [7]

In 1966, Dr. Mary O. Amdur, a toxicologist at the Harvard School of Public Health, reported her studies dealing with the physiological responses of guinea pigs to sulfur dioxide. Dr. Amdur concluded that at concentrations found in urban atmospheres, SO_2 could have no harmful effect on the health of man.* [8]

In more recent studies, Dr. Amdur found that concentration alone is not sufficient to predict irritant potency; particle size is of extreme importance. Toxicological studies on experimental animals have similarly shown that some of the oxidation products of SO_2 have a greater irritant capability than the parent compound. It is a mistake, Dr. Amdur claims, to establish standards on the basis of SO_2 concentrations alone. They will not really protect the public. [9]

At the conference, "Man's Health and His Air Environment" (University of California, December 1970), Dr. James L. Whittenberger of the Harvard School of Public Health described his experiments on the effects of sulfur dioxide on pulmonary function. He noted the increased airway resistance in guinea pigs when sulfur dioxide was combined with inert aerosol. When, how-

---

* Addressing a Senate committee in May 1967, A.J. Clark and G.N. Stone of the Central Electricity Generating Board, London, said that after twenty years of intensive study, the British National Medical Council could not implicate SO_2 as a cause of illness or death.

ever, the same tests were done with human subjects, this enhancement did not occur. Dr. Whittenberger remarked on the danger of extrapolating results from experimental animals to man.

At the October 1967 National Meeting of the American Public Health Association, Dr. Eric Cassell and colleagues of the Department of Community Medicine, Mt. Sinai School of Medicine, reported that their three-year study of air pollution levels and death rates in New York City failed to establish a significant correlation between these two conditions, since their data showed several associations: periods of high pollution and low death rates, low pollution and high death rates, and high pollution and high death rates.

The report of the Environmental Pollution Panel of the President's Science Advisory Committee (White House Conference, 1965) said: "While we all fear, and many believe, that long-continued exposure to low levels of pollution is having unfavorable effects on human health, it is heartening to know that careful study has so far failed to produce evidence that this is so, and that such effects, if present, must be markedly less noticeable than those associated with cigarette smoking. Attempts to identify possible effects of ordinary urban air pollution on longevity or on the incidence of serious disease have been inconclusive."

This evaluation was substantially buttressed by a report made public by the California State Department of Health in December 1967. Its main conclusion condemned cigarette smoking as the primary factor in the generation of lung cancer. Results of a study of some seventy thousand deaths over a five-year period specifically ruled out smog as a cause of cancer. Accounting for such variables as length of residence, age, and smoking habits, the researchers found that the lung-cancer death rate was significantly higher in the San Francisco Bay and San Diego areas than in Los Angeles County, the most smog-ridden area of California. The study also showed that heavy smokers were five times more likely to die of lung cancer than non-smokers. These findings tend to support Dr. Hammond's earlier study.

Recently, Walborg S. Wayne of the U.S. Department of Health, Education and Welfare, in collaboration with Dr. Paul F. Wehrle, a pediatrician at the School of Medicine of the University of Southern California, reported the results of their year-long study of absenteeism in two Los Angeles elementary schools. Analysis of their data showed that "absence rates were highest in the winter and usually greater on Monday and Friday than on other days of the week." They also found that ". . . in contrast, oxidant levels were lowest in the winter and usually higher in the middle of the week than on Monday and Friday." They concluded that "no evidence of statistically significant associations between absence rates and oxidant levels could be found." [10]

In their recent report, "Air Pollution and Health," the Royal College of Physicians of London noted that "the increasing mortality from bronchitis in men is more closely linked to increased cigarette smoking than to any greater exposure to urban air pollution." They went on to say that "there is no consistent excess of deaths from lung cancer in men especially exposed to polluted air in streets, as policemen, bus conductors or truck drivers." [11]

In 1969, D. D. Reid analyzed the circumstances related to the onset of bronchitis in children. He noted a higher mortality among pre-school children living in urban areas. In children of school age, however, the pattern was reversed and rural children had a higher rate of bronchitis mortality. Dr. Reid suggested a possible explanation. He believes that the rural pre-school child, living in small communities with fewer opportunities for contact, is less exposed to infection than the town child and, therefore, less likely to suffer serious respiratory disease. When the child first attends school, the crowding and greater opportunity for cross-infection, combined with a relative lack of immunity, place him at a disadvantage. This is reflected in higher bronchitis mortality rates. Semi-skilled and unskilled workers and their families tend to live in the large industrial cities and, as already noted, respiratory mortality is especially high among children of such families. The higher mortality rates in large cities may thus reflect the social class composition of their populations, rather than higher levels of pollution. These observations suggest that to attribute an urban excess of respiratory mortality solely to air pollution may be unjustified and that account must be taken of other factors, such as social class and the home environment.[12]

In England, Colley and Reid found a definite gradient for past history of bronchitis and cough, with lowest rates in rural areas, peaking to a maximum in the most heavily polluted areas.

These differences were most clearly seen among children of semi-skilled and unskilled workers. In South Wales, where levels of smoke and, therefore, particulate matter are relatively low, the respiratory morbidity rates were far in excess of those found in towns in England proper with comparable levels of pollution. Colley and Reid pointed out that there may be some special circumstances in South Wales unrelated to pollution that produced these high levels of illness.[13] Unfortunately, similar studies have not been done in the United States.

Whereas biological scientists have been unable to show a causal relationship between air pollutants, more properly the entire spectrum of air pollution, and disease, two economists appear to have bridged the gap. Lester Lave and Eugene Seskin sifted the literature dealing with air pollution and health, studied the reported data, and subjected it to multiple regression analysis. They concluded that "an objective observer would have to agree that there is an important association between air pollution and various morbidity and mortality rates." They also believed that the data showed that if air pollution levels in urban areas were reduced by 50 percent, the total sickness and death due to bronchitis would be reduced by 25 to 50 percent. As economists, they noted that savings in medical costs and lost earnings of $2 billion per year would result. A particularly damning item also comes from their analysis. They show that many of the investigations reported are not worth the time spent doing them. The rush to publish and get into newsprint appears more compelling than solid research. Poor research helps no one. It does confound many.[14]

There is an obvious gap between what we know and what we believe. Yet scare tactics in the press and on radio and television regularly exhort the community to greater vigor in combatting pollution lest horrible death or disease be our lot. This is unjustified. Some people demand quick action—any kind of action so long as something is done. While it is tempting to motivate people by appealing to their fear of illness and injury, Dixon has shown that such continuous pressure produces the opposite effect.[15]

In such an atmosphere even thoughtful people are misled and frightened, and feel that illness and death as the consequences of community air pollution are well-established facts. Of course, they must also wonder why, if this relationship is true, there is any delay in getting the clean-up job done.

A useful guide for all concerned citizens—air pollution researchers, administrators, clinicians, politicians, and laymen—is "Air Pollution Epidemiology," Dr. John R. Goldsmith's cogent critique of the air pollution morass. In this short but incisive essay, he indicts the concerned parties for attempting "to deal with a manageable part of the problem while ignoring the bulk of it." [16]

One would hope this article obtains wide circulation and consideration. Perhaps then many of the questions will get satisfactory answers and much of the murkiness and fuzzy thinking shrouding the subject will be dissipated.

In a recent article, M. A. Crenson of the Johns Hopkins University points out that just prior to World War II, the U. S. Bureau of Mines published sulfur dioxide values obtained in the period 1914–1939. Comparison with figures obtained in the 1960s, clearly shows that over the past forty years SO_2 has markedly declined. In some cities the SO_2 levels are a third to a fourth less than the prewar levels. Similar values were found for particulate matter. While Professor Crenson suggests air pollution requires serious attention, he wonders "whether it warrants a national crusade." He goes on to remark that "for a politician who wants to bring his constituency together (or who simply wants to get elected and stay elected) dirty air offers a relatively inoffensive means for arousing support." And he adds that

> it may be argued that much of the exaggeration which appears in national political discussions is merely "rhetoric." But it would be a mistake to assume that rhetoric doesn't count. The rhetorical commitments of high officials have a way of becoming the real commitments of lower officials, and political leaders have been known to convert themselves to a cause by the power of their own oratory. Verbal crusades easily become actual crusades. Unfortunately, our experience during the past half dozen years suggests that this nation can handle only so many crusades at one time.[17]

This fact notwithstanding, I would still urge the mounting of a vigorous campaign for development of a city-wide rapid transit system, preferably a subway, for the sprawling, automobile-infested Los Angeles area. This would unquestionably be the giant step toward major reductions in photochemical smog. I'd crusade for that.

References

1. L. Pearson and E. S. Skye, "Air Pollution Affects Patterns of Photosynthesis in *Parmelia sulcata,* a Corticolous Lichen," *Science* 148 (1965): 1600.

2. L. H. Weinstein and D. C. McCune, "Effects of Fluoride on Agriculture," *Air Pollution Control Association Journal* 21 (1971): 410.

3. Q. M. Myrvik and D. G. Evans, "Metabolic and Immunologic Activities of Alveolar Macrophages," *Archives of Environmental Health* 14 (1967): 92.

4. M. Corn and G. Burton, "The Irritant Potential of Pollutants in the Atmosphere," *Archives of Environmental Health* 14 (1967): 54.

5. S. W. Tromp, "Biometeorology and Asthma in Children" (Paper delivered at the 8th AMA Conference on Air Pollution, Los Angeles, California, March 2–4, 1966).

6. W. Winkelstein, "Air Pollution Respiratory Function Study" (Paper delivered at the 8th AMA Conference on Air Pollution, Los Angeles, California, March 2–4, 1966).

7. D. O. Anderson and B. G. Ferris, Jr., "Community Studies of the Health Effects of Air Pollution: A Critique," *Air Pollution Control Association Journal* 15 (1965): 587.

8. M. O. Amdur, "Respiratory Absorption Data: SO_2 Dose-Response Curves," *Archives of Environmental Health* 12 (1966): 729.

9. M. O. Amdur, "Aerosols Formed by Oxidation of Sulfur Dioxide: Review of Their Toxicology," *Archives of Environmental Health* 23 (1971): 459.

10. W. S. Wayne and P. F. Wehrle, "Oxidant Air Pollution and School Absenteeism," *Archives of Environmental Health* 19 (1969): 315.

11. *Air Pollution and Health: A Report for the Royal College of Physicians* (London: Pitman Medical and Scientific Publishing Company, 1970).

12. D. D. Reid, "The Beginnings of Bronchitis," *Proceedings of the Royal Society of Medicine* 52 (1969): 31.

13. J. R. T. Colley and D. D. Reid, "Urban and Social Origins of Childhood Bronchitis in England and Wales," *British Medical Journal* 2 (1970): 213.

14. Lester B. Lave and E. P. Seskin, "Air Pollution and Human Health," *Science* 169 (1970): 723.

15. J. P. Dixon and J. P. Lodge, "Air Conservation Report Reflects National Concern," *Science* 148 (1965): 1600.

16. J. R. Goldsmith, "Air Pollution Epidemiology: A Wicked Problem, an Informational Maze, and a Professional Responsibility," *Archives of Environmental Health* 18 (1969): 516.

17. M. A. Crenson, "Is Air Pollution Really a Threat?" *The Johns Hopkins Magazine,* December 1970, p. 23.

Suggested Reading

Urban Air Pollution: With Particular Reference to Motor Vehicles, Geneva: WHO Tech. Dept. Ser. no. 410, 1969.

Morgan, G. B.; Ozolins, G.; and Tabor, E. C. "Air Pollution Surveillance Systems." *Science* 70 (1970): 289.

Huess, J. M.; Nebel, G. L.; and Calucci, J. M. "National Air Quality Standards for Automotive Pollutants: A Critical Review." *Air Pollution Control Association Journal* 21 (1971): 535.

ACCIDENTS

*Popular opinion is the greatest lie
in the world.*

Thomas Carlyle

On a crisp September day in 1899, Mr. H. H. Bliss stepped from a trolley car in New York City and was struck down by a horseless carriage, thus becoming the first person to be killed by an automobile. Since that day, more than 1.5 million men, women, and children have been killed by motor vehicles. Somebody's home catches fire every fifty-seven seconds of the day and night. Literally millions of injuries, both fatal and non-fatal, occur each year in the home, at work, and at play. In 1971, 114,000 of our citizens died as a result of accidental injury. Today, accidents constitute a greater threat to the health of the community than do all communicable diseases combined; only heart disease, cancer, and stroke have higher annual death rates.

Our rapidly changing environment is the prime reason for these statistics. New scientific advances are being applied in industry, in agriculture, and in the home faster than ever before in history. Employing unfamiliar fuels, machinery, chemicals, and household paraphernalia creates new hazards. In industry, potential sources of accidents are constantly arising as a result of the introduction of new processes and materials (see Chapter 14), while in the home, new patterns of living engender new accident risks. Approximately thirty thousand accidental deaths in the home were recorded in 1970 and over twenty million disabling injuries occurred within and around the home. Table 17 indicates

TABLE 17.

Deaths by accident, all age groups, 1970.

Motor vehicle accidents	54,000
Home accidents	33,100
Work accidents	14,000
Fire and burns	8,600
Poisoning	2,400
Drowning	1,600
Total	113,700

the frequency and distribution of accidental deaths in the United States in 1970. Perhaps even more dramatic is the number of disabling accidental injuries that do not result in death. Exclusive of motor vehicle injuries, over forty-two million * injuries from all causes are reported each year. This means that just about one person in four can expect a disabling injury during the year.

This grim problem is not unique to the United States. In June 1967, for example, the Supreme Court of the Soviet Union ordered a legal crackdown on officials whose neglect of safety rules led to accidents in Soviet factories and farms.

In economic terms, sixty-eight thousand hospital personnel and fifty thousand hospital beds are needed each year to care for accident victims. Accidents cost the community approximately $15 billion a year in lost earnings and productivity, medical ex-

* In a world of large numbers, I fear that a figure such as forty-two million, rather than conjuring up the calamitous conditions now existing, will be shrugged off as just another large number. Forty-two million is equivalent to the population of Alabama, Arkansas, Arizona, California, Idaho, Montana, Nevada, Pennsylvania, and Wisconsin combined.

penses, property damage, and insurance overhead. Off-the-job accidents alone have been estimated to cost leading industries more than seven billion dollars a year.*

Accidents are usually measured in terms of the frequency and severity of injury and the cost of property damage or medical care or man-hours lost from work. Indices such as these are of practical value for insurance, engineering, and legal purposes. However, why a driver, for example, sustained a fractured skull is not the same question as why he drove his car into a tree. The question that is being asked more and more today is this: Do accidents occur by chance alone, or do they occur because we set up certain conditions? Are accidents accidental?

In common usage, the word *accident* is defined as a suddenly occurring, unplanned, unintentional event that leads to personal injury, death, or property damage. However, experts in this field say that less than 10 percent of all "accidents" are unplanned, unintentional, chance events. If this is true, then 90 percent of all accidents must be attributed to purposeful acts; that is, they are the result of acts of omission or commission on the part of some of the people involved. This puts the problem in a new light.

Americans put up with the nationwide slaughter on highways and with all manner of "accidental" injuries because they believe that accidents are fortuitous events—strokes of bad luck beyond one's control. In fact, it is being revealed time and again, as more accident research is conducted, that human failure is a component of most accidents. Human failure can manifest itself as inattention, distraction, haste, and preoccupation, which in turn are often related to anxiety, anger, fear, hate, frustration, and guilt.

At the University of Michigan, a study of ninety-six drivers involved in traffic accidents showed that 20 percent had been subject to emotional disturbance just prior to the event. Dr. Melvin J. Selzer, a psychiatrist at the university, said that most of the victims "had had violent quarrels, for the most part with women." Most accident researchers also agree that teenagers are particu

---

* How much is a billion dollars? If you had one billion dollars on the day Christ was born some two thousand years ago, and if you spent one thousand dollars every day from that time until the present, you would still have over two hundred million to spend.

larly prone to driving accidents. As both drivers and victims, teenagers have nearly twice the average rate of traffic fatalities. Another study at the University of Michigan found that teenage problem drivers drove to express a need for recognition, to vent antisocial urges, and to escape authority.

According to Professor Ross A. McFarland of Harvard University, accidents must be studied as a non-contagious mass disease of epidemic proportions; research, he believes, should concentrate on the interactions between the host (the individual), the agent (the object involved in the accident), and the environment. Accidents can be controlled only by analyzing their incidence in relation to complex causal factors throughout the environment, not just by searching for loose boards or faulty steering wheels.

There are five steps in the strategy used to attack any public health problem. These steps are as applicable to designing an attack on accidents as they are to attacks on diseases such as typhoid or smallpox:

1. Collection and analysis of data: place of accident, time, age of victim, sex, season of year, etc.

2. Examination of apparent relationships to discover possible causative factors.

3. Establishment of a hypothesis regarding causation and testing of the hypothesis under controlled conditions.

4. Development of control measures and testing to determine their effectiveness.

5. Incorporation into accident prevention programs of control measures which prove to be effective. To apply this methodology to a problem of national scope, nationwide collection of data is essential.

When accident reports from around the country are collected and analyzed, graphs such as Figure 63 can be constructed. Figure 63 shows that accidents are the leading cause of death for all age groups from one to thirty-four years of age. Among older people, the death rate from accidents is also quite high. Although some 10 percent of the national population is over sixty-five, more than 25 percent of all those who die in accidents are sixty-five or over. Older people are particularly prone to falling, and since

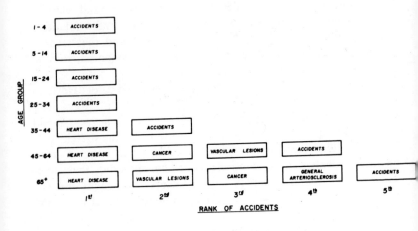

Figure 63. Accidental death.

their bones are less resilient than those of younger people, they often suffer serious fractures requiring long recuperative periods.

Tabulated data clearly point to the excessive risk of motor-vehicle deaths among males aged fifteen to twenty-four. Figure 64 shows death rates by age and sex. It is evident that a striking change in the pattern of motor vehicle death rates has occurred. Young people are definitely in the lead. This strongly suggests the need to probe more deeply into the underlying reasons for this correlation. The research at the University of Michigan mentioned above is a step in this direction.

The collected data also highlight the difference between the sexes. Up to age eighty-five, the accidental death rate is 2:1 in favor of men. Either men are at greater peril in our society or they are more susceptible to accidents than women. Between twenty and twenty-four years of age, the ratio climbs to 6:1.

It is now well documented that the motorcycle is the deadliest vehicle on the nation's highways. In 1970, some 2,400 cyclists were killed in the United States. According to data collected by the Federal Highway Administration, the 1970 motorcycle death rate is approximately six times greater than the motor vehicle (automobile, truck) death rate, on the basis of miles trav-

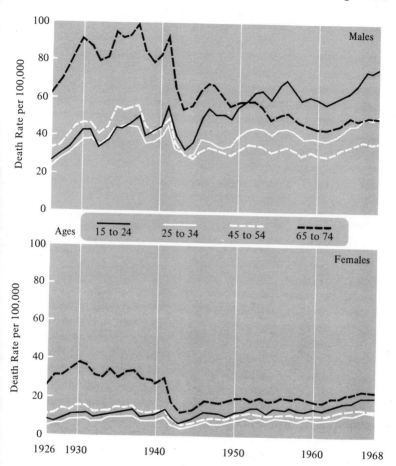

Figure 64. Death rates from motor vehicle accidents by selected age groups and sex in the United States 1926–1968. (By permission, Statistical Bulletin, *April 1971, Metropolitan Life Insurance Company.)*

eled. If calculated on the basis of number of motorcyclists, rather than miles, the risk to the motorcyclist is 20 times greater. Dr. Armand M. Nicholi, Jr., a psychiatrist at Harvard University, believes this rate is directly related to the motorcycle's symbolism:

"a powerful emotional prosthesis for the masculine self-image. It gives a sense of strength, of virility, or potency; of doing something and getting somewhere." Dr. Nicholi firmly believes these people need psychiatric care if motorcycle accidents are to be reduced.

The highest accidental death rates in the United States occurred in four Western states—Montana, Wyoming, Idaho, and Nevada—and two Southern states—Arkansas and Mississippi. These Western states also reported the highest rate of motor-vehicle fatalities. Among the causes for which the death rates were higher in these states than in the country as a whole were accidents involving firearms, aircraft, and drownings. Curiously enough, Alaska had the highest overall accidental-death rate and the highest rates for accidents involving aircraft, fire, explosions, firearms, and drownings.

Significant variation depending on the season of the year is also well documented. The peak accident months are June, July, November, and December. Increases in drownings occur in June and July, while sharp increases in motor vehicle accidents, falls, fires, and explosions occur in November and December. With this type of information, the emphasis of an accident control and prevention program can be modified as required.

What of environment as a variable? More than a quarter of all accidental deaths occur in the home. Farm work is a definite threat to safety; a third of all farm deaths are attributed to the misuse of farm machinery. The danger to life and limb in our homes and places of work is dramatized by the fact that during World War II the casualty lists (death and injury) for the armed forces of England averaged 8,126 per month for the six-year period 1939–1944. During this same period, there were 22,000 industrial casualties per month. The armed forces of the United States averaged 23,000 casualties a month during World War II, while industrial casualties averaged 161,000 during the same period.

On the basis of the collected data, experts suggest that there can be no simple solution to the accident prevention problem. Accidents result from the reaction of man to his environment. From moment to moment the accident susceptibility of individuals changes, depending upon poorly understood physical, physiological, and psychological factors. Man constantly moves from one environment to another: he leaves home, proceeds to a place of work, and engages in various recreational activities. The very environment in which he customarily moves changes, often imperceptibly, sometimes radically. Not only does it vary with the seasons and with the time of day or night; it is often changed by the actions of other people—skates left on a staircase, a cupboard door left open, competitive traffic, or faulty machinery. There is very little if any stability to any of these factors.

From Figure 65, it appears that fatalities from motor vehicle

Country	Average annual death rate per 100,000 1967–68	Average annual death rate per 100,000 1965–66	Percent change
United States	27.2	26.3	+3.4
Canada	26.4	26.4	0.0
New Zealand	20.0	20.9	−4.3
France	26.2	24.8	+5.6
Denmark	22.3*	21.3	+4.7
Australia	27.7	27.9	−0.7
Netherlands	22.7	20.6	+10.2
Finland	20.3	23.2	−12.5
Great Britain **	12.8	14.6	−12.3
West Germany ***	28.1	27.5	+2.2
Norway	12.6	11.7	+7.7
Italy	17.9	17.3	+3.5
Japan	15.6	15.1	+3.3

* 1967 only.
** Includes England and Wales, Northern Ireland, and Scotland.
*** Includes West Berlin.

Figure 65. Mortality from motor vehicle accidents, selected countries, 1967–68 compared with 1965–66.

accidents are not the same throughout the developed countries of the world. Some, such as Finland and Great Britain, have made major reductions in the rate, while in others the accident rate continues to grow. Perhaps by studying the methods employed in Finland and England we might obtain clues that could help reduce our own high rates.

As noted earlier, it is now believed that 10 to 15 percent of all "accidents" are solely fortuitous events to whose causation the victim made no contribution whatever. On the other hand, the remaining 85 to 90 percent appear to have been brought about by the victim himself.

A trailer truck, traveling at night, goes off the road and turns over in a riverbed. The accident report reads: "Driver asleep at the wheel."

An eight-year-old boy is struck down by a city bus. The accident report reads: "Ran in front of vehicle."

A lawyer, homeward bound from a late party, misses a turn and rams a culvert buttress. The accident report reads: "Driver inattention."

A garage worker pins another employee against a wall while testing a car. The accident report reads: "Shifted the wrong gear."

Let's look at the four accidents just cited. In the first one, further probing revealed that the dead driver, in order to earn more money to pay debts, had driven for three nights without sleep and was keeping awake on amphetamine. An autopsy on the eight-year-old boy disclosed a tumor that deprived him of sight on the side on which he was struck. The lawyer recalled that he had reached for the cigarette lighter in his new car and had turned out the headlights instead. The garage worker admitted that he had been under severe emotional stress after learning that his child was mentally retarded.

Researchers seeking to isolate all the tangled components that make up any single accident have suggested a useful tool: the accident syndrome. A syndrome is usually understood to be a group of related symptoms that together characterize a disease. The components of the accident syndrome as put forth by Schulzinger [1] are depicted in Figure 66.

The universal risk is considered a constant factor. From the day of his birth an individual lives in peril; anything, including death, can occur at any time. For the most part, the universal risk becomes part of the syndrome because of fear of injury. Many accidents are brought about because of a state of mind induced by knowledge that danger exists; the dread of an accident may well be a factor in its cause. A nervous, jumpy, nagging passenger may, for example, upset an otherwise reliable driver to the point

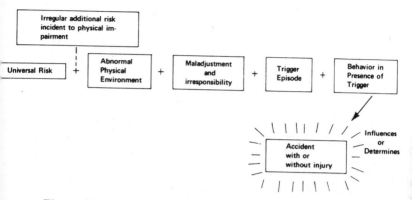

Figure 66. The accident syndrome. (From Schulzinger, M. S., The Accident Syndrome, 1956. Courtesy of Charles C. Thomas, Publisher, Springfield, Illinois.)

where he has an accident, when ordinarily no accident would have occurred.

Irregular additional risk is set above the other components of the syndrome as it does not have to enter into the equation. It can enter the syndrome as an individual's physical defect or handicap. The fact that a person is a diabetic, which would be an irregular additional risk, would enter the syndrome only if insulin deficiency initiated a series of metabolic events resulting in coma. Similarly, epilepsy and cardiovascular disease can increase the risk of accident. However, many physically handicapped persons compensate for impairments and may in fact have fewer accidents than people without handicaps.

In the May 1967 issue of the *British Medical Journal,* an English physician reported that about 9 percent of all automobile drivers studied had some form of disability. Among the disabilities found were eye defects, coronary conditions, epilepsy, and severe hypertension.[2]

Not so obvious are those without "true" handicaps. An individual of 6′3″ or over does not have the line of vision needed for ready observation of overhead traffic lights. In many automobiles, windshields are tinted more heavily at the top; this restricts the vision of very tall people at night. On the other end of the scale, short people have difficulty reaching automobile pedals. Individuals at the extremes in stature also have difficulty with doorways, furniture, machinery, tools, and household appliances.

Abnormal physical environment, the third factor in the syndrome, is not at all sharply defined. Nevertheless, certain points can be noted. Extremes in weather, such as heavy downpours, can obstruct vision and make conditions ripe for skidding. Poor ventilation, upsetting odors, sudden startling noises, and excessively hot weather, as well as sustained periods of cloudiness and rain, may contribute to accidents.

Although abnormal physical environment remains hard to pin down, it is clear that maladjustment and irresponsibility, which lead to the blunting of good judgment, are at the core of the accident syndrome. The main psychological or physiological elements that sharply increase the probability of accidents in maladjusted persons are anxiety, fear, hostility, worry, fatigue, frustration, and a host of other states resulting from pressure in the home, on the job, and in the community. Some 250 factors contributing to the blunting of good judgment and hence to accidents have been suggested. Experts in accident prevention look to this area as the most promising for reducing accidents. Mechanical devices and educational programs appear to be achieving less and less.

The most readily observable portion of the syndrome is the "trigger episode"—the nail that is stepped on, the blown tire, the fire, and the bullet entering the body. To students of accident prevention, this is the least important part of the syndrome, since the prospective victim will almost invariably reach some accident trigger. The maladjusted person ready for an "accident" may find his trigger anywhere: at home, at work, on the street. The trigger is only the detonator of a far more powerful cause or combination of causes. Consider for a moment how you would appraise a blown tire in the light of the syndrome theory. Check your ideas with Figure 66.

A particularly important aspect of the syndrome is the individual's behavior in the presence of the trigger. An individual's pattern of behavior when confronted with a sudden decision or with danger will frequently determine whether the forces set in motion will result in a near miss or an "accident." In addition, behavior may affect the severity of the accident. For example, if clothing is ignited, one person may try to smother the flames by wrapping himself in a coat or blanket. Another person, in stark panic, may run aimlessly, and as a result may die or suffer severe injury. Behavior in such a case is determined, at least in part, not by the immediate situation, but by long previous adjustment—one's life situation—that paves the way for disastrous mishaps or survival. Perhaps in Figure 66 this factor should be related directly to maladjustment rather than linked to the trigger episode.

Even if all the factors making up the syndrome are present, it does not follow that an accident with or without injury is inevitable. In the main, however, it does occur. Viewed in this manner, accidents appear to be set in motion by a constellation of events. And it may well be that this type of theorizing offers means to break the links at various points in the accident chain. The accident syndrome theory may be a tool that will lead to significant reductions in "accidents."

Accidents are the primary threat to the life and safety of children. Each year about fifteen thousand boys and girls under the age of fifteen die as a result of accidents. About seventeen million, or one in three, are injured each year. Although most of those accidents are not fatal, many children are maimed for life. The suffering, the schooldays lost, and the expenses involved are never reflected in the statistics; perhaps they should be.

In the one-to-four age group, motor vehicles are the chief cause of accidents. In most of these accidents, children are run over in driveways and streets. Drownings account for another large number of deaths, and, curiously enough, do not always occur at the beach or in pools. Many children, left unattended, drown at home or close to home in fishponds, cesspools, wells, creeks, and brooks.

Surprisingly, it is now a well-documented fact that injury rates among children are highest for those whose parents are college graduates. Could it be that college graduates (particularly mothers and teachers) give children credit for having better judgment than they actually possess?

Over half of the non-fatal accidents to children under fifteen occur at home. The part of the body most frequently injured is the head, in contradiction to the statement often made by parents that hands and arms are most frequently injured.

As in the case of the infectious diseases that affect a community, the occurrence of accidents in a specific portion of a population involves important, though at present poorly understood, interrelationships between host, agent, and environment. An analysis of the causes of childhood accidents can be attempted by studying the interrelationships between the host (the child), the agent (the tool or instrument involved), and the environment (the external circumstances). From the physician's point of view, the injured child is of primary concern, whereas to the epidemiologist the number of accidents, their time and place of occurrence, and the possible relationship of these events to the group at risk are of greater concern. These may lead him to an understanding of the cause of an accident and ultimately to means for prevention and control.

A particularly fruitful area of study may be the narrowly averted accident. It might reveal "carriers" of accidents. Reports from time to time have hinted that there may be children who involve others in dangerous games or activities. While these human infectors manage quite well to avoid harm to themselves, they appear to involve their playmates in accidents resulting in injuries or narrow misses. A good example of this type of child was reported from England, where "last across the road" was a popular pastime. In this game, the bigger, more agile child ran across a road or street in front of oncoming traffic; of course the smaller, less agile children were often caught in the path of onrushing cars. Concerted instruction in the schools has all but eliminated this "game."

Everyone is familiar with the child who shouts "I dare you do it," and the children who take the dare and all too often wind up with an injury. The absentminded child who injures himself or others through lack of awareness of his surroundings is also well known. What is not well known is why he does this. Investigations of the individual's personality problem may be a means of controlling these types of induced accidents.

From the collection and interpretation of epidemiological data it has been learned that accidents are the leading cause of death in people up to age thirty-four. In childhood, mortality from accidents is highest at the preschool age, lowest among grade school children, and higher among adolescents. The fifteen-to-twenty-five age group is the greatest contributor to accidents with motor vehicles. These facts suggest where control and prevention programs might best be directed, given (as is too often the case) a limited budget.

Because of its unique culture, climate, geography, and general environment, each country must study its own population to ascertain its peculiar accident patterns. Perhaps then "accidents will happen" less frequently.

Alcohol has a profound effect on behavior. It also has a major impact on traffic deaths. Postmortem examinations of fatally injured drivers show that some 60 percent of them had alcohol levels of more than .05 percent in the bloodstream; some 35 to 40 percent of the victims had alcohol levels of more than .15 percent.

In New Jersey, recent tests conducted under the state's Alcohol Determination Program showed that for four successive years more than 50 percent of drivers killed had an alcohol content in their blood of .15 percent or higher. A 150-pound man who drinks an ounce of whiskey or a bottle of beer will have a blood-alcohol concentration of .02 percent. The same individual will have a concentration of .15 percent after consuming ten ounces of eighty-proof liquor; this concentration is sufficient to cause loss of balance, emotional instability, and a slowing of responses to external stimuli.

Studies conducted over the past ten years clearly indicate that alcohol is not only a very significant contributor to fatal auto accidents, but also increases the risk of all types of accidents, particularly in the home. As yet, researchers are not certain why drivers drink so much. It may be a response to generalized pressure in society generated by our faster-paced way of living, or it may be that the drunk drivers are pathological drinkers. Before prevention programs can be instituted, however, these alternatives will need a great deal of additional study.

Although the riddle of alcohol and accidents may not be solved in the near future, safer car design and road engineering may help reduce motor vehicle injuries and fatalities.

Speed is not necessarily a major factor in collisions: most collisions occur in fair weather, on good roads, within twenty-five miles of the driver's home, at speeds less than fifty miles an hour.

On our overcrowded thoroughfares, driving is an intricate task. How well are we naturally equipped with vision, hearing, judgment, and quick response to stimuli? Given the complexity of several simultaneous, split-second circumstances that converge to cause an accident (rain, inattention, fatigue, drunkenness, foot placed on accelerator instead of brake pedal, etc.) what chance does a driver have? If, as has been assumed, accidents cannot be eliminated, it may be necessary to design cars with the express purpose of minimizing injury in the event of a collision. Although there will never be a fully crashproof car, surely a vehicle can be designed so that in a collision its occupants will not be hurled about by the sudden deceleration.

A major area of current research is the "second collision": the impact of a passenger against the interior of his vehicle after its collision with an exterior object. Milliseconds after a vehicle comes to a crash halt, there is a collision between the passengers and the inside of the car. If a passenger is not restrained by a seat belt or harness, he will be hurled upward and forward toward the point of impact with tremendous force. It has been calculated that at the moment of impact, a 175-pound man in a car traveling 50 mph will be hurled against the front of the car with a force of almost four tons.

The concept of the second collision goes back to a chance observation by Hugh De Haven, who had been a Canadian aviation cadet during World War I. De Haven, the sole survivor of a two-plane collision, rejected the notion that good luck alone saved him. Studying the problems of accident-induced injury, he noticed that such unlikely items as clotheslines saved people who fell from great heights. He was one of the first to show that seat belts could greatly reduce injuries from the second collision. (Pilots in World War I used seat belts, but unhooked them when crashing seemed imminent; they believed the belts would cut them in two.)

At the Institute of Transportation and Traffic Engineering (University of California, Los Angeles) studies are underway to ascertain the effects of impact on vehicle and passengers, as a prelude to improved vehicle design.

Figure 67 shows the result of a head-on collision of two school buses of different design. Using dummies to simulate school-children, the type and extent of injury can be determined. The complete accident is filmed by strategically placed motion picture cameras; the film is used to study the impact and its results. From Figure 67, it is obvious that a 1944 model bus with a front-mounted engine protected the children far better than one with a rear-mounted engine. Additional studies at the Institute of Transportation and Traffic Engineering deal with the measurement of

Figure 67. Experimental collision. On the left is a 1965 school bus with thirty-six occupants; on the right is a 1944 school bus. Each was traveling at thirty miles per hour at the moment of the head-on collision. (Photo courtesy of the University of California.)

collision impact forces on passengers and with finding new ways to design the interior of vehicles in order to limit injury. Studies such as these should go a long way toward reducing collision injuries and fatalities.

A completely different approach to solving the motor-vehicle accident problem is concerned with human behavior and employs electronic driving simulators in a newly created Public Health Service laboratory in Rhode Island. The new laboratory, the first of its kind in the country, is devoted to the study of behavior patterns that may relate to accidents.

The electronic simulators create the illusion of actually driving a car. Each simulator has the usual driving controls, so that a subject seated in an actual car can react just as he would in his own car to various driving situations programmed on analog computers and presented to him on a huge television screen.

Figure 68 shows a twelve-by-eighteen-foot model of a portion of Akron, Ohio. Because of the angle of the lens on the

Figure 68. Model of a portion of Akron, Ohio and an electronic TV camera.

Figure 69. *TV camera focusing on a point in the Akron model.*

camera, it appears to the driver that he is looking across the replica and not down on it. As he presses the accelerator, electronic impulses move the camera forward over the "road." Figure 69 is a close-up view of the TV camera suspended above a point on the road.

With the aid of the simulators, research can be undertaken that would not be feasible on the highway. Drivers can be exposed to the most hazardous conditions, an accurate record of their responses can be compiled, driver behavior in many different situations can be observed, and many different drivers can be observed in an identical situation.

Figure 70 shows the test system developed by Liberty Mutual Insurance Company. Its decelerator test sled and human-like dummy can simulate crash effects on a passenger with and without seat belt.

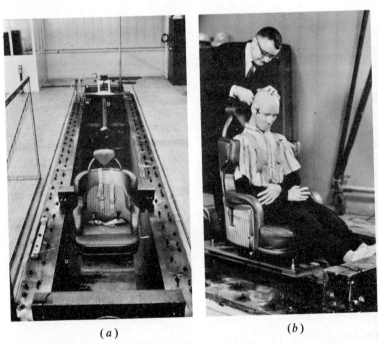

(a)   (b)

Figure 70. A driver testing system. (a) the decelerator test sled; (b) the dummy used to study effects of deceleration. (Photos courtesy of Liberty Mutual Insurance Company.)

If a disease threatened every tenth person in this country (particularly our young people) with illness or death, there would undoubtedly be a tremendous popular outcry to check the havoc. Tuberculosis, poliomyelitis, cancer, and heart disease have provoked such a public response. As a consequence, the incidence of several of these diseases has been reduced, and others are being intensively studied. Yet the epidemic on the highways, which has taken over 1.5 million lives, permanently crippled four million people, and cost ninety billion dollars in property damages, continues unabated. Why is this? Why don't people seem to care about death and injury resulting from accidents?

Some people may spend a great deal of time and effort agitating against an elusive hazard such as fluoridation of water supplies, but give no thought to the proven daily slaughter on our highways. Did you ever hear anyone asking an automobile dealer or manufacturer for a guarantee of safety before purchase? Consider this: someone eagerly pays three to six thousand dollars for a car, without so much as a comment about its safety, yet the same person demands a guarantee of safety each time he purchases a twenty-five-cent loaf of bread. Why this inconsistency? Perhaps research in this area will uncover information that will lead to greater safety in our lives.

Another area that needs more research is how the strictness of law enforcement and the type of penalties levied affect the accident rate, particularly multiple offenses by individual drivers. A recent study by Stanley Schuman of the University of Michigan has shown that a one-time reprimand is an exercise in futility.

Dr. Schuman and a team of researchers reported on the reduction of young driver crashes among students in a Michigan high school. An attempt was made to develop a program of preventive rather than remedial countermeasures to reduce accident rates. With the aid of a school system in the greater Detroit area, a "booster" program was developed. Nineteen students, sixteen male and three female, were randomly selected for experimental treatment. A control group of students (compared as to sex, age, grades in school, and number of previous accidents and violations) was also established.

The "experimental" or treatment group participated in a series of seven two-hour sessions over a seven-week period. The objective was to provide an open, informal setting for discussion of actual road experiences, diagnosis of components of accidental situations, and understanding of the stages of decision-making behind the wheel that occur either consciously or unconsciously, deliberately or impulsively, depending on the maturity of the driver. Reinforcement of this initial counter-measure took the form of personal letters to each of the participants (in the experimental group only) six and twelve months after the workshop. These letters either congratulated the student for having maintained an accident-free record, or expressed mild concern if an accident had occurred. At the end of six months, the investigators found no difference between experimental and control groups. After that, a significant reduction in accident rates was observed in the experimental group. Dr. Schuman and his colleagues believe that time is required for this treatment to take effect. They also point out the ineffectiveness of a "single" hearing type of program.[3]

The numbers in this study were, of course, too small to allow generalizations to be made. We need additional studies by investigators in a number of states using this and other treatment counter-measures. Perhaps then a suitable, widely applicable means of reducing second offenses can be adopted.

The yearly death toll from motor vehicle accidents is appalling. Even worse, it has become a fact of life that apparently is acceptable to most people. Table 18 compares the number of motor vehicle deaths and deaths of United States military personnel in Vietnam. The yearly figures have been over fifty thousand for the past six years. In the face of such carnage, it is difficult to comprehend how great numbers of people can become incensed over the loss of life in Vietnam, yet remain silent about death on our streets and highways.

Is it that most people do not (will not?) see that they alone can solve this problem? Certainly, automobiles and highways can be redesigned, but personal responsibility will always be the determining factor. And perhaps we are not yet willing to accept it.

Having participated in a number of "Earth Day" and Environmental Week activities at schools around the country, I have seen the complete lack of attention concerned environmentalists give to accidents, especially motor vehicle accidents. The reason for this continues to elude me. It has been suggested that the high

TABLE 18.

Comparison of number of motor vehicle deaths and Vietnam deaths.

	Motor vehicle deaths	Vietnam deaths
1971	55,100	1,350*
1970	54,800	4,221
1969	56,000	9,414
1968	55,110	14,592
1967	52,900	9,378
1966	53,000	5,008
1965	49,000	1,369
1964	47,000	147
TOTAL	423,670	45,479

* As of November 21.

accident rate is a problem for which those in the 15-25 age group must be responsible. Here is a major environmental problem on which young people can take direct action. It deserves their consideration.

References

1. Morris Schulzinger, *The Accident Syndrome* (Springfield, Illinois: Charles C. Thomas, 1956).
2. Rees Dewi, "Physical and Mental Disabilities of 1,190 Ordinary Motorists," *British Medical Journal* 1 (1967): 593.
3. Stanley H. Schuman, R. McConochie, and D. C. Pelz, "Reduction of Young Driver Crashes in a Controlled Pilot Study," *Journal of the American Medical Association* 218 (1971): 233.

Suggested Reading

Taggart, P., and Gibbons, D. "The Motor Car and the Normal and Abnormal Heart." *Triangle, Sandoz Journal of Medical Science* 10 (1971): 63.

NOISE

*Humanity either makes, or breeds, or tolerates all its af-
flictions, great or small.*

H. G. Wells

On April 21, 1966, Theodore Kupferman, representative
from Manhattan's Seventeenth Congressional District, rose in the
House of Representatives to address his colleagues. As he spoke, it
became obvious that an insidious environmental problem created by
modern technology had inspired a champion who would assume responsibility for the political action necessary for its control and
prevention. He said: "Another serious environmental problem
which demands our immediate attention is that of excessive noise.
I call it 'noise pollution.' Accordingly, I have introduced a comprehensive bill to provide for a study of the complex noise situation in the United States with a view toward finding ways and
means of eliminating unnecessary noise in general on the inhabitants of our cities and towns." [1] With these words, political
involvement was initiated: community pressure had seen to that.

It has been argued that because noise produces no dramatic ill effects that we are yet aware of, the public has been largely uninterested in its suppression. It may be more to the point to say that the degree of annoyance and discomfort that people will endure is astonishing.

Although some amount of noise is a necessary and probably unpreventable adjunct of our machine civilization, it would appear that unless some definite steps are taken to reduce the present inordinate levels in industry and in the community generally, more and more people may become auditory cripples.

Fortunately, in the past few years large segments of the population have expressed an increasing determination to revolt against noise. A measure of this resentment is seen in the number of articles on the subject that regularly appear in newspapers and popular magazines. In New York City, one of the most cacophonous of cities, concerned citizens have banded together to assure that their voices are heard above the din. In fact, Citizens for a Quieter City, Inc., was the motivating force behind Congressman Kupferman. KEEP NEW YORK PLASTERED: To the uninitiated, these clever signs in buses and subway trains may at first appear to support wholesale inebriation. They really show that New Yorkers are opting for thick plaster walls as a means of reducing noise levels in multi-unit dwellings, instead of the currently employed thin sheetrock.

Ramazzini mentioned the deafness of coppersmiths in his book *Diseases of Workmen,* published in 1700 (see Chapter 13), and some hundred years ago isolated references were made to the hearing losses among blacksmiths and, later, boilermakers. But the range of adverse effects of noise has only recently become known.

During the past twenty-five years, the increasing mechanization and industrialization of our society has sharply increased the frequency and magnitude of noise-induced hearing loss, and this problem has come to the attention of the medical profession, industrial leaders, governmental agencies, labor unions, and workmen's compensation boards. Past lack of interest was due in part to the absence of accurate means of measuring noise and hearing loss.

The magnitude of the problem may be inferred from the

fact that conservative estimates place the number of Americans who need hearing aids at eight to ten million; the rate of hearing-aid use in urban communities is believed to be about seven per one thousand people. Estimates place at 170,000 the number of men between fifty and fifty-nine who are eligible for workmen's compensation because of hearing impairment. Industrial surveys have shown that 20 percent of the people who are given hearing tests for employment have hearing losses; factory workers appear to have double the rate of hearing loss of office workers in comparable age groups. Because there is a loss in hearing acuity associated with the process of aging, it is often difficult to distinguish between noise-induced hearing loss and natural loss. In addition, men and women differ in the ability to hear. Generally, women have better and less variable hearing than men of the same age. The major break in the audibility curves of men occurs at about age thirty-two; in women it occurs about five years later.

While it is well known that sudden, severe exposure to loud noise can cause deafness, it is the insidious loss of hearing caused by chronic, long-term exposure to critical noise levels in industry and the community that needs extensive investigation.

We can define noise in terms of particle displacement, variations in pressure, and particle velocity in an elastic medium, or we can accept the concept advanced by the British Committee on the Problems of Noise, which with characteristic British pithiness defined noise as "unwanted sound." It has also been defined as any sound regarded as a nuisance. While wholly satisfactory, these latter definitions share a measure of subjectivity: that is, different people are annoyed by different sounds, depending upon individual thresholds. To some people, even certain weak sounds may be offensive. Generally, however, nuisance increases with frequency and pitch.

Sound (noise) in industry, in the home, or in traffic is a by-product of the conversion of energy. No process using power is completely efficient; some energy is inevitably wasted. Most of this is converted into heat; but some is converted into sound, as when surfaces vibrate or turbulence is set up in air. All noise sources send out sound waves, which vibrate at various frequencies. The number of vibrations per second—the number of times per second that the sound waves emitted exert a pulsating pressure (sound pressure) on the ear—is the frequency of the sound, usually described in cycles per second (cps) or Hertz (Hz) or vibrations per second (vps).

A cannon shot roars out its sound waves, while the drop of a pin is hardly audible. Thus, sound is also characterized by its pitch, its degree of highness or lowness. Low pitch implies a slower rate of vibration, or fewer cycles per second, than high pitch, in which the same type of pulses strike the ear more often each second. Thus, although pitch depends in part upon the frequency of the sound stimulus, it is primarily a function of the amplitude or depth of the sound wave.

Another essential characteristic of sound as it affects the perception of noise is loudness or intensity. Loudness is a sensation that is decided by the nerve stimulus that reaches the brain. It is a highly subjective perception. Each person experiences his own degree of loudness because the stimulus received depends on the intensity of the sound energy reaching the nerve and the sensitivity of the nerve. Here again, wide ranges of individual difference are found. The human ear can translate sound between approximately twenty and two thousand cycles per second into nerve impulses. This means that the ears of healthy young adults are sensitive to a wide range of frequencies. For the most part, our ears are most sensitive to the range of 500 to 4,000 cps, which includes conversational speech.

The range of a piano may help to give an idea of the frequencies of the various sounds. The keys range from the lowest note, A_0, which emits pulses that vibrate at the rate of 27.5 cycles per second, through middle C, with a frequency of 286 cps, to the highest note, C_8, which generates 4,186 cps. Men's voices range from the lowest basso, at 80 cps, to tenor, producing sounds at 300 cps—just above middle C. It is not uncommon for sopranos to reach 850 cps. Some few trained voices have been known to exceed this.

Few, if any, people can hear sounds above 20,000 cps. In these regions the ears of animals are particularly keen. "Silent" dog whistles are silent to human ears only because they emit vibrations with frequencies well above twenty thousand, to which dogs readily respond.

The ear is least sensitive at the low frequencies. For example, its sensitivity to a tone of 100 cps is only 1/1,000th that to one at 1,000 cps. Von Békésy points out that this is a physical necessity. If it were not so, we would hear all the vibrations of our own bodies. He notes that "the ear is just insensitive enough to low frequencies to avoid the disturbing effect of noises produced by muscles, bodily movements, etc. If it were any more sensitive to these frequencies than it is, we would hear the vibrations of the head that are produced by the shock of every step we take when walking."

"What noise annoys an oyster?" Although no adequate way to measure the annoyance level of noise has been devised, we know that the annoyance level is often directly related to loudness. Studies have found that loud sounds are more annoying than those that are of similar character but not as loud. To ascertain loudness level and to determine whether a noise is a potential hazard to the hearing mechanism, an accurate sound measuring system must be employed. Several general types are available.

For preliminary screening of a site for possible hazards, the sound-survey meter, as seen in Figure 71, is appropriate, although a number of other instruments are commercially available. This meter is well suited for measuring noise levels in manufacturing plants as a means of locating areas where the possibility of hearing damage exists. It is often used by architects, planners, and engineers to study possible sites for schools, hospitals, office buildings, and express highways in relation to existing housing. Sound-survey meters are small, simple, and relatively inexpensive. For more precise measurements, a sound-level meter (Figure 72) is generally employed. This unit is more sensitive and far more accurate than its smaller counterpart, and it too is available in a variety of models and accessories.

Recall that sound is a transmission of energy in the form of vibrations that constitute variations in pressure of air, liquid, or solid media. Acoustical instruments for measuring variations in sound pressures are usually calibrated in dB, decibels.

The magnitude of these pressures is relatively small and is measured in dynes per square centimeter. The standard reference level used in measuring sound levels in decibels is equivalent to a sound pressure of 0.0002 dynes/cm². This is close to the faintest sound (the threshold) that can be heard by a healthy

Figure 71. A simple sound-survey meter.

young adult in a quiet location, and is equal to zero decibels.
The decibel is a dimensionless unit. It simply expresses a ratio
between two sound intensities: the reference pressure * and the
source being measured, whether it is a pneumatic hammer, a
speech, a food blender, or a subway train.

Between the threshold of hearing, the lowest pressure to
which the human ear responds, and the greatest intensity that the

---

* Often the term *microbar* (μ bar) is used as the reference, one microbar being equal to 1 dyne/cm².

Figure 72. Precision-type sound-level meter.

ear can interpret as sound but not as pain, the average individual can distinguish about 130 steps in intensity. In other words, the range of hearing covers approximately 130 decibels. Figure 73 lists some commonly encountered sound-pressure levels.

The number of decibels, while indicative of the sound level, tells nothing about the frequency distribution of the component frequencies. Deafness, whether temporary or permanent, is better correlated with frequencies than with overall intensities. While overall noise levels can indicate the need for noise reduction or control, they provide no information about the particular frequencies that are causing the noise problem. Most noises in our urban communities are complex, since the noise emanating

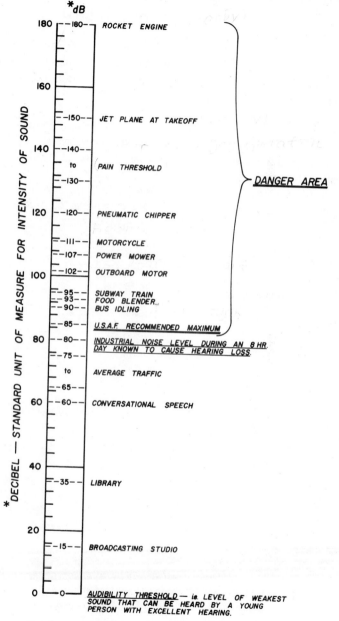

Figure 73. Noise levels in urban communities.

from a single source is usually composed of sounds of many frequencies, varying in intensity.

The response of the human ear to a certain sound pressure depends upon the frequency of the sound. While sensitivity is greatest between 500 and 4,000 Hz (cps), it falls off for both lower and higher frequencies.

When adolescents with good hearing are tested, a characteristic profile of the efficiency of hearing at several frequencies is obtained. This is portrayed in Figure 74. The curve shows that at low frequencies the sound-pressure level must be relatively high before the tone can be heard. By contrast, tones in the range 200–10,000 cps can be heard even though the levels are very low. This variation in hearing acuity depending on frequency is

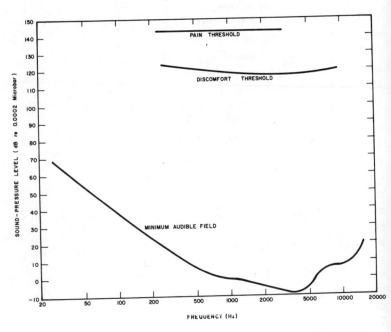

Figure 74. Thresholds of hearing and tolerance. MAF is the minimum audible field. [*From* Handbook of Noise Measurement (*West Concord, Massachusetts: General Radio Company*).]

one of the reasons it is essential to know the frequency rather than the overall noise level if a noise problem is to be dealt with intelligently. For example, a value of 90 dB was obtained near a steel-rolling machine. Analyses of the frequencies involved showed that the greatest intensity was in the low range—where the ear is least sensitive. The intensity was 81 dB, almost ten times less, in the higher ranges, where the ear is more sensitive.

To resolve the spectrum of frequencies of a sound, a frequency analyzer must be used. For the most part, an octave-band analyzer is employed. Octave bands are arbitrary spreads of frequencies in which the upper limit is twice the lower. Generally, the bands chosen are 20–75, 75–150, 150–300, 300–600, 600–1,200, 1,200–2,400, 2,400–4,800, and beyond 4,800. With both the sound-level meter and the octave-band analyzer, readings should be taken at several points in and around the area being studied and, if for an industrial machine, as near to the ear of the operator as practically feasible.

When sound waves reach the outer ear, they initiate vibrations in the eardrum—the tympanic membrane, which can be seen in Figure 75. These vibrations are transmitted to three ossicles, the bones of the middle ear: the hammer (malleus), anvil (incus), and stirrup (stapes). Figures 76 and 77 show the relation of these three to the tympanic membrane. From the position and shape of the bones, it is not difficult to understand how they transmit vibrations to the inner ear.

The stirrup, a tiny bone weighing approximately 1/30,000 of an ounce, drives the perilymph (fluid) of the cochlea back and forth, piston-fashion, according to the rhythm of the vibrating sound pressure. These movements of the stirrup, and particularly of its footplate, magnify the original vibrations some twenty times and initiate vibrations in the basilar membrane,* which in turn transmits the vibrations to the haircells of the organ of Corti, within the cochlea; the endings of both branches of the auditory nerve are also contained within the spiral cochlea (see Figure 77). Here, mechanical motion is converted to nerve impulses. These impulses, carried by the auditory nerve to the brain, are

---

* Because of its filtering and analytical functions the basilar membrane is of interest in hearing research. Since it is embedded in the skull, however, direct study is extremely difficult.

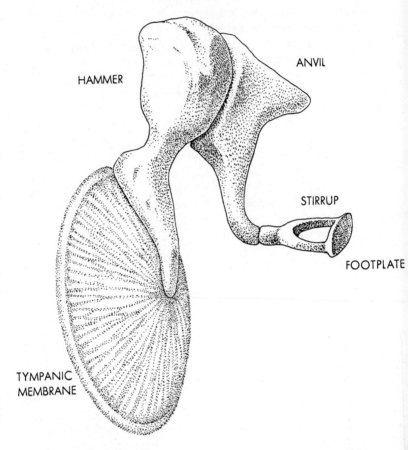

Figure 75. The middle ear. (Source: Georg von Békésy,
"The Ear," Scientific American, August 1957.)

then perceived as sound. It is in the inner ear that the vestibular
and cochlear branches of the acoustic nerve receive their signals, and it is within the cochlea that translations of sounds are
made. If the translations are muddled or weak, the acoustic nerve
obtains and transmits faulty impulses to the brain. This is manifested in some degree of hearing loss.

It may be concluded, therefore, that noise-induced hearing

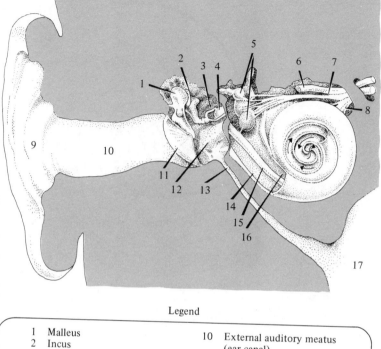

Legend

1	Malleus	10	External auditory meatus (ear canal)
2	Incus	11	Ear drum (tympanic membrane)
3	Crura of stapes		
4	Footplate of stapes in oval window	12	Promontory
		13	Eustachian tube
5	Semicircular canals, utricle, and saccule		Cochlea
			14 Scala tympani
6	Cochlear nerve		15 Cochlear duct containing organ of Corti
7	Vestibular nerve		16 Scala vestibuli
8	Facial nerve	17	Pharynx
9	Pinna		

Figure 76. Pathways of sound reception.

loss is due not only to ill effects on the eardrum, as so many erroneously believe, but also to damage to the internal ear—to the cochlea, the organ of Corti, and the acoustic nerves.

Incidentally, the eardrum is not the only avenue by which we hear. Sound energy can be carried to the inner ear by way of

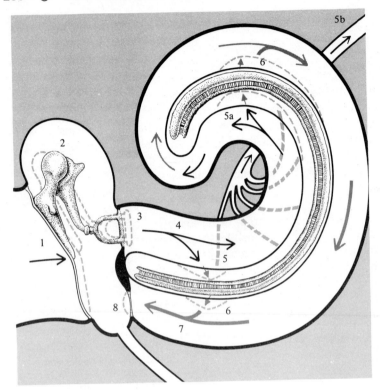

Legend

1 Sound waves impinge on ear drum, causing it to vibrate. 2 Ossicles vibrate as a unit. 3 Stapes moves in and out of oval window. 4 Sound waves transmitted up scala vestibuli in medium of its contained peri- lymph. 5 Short waves (high frequency, high pitch) act at base of cochlea. 5a Long waves (low frequency, low pitch) act at apex of cochlea. All waves act by distorting Reissner's membrane and basilar membrane of cochlear duct and its contained organ of Corti, thus stim- ulating hair cells which are in contact with the tectorial membrane. 5b Impulses then pass up cochlear nerve. 6 Wave transmitted across cochlear duct in medium of endolymph, from scala vestibuli to scala tympani. (Note: waves may also travel around helicotrema at apex of cochlea.) 7 Waves descend scala tympani in medium of its contained perilymph. 8 Impact of wave on membrane of round window causes it to move in and out at round window in opposite phase to oval window.

Figure 77. Transmission of vibrations from drum through the cochlea.

the bones of the skull. The sounds we hear when we click our teeth or move the tongue around the mouth come through the skull. Much of the sound we receive when the ears are plugged or covered also comes in this way. This distinction is an aid in diagnosing deafness. Von Békésy noted that "if a person can hear bone-conducted sounds but is comparatively deaf to airborne sounds, we know that the trouble lies in the middle ear. But if he hears no sound by bone conduction, then his auditory nerves are gone and there is no cure for his deafness. This is an old test long used by deaf musicians. If a violin player cannot hear his violin even when he touches his teeth to the vibrating instrument, then he knows he suffers from nerve deafness, and there is no cure."

Deafness is far from being solely of occupational origin. Any diagnosis of occupational deafness must first rule out the possibility of loss of hearing accompanying advancing age. Sensory presbycusis, one form of the natural aging process, is characterized by hearing losses in the high-frequency ranges. Other forms produce losses of hearing in all frequency ranges, as evidenced by flat audiometric curves. (This point will be discussed further on.) Thus, it is difficult to prove that a case of deafness is solely of occupational origin. In addition, tumors, infections, or blows on the head can also produce loss of hearing. In fact, before World War II, ear infections were the leading cause of deafness. Figure 78 shows two relatively simple tests used to determine types of hearing loss.

Progressive noise-induced deafness is known to occur through continuous exposure to sound levels above 80 dB over an eight-hour day. Exposure to excessive noise is initially seen as a temporary threshold shift (TTS), which is the difference between the post-exposure threshold and the pre-exposure threshold.

Accumulating evidence indicates that levels of noise below 75 dB are not dangerous. Levels about 80 to 85 dB in the frequency range of 1,200 to 4,800 cps, however, seem to be unsafe. In fact, as noise-induced deafness progresses, the ability to hear the high-pitched sounds of speech is lost first. The most common complaint of people with noise-induced deafness is "I can hear, but I don't understand." The first sounds to be lost by the nerve-

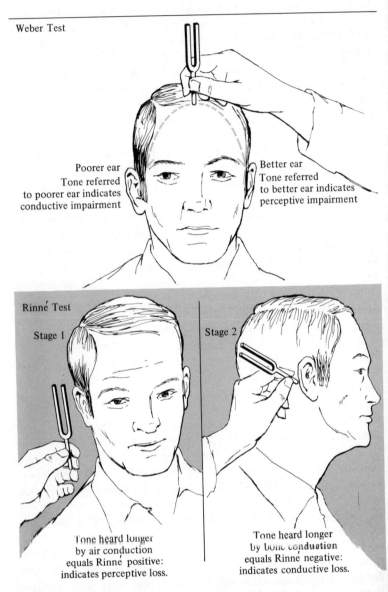

Weber Test

Poorer ear
Tone referred
to poorer ear indicates
conductive impairment

Better ear
Tone referred
to better ear indicates
perceptive impairment

Rinné Test

Stage 1

Stage 2

Tone heard longer
by air conduction
equals Rinné positive:
indicates perceptive loss.

Tone heard longer
by bone conduction
equals Rinné negative:
indicates conductive loss.

Figure 78. Simple tests of hearing.

deaf are the fricative consonants *f, s, th, ch,* and *sh.* It becomes increasingly difficult to discriminate between such words as *sick, thick, flick,* and *chick.* With greater hearing loss the explosive consonants *b, t, p, k, g,* and *d* become difficult to distinguish.

Recovery from a temporary shift of from 30 to 40 dB may take several hours. For a shift of 50–60 dB, even several days may be insufficient. Despite these figures, it should not be assumed that nerve deafness depends solely upon the noise level. A good deal depends upon the total noise exposure. This includes the overall noise level, the time distribution (whether the noise is continuous or intermittent), and the total duration of exposure during a lifetime. It is this combination of factors working in concert that constitutes the hazard of noise.

A step in the direction of controlling or preventing nerve deafness has been the development of damage risk criteria. Figure 79 indicates the combination of sound-pressure level and frequency that may be tolerated without danger. From the graph, it is clear that the tolerable exposure periods decrease with an increase in decibels for the same octave band. For example, at 150 to 300 Hz, sound intensity is ten thousand times greater at 130 dB than at 90 dB. Thus the difference between ten minutes and eight hours of tolerable exposure becomes understandable. Briefly, then, a damage-risk criterion specifies the maximum sound-pressure level of a noise to which a person may be exposed without risk of hearing loss.

E. R. Hermann, an engineer at Northwestern University, has developed a mathematical equation that may aid in explaining the mechanism of noise-induced deafness.[2] His calculations indicate that the ill effects of noise follow a first-order differential equation. Simply translated, the equation suggests that the loss of hearing proceeds as if the sound waves or pressure acted adversely upon one structure or organ or some cell within a critical organ. If, as current theory holds, the conversion of sound from mechanical to electrical impulses occurs in the hair cells of the organ of Corti, then this theoretical calculation fits nicely. Apparently, severe mechanical stress on the hair cells causes them to become fatigued and unable to transmit impulses to the auditory nerves. When physiologists test this model, experimental evidence might unveil the actual mechanism of this failure, which might ulti-

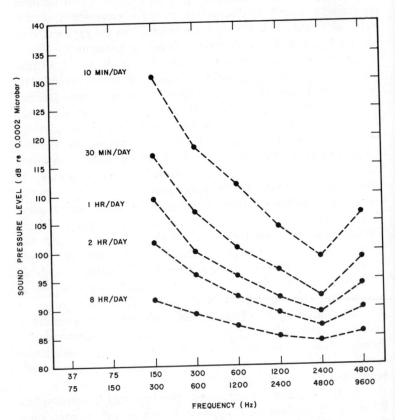

Figure 79. Damage-risk criteria for a single daily exposure.

mately make it possible to perform beneficial surgical or prosthetic intervention. Benefits would accrue even if the organ of Corti did not prove to be the primary site, because other experiments would follow naturally and ultimately lead to a better understanding of noise damage.

In September 1968, Dr. David M. Lipscomb of the University of Tennessee's Noise Study Laboratory reported on the effects of rock music on the ears of guinea pigs. Dr. Lipscomb and his colleagues recorded music in a Knoxville discotheque and then played it back to an audience of guinea pigs. After some ninety hours of intermittent exposure to the music, the cells of the cochlea were photographed (Figure 80). They "had collapsed and shriveled up like peas." [3] On the left in the figure (A) are normal cells, removed from the protected left ear, which had been fitted with a thick plastic plug to resist the incursion of sound. The right ear (B), with no such plug, sustained significant damage. Two cells (arrows) are in the process of collapsing. In this segment of the ear, 19 percent of the total sensory cell population was found to be irreversibly destroyed. These findings have subsequently been substantiated in studies using large numbers of guinea pigs. In addition, the experimental animals manifested the by now classical Selye stress reaction triad of swollen adrenal glands, atrophied thymus, and duodenal ulcers.

Support for Dr. Lipscomb's findings has come from a most unlikely source. In August 1971, rock music played by 14 groups at a pop festival was blamed for the deaths of 200 prize hens at a poultry farm near Udine, in the north of Italy. Veterinary

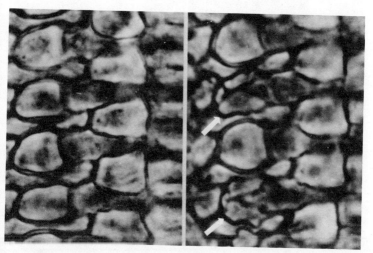

Figure 80. Effect of noise on sensory cells of cochlea. (Photo courtesy of David Lipscomb, University of Tennessee.)

surgeons said that 5,000 hens became frantic and piled up against fences. Many were suffocated or pecked to death. Unfortunately (or fortunately, depending upon your point of view) the organizer of the festival was also the owner of the poultry.

Recently, studies at Dr. Lipscomb's Noise Study Laboratory have developed additional evidence to support his contention of noise-induced ear damage. The results are shown in Figure 81. This is a composite photomicrograph (enlarged 1,000 times) depicting the contents of the capillary (A) immediately beneath the organ of Corti in the cochlea of a rat. This tissue was re-

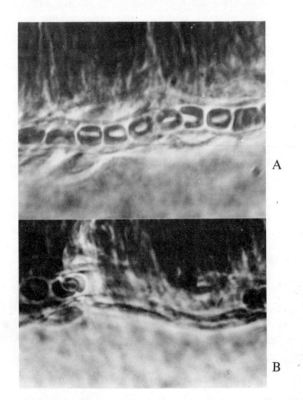

Figure 81. Effect of noise on blood supply to organ of Corti. (Photo courtesy of David Lipscomb, University of Tennessee.)

moved from a control animal (unexposed to noise), whereas the tissue section in part B was obtained from an animal that had been exposed to high noise levels. In addition to the obviously diminished blood supply in the cochlea, there is an interruption (not shown) of blood flow in the vestibular end organs. This occurs after 48 hours of continuous exposure to 110 dB broad band random noise levels.[4]

It is interesting that shortly after the first publication of these findings in newspapers around the country, purveyors of this music quickly pointed out that guinea pigs are not people and that the assumption that damage occurs in human ears cannot be extrapolated from animal studies. This is quite correct; but one wonders if the people who cry "foul" in this instance are not among those who are so quick to accept evidence of potential toxicity from animal feeding studies as directly applicable to man.

In somewhat similar studies, Dr. Frederick L. Dey of New London, Connecticut, tested the effects of rock-and-roll music on teenagers. He recorded his sound levels in a local discotheque, then played them back to young adults. In his experiments, Dr. Dey had 15 men listen with one ear to a recording of hard rock. Six of them had exposures of from 5 to 30 minutes over a 4-day period at both 100 and 110 dB levels. The other nine were exposed to 100 dB sound for only 30 minutes. Because the temporary loss of hearing was so great in those exposed to the 110-dB level, Dr. Dey scrapped plans to play the music at 120 dB or to prolong the exposure to two hours. He wrote, "It is not likely that society could insist that our young restrict themselves to so mild a sound as 100 dB for two hours, so we shall have to reconcile ourselves to damaging the 14 percent most susceptible and later providing a variety of social rehabilitative and Medicare support to which these persons certainly will eventually turn." [5] That's quite a statement. Society can do nothing to prevent the damage, but will have to pay for it after it occurs!

Until a few years ago, deafness was thought to be the only ill effect of noise. Few, if any, reports even hinted at other effects. In 1965, Dr. Samuel Rosen of Mount Sinai Hospital, New York, published the results of his studies of the Maabans of the Egyptian Sudan, among whom he found an association between sustained noise level and arteriosclerotic heart disease.[6] In an earlier study,[7]

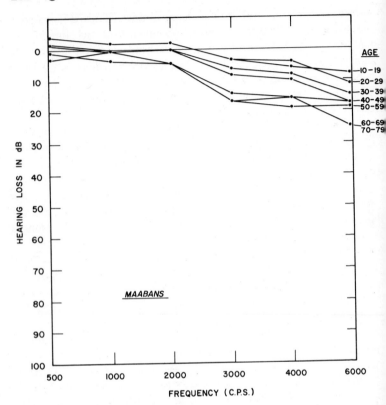

Figure 82. Comparison of hearing loss in Maabans and Americans. (Source: Dr. Samuel Rosen, Archives of Otolaryngology.)

Rosen and his group had found that in primitive villages, compared with urban centers, there was very little noise. They also noted that Maabans of age seventy had hearing acuity similar to that of young boys, and that they also had low blood pressure. Dr. Rosen reported that the Maabans had better hearing than men and women of all age groups in the United States. This comparison is shown in Figure 82. He explained that noise appears to cause a narrowing of the arteries that may affect the hearing mechanism. This point was corroborated by recent research in Germany, which found that vasoconstriction persists as

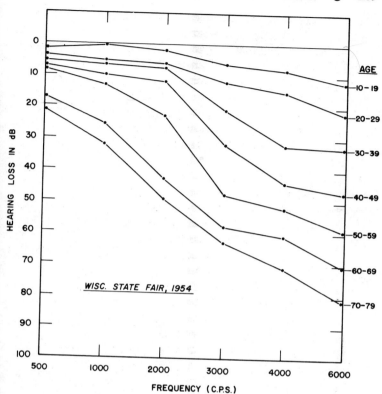

long as noise continues. Russian scientists also reported pain in the region of the heart and electrocardiographic changes in persons exposed to continuous noise at levels of 85 to 120 dB. Dr. Rosen stated that "diminished hearing in people age fourteen to twenty-nine may be the beginning of the long process that eventually shows up as atherosclerosis or coronary artery disease." If this were to be demonstrated conclusively, it would be one of the most dramatic examples of the role of the technological environment in chronic degenerative disease.

An additional piece of evidence found by Dr. Rosen tends to support the noise-deafness theory. Among the Maabans there was no difference in auditory acuity between men and women. This is in sharp contrast to the populations in the United States and industrialized Western Europe, where men show greater hearing losses than women of the same age. Presumably, this is due mainly to the higher noise levels encountered by the men on the job. In March 1967, speaking to a group of concerned citizens, Dr. Rosen said that "the reflex effect which causes contraction of the blood vessels occurs with equal intensity during sleep as during wakefulness. Not only do noise signals make the blood vessels contract, but the skin becomes pale, muscles constrict, and adrenalin is shot out into the bloodstream. This adrenalin output causes tension and nervousness. If chronic, it can elevate blood pressure."

Measurements of auditory acuity or hearing loss can be quickly obtained by an audiogram. This is a measure of the threshold of hearing at standardized frequencies. The audiogram indicates how much sound pressure on the eardrum is required for the sound at each of the six frequencies (500, 1,000, 2,000, 3,000, 4,000, and 6,000 cps) to be just barely audible. If a standard sound must be raised 10 or 15 dB higher to be heard, then a 10- or 15-dB loss of hearing has been sustained.

An audiometer is an instrument that can produce sounds, usually pure tones at predetermined frequencies; part of the instrument is an attenuator that controls the intensity of the tone. The individual being tested dons a set of earphones and responds by pressing a button each time the test tone is heard. When both ears have been tested, a graph of threshold of hearing in dB versus frequency is plotted: this is the audiogram. It is particularly useful in detecting threshold shifts long before the individual notices difficulty in conversation, and in evaluating noise-control measures.

When it has been established, at least in the industrial setting, that a loss of hearing has resulted from exposure to excessive noise, it may be possible to reduce the level of noise at its source. Should this prove impracticable, exposure levels can be reduced by reassigning sensitive or susceptible individuals to a quieter area. If both of these measures are unsuitable, acoustical barriers can be imposed between the noise source and the ear. Individual acoustical barriers run the gamut from a wad of cotton placed at the entrance to the auditory canal to muff-type ear defenders, used with increasing frequency by airport mechanics.

Although dry cotton plugs provide little, if any, attenuation, many people continue to use them. Insert-type plugs made of rubber, plastic, or wax are far superior to cotton; muff protectors are better yet. Figure 83 shows the degree of attenuation achieved with a muff, with an insert-type plug other than cotton, and with cotton. Unfortunately, too many workers in high noise areas discard or fail to wear plugs or muffs. When asked, "Why don't you wear the ear protectors?" they may reply, "What's that, can you speak a little louder?"

In addition to employing barriers at the entrance to the auditory canal, environmental control can be instituted to protect people from noise. This includes designing equipment so as to reduce its noise level, muffling apparatus with sound-absorbing materials, or isolating noisy processes or machines. Any inelastic material of low density, such as ground cork, hairfelt, fiberglass, or rubber compositions, is a good insulator.

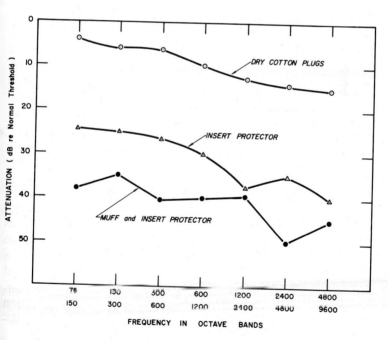

Figure 83. Degree of noise attenuation achieved with three types of ear protectors.

Sound waves travel with greater velocity through many solid materials than they do through air. For example, sound waves have a velocity of 11,000 to 16,000 feet per second in wood— 14,000 in oak and approximately 16,000 in Norwegian spruce— 16,000 in glass and steel, and 17,000 in aluminum. Sound travels through air at a velocity of 1,130 feet per second. Small wonder, then, that street traffic noise can be heard so easily in homes and offices.

According to the mass law, the heavier the wall, the more effectively it will damp noise. But heavy walls are costly; hence the growing use of lightweight materials, which permit more noise to get through. To damp noise without heavy walls, walls of various materials can be divided into two walls with an air space between them. The need for more weight (density), or more space, or both, makes it difficult to design economical structures that keep noise out. The Lead Institute has been investigating the potential use of thin lead sheets as insulating material. Lead's mass and its malleability, even in thin sheets, make it highly resistant to the passage of sound waves. Lead is readily available and is comparatively low-cost.

Although sonic booms have long been blamed for a variety of ill effects, fatalities were not among them until quite recently. On August 6, 1967, the *New York Times* carried an account of a group of French farmers in the village of Mauron, Brittany, who had gathered for lunch and who became the first casualties of a sonic boom. Witnesses heard a "thunderous" sound that shook timbers loose and brought eight tons of barley stored in the loft down on the diners below. Three were killed and another was seriously injured.

A sonic boom is not the result of breaking the sound barrier, as many mistakenly believe; it is, in fact, an intense pressure wave. This pressure, generated by the nose and tail of planes traveling above 660 miles per hour, strikes the earth and, shortly thereafter, the ear. Reduced speeds are less economical, but increasing public and governmental dissatisfaction with current noise levels in urban communities has convinced the airlines that they must reduce aircraft noise even if it entails economic sacrifices.

The scream of jet engines is caused by exhaust nozzles and the stationary-vane inlet assemblies of compressors. The vane assembly noise, initially troublesome only when the engines were throttled back for landing, became the dominant noise when turbo-fan jets were introduced. The principal factors contributing to the noise turned out to be the number and design of stationary and rotating blades, the spacing between the rotor and stator, and the rotational velocity of the rotor. As yet, engineers have had difficulty in redesigning these parts so as to reduce noise levels without severe loss in power output.

By July 1971, the British Aircraft Corporation Concorde 002 (which flies at speeds up to 1,800 mph) had been modified to reduce its noise level appreciably. The major breakthrough in noise reduction has resulted from the new design of the final jet nozzle assembly. The Concorde uses "buckets" that close over the jet effluxes to reverse thrust as a means of slowing the plane after landing. For yet unexplained reasons, it appears that if the buckets are slightly closed during the run, the device actually significantly reduces the noise made during takeoff. Although this slight closure involves some loss of engine power, the engines make much less noise. This, coupled with the reset of the nozzles to reduce jet velocities, further reduces the noise level.

Noise can have a strong effect on human behavior. The Chinese have known some of this for thousands of years. They learned rather early that to a man in quiet isolation the sound of slowly but steadily dripping water rapidly assumes the proportions of a loudly beaten drum. Such noise could drive a man mad or break his will. On the other hand, silence or very quiet conditions are difficult for city people to tolerate; sound and noise have become an intimate part of their lives. In a recent article, Dr. Gilbert C. Tolhurst of the University of Massachusetts wrote, "Relative silence is a condition that few individuals have experienced. The usual reactions are extreme apprehension, fear or panic. It is truly an eerie first experience to be in a situation where one can hear one's own heart beat clearly, the vertebrae grate upon each other as one rotates his head from side to side, and where each breath is most apparent, both upon inhalation and exhalation, no matter how one may try to breathe easily. It seems that with but few exceptions, man has adapted to his 'noisy' environment so well during his maturation that profound silence is a condition to be avoided." [8]

Recently the New York State Supreme Court ruled that one of the inescapable hazards of living in a modern community is the sound of gunfire. It seems that the city of Cortland, New York had tried to prevent a sportsmen's club from firing high-powered rifles because the noise disturbed many of the residents. The judge, in deciding the case, held that persons living in an organized community must suffer some damage, annoyance, and inconvenience from each other. He went on to say that for these inconveniences they are compensated by the advantages of a civilized society! Perhaps if the judge lived closer to the rifle range he would not have been able to write so detached an opinion.

The courts' progress in dealing effectively with the demands of an aroused citizenry was seen in October 1971, when Superior Court Judge Milton Feller (New Jersey) awarded $164,119 to the Elizabeth, N.J., Board of Education for damages caused by noise coming from new highways. Judge Feller made the award when he found normal conduct of classes in William F. Halloran School No. 22 to be impossible after Interstate Highway 278 was built next to it. The suit was filed against the State Department of Transportation, which, of course, will appeal the decision. The real problem here is how the award will affect the classes. The mistake was placing the highway near the school. Communities must learn to be wary of plans made by often single-minded government bodies, for whom roads are a good in themselves. Figures 84 and 85 show the type of studies that should be done if noise levels are to be kept at acceptable levels.

The effect of aircraft noise on health is a regular and continual source of controversy when sites for much-needed new airports are discussed. Although there is a good deal of popular sentiment associating noise with mental breakdown, it has been unusually difficult to obtain adequate clinical evidence of adverse effects of aircraft noise on mental health.

Recently, a team of British physicians and statisticians reported on a study of the possible association between aircraft noise and admissions to a mental hospital of the population living in the Borough of Hounslow, which is considered to be a "maximum noise area" (MNA) because of aircraft using London's nearby Heathrow Airport. The MNA is defined as an area whose

Figure 84. A state trooper positions the new CBS Laboratories electronic Highway Noise Monitor near a Connecticut highway. Traffic noise levels are monitored by a highly sensitized microphone (foreground), which triggers the electronic device (background) containing a noise level chart recorder and a split-image camera. The device is actuated automatically when a vehicle exceeds noise level limits and produces a photograph of the offending vehicle and its marker plate with a superimposed picture of the noise level reading at the time of the violation. The new system will go into effect on Connecticut highways as part of the Connecticut Research Commission's all-out war on noise pollution. (Photo courtesy of CBS Laboratories.)

sound levels are above 100 decibels. The investigators examined the records of all patients both from within and without the MNA who were admitted to a specific mental hospital over a three-year period. The address of each admission was spotted on a large map of the district. The distribution of the spots showed that hospital admission rates were substantially higher from

Figure 85.   Split-image photograph of a noise-level violator taken by the CBS Highway Noise Monitor. (Photo courtesy of CBS Laboratories.)

within the MNA than outside of it. "Furthermore," the investigators wrote, "the type of person most affected is the older woman who is not living with her husband and who suffers from neurotic illness." They concluded that "the high intermittent noise levels from aircraft using Heathrow Airport may be a factor in increased rates of admission to mental hospitals." [9]

It would be particularly useful if a similar study were made in the United States. Areas adjacent to Kennedy, LaGuardia, O'Hare, and Los Angeles airports would serve as excellent test areas. Many people who live in the area around the Kennedy Airport landing and takeoff pattern in New York report many sleepless nights spent counting the planes—almost one every thirty seconds.

The National Management Association has reported the experience of a large insurance company that undertook a "quiet please" campaign. When the company set about eliminating irritating but commonly accepted office sounds, the wheezing and clacking of a dozen different pieces of machinery, they found that typing errors dropped 29 percent, machine operator mistakes fell 52 percent, absenteeism fell 37 percent, and employee turnover fell 47 percent, while efficiency, morale, and cooperation rose precipitously. One would hope that this is not just another example of the Hawthorne effect. Some 50 years ago, Western Electric decided that the way to increase efficiency was to increase the lighting in its Hawthorne, N.J. plant. After experimenting with a number of variations, they found that no matter what they did, including decreasing the available light, efficiency increased. The mystery was solved when some clever manager realized that it wasn't the lighting that increased efficiency, but the simple fact that management was showing concern about the workers. Nevertheless, it is difficult to know how typists in a typing pool survive day after cacophonous day.

A rather wry response to the disturbing effects of on-the-job noise was the solution contrived by one of New York's major banking firms. Over a period of months, employees in the bank's central check-tabulating department increasingly complained that the noise of the machines was making their lives intolerable; it was psychologically and physiologically irritating. The bank's answer was not to try to reduce the noise levels; instead, it "hired the handicapped"—deaf workers were brought in to staff that department. Obviously this solution totally misses the point.

One can only wonder about the possible effects of household noise on the woman of the house. During the day she is subjected to the dishwasher, garbage disposal, electric food mixers and blenders, vacuum cleaner, clothes washer and dryer, doors slamming, phone ringing, baby crying, radio and television, and the end of all noise, the full blast of rock music if there are teenagers around.

Nevertheless, although a variety of adverse effects of noise have been reported—losses in work capacity, disruption of rest and sleep, annoyance reactions, and general mental distress—little evidence to support these reports has been developed. A great deal remains to be done.

The two main reasons for the lack of progress toward noise abatement are the widespread apathy of both government agencies and the public toward the problem and the cost of the remedy. Although noise has increased noticeably in suburbia and rural areas, it is most of all an urban problem because of cities' greater population densities. Several European cities, notably Paris, have long emphasized noise abatement with the help of nationwide and local private groups organized to achieve that goal, and they have succeeded admirably in attaining a quieter environment than can be found in New York, Chicago, London, or Rome. Honking of horns, a national pastime in Rome, has been outlawed but for emergencies in Paris. The Paris subway is well known for its quiet rubber-wheeled trains. To the dismay of many, this innovation has been discarded as too costly by the planners of New York's subway system. And in many European cities building codes are stricter than most American cities with respect to sound insulation in home and apartment construction.

The quietest city in the United States, if annual awards are any judge, is Memphis, Tennessee. Memphis has won more than a dozen annual awards for its noise abatement program. City officials add with some pride that the impetus for a quieter city (Memphis long had a reputation as a brawling river town) came from "Boss" Crump and his powerful political machine. E. H. "Boss" Crump, while a personification of the political boss, decided in the late 1930s that he wanted to live in a quiet city. He had several strict noise-control ordinances passed that are still in force. Consider a few of Crump's ideas. In part, the ordinances state that unnecessary horn blowing is illegal and that vehicles making "loud and unnecessary grating, grinding, rattling, or other noises are outlawed." It's as simple as that. But also prohibited are yelling, shouting, hooting, whistling, and singing in the streets between 11:00 p.m. and 7:00 a.m., playing radios or television sets loudly enough to be heard outdoors between the same hours, and the use of noisy construction equipment between 7:00 p.m. and 6:00 a.m. Is it really necessary to bring back the political boss and his controlled votes in order to obtain quieter cities? I wonder.

References

1. T. Kupferman, "Noise Pollution," *Congressional Record,* April 12, 1966, p. 8339.

2. E. R. Hermann, "An Epidemiological Study of Noise," *Proceedings XIVth International Congress of Occupational Health,* Madrid, Spain, September 12–13, 1963.

3. David M. Lipscomb, "High-Intensity Sounds in the Recreational Environment," *Clinical Pediatrics* 8 (1969): 63.

4. David M. Lipscomb, "Non-Occupational Noise and the Effect upon Hearing of Young Persons: A Report Presented to the House of Representatives, Committee on Health and the Environment," Washington, D.C., June 22, 1971 (University of Tennessee Noise Study Laboratory).

5. Frederick L. Dey, "Auditory Fatigue and Predicted Permanent Hearing Defects from Rock-and-Roll Music," *New England Journal of Medicine* 282 (1970): 467.

6. S. Rosen and P. Olin, "Hearing Loss and Coronary Heart Disease," *Archives of Otolaryngology* 82 (1965): 236.

7. S. Rosen et al., "Presbycusis Study of Relatively Noise-Free Population in Sudan," *Annals of Otolaryngology, Rhinology, and Laryngology* 71 (1962): 727.

8. Gilbert C. Tolhurst, "Acoustic Fatigue of Humans Exposed to Noise," *Naval Research Reviews* (Office of Naval Research, Washington, D.C.), August 1971, pp. 20–30.

9. I. Abey-Wickrama et al., "Mental Hospital Admissions and Aircraft Noise," *The Lancet* 2 (1969): 1275.

Suggested Reading

Burns, William. *Noise and Man.* Philadelphia: J. B. Lippincott, 1969.

Kryter, Karl D. *The Effects of Noise on Man.* New York: Academic Press, 1970.

Tobias, Jerry V., ed. *Foundations of Modern Auditory Theory,* vol. 1. New York: Academic Press, 1970.

Ward, W. Dixon; and Fricke, James E., eds. *Noise as a Public Health Hazard: Proceedings of the Conference.* Washington: The American Speech and Hearing Association, 1969 (report no. 4).

13

OCCUPATIONAL HEALTH

*Modern man is the victim of the very instruments
he values most. Every gain in power, every mas-
tery of natural forces, every scientific
addition to knowledge, has proved potentially
dangerous; because it has not been accompanied
by equal gains in self-understanding and self-discipline.*

Lewis Mumford

"Of what trade are you?" Yes, "of what trade are you?"
Because we spend most of each day at some occupation, physicians
have long asked their patients, "Of what trade are you?" "Where
do you work?" "What do you do?"

Although the association between occupation and ill health
and disease was first recorded by Pliny the Elder, who advocated
the use of protective masks for workers in mining and grinding
operations in the first century A.D., it is Bernardino Ramazzini
who is considered the father of occupational health and hygiene.
In his book *De Morbis Artificium Diatriba* (*The Diseases of*

Workmen), published in 1700, he described the occupational diseases of his day and suggested preventive measures. Ramazzini first asked, "Of what trade are you?" 272 years ago, and the question is still being asked today—not because we have not progressed, but because new industries, new chemicals, and new stresses confront each new generation of workers, and old diseases reappear in new industries.

Optokinetic nystagmus is a disease of the twentieth century. Also called "conveyor belt sickness," it was first described in 1966, when a number of women in a potato chip factory in Michigan became strangely ill. The symptoms were giddiness, fainting, nausea, and general mental confusion. When samples of air in the factory were shown to be free of toxic gases capable of producing this set of symptoms, a study of the physical conditions in the factory was undertaken. Because all of the women involved worked on conveyor belt lines, these belts were studied, and it was not long before the answer was apparent. When conveyor belts move at speeds up to thirty-two feet per minute, little or no vertigo is experienced by workers inspecting food products or other items carried along on the belt. When, however, the belts fly along at speeds above thirty-two feet per minute, workers trying to focus their eyes on the items experience dizziness, nausea, and mental confusion. Optokinetic nystagmus results from the inability of the eye to respond rapidly enough to keep pace with the units speeding by on the belt. As the eye follows individual objects carried along a moving belt, it constantly establishes new focusing points. The eye picks out one object, follows it for a distance, leaves it, picks out another object, follows it, and repeats the process. When the belt speed increases beyond thirty-two feet per minute, the number of focusing points per minute must also increase. Thus, when objects on a belt fly by more rapidly than the eye can focus upon them, involuntary contractions of the eye muscles occur. These contractions cause the eyeballs to move back and forth like pendulums, which triggers the giddiness, fainting, nausea, and general mental confusion.

Trichlorethylene (an organic solvent) is a potential hazard for workers in the modern office. In order for banks or other commercial organizations to process thousands of checks automatically, magnetic ink is used for imprinting. In case of error, trichlorethylene is used to erase the original impression. As a consequence, dangerous concentrations of TCE can occur in the immediate environment, causing irritation to the skin, eyes, and mucous membranes.

Carbon monoxide generated in trace amounts by normal metabolic activity is usually of no consequence. In the sealed microenvironment of a space vehicle, however, it can attain toxic levels if uncontrolled.

These are but three random examples of the stresses imposed by the new technologies of a highly industrialized society in which people are being exposed to new techniques, new materials, and new stresses. Although these three examples of occupational hazards were unknown to Ramazzini, they have a heritage extending back to two hundred years ago, when the factory system was established in England. The series of inventions and discoveries, both purposeful and accidental, that occurred in the seventy years between 1760 and 1830 and began to cause many of the environmental problems we have today is generally referred to as the Industrial Revolution.

In the years before 1760, production of textiles was limited by the speed of the individual spinners; a good weaver could use up the production of a half-dozen home "spinsters" rather quickly. In fact, he would often have to stop weaving until he could accumulate a supply of thread. In 1768, James Hargreaves, a poor wool spinner, upset his spinning wheel. While lying on its side the wheel continued to spin and wind the wool. Hargreaves wondered why several spindles could not be kept in motion by a single wheel. This idea led to the construction of the spinning jenny, in which eight spindles were kept turning by a single wheel. With the introduction of this machine, the Industrial Revolution was initiated. With sufficient driving power any number of spindles could be kept spinning. Two years later, in 1770, this power was supplied by Richard Arkwright's water frame. It accomplished two things: the spun thread was passed through two pairs of rollers, and because the second pair revolved faster than the first, it stretched out the thread, making it a good deal finer; and driving power was supplied by a water wheel.

In 1779, Samuel Crompton combined the water frame and

the spinning jenny into one unit called the spinning mule, which provided stronger and still finer thread. The next problem was how to weave the thread faster. Crompton's mule had reversed the original limiting factor, and the weaver was now too slow to keep pace with the amount of spun thread that could be produced. In 1783 a clergyman, Edmund Cartwright, working with a local blacksmith, constructed a power loom that was to be the death-blow to domestic work and the beginning of the factory system. Cartwright's power loom used the energy of two strong men, but soon they were replaced by water power, which was superseded by steam power. The use of coal and the steam engine had been developing almost simultaneously with the profound changes in the textile industry. The Industrial Revolution wrought changes with enormous consequences. It altered the whole character of work. The use of power looms led to the construction of large factories to accommodate hundreds or thousands of workers and the machines they would use. Because the factories needed sources of energy and ore they were built close to the coal- and iron-producing areas. Thousands upon thousands of people migrated from their homes in rural areas to these new locations, with the result that new, densely populated areas developed rapidly. It was in these new industrial centers in both England and the United States that many of our present-day problems developed. The mushrooming of cities proclaimed the changing character of our nation. Foundries, factories, and mills created a new industrial metropolis, whose towering smokestacks belching dark effluents marked the approach of a new age.

When Abraham Lincoln was inaugurated in 1861, fewer than one-sixth of the American people lived in cities with populations of ten thousand or more. By 1900, more than one-third of the population lived in cities of this size. And, as the country surged forward, ever-increasing production became the goal. Workers spent long hours in the dirt and wastes generated by the industrial processes. Few factories or foundries provided washrooms, and the worker brought home these wastes on his skin, hair, and clothing. Dust, grime, and toxic fumes were regarded as the necessary by-products of an industrialized society. Little was known, and few were concerned, about the effect of this industrial environment on human life; employers were not legally responsible for the safety or health of their work force. In addition, extreme heat or cold, dampness, noise, poor lighting and ventilation, and overcrowding were the rule. Children outnumbered adults in some factories. They worked under the same conditions and spent twelve to fourteen hours, seven days a week, on the job. Small wonder that occupational illness emerged as a major consequence of industrialization.

The workers were not unaware of the health hazards of their jobs. Such terms as "miner's asthma," "brass-founder's ague," "hatter's shakes," "filecutter's paralysis," "baker's itch," and "mulespinner's cancer" were part of their language and bitter experience. Many felt that to change jobs would be simply to exchange one set of hazards for another. Although employers realized that their workers suffered bad health and often early death, they preferred to attribute it to poor conditions at home.

With the advent of the labor movement there was a drive for better working conditions, and public awareness combined with enlightened industrial leadership began to bring improvements. By the early 1940s our country was on the threshold of the technological age. New industries, new products, new chemicals brought new hazards to the workers, and old hazards appeared in new industries. Lead was used in the manufacture of storage batteries and rubber tires. Thus lead poisoning, a problem in ancient Rome, became a problem once again. The development of X-ray tubes and fluorescent lamps, for example, introduced new materials into industry. Their toxic properties were not known, and workers became ill before suspicion fell on these products. Skin lesions and ulcers were common among workers in the chromate industry, and the cancer rate among electroplaters was higher than among workers in other industries. With the development of the giant petroleum industry, a multitude of by-products—insecticides, solvents, greases, and drugs—brought new and unfamiliar hazards to workers. Naphtha, benzene, carbon tetrachloride, and acetone were used in thousands of new industrial processes. But the same volatile proportion that make solvents so useful as cleaners, thinners, and dryers also made them potentially hazardous when used without proper protection or ventilation.

Today, more Americans are at work than ever before. In

1971, the Bureau of Labor Statistics in its publication, *Employment and Earnings,* estimated the non-agricultural work force at approximately 70 million. This represents about 33⅓ percent of the total population.

Although potentially hazardous materials are widely used, knowledge and experience gained over the years have made healthier working conditions possible. However, the danger of occupational accident has by no means vanished. In 1969, 2,200,-000 occupational injuries were reported. Of these, 14,200 were fatal and 90,000 resulted in permanent impairment. Curiously enough, between 1963 and 1971, the on-the-job accident rate has remained relatively constant—just over 2 million each year.

New processes and advanced technology with their more complex tools and machinery, and new chemicals and new materials, are always raising new hazards to health. Table 19 shows the incidence of nonfatal injuries among a specific segment of the labor force. From this graph it is clear which are the "dangerous (manufacturing) trades." It is also clear that manufacturing accidents have been increasing. But it is not clear whether this can be attributed solely to an increase in the labor force. It is more likely that an increase in the labor force accounts for only a portion of the increase in accidents; carelessness, inadequate safety facilities, and inadequate training probably account for the lion's share.

As reliable statistics on the true incidence of occupational diseases for the general labor force are unavailable (it is extremely difficult to obtain such information), the data for federal employees (3 million), shown in Table 20, suggest that the national problem is at least several orders of magnitude higher. This supposition is buttressed by the data from California alone. Table 21 shows the occupational diseases reported to the California State Department of Health in 1969. Both surveys show that dermatitis is the leading occupational illness. In fact, it is estimated that 1 percent of the total labor force is affected by occupational dermatoses each year. Although only one chemical injury appears to occur for every ten cases of dermatitis, chemical injury is usually far more severe.

Each year hundreds of new substances are synthesized and brought into use in many industrial processes; many of them are

TABLE 19.

*Work injury frequency rates in the manufacturing industries,
United States, 1958 and 1967.*

Number of Disabling Injuries per Million Employee Hours Worked

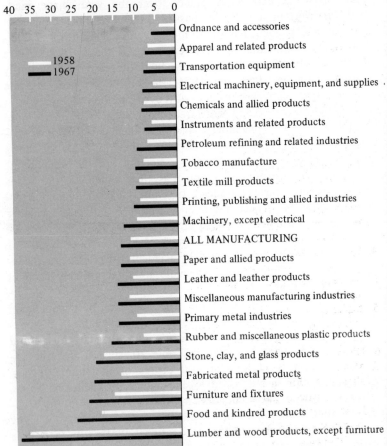

40   35   30   25   20   15   10   5   0

1958
1967

Ordnance and accessories

Apparel and related products

Transportation equipment

Electrical machinery, equipment, and supplies

Chemicals and allied products

Instruments and related products

Petroleum refining and related industries

Tobacco manufacture

Textile mill products

Printing, publishing and allied industries

Machinery, except electrical

ALL MANUFACTURING

Paper and allied products

Leather and leather products

Miscellaneous manufacturing industries

Primary metal industries

Rubber and miscellaneous plastic products

Stone, clay, and glass products

Fabricated metal products

Furniture and fixtures

Food and kindred products

Lumber and wood products, except furniture

Note: The term "injury" includes occupational disease.
Source of basic data: *Handbook of Labor Statistics 1969.* Bureau of Labor Statistics Bulletin No. 1630

inherently dangerous. The introduction of a large number of volatile solvents has precipitously increased the list of potential poisons. In addition to the obvious hazards of chemicals, dusts, and
fumes, many jobs involve potentially harmful conditions: ex-

TABLE 20.

Incidence of alleged or suspected occupational diseases as reported in twenty-eight states and for federal employees during a year.

	Total
ALL DISEASES	43,307

1. Systemic effects due to chemical agents   2,252
   ammonia, 24; anilin, 23; arsenic, 16; benzol or its derivatives, 16; beryllium, 9; carbon bisulfide, 6; carbon monoxide or dioxide, 233; carbon tetrachloride, 32; chlorine, 29; chrome, 154; cyanide, 15; halogenated hydrocarbons, 14; insecticides, 323; lead, 491; mercury, 14; petroleum products, 23; phosphorus, 5; sulfur dioxide, 14; zinc, brass, 84; gases not specified, 202; paint solvents, 33; miscellaneous and not known, 492.

2. Dust diseases of the lungs   1,999
   asbestos, 21; anthracosilicosis, 233; silicosis,* 1,615; pneumoconiosis, other and not specified, 130.

3. Respiratory disorders   667
   bronchitis, influenza, pneumonia, 79; respiratory irritations and not specified, 588.

4. Disorders due to physical conditions   4,127
   pressure abnormalities, 58; effects of repeated motion, pressure, or shock, 3,748; effects of heat and cold, 304; all other,** 17.

5. Infective and parasitic diseases   1,148
   anthrax, 69; brucellosis, 50; tuberculosis, 811; communicable and not specified, 218.

6. Diseases of the skin   23,502

7. Miscellaneous conditions   9,612
   allergies (other than skin), 211; cancer, 7; conjunctivitis, 2,034; blisters, abrasions, 567; effects of bites, stings, 1,635; heart disease, 10; neuritis, arthritis, 144; all other, indefinite not specified, 5,004.

   * Includes 134 cases reported of silicotuberculosis.

   **Includes 14 cases of loss of hearing, 3 due to radiation.

cessive heat, continual dampness, sudden variations in temperature, poor lighting, and continuous vibration. The highest death rates are found in occupations that combine a high probability of accidents with exposure to dust, particularly silicon dioxide. These

LE 21.

*pational disease rates per 1,000 workers by industry and sex
lifornia, 1969.*

INDUSTRY	TOTAL		MEN		WOMEN	
	Reports	Rate	Reports	Rate	Reports	Ra
	18,153	2.6	13,960	3.3	4,193	1.
griculture	1,986	8.5	1,688	8.6	298	8.
Farms	1,624	7.7	1,333	7.6	291	8
Spray, pest control and other agricultural services *	362	16.2	355	16.7	7	
ineral Extraction	58	1.8	58	1.9	—	
onstruction	1,157	3.8	1,151	4.0	6	
anufacturing	7,814	4.7	5,742	4.7	2,072	4
ransportation, Communication, and Utilities **	1,334	3.4	763	2.8	571	5
Transportation	891	4.6	375	2.3	516	16
Communication	172	1.3	118	1.9	54	0
Utilities **	271	4.7	270	5.4	1	
rade	1,170	0.8	872	1.0	298	0
inance, Insurance and Real Estate	141	0.4	101	0.6	40	0
ervice	1,708	1.3	1,124	1.9	584	0
ate and Local Government	2,759	2.6	2,441	4.4	318	0
State	585	2.6	475	3.4	110	0
Local	2,174	2.6	1,966	4.7	208	0
Not Stated	26		20		6	

* Includes only operators who service farms and other agricultural establishments. Structural and other pest control operators are included with Service.

** Includes privately owned utilities only. Publicly owned utilities are included with Local Government.

a Not computed if fewer than 10 reports of occupational disease.

SOURCE: State of California, Division of Labor Statistics and Research, *Doctor's First Report of Work Injury* and, by private communication, employment estimates of workers covered by the California Workmen's Compensation law. Statistics compiled by State of California, Department of Public Health.

conditions are present in lead, zinc, hard-rock, and gold mining. On the other hand, clerical workers and professionals, such as physicians, university professors, and clergyman, especially Anglican clergymen, have the lowest death rates of all occupational groups. As might be expected, the risk of accidental death or injury is highest in building wreckers, electric light and power linemen, handlers of explosives, and window cleaners.

For its statistical purposes the Bureau of Labor Statistics uses 2,000 man-hours as the length of the average work year. Assuming the average work day is 8 hours, an employee works an average of 250 days per year. Multiplying this figure by the non-agricultural work force gives an estimated total of 17,405,-500,000 man-days worked per year by the non-agricultural work force. In 1970, this work force incurred a loss of 45,000,000 man-days from disabling injuries. Workmen's Compensation—cash paid out to workers and their dependents—has reached the $2 billion mark. Programs directed at promoting the health of the worker can reduce this loss. It has been estimated that if the overall annual rate of sickness and injury absence could be reduced by only one day, an increase of $10 billion in the GNP as well as a substantial reduction in personal suffering would result.

A major problem for investigators studying occupational exposure problems is determining the concentration of chemicals, dusts, or fumes to which a worker may be exposed without injury during his working day, five days a week, fifty weeks a year. This is particularly difficult to ascertain because the spectrum of workers in any industrial plant includes both men and women from seventeen to sixty-five, of all sizes, shapes, and genetic constitutions, and varying in degree of general health from day to day. To develop a value suitable for all these variables would be impossible. But information of this type is important in evaluating health hazards and establishing controls.

Toward this end, in 1969 the Bureau of Industrial Health and Air Pollution Control of the Michigan Department of Health introduced the personal air sampler. It has paid off handsomely in ascertaining the individual employee exposure to dust in the immediate work area. The device, shown in Figure 86, is a

Figure 86. The personal air sampler. (Michigan Department of Public Health.)

battery-operated pump that sucks a sample of air through a micropore filter over a period of from one to three or more hours. This extended sampling period produces results representative of the workers' actual exposure. Because of the wide variety of dusts capable of producing pneumoconiosis that procedure is uniquely useful for long-term measurement of highly toxic particles.

All chemicals vary in their degree of toxicity simply on the basis of the quantity consumed. This variation in degree of response to an amount of chemical—the so-called spectrum of toxicity—is described in Table 22.

TABLE 22.

*Spectrum of toxicity.**

	LD_{50} **	*Lethal dose*
Extremely toxic	<1 mg.†	taste
Highly toxic	<50 mg.	teaspoon
Toxic	50–500 mg.	an ounce
Moderately toxic	0.5–5.0 gm.	a pint
Slightly toxic	5–15 gm.	a quart
Non-toxic	>15 gm.	More than a quart

* Bear in mind that 1000 milligrams (mg.) equal 1 gram (gm.) and that 30 gm. are just about an ounce.

** LD_{50} is the notation used by biological scientists to express that dose in milligrams per kilogram of body weight that kills 50 percent of the test animals.

† The notation < means "less than," and > means "more than."

Thus, it can be seen that quite a wide range (an increase of more than fifteen thousand times between <1 mg. and >15 gm.) exists in degree of toxicity. To be harmful to health, some chemicals must be consumed in large doses, while others need be taken only in small amounts. This is why there is such difficulty in determining and establishing levels of chemicals that workmen can be exposed to without harm.

The American Conference of Governmental Industrial Hygienists (ACGIH) each year publishes lists of standards it has set for allowable occupational exposure to chemicals based on an eight-hour working day and a five-day week. These standards are called Threshold Limit Values, or TLV's. Although TLV's exist for hundreds of chemicals, they do not exist for hundreds of others. These values are based on information gathered from industrial experience and experimental studies with animals and human subjects. Thus it will require many years and much research to gather data on all industrial chemicals. It is important to note that TLV's are only guidelines, not absolute values. As new data become available, a value published one year can be reduced or its threshold increased the following year. These standards are pegged to allow the concentration of airborne substances to fluctuate a reasonable amount above and below the listed TLV, with the understanding that the average value for the eight-hour day does not exceed the standard.

In remarking on the difficulty of determining these values, one must consider the age differences among workers in a factory, as well as the differences in body type and genetic constitutions. These will all have an effect on the individual's reaction to a specific concentration of chemical. The TLV's are based on the reasonably healthy adult; they are not applicable to continuous exposure of the very young and very old, the indisposed, or the diseased.

The American Standards Association (ASA) has also studied the problem of occupational exposures and has set standards called Maximum Allowable Concentrations, or MAC's. These are issued with the proviso that they are only guides in the control of health hazards and are not to be regarded as fine lines between safe and dangerous levels. Rather, they represent a ceiling above which concentration should not be allowed to rise at any time during the working day. Below these MAC's only the most susceptible or sensitive individual should show ill effects.

It is the rare industrial environment that has only a single chemical circulating. It is much more likely that several chemicals are present at the same time. How then is an estimation of a safe or hazardous condition to be made?

Experience and experiment have shown that certain combinations of chemicals have an additive effect. That is, their combined effect, rather than the effect of either individually, must be evaluated. To express this, an equation relating observed atmospheric concentration (C) to the TLV of that specific chemical (T) can be set up. For example,

$$\frac{C_1}{T_1} + \frac{C_2}{T_2} + \frac{C_3}{T_3} + \ldots \ldots \frac{C_n}{T_n} - 1$$

This expression says that when the ratios of each of the chemicals are added together their value can be equal to unity, one. If their value is less than unity, the TLV is not exceeded; if it is one, the condition is borderline; and if it is more than one, the TLV is exceeded and the chemicals can be assumed to be potentially hazardous.

If experience indicates that the effects of each chemical are in fact independent of those of the other, the ratio $\frac{C}{T} = 1$ must be ascertained for each substance independently, and the TLV is exceeded only when at least one constituent has a value higher than one.

Inhalation is one of the most important means of entry of toxic materials into the body. However, of the various means of exposure, skin contact, as shown in Tables 20 and 21, accounts for more illness and lost time than any other mechanism.

In contact with the skin, a chemical can induce injury in one of three ways: it can react with the skin surface and produce a localized irritation; it can penetrate the skin to combine with tissue proteins, producing a more diffused sensitization; or it can penetrate through a hair follicle, enter the bloodstream, and thereby act as a systemic poison. In this case, any tissue or organ can be affected if it comes in contact with the circulating blood.

Trichlorethylene, a widely used solvent, can dissolve lipids from the skin, causing chapped or cracked skin. Corrosive acids and alkalis attack the skin directly, causing burns and tissue destruction. Aniline and tetraethyl lead can be absorbed through the skin. Aniline has a great affinity for hemoglobin, the pigment of red blood cells. When it combines with hemoglobin, it produces an oxygen deficiency in tissue by preventing the normal transport of oxygen by hemoglobin, thereby giving a cyanotic tint to the skin, tongue, and mucous membranes. Tetraethyl lead, on the other hand, has an affinity for the central nervous system. Severely exposed individuals suffer from convulsive seizures, tremors, and periods of manic behavior, accompanied by auditory and visual hallucinations. Nightmares are not uncommon. The large majority of occupational intoxications that affect the internal integrity of the body results from breathing airborne substances. Chemicals inhaled into the lungs can produce damage there or pass to other organs by way of the pulmonary blood system. However, the type and severity of the action of the potentially toxic agent depend on such factors as the chemical structure of the substance, the amount inhaled, the rate of absorption, and the individual's susceptibility and rate of physical activity. An individual inhaling one ounce of alcohol as vapor would feel the effects much faster than if he drank the same quantity. Most solvent vapors and gases, when inhaled, produce their effects in a relatively short time.

Chronic occupational poisoning can also occur via the alimentary canal. Illness or injury by ingestion and swallowing occurs when contaminated hands, food, or cigarettes are placed in the mouth, or when a worker licks a brush containing a harmful material. Lead, mercury, radium, and arsenic have produced illness in this way.

Physical conditions, such as abnormally high or low air pressure, sudden changes in temperature, excessive vibration, and noise, can also cause injury. In the unique case of ionizing radiation and ultraviolet radiation, internal and external tissue injury, respectively, can be induced. The human being, a hardy creature, apparently can tolerate a wide range of physical stresses, but in many instances industrial processes may exceed this tolerance. The noise in can manufacturing plants and in foundries can cause both temporary and permanent hearing loss. The severe cold in food-freezing plants can induce frostbite and tissue death, while excessive heat often produces heat exhaustion, heatstroke, and muscular cramping. Operators of pneumatic drills, tampers, and pounders can develop injuries of the bones, joints, tendons, ligaments, and blood vessels. "White fingers" is a condition seen in men who constantly grip tightly the handles of their tools, thereby inducing circulatory changes. The most dangerous of these vibratory tools are those with frequencies of two thousand to three thousand blows per minute.

With every breath we take, we inhale some dust. Most dusts are harmless. Certain dusts, however, can produce pathological changes in lung tissue, converting healthy spongy tissue into useless fibrous or scar tissue. Dusts consist of solid particles suspended in air. They are usually considered to range from 0.5 to 150 microns in diameter. Street dusts, plant pollens, and sand, for example, are so large that they either settle out rapidly or are trapped in the nose and upper respiratory passages and thus rarely reach the alveoli. On the other hand, industrial dusts resulting from grinding, drilling, sawing, and the like are about 5 microns or less in diameter and can penetrate to the depths of the lung. The greater the energy used in grinding and the harder the material being ground or broken up, the finer and, therefore, the more dangerous to human health, are the resulting particles (see Chapter 10). It is the particles from 1.0 to 0.1 microns that remain suspended in inhaled air and are the most dangerous. In lung specimens of men who have died of dust-induced diseases, the particles most often found measure 1 micron in diameter.

Some twenty pulmonary diseases caused by industrial dusts have been described and are classified as pneumoconioses. This word literally means "dust retained in the lungs." Of these twenty diseases, six are considered the major pneumoconioses—the most common and the best understood. These are silicosis, asbestosis, talcosis, shaver's disease, diatomite pneumoconiosis, and coal worker's pneumoconiosis.

Silicosis, the most important of the six, has been well known for centuries. Ramazzini called it miner's asthma; others called it rock tuberculosis and grinder's consumption. Silicosis can occur in workers exposed to mineral dusts containing free silica, such as sandstone, flint, quartz, chert, or agate. The disease occurs most often in workers who manufacture and pack abrasive soap powders, in sandblasters working in enclosed tanks,* and in drillers working in tunnels. The most detailed descriptions of silicosis were obtained from studies of South African gold miners who inhaled large amounts of silica when mechanical drills were introduced in the 1880s and 1890s. However, the typical chronic pulmonary condition is also produced after ten to fifteen years of exposure to dust by potters, foundrymen, stonecutters, tile and clay producers, and glassmakers.

When crystalline silica particles are in contact with lung tissue over a period of years, characteristic fibrous nodules develop. These increase in size until round, hard, discrete nodules of from two to four millimeters in diameter are studded throughout the lung. As a result of this loss of spongy tissue to nodule forma-

---

* Sandblasters are well aware of the hazards of their trade; one of their grim jokes is, "Join the Navy and see the world—become a sandblaster and see the next."

tion, shortness of breath, difficulty in breathing, chest pains, and a racking cough are experienced by the silicotic individual. The most important consequence is tuberculosis; the more advanced the lung damage, the greater the likelihood of infection by the tubercle bacillus.

Raw asbestos is found in many countries. The largest mines are in Canada, South Africa, and the Soviet Union. It is a unique material in that it will not burn and thus has many uses, such as in protective clothing for firefighters, pads for ironing boards, brake linings, and boiler and pipe insulation. Chemically, asbestos is a hydrated magnesium silicate found in such minerals as chrysotile (white asbestos), crocidolite (blue asbestos), amosite (brownish) and anthophyllite (white). Chrysotile is the most common fiber and accounts for 80 percent of asbestos used. It is a fibrous material and its dust is composed of microscopic fibrils. It has been well demonstrated that the fibers measuring twenty to fifty microns in length are the most active in the initiation of asbestosis. These fibers must be less than 1 micron in diameter if they are to reach the terminal bronchioles on repeated inhalation. These characteristic fibers are produced during the mining and processing stages of asbestos production.

Although asbestos has been known and used for some two thousand years, it was only in 1927 that asbestosis was described as a clinical entity. In this disease, the lung lesion is not the discrete nodule seen in silicosis but rather a diffuse fibrous infiltration with thickening of the pleural wall. Within the fibrous material are dumbbell-shaped nodules that have formed around asbestos fibers. After many years of concentrated occupational exposure, coughing, expectoration, loss of appetite, and consequent loss of weight occur, followed by progressively increased shortness of breath. In some cases clubbing of the fingers has been reported.

Recent evidence suggests that the general public is exposed to levels of chrysotile asbestos far lower than those encountered in industrial situations; consequently these levels do not appear to be a danger to the health of the general public.

Crocidolite asbestos has been implicated in a rare form of malignant tumor of the pleura known as mesothelioma. Standards for levels of this form of asbestos are usually ten times more stringent than those for chrysotile.

In a recent study, Selikoff, Hammond, and Churg reported that as a group, asbestos insulation workers have a high rate of dying of bronchogenic carcinoma, but that asbestos exposure alone is not the full explanation. They found that asbestos workers who smoked had about 92 times the risk of dying as non-asbestos workers or nonsmoking asbestos workers. They concluded that among asbestos workers "those now smoking should stop immediately." [1]

More recently, a report, *Asbestos: The Need for and Feasibility of Air Pollution Controls,* issued by the NRC-NAS, noted that "at present, there is no evidence that the small number of fibers found in most members of the general population affect health or longevity." The report went on to say that "the major potential for risk appears to lie on those with indirect occupational contacts, household contacts, or residence in the immediate neighborhood of an asbestos source; and even there the actual risk is poorly defined." However, the NRC-NAS does suggest that it would be highly imprudent to permit additional contamination of the public environment with asbestos.[2]

Most recently, a team composed of researchers from Harvard School of Public Health and Boston University School of Medicine studied the effects of low concentrations of asbestos in shipyard pipe coverers. They found that this type of worker ran a considerable risk of developing asbestosis in an environment of low concentrations, but that the effects of the disease usually take about 20 years to become manifest. The researchers emphasized the need for developing lower TLV's for this occupation.[3]

On June 7, 1972, the U.S. Bureau of Labor issued a new set of standards for dust control in the 500 asbestos plants around the country. For the 200,000 industry employees this is an event of historic importance. For most of its 50 years the asbestos industry has gone totally unregulated. The new standards set a mandatory limit of 5 fibers per cubic centimeter of air. Of course this will mean outlays of large sums of money for the equipment needed to purge the air of particles. It should be worth it.

Whereas disease from asbestos, silica, and other dusts has

been known for centuries, the toxic nature of beryllium has been recognized only since 1933. As a result of the need for radioactive material before and during World War II, beryllium, a light-weight grayish-black metal obtained from the ore beryl, was used in substantial quantities in atomic reactors. When beryllium dust is inhaled by workers engaged in the manufacture of X-ray apparatus, neon tubes, fluorescent lamps, and non-sparking tools, both acute and chronic systemic effects, as well as contact dermatitis, can occur. The acute form occurs in response to high concentrations inhaled during a brief exposure, and resembles bronchitis and pneumonia. Symptoms can appear as early as seventy-two hours after exposure. They usually subside after hospitalization for thirty to ninety days and do not recur unless the individual is again exposed to beryllium dust. The chronic disease can occur from a month to twenty years after exposure. A striking feature of the chronic case is that even people who live in the vicinity of plants generating beryllium dust have become victims. Chronic cough and shortness of breath are typical symptoms. On X-ray examination of the lungs, fine nodules dispersed throughout the tissues are seen. Unlike silicosis and asbestosis, beryllosis can be treated, and often dramatic improvements are possible. The use of steroid compounds such as cortisone and ACTH can arrest the disease, and in some cases have even reversed the degeneration of the lungs that occurs. Beryllium is the only non-radioactive element that has produced cancer of the bronchi in laboratory animals, but evidence linking it with human lung cancer is not strong.

Even though Ramazzini observed and recorded the asthmalike respiratory condition produced in workers by flax dust,* it was not until more recent times that inhalation of textile dusts gained acceptance as a cause of lung disease. Workers exposed to dust in the processing of cotton, flax, and hemp experience tightness of the chest, dyspnea (labored breathing), and cough within hours after they return to work on Mondays after a weekend's absence.

The effects of dust exposure have been explained by the

---

* "For a foul and poisonous dust flies out from these materials, enters the mouth, then the throat and lungs, makes the workers cough incessantly, and by degrees brings on asthmatic troubles."

presence of a chemical in the dust which, after long-term, low-level exposure, can trigger a hypersensitivity (on Mondays) in the form of a bronchoconstriction in people with a history of prior exposure. Byssinosis, as this condition is called, has three clinical stages or grades: grade 1, symptoms only on Monday; grade 2, symptoms Monday and on other days of the week; grade 3, continuous dyspnea and chronic cough. This usually occurs after ten or more years of exposure.

Because of the large number of people employed in carding and spinning in textile mills, and because preliminary prevalence studies indicate that some 17,000 workers have byssinosis in any one of its stages, it is important to study this disease and the occupational environment that contributes to it, if it is not to progress to chronic obstructive pulmonary disease.

During the past several years, much has been written about "black lung," a coal-dust-induced pneumoconiosis. Here too, shortness of breath is the key symptom. A man working in a coal mine is presumed to have black lung if he has been exposed to coal dust for at least ten years. Diagnosis is based on the performance of the lung as well as its appearance on X-ray examination. In February 1969, 43,000 angry West Virginia coal miners walked off their jobs in an unprecedented wildcat strike to take their grievance directly to the state legislature. They were anxious to express their views on a bill allowing them to collect workmen's compensation.

More recently a study by William D. Inglis and William H. Anderson, two physicians in Louisville, Kentucky, reported that inhalation of coal dust does not appear to be a primary cause of premature disability and lung disease. After studying seven hundred Kentucky miners, they observed that "a reduction in cigarette smoking can be expected to result in a significant reduction in disabling chronic obstructive pulmonary disease in the miner."

We need other investigators to undertake controlled studies that will lead to definitive data on coal dust and pneumoconiosis.

The evaluation of occupational hazards, a necessary first step for establishing controls, requires that a well-directed plant survey be undertaken. The survey should delineate which operations or physical aspects of the contained environment constitute a potential danger to those in the area. This must not be a superficial study by semi- or non-professionals. Industrial hygiene engineers or others trained in environmental or public health should be involved in the planning, direction, and actual surveying. It is simply too difficult to evaluate a sample, condition, or process without firsthand knowledge of the individual plant in operation.

Surveys of the frequency and types of occupational injuries (I avoid using the word *accident,* since many industrial injuries may not be chance occurrences; see Chapter 11) have revealed that 25 percent of all disabling industrial injuries occur to the hand. Thus, protection of the hands should be a major concern of employer and employee.

The most effective way to insure a safe environment is to eliminate hazardous chemicals, devices, and practices. Practically, this may not be possible or even necessary. Safety does not mean the complete eradication of all potentially harmful agents. It only means that such materials are used judiciously. The TLV's and MAC's already discussed imply that certain chemicals are dangerous when they exceed certain concentrations; they do not imply that the very presence of these chemicals is to be disallowed.

Accordingly, the first step in creating a safe environment is to ascertain the amount and type of contamination in the work areas. It may be that simple dilution of contaminated air by ventilation with uncontaminated air will solve the problem. If an operation is inherently dangerous, such as the use of tetraethyl lead, the entire operation can be isolated from the general work area and the individuals performing the operation can be fitted with protective clothing, such as self-contained half-masks and full-face respirators, or supplied with air hoods and helmets (Figures 87, 88). Personal, self-contained air conditioning units with self-regulating temperature controls are now available for workers who must be totally enclosed in protective suits. Hard hats, shin guards, and toe and foot guards are also available. There are protective aprons of many kinds, including the "kickback" type to prevent abdominal injury to sawyers as lumber is ejected by power-driven saws. Gloves, goggles, ear guards, and protective creams can further reduce injuries.

While walking through the lobby of a large hotel in New York City recently, I saw a procedure that seemed guaranteed to

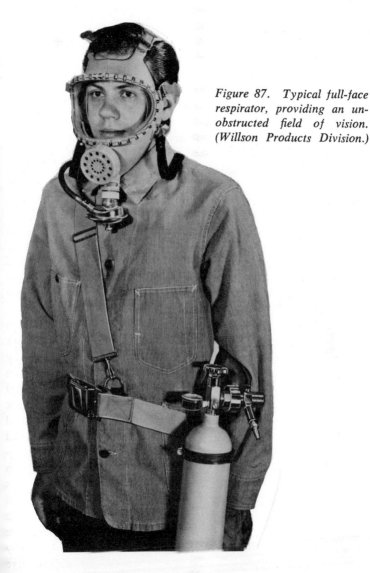

Figure 87. Typical full-face respirator, providing an unobstructed field of vision. (Willson Products Division.)

produce injury to the men using it. Two men were attempting to stretch and straighten a large wall-to-wall rug. Each was on his hands and knees moving sideways across the rug. As he moved,

Figure 88. Protective breathing apparatus for individuals whose larynx has been removed. (Willson Products Division.)

each moved a rug-stretcher held in his right hand firmly down and forward. The metal prongs on the bottom grasped the rug and held it as each man brought up his left knee and imparted a resounding whack to the padded knob of the stretcher; this stretched the rug considerably, but it took at least eighteen such knee-kicks by each man to finish the job properly. Although I didn't inquire, I'm ready to wager that shooting pains in the leg and even occasional limping have occurred more than once to these men. New tools such as the rug-stretcher and new processes often engender new occupational hazards. Surely a less troublesome way of stretching rugs, for example, could be devised.

"Laser" is the acronym for Light Amplification by Stimulated Emission of Radiation. And laser is a device for producing an intense unidirectional beam of light. However, the light produced can be so intense that it can pierce a steel beam. If one scientific and technological development of the past fifteen years can be considered the most potentially useful as well as the most potentially harmful, lasers would in all likelihood receive the designation. Laser technology is an excellent example of how the advance of knowledge creates new hazards. However, as its potential for harm is so great, and public and professional concern with the adverse side effects of new technologies is at a high level, evaluation of laser hazards is proceeding well. As lasers emit electromagnetic radiation, they come under P.L. 90-602, the Radiation Control for Health and Safety Act (1968). Under the law, manufacturers of laser products must comply with pre-set standards and are then responsible for providing adequate protection against emissions of harmful rays.

Implications for health hazards come from two sources: industrial workers who use laser devices and work in close proximity to laser beams; and the general public, who will begin to use more and more products with the possibility of greater exposure. As laser beams are known to produce skin burns and damage to the retina of the eye, it was of more than passing concern that a recent survey among construction workers revealed an almost total disregard for the use of safety goggles to prevent eye injuries. Apparently, neither the workers nor the supervisory personnel are aware of the inherent dangers of lasers.

A great deal of protection can be afforded workers by general good housekeeping practices. Regular removal of waste materials prevents hazardous substances from building up on floors and ledges. Materials spilled on floors and tables should be cleaned up immediately. Where feasible, a special team or individual could be trained to handle this.

One of the most important preventive measures is regular examination of employees by competent medical personnel trained to evaluate occupational problems. Examinations at three- or six-month intervals could pick up early signs of illness, spot susceptible individuals, and determine whether an illness is in fact the result of some in-plant exposure. Medical records can help pinpoint particularly hazardous operations in the plant. Spot maps, like those used to study diseases of epidemic proportions, can signal the process or area in a plant where numerous cases of some illness have occurred. Once these areas are located, conditions can be modified.

Personal hygiene is also important in any program of prevention. Copious use of soap and water can markedly reduce the incidence of skin diseases. This simple expedient is often neglected by many people who come in contact with potentially toxic materials. In-plant washing facilities should include shower rooms.

The working environment need not contribute the amount of illness and injury it presently does. Moving in the direction of substantially improving this habitat, the new, comprehensive Occupational Safety and Health Act of 1970 (P.L. 91-456) became effective on April 28, 1971. Under the new law, every employer engaged in a business affecting commerce will be subject to stricter safety and health standards: federal on-site inspectors; fines up to $1,000 for non-serious violations, $10,000 for repeated violations; and the Federal District Court partially or totally closing a business if these warnings are ignored. Under the act, employees can demand immediate inspections and they or their representative must be permitted to accompany the inspector. Funds will also be available for studies dealing with occupational health and safety.

To underline the new spirit embodied in the law, the first citation issued under the act occurred in May 1971. It accused the Allied Chemical Corporation's Moundsville, West Virginia, plant of maintaining hazardous conditions that evoked symptoms of mercury poisoning in scores of workers. Specifically, the complaint charged that the levels of mercury vapor in the air greatly exceeded existing TLV's. Apparently the company is proceeding satisfactorily to correct the conditions that produced the classical neurological symptoms of mercury poisoning.

It became obvious that control and prevention of occupational hazards are the responsibility of all personnel in a plant, both workers and management. Improvement in working conditions can only benefit both.

Perhaps the ultimate occupational hazard was brought to light recently in Sydney, Australia. According to the spokesman for The Hospital Research Employees Association, shift workers should get more money to compensate for their disrupted sex life. He maintained that only increased wages could compensate for the "enormous strain placed on marital and general family relations by someone working irregular hours." He went on to say that "the sexual activities of a shift worker definitely are interfered with by the odd hours worked. Unmarried employees also suffer as shift work drastically limits their opportunities to mingle with members of the opposite sex." Let us hope all occupational 'illnesses" will be as amenable to solution as this.

References

1. I. J. Selikoff, E. Cuyler Hammond, and J. Churg, "Asbestos Exposure, Smoking and Neoplasia," *Journal of the American Medical Association* 204 (1968): 104.

2. *Asbestos: The Need for and Feasibility of Air Pollution Controls* (*Biological Effects of Atmospheric Pollutants*) (Washington: NAS-NRC Division of Medical Sciences, 1971).

3. R. L. H. Murphy, B. G. Ferris, W. A. Burgess, J. Worcester, and E. A. Gaensler, "Effects of Low Concentrations of Asbestos: Clinical, Environmental, Radiologic and Epidemiologic Observations in Shipyard Covers and Controls," *New England Journal of Medicine* 285 (1971): 1271.

Suggested Reading

Bouhuys, Arend; Wolfson, R. L.; Horner, D. W.; Brain, J. D.; and Zuskin, E. "Byssinosis in Cotton Textile Workers: Respiratory

Survey of a Mill with Rapid Labor Turnover." *Annals of Internal Medicine* 71 (1969): 257.

Permissible Levels of Occupational Exposure to Airborne Toxic Substances. 6th Report of the Joint ILO/WHO Committee on Occupational Health. Geneva: WHO Tech. Rept. Series no. 415, 1969.

Bradley, F. J.; Roberto, S. N.; and Ratajack, R. J. "Evaluation of Laser Hazards in the Construction Industry." *Industrial Hygiene Review* (New York State Department of Labor–Division of Industrial Hygiene) 13 (1971): 7.

Lutz, A. M., and Steward, H. "Trends in Laser Applications: Public Health Implications." *Journal of the American Public Health Association* 61 (1971): 2277.

CHAPTER
14

IONIZING RADIATION

The rediscovery of the kingdom of nature might also make it possible to love as well as to use the new world that is coming into being.

Scott Buchanan

Unquestionably the most important scientific discovery of this century was the demonstration that the energy of atoms could be released and controlled. Success on December 2, 1942 proved the feasibility of splitting the atom and harnessing astounding amounts of energy. However, some sixty years ago it was learned that there are traces of radioactivity all around us, that we are subject to natural radiation through our existence. It wasn't, of course, until the explosion of a nuclear device that the public health aspects of radiation assumed importance.

Before we discuss the effects, uses, and problems of relatively large quantities of man-made radiation, some facts about low-level natural background radiation may be helpful.

The natural radiation to which each of us is exposed may be from external sources: granite floors or walls containing traces of radium that emit gamma radiation; the soil upon which we build our homes; or cosmic rays. Internal natural irradiation is emitted by potassium-40, an essential constituent of living tissue. We take natural radioactive materials into our bodies with every breath we take, with the water we drink, and with the food we eat.

Recently we have begun to be irradiated by man-made radioactive materials such as cesium-137, a gamma emitter produced during atomic explosions and deposited by rain in a thin layer on the surface of the earth. In this form, it can be an external source of irradiation; the same element may be ingested in milk and meat obtained from animals pastured on grasslands on which the fallout was deposited. This type of man-made or artificial external and internal irradiation is not part of the natural background. Table 23 shows the sources of natural low-level irradiation.

The predominant natural alpha radioactivity of our environment comes from the long-lived isotopes of uranium and thorium. Both of these elements have half lives comparable with the age of the earth. Most soils contain traces of radium derived from uranium and thorium present in the original rock that, on weathering, became a constituent of soil.

The background of gamma radiation at any given location on the earth is roughly proportionate to the concentration of radioactive material, and thus also varies with the soil type. For example, over igneous rock (rock of volcanic origin) radiation may be as high as one hundred or two hundred millirems per year; over chalk deposits, it may be as low as twenty-five millirems per year. Table 24 is a selected sampling of natural background sites around the world, and Figure 89 shows how natural radiation from different sources is varied.

The unusually high natural backgrounds in Kerala, India and Espirito Santo, Brazil have been cause for cautious concern. Studies are under way in both cities to uncover possible hazards to health from long-term residence in this environment. It is still too early to tell whether decreased life expectancy, congenital malformations, metabolic errors, and cancer are more common in these areas than in cities with far lower natural radiation levels.

In the lower atmosphere, the dose rate from cosmic radiation is primarily a function of elevation, and secondarily of latitude.

TABLE 23.

Sources of natural background irradiation.

Sources of Irradiation	Dose rate (millirems* per year)		
	Gonad	*Bone Marrow*	*Haversion Canal*
External irradiation			
Cosmic rays ** (including neutrons)	50	50	50
Terrestrial (including air)	50	50	50
Internal irradiation			
Potassium-40	20	15	15
Radium-226 (and decay products)	0.5	5.4	0.6
Radium-228 (and decay products)	0.8	8.6	1.0
Lead-210	0.3	3.6	0.4
Carbon-14	0.7	1.6	1.6
Radon-222 (absorbed in bloodstream)	3	3	3
	125	137	122

    * The rem, an acronym for "roentgen equivalent man," is a unit of absorbed dose of ionizing radiation that accounts for biological effectiveness. A dose in rem is numerically equivalent to a dose in rad. The rem is useful to measure permissible exposure levels and where mixtures of radiation must be considered, as it takes into account the biological damage produced by a given unit of energy. For X- and gamma rays the rem and rad are the same. A millirem (mrem) is 1/1000 of a rem.

    A roentgen (R) is a unit of exposure to either X- or gamma radiation.

    The curie is a unit of radioactivity. A material or substance is said to have an activity of one curie if it is transformed at the rate of 3.7×10^7 disintegrations per second.

    ** The radioactive activity of cosmic rays increases with altitude; thus Denver, the "mile-high city," is exposed to greater radiation than New York City, at sea level.

At sea level the dose rate from cosmic radiation is about 30 mrem per year in Florida and approximately 35 in Alaska. On the average, the annual cosmic ray dose equivalent in the United States is about 45 mrem.

    The contribution from the ground varies from place to place. Terrestrial dose rates range from about 30 mrem per year in

TABLE 24.

*Dose of irradiation to gonads and bones
from natural external sources, including cosmic rays.*

Region	Dose (rem/year)
New York City	75
Granitic regions of France	190
Espirito Santo, Brazil	320
Kerala, India	900

Dallas to about 130 in Denver. The two sources taken together result in an average annual dose around the United States of some 125 mrem. It is unlikely to be much less than 100 mrem for any individual and highly unlikely to be greater than 400 mrem for any segment of the population, no matter where they live.

Radiation, in its broadest sense, means the transfer of electromagnetic waves through space. Radiation is energy in motion, and it produces an effect only if energy is transferred to matter. Accordingly, a major effect of radiation on matter is to increase its energy content. In addition, chemical bonds are broken, permitting ions and chemical radicals to re-form in unique ways. Radiation creates new chemical species.

The radiations or rays emitted by radioactive elements are called alpha (α) rays, beta (β) rays, gamma (γ) rays, and X-rays. All of these taken together are referred to as *ionizing radiations*. They are called ionizing because when they strike atoms of the material through which they pass, they knock out an electron. This removal of an electron confers great reactivity on the atom, which is now positively charged, or ionized. This is simply another way of describing the increase in energy content. Ionization is the mechanism by which radiation causes physical, chemical, or biological changes.

Now although these rays are highly energized, they are not equally dangerous. By dangerous, we mean capable of penetrating matter. Figure 90 illustrates this concept. Alpha particles are the least penetrating. They can be stopped by a thin sheet of paper, a thin film of water, or the outer layer of skin. (Alpha particles can be dangerous if they are inhaled or ingested, because they

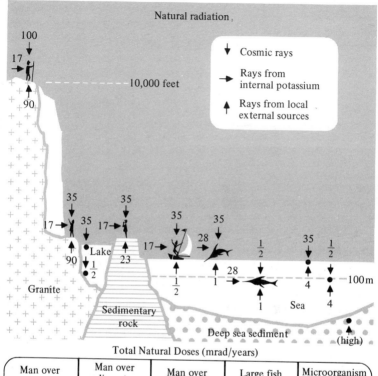

Figure 89. The multiplicity of sources from which we receive impingements of material radiation, and differences in intensity according to location. The numbers within the circles represent averages and do not include exceptionally high natural background areas. (Source: NAS-NRC Publication No. 551, The Effects of Atomic Radiation on Oceanography and Fisheries.)

Man over granite		Man over sedimentary rock	Man over sea	Large fish in sea		Microorganism in sea ●	
10,000	m.s.l.	75	52	surface	100m	surface	100m
207	142			64	30	39	5

Total Natural Doses (mrad/years)

can penetrate into soft tissue.) Beta particles are stopped by a 1 mm. thickness of aluminum. They can penetrate at least half an inch into skin or tissue. Gamma particles are the most danger-

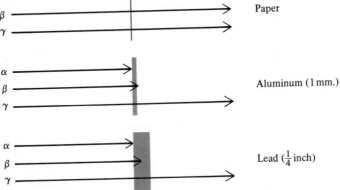

Figure 90.   Penetration capabilities of three types of particles.

ous because of their extremely great ability to penetrate matter. They penetrate organs, tissues, and bone; thus it is the gamma ray that shielding must protect against. Our clothing is sufficient to protect against both alpha and beta radiations, but not against gamma radiation.

One of the problems of radioactivity is its persistence, resulting in continuous ionization. The relative persistence of radiation is determined by the length of time it takes for half the atoms of some radioactive substance to disintegrate: This is the half life of the specific substance, and it is as characteristic of the substance as fingerprints are of a person. Half lives vary from fractions of seconds to millions of years. Table 25 gives the half life of eight representative radioactive elements.

At the end of one period the element has lost half of its activity; at the end of the second period, half of the remaining activity has been lost, leaving a quarter of the original activity. At the end of the third period half of that quarter is lost, and so on as the amount remaining approaches zero. Thus, the shorter the half life the less dangerous the element is, while the longer the half life the longer the period over which the element is able to emit radiation, which causes ionization and, thereby, injury. In

TABLE 25.

Half lives of radioactive elements.

Element	Half Life
Nitrogen-16	8 seconds
Bromine-85	3 minutes
Sodium-24	14.8 hours
Iodine-131	8 days
Cesium-137	33 years
Radium-226	1,600 years
Carbon-14	5,600 years
Thorium-232	10 billion years

biological terms this means that an element with a relatively long half life, such as strontium-90 from fallout debris (which has a half life of twenty-eight years), can remain sufficiently long in tissue to become carcinogenic. On the other hand, certain radioactive agents with half lives of ten hours to ten days are used to treat disease; this is sufficient to deliver the required dose, but not long enough to cause injury.

The power of a nuclear weapon is due to the almost instantaneous transformation of atomic mass into energy. According to Einstein's formula $E = mc^2$ (energy equals mass multiplied by the square of the velocity of light) the fission of a single atom of uranium-235 will yield roughly two hundred million electron volts. Thus weapons having thousands of times the destructive force of TNT can be constructed.

The energy in a typical air burst produced by a thermonuclear device has been found to be distributed as follows: blast and shock, 50 percent; thermal radiation, 35 percent; initial nuclear radiation, 5 percent; and residual nuclear radiation, 10 percent. The immediate effects of this set of responses would be mechanical injuries, injuries due to heat, and those due to radiation.

The mechanical injuries would be caused directly by the blast's shock wave and secondarily by flying debris and collapsing buildings. Tests with dummy figures at the Nevada test site indicate that a man standing or walking in the vicinity of the blast could be picked up and hurled twenty feet. The injuries caused by heat or by thermal radiation result from direct exposure to extremely high temperatures. Temperatures within the fireball of a one-megaton device range up to one million degrees Fahrenheit; this is comparable to the temperature in the center of the sun. Accordingly, anything within three thousand feet of the fireball would be vaporized. Varying degrees of flame burns from spreading fires would also occur.

The injuries we are most concerned with are those resulting from intense, acute doses of gamma radiation received in less than a minute, and those from the delayed effects of fallout. Since a great deal has been written on the effect of radiation on various body tissues, on the carcinogenic effects and even the genetic effects to be expected, let us focus on the factors that affect survival.

The lethal dose of radiation is generally designated as the LD_{50-30}: that is, the dose of radiation that would be expected to kill 50 percent of a population within thirty days. For obvious reasons, this has never been determined experimentally for humans. Thus, animal studies and the data from Hiroshima and Nagasaki must be used to predict the expected LD_{50-30}.

It has been suggested that 450 roentgens of radiation is the human lethal dose. However, this value has been obtained from animals given no supportive or protective treatment. Consequently, estimates of the lethal dose obtained in a single day have been scaled upwards of 600 to 700 R. Furthermore, if the dose were divided—if it were given over several days or weeks—probably a great deal more could be sustained with survival. Thus, a dose of 1400 R is currently being suggested as the upper limit at which survival is possible. Evidence for this comes from experience with overall body irradiation of patients with incurable cancer.

On March 1, 1954, a thermonuclear device was detonated from a barge in the Marshall Islands. At that time, twenty-eight American airmen were gathering weather data on the island of Rongerik, 160 miles from Bikini, the point of detonation. As a consequence of the blast, radioactive debris fell in such abundance that the monitoring detectors were completely disrupted. In addition to the airmen on Rongerik, a number of people lived on the nearby islands of Rongelap, Utirik, and Alinginae. Several days after the detonation, it was learned that a Japanese fishing vessel, the Fukuru Maru, had been inside the fallout area.

Although the fallout was so great as to be visible, neither the sixty-four residents of the islands nor the twenty-three fishermen took any precautions to reduce their exposure. As a consequence, all of these people lived in intimate contact with the most radio-active environment ever known to exist. The Japanese fishermen described the fallout dust as being as heavy as a snowfall. It covered the hair and came into direct contact with skin and eyes. Food and water were heavily contaminated. More than two days after the blast, the islanders were taken to a military hospital on the island of Kwajalein for medical examinations. The fishermen had been in contact with this severe fallout for thirteen days before they reached their home port, and only then did they learn why they were ill. All twenty-three of them were hospitalized. Itching and burning of the skin were felt by most of those who had been exposed; ulceration of the skin and severe loss of hair usually followed. It was found that the severity of the ulceration and hair loss for both the fishermen and the islanders was directly related to the amount of clothing they had been wearing. The most severe burns occurred among the fishermen who did not wear hats. Effects on the blood were related to the degree of the whole-body gamma irradiation dose.

Figure 91 shows changes in skin pigmentation as a result of beta radiation. On the top (part A) is a burn on the neck of a Rongelap Islander one month after accidental exposure. On the bottom, part B shows the same person one year later. Complete recovery has been effected.

Since both islanders and fishermen had been so totally blanketed with fallout the amount of radiation ingested and inhaled was undoubtedly at a maximum. The islanders had drunk water from exposed sources and eaten food that was completely exposed to the atmosphere. Because the Japanese ate fish that had come in contact with the contaminated deck of their ship, they ingested a large internal dose. Chemical analysis of urine specimens indicated that the natives had received from 100 to 150 R to the thyroid in addition to a whole-body dose of 175 R.

Six months after leaving the hospital, one of the fishermen died of a diseased liver. The amount of radionuclides in his tissue

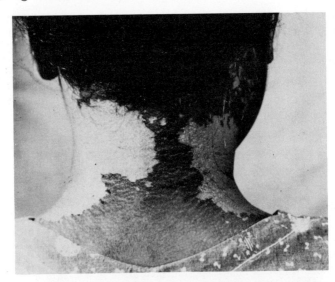

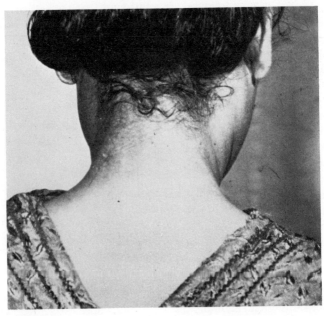

Figure 91. Effects of beta radiation on the skin. (Photos courtesy of Brookhaven National Laboratory.)

was so low that death from radiation due to isotopes with long half lives was ruled out.

In 1960, the islanders were examined again. Both those who had been exposed and those who had not were in generally good health. There was no evidence of disease that could be related to the effects of fallout.

In May 1966, five natives from Rongelap were brought to New England Deaconess Hospital in Boston because they had developed thyroid gland nodules as a result of ingesting radioactive substances. These growths were removed, and examination showed them to be non-cancerous.

Thirteen of the original eighty-seven islanders and fishermen died as a result of the fallout. According to Dr. Robert Conrad, Physician-in-Charge at Brookhaven National Laboratories, the survivors have recovered completely from the ill effects of radioactive fallout.

From repeated examinations of the exposed islanders, fishermen, and airmen, several conclusions emerge: inhalation and ingestion of radioactive substances appear to be very much less of a problem than originally believed, and burns from fallout can be minimized or completely avoided by using proper clothing, washing exposed parts quickly, or remaining indoors.

In 1954, following a long series of atomic and hydrogen weapons tests, scientists drew public attention to the fact that the atmosphere, the oceans, and the land surfaces of our planet were being contaminated by radioactive fallout. Atmospheric testing of nuclear devices is known to produce in its fallout such isotopes as iodine-131, a short-lived species; strontium-90 and cesium-137, which decay within a human lifetime; and carbon-14, whose half life is approximately 5,600 years. The scientists revealed that great quantities of radioactive substances ejected into the air by each detonation were caught up by air currents, carried across the globe, and deposited on land and sea. These radioactive elements were then rapidly absorbed by edible food crops and ingested by man. As a consequence of the significant rise in environmental radioactivity, the scientists warned of the potential dangers to humanity and asked for a cessation of all nuclear weapons testings. To assess the problem, the United Nations convened a committee of leading scientists from fifteen countries.

After three years of deliberations, the committee submitted its report. It stated that if atomic weapons tests continued, hundreds of thousands of people would die or become ill due to altered hereditary mechanisms, leukemia, and other forms of cancer.* Subsequently, an international test-ban treaty was proposed.**

During the past ten years, the subject of the genetic effects of radiation has been discussed at such length that it hardly seems possible that anything remains to be said. Nevertheless, I want to present several findings that cannot be ignored in evaluating the potential or actual hazards of man-made radiation.

Without doubt, the outstanding opportunity to study and analyze the possible mutagenic effects of radiation in man arose as a consequence of the atomic bombing of the Japanese cities of Hiroshima and Nagasaki on August 6 and 9, 1945. But it is often said that today we know little more about the effects of ionizing radiations on people than we did in July 1945. Is this so? What has been gleaned from years of studying the Japanese population?

Recognizing the importance of a careful appraisal of ill effects to the survivors of the bombing, the National Academy of Sciences-National Research Council established the Atomic Bomb Casualty Commission (ABCC) and charged it with responsibility for investigating the effects of the bombing. In 1947, the Commission entered the devastated cities. The immediate genetic interest in Hiroshima and Nagasaki stemmed from the demonstration in 1927 by Nobel laureate H. J. Muller that X rays could produce mutations in fruitflies. Although the bombing of Hiroshima and Nagasaki offered the most propitious opportunity to study the genetic effects of radiation in man, the doses received by the survivors, surprisingly enough, were low by comparison with those used in laboratory experiments with animals. The ABCC designed a population study of approximately three hundred thousand people—probably the largest of its kind ever attempted—in which it proposed to obtain evidence of potential and actual genetic damage.

* These predictions were based primarily on mathematical calculations rather than studies of irradiated populations.

** This became a political hot potato. Candidates in the 1964 presidential election took opposing sides on what became an important public issue.

To accomplish such a monumental task, two major requirements had to be satisfied: one was an unexposed control population comparable in age, sex, weight, height, diet, occupation, etc., to the exposed population; the second was a set of criteria or indicators by which to assess damage. The question posed by the ABCC was not, "Is there damage?" but rather, "Can the damage be detected?" This concept recognized that genetic damage need not manifest itself in gross or dramatic aberrations. Thus, the indicators of genetic damage around which the population study was designed were: increase in stillbirths * and neonatal deaths,** increase in deaths during the first months of life; increase in congenital malformations; decrease in birthweight; altered sex ratio; and impaired physical development at nine months. The relative broadness of these indicators created the need for an adequate control population.

Today, analysis of the data for all of the indicators chosen indicates few clearly discernible trends.[1] There were no clear relationships between the radiation dose experienced by the parents and the frequency of stillbirths and neonatal deaths, birthweight, and congenital malformations. In a 1953 summary of the data an equivocal relationship with sex ratio appeared. However, when thousands of additional cases were studied, the combined total annulled that relationship. Additionally, there were no differences in the frequency of deaths during the first nine months of life, a particularly sensitive criterion of infant viability, among infants born to exposed and non-exposed parents.

The ABCC calculated that, allowing for shielding, the population of Hiroshima and Nagasaki had received about 100 to 175 rads † of gamma irradiation. This is just about equal to the dose received by the exposed islanders and fishermen after the 1954 detonation in the Marshall Islands.

How are we to interpret the apparent absence of radiation

---

* A stillbirth is a fetal death which occurs after twenty eight weeks of gestation.

** A neonatal death is one occurring before the twenty-eighth day of life.

† The rad is a unit of absorbed dose, differing from the roentgen (R), which is used as a unit of exposure.

effects in the offspring of exposed parents? Evidence from labora-tory experiments, which can direct larger doses to any organ or tissue than could the bombings, has clearly shown genetic effects in plants and mice; it is difficult to conceive that man is unique in his response to gamma radiation. Consequently, we must turn back to the indicators or criteria chosen to demonstrate muta-tions (inherited changes in genes and chromosomes) or other genetic effects; rather than conclude that the atomic bombings had no harmful genetic effects, we should, perhaps, more rightly conclude that thus far such effects have not been demonstrated.

Support for this position comes from two independent but parallel studies. Dr. William Beierwalter of the University of Michigan observed chromosomal abnormalities in human subjects following irradiation with iodine-131. He has been unable to relate these abnormalities to actual or potential genetic or somatic defects.[2] A. D. Bloom and his team examined chromosomal ma-terial from leucocytes (white blood cells) of survivors of the bombings in Hiroshima and Nagasaki and found no alteration in the number or condition of the chromosomes.[3] Thus, it bears re-peating that the amount of radiation a person can receive and survive without lasting effect remains unknown; but the effects of the atomic bombings on the survivors have not been as grim as many had predicted. However, it must be added that twenty years is a relatively short period; it may well be that more time is needed for effects to become apparent.

The problem of evaluating injury to a population becomes progressively more difficult as the potentially harmful agent is steadily reduced. Radiation studies illustrate this point. In the early years, the permissible exposure level was set at 100 milli-roentgens per day. When damage was observed in experimental studies on animals, the permissible level was reduced to 300 mr/week. Still more research suggested that further reductions should be made, so that by the early 1960s, 100 mr/week became the permissible exposure for man. These reductions were made despite the fact that studies with human subjects at each of these permis-sible levels failed to show evidence of illness or injury. It should be noted that each successive reduction in permissible level re-quired a significant outlay of money and engineering effort and was done to accommodate calculated scientific judgment of possible mutational damage to human genes.

In 1957, Ehrenberg, Ehrenstein, and Hedgran of the University of Stockholm reported that increased numbers of spontaneous mutations could be expected with increased temperature of the gonads. They suggested that mutations during the past several centuries were due to men's wearing trousers, which can increase testicular temperatures by three degrees Centigrade. By calculating the increase in mutations and by extrapolating to men aged twenty to forty, as had been done for ionizing radiation, the researchers concluded that the harmful genetic effect of our clothing was one hundred to one thousand times greater than that from all the radiation to which we are now exposed. They suggested that the kilts worn by Scots were far less conducive to temperature increases. In addition, they noted that regularly taken hot baths raise the gonadal temperature to levels conducive to mutational changes.[4]

Interestingly enough, in April 1967, Derek Robinson and John Rock of the Rock Reproductive Clinic in Brookline, Massachusetts, reported that men who wore tight insulating garments for six to eleven weeks had severely depressed sperm production. They noted that even athletic-type undershorts can raise the temperature of the testes and hinder sperm production. Perhaps there is a message here for population control.

Johannes Clemmesen of the Copenhagen Cancer Registry (where the world's oldest national cancer registry is maintained) recently reported that testis carcinoma, a relatively rare malignancy, appears to be on the increase among middle-aged men. He pointed out that the incidence of the disease has risen from 3.2 to 6.3 per 100,000 in the past twenty years. According to Dr. Clemmesen, this gonadal malignancy may be due to increased use of jockey shorts, which is believed to raise testicular temperature and thus foster tumor growth.[6]

Some twenty years ago, nuclear weapons testing began in Nevada. During that time, large numbers of people near the test sites were exposed to radioactive fission products. As a consequence of these tests, iodine-131 rained down to settle on crops grazed upon by cattle. Ingestion by cattle implies concentration in milk, which can be conveyed to those who drink milk. In children, the iodine concentrates in the thyroid gland, where it can induce nodule formation.

Recently, Weiss and co-workers, working under a contract from the Utah State Division of Health, attempted to ascertain if the radioactive fallout from this testing produced abnormalities in children living in southwestern Utah and a portion of Nevada and Arizona. To identify children with abnormal thyroid glands, all schoolchildren between the ages of eleven and eighteen were given a physical exam by a team of physicians. They found thyroid nodularity "with equal frequency among children potentially exposed and those not exposed." They went on to remark that "within the limitations of the study there was no evidence that children of southwestern Utah and adjacent areas of Nevada and Arizona near the test site have received enough radiation to produce significant thyroid disease." [7]

In attempting to formulate radiation protection standards, the Federal Radiation Council in 1960 wrote that "if beneficial uses were fully exploited without regard to radiation protection, the resulting biological risk might well be considered too great. Reducing the risk to zero would virtually eliminate any radiation use, and result in the loss of all possible benefits. It is, therefore, necessary to strike a balance between maximum use and zero risk. In establishing radiation protection standards, the balancing of risk and benefit is a decision involving medical, social, economic, political and other factors. Such a balance cannot be made on the basis of a precise mathematical formula but must be a matter of informed judgment."

This point of view is often discounted by people who are primarily concerned with damage to the protoplasm of unborn generations. Of course, obtaining direct evidence *now* either to support or discount such fears is impossible. Recently, however, Dr. E. L. Green, director of the Jackson Laboratory at Bar Harbor, Maine, reported that his studies of eighteen generations of mice (equivalent to five hundred to six hundred human years) revealed that accumulated ancestral radiation had very little physical effect.[8] He indicated, too, that population survival may not be endangered by radiation, as had been thought. Perhaps these findings will bring some measure of comfort to those who rail against air pollution but denounce all plans for clean sources of power in the form of nuclear power plants.

Speaking on technology and the life sciences at a symposium on "The Impact of Engineering on the Bio-Sciences," Dr. Alvin Weinberg presented an example of the type of problem the public demands that scientists resolve, but which is beyond the capability of science.

> . . . . we believe that in mice 30 rads given at high dose will double the spontaneous mutation rate in a single locus. . . . Can we devise an experiment to determine directly whether 150 mrad (the yearly dose allowed by the old standards) will cause an 0.5 percent increase in mutation rate? The answer is no; it will take 8 billion mice to show directly the expected 0.5 percent effect. Here is a question raised by science, yet is unanswerable by science; yet upon whose outcome may depend the public acceptance of a most important technology—nuclear energy.[9]

In October 1971, speaking at the Astronautical Congress in Brussels, Dr. Charles Berry revealed that the Apollo 14 astronauts received a radiation dose of 1,140 mrem. This is about four times the dose presently permitted individuals under the 1960 AEC guidelines. Dr. Berry called the level "of no hazard or biological significance."

In January 1971, dose-limiting recommendations for permissible exposure levels were published by the National Council on Radiation Protection. These are now in the process of evaluation by the Criteria and Standards Division of the Environmental Protection Agency. Table 26 lists several proposed values. However, until these new values are discussed and accepted, the basic exposure levels or protection standards for the general population remain: workers—5,000 mrem/yr; individuals—500, with 170 as an average for a sample of the population.

Because development and acceptance of standards involve value judgments (which should be based on reliable evidence) that can vary substantially from individual to individual, they will and perhaps must remain controversial and subject to con-

TABLE 26.
NCRP recommended guidelines, 1971.

Maximum Permissible Dose			
Equivalent for occupational exposure	5,000	mrem	in one year
Skin	1,500	″	
Hands	7,500	″	(2,500/Qtr.)
Forearms	3,000	″	(1,000/Qtr.)
Dose limits for the public			
Individual	500		
Student	100		
Population dose limits			
Genetic	170		
Somatic	170		

tinual appraisal. They also fall within what Weinberg calls trans-science: questions beyond the ability of science to answer; questions that only the public can answer for itself.

Any discussion of the hazards of ionizing radiations would be misleading and unfair if adequate emphasis were not given to the many benefits obtained from this relatively new energy source, through new procedures in medicine and public health, agriculture, food preservation, and a host of industrial practices.

Although physicians and dentists have used radiation in the form of X-rays for a generation, the many additional possibilities for serving man are only now being widely explored. A property of radiation gaining wide usefulness is its ability to cause the regression and often the complete disappearance of malignant tumors. The use of radium has been a standard therapeutic procedure for years. Sealed in needles or tubes and implanted in a tumor or placed on the surface of a malignant growth, its alpha and gamma emissions can suppress the uncontrolled proliferation of cancerous cells.

The administration of radioisotopes orally or intravenously is gaining wide acceptance as a therapeutic tool. Radioiodine-131 is the isotope most frequently employed. Its usefulness depends upon the ability of the thyroid gland to take up and concentrate the stable isotope. In this way, selected areas receive a large dose of highly localized radiation.

Another more recent innovation is the technique of dilution-analysis. With this method, a known quantity of iodine-131 or chromium-51 is tagged to a protein such as albumin and injected into the bloodstream. After allowing time for the tracer or "tag" to become distributed, a sample of blood is obtained and its radiation measured. In this way an accurate determination of blood volume can be made. A variation of this procedure is used to determine circulation rate, thereby supplying evidence of circulation impediments.

By placing a radioactive "tag" on insects, the flight range and flight patterns of disease-carrying species can be traced. As the tagged specimens are trapped days or weeks later, their place of capture is spotted on a map. Control and prevention programs thus have a greater chance of success.

In Figure 92, a rat is shown in a metabolic chamber. Radioisotopic tests are an important supportive test in toxicological studies showing where chemical compounds—food additives or drugs, for example—go in the body. After the animal is dosed, it is placed in a metabolic chamber where its air, feces, and urine are collected and later analyzed.

In agricultural research, the radioactive calcium-45 isotope has been successfully used to study the uptake of the stable isotope by the roots of plants. Increased crop yields have resulted from this study. In other experiments, tracer studies showed that nutrients could be applied to the leaves of fruit trees to increase the yield of fruit.

Over the past few years, a new revolution has come upon the agricultural scene. The green revolution refers to the high-yielding varieties of crops, especially grains, that are being derived from radiation-induced mutations. Indeed, induced mutations may also be used to improve the food quality of the crop to combine nutritional value with high yield. The high-yielding rice and wheat have a short, stiff straw. This means that added fertilizer produces more grain instead of more stalk or leaf, and it also means that the plant does not break or bend in high wind and rain. The Japanese rice variety Rei mei had its straw reduced by gamma radiation. The better baking quality of the mutant wheat Sharbati Sonora is shown in Figure 93. The parent Mexican variety (Sonora-64) and Lerma Rojo, grown in India,

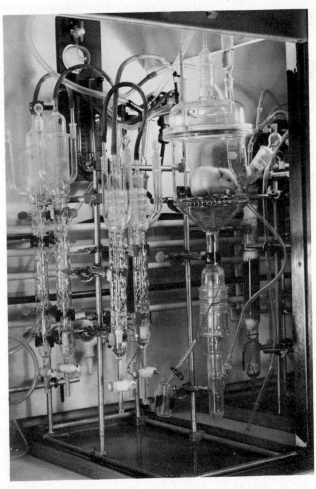

Figure 92. Metabolic chamber.

produce smaller, denser loaves. Radiation is also used to breed new mutant varieties that have greater resistance to the depredations of insects and disease.

For the past twenty years, research studies dealing with the preservation of foods by ionizing radiation have been in progress. The work begun at the Massachusetts Institute of Technology

Figure 93. Effect on baking quality of radiation-induced mutant wheat. (Courtesy of International Atomic Energy Agency, Vienna.)

in 1948 has culminated with the acceptance and certification by the Food and Drug Administration, Department of Agriculture, and Department of Defense of half a dozen irradiated foods as safe, nutritious, and suitable for sale to the public.

As laboratory experiments yielded new data on the biological effects of radiation, it was learned that a specific dose could inhibit the sprouting of potatoes and onions. It was also found that higher doses could kill insects and worms, that still higher doses could remove bacteria, and that in the process of irradiation the treated foods remained relatively cool and raw. These observations suggested a new means of food preservation. Table 27 shows the dose range for several food-preservation processes.

Radiation preservation or Radification, the new inclusive term proposed for all irradiation procedures, will not replace such conventional methods as canning, freezing, drying, and pickling, but it could in the near future increase the shelf life of such highly perishable items as shellfish.

For many years, food preserved by irradiation was thought to be toxic and consequently unfit for human consumption. Recently, the U.S. Army Medical Service completed a ten-year study of twenty-one food items. They found no evidence of harm or hazard; nor is there evidence that irradiated foods can cause cancers or mutations.

TABLE 27.

Irradiation dose range required for
various food-preservation processes.

Process	Rads
Inhibition of sprouting carrots, onions, and potatoes	4,000–40,000
Inactivation of trichina (roundworm)	20,000–50,000
Destruction of grain- and cereal-infesting insects	100,000–500,000
Sterilization of foods (removal of all microbes)	2,000,000–5,000,000
Enzyme inactivation	up to 10,000,000

In June 1966, two hundred scientists from twenty-eight countries met in Karlsruhe, West Germany, to review the current status of food preservation by ionizing radiation. They agreed that irradiation did not produce dangerous radioactivity in foods.[10] The participants ate bacon that had been irradiated and kept at room temperature (20 to 38° C) for twenty-one months. The Russian scientists indicated that they hoped to be able to offer irradiated caviar in the next meeting. Thus far, the Soviet Government has released several fruits and vegetables, meats, and meat products for public consumption.

As exponentially growing populations seek to feed themselves on already inadequate food supplies, the potentials of irradiation preservation cannot be overlooked.

Some fifty countries around the world are studying the feasibility of preserving a wide variety of foods by irradiation. In most, including the United States, onions, potatoes, and wheat have been cleared for human consumption (Figure 94). In the Soviet Union and the Netherlands, many additional items are at the point of certification: asparagus, strawberries, mushrooms, and shrimp in the Netherlands, and eviscerated poultry in bags, fried meat, and entrecôte steaks in plastic bags, as well as beef, pork, and rabbit products in the U.S.S.R.

The use of relatively low doses of radiation to remove insects in stored grain is known as disinfestation. Its use to destroy parasites in meat products, food poisoning microbes or pathogens generally, is currently being called radicidation. Partial removal,

Figure 94. Comparison of irradiated and untreated potatoes shows how sprouting is inhibited. (Courtesy of International Atomic Energy Agency, Vienna.)

the reduction of organisms to levels low enough to increase shelf life, formerly called pasteurization, is now termed radurization. The largest doses, used for the total destruction of all microbes to produce a sterile product, is called radappertization. This is an attempt to respect the memory of Nichols Appert, the French confectioner and father of canning. With all due respect to Appert, I would suggest we have enough suitable terms now. There is no need for additional terminology. Nevertheless, the techniques are being developed and foods so processed should be commonplace within five years.

The metabolism of cattle has been studied using tracers that show the pathway of food utilization. Knowledge of this kind is useful for upgrading both milk and beef production. Chapter 5 presents additional uses of radiation that ultimately benefit man.

In industry, the uses of radiation appear limitless: leak detection; measuring liquid levels and thickness; monitoring pipeline flow; actuating cutoff valves; and inspecting the integrity of weldings and castings.

The radiation sterilization of such pharmaceutical products as sutures has advanced to the point where these are commercially available. Human blood vessels and bones that have been sterilized by radiation are successfully used for transplants in many hospitals.

Research into ways of improving the performance of automobile, bus, airplane, and tractor engines has attempted to establish the causes of friction, corrosion, and wear. In the Soviet Union, for example, the use of radioactive piston rings in a single-cylinder diesel engine showed that rings were fully broken in after six hours and that the rate of wear dropped sharply thereafter and remained constant. It was also found that the rate of wear on a piston ring was directly related to the size of dust particles: those measuring 10 to 20μ were the most abrasive.

In the Soviet Union, France, and the United States, large sums of money have been saved in oil-well drilling operations by using radioisotope tracers to track underground water movement and to locate oil-bearing geological formations. Particularly helpful has been the use in France of radioactive sulfur and phosphorus to discover small fissures in rock. This type of information is useful to civil engineers, who can avoid placement of dams in such areas, thereby avoiding dam breaks.

In Japan, radioactive cobalt has been used to study air pollution. Radioactive cobalt sulfate is placed in a smoke stack emitting polluting gases. The cobalt mixes with the effluent and is carried along with it. By taking air samples at various locations, the diffusion of the stack gases can be plotted. If necessary, each stack in a given community can be tagged with a different radioactive tracer so that the polluter can be determined.

In the United States, several new irradiated products are already being mass-produced. For example, the Atlantic Richfield Company is marketing parquet flooring that has been irradiated to produce a stain-resistant surface. Irradiation of fabrics can increase their resistance to soiling and creasing. Fabrics with these qualities are being produced by the Deering-Milliken Company.

Beer drinkers will be happy to learn that Russian investigators who tagged lactic-acid bacteria found a way to reduce the time needed for fermentation from six days to one day, and improved the quality of the beer in the process.

The future holds still more promise. While we must be cautious with this unique source of energy and continue to evaluate its potential for harm, we must not be so circumspect that we fail to take advantage of the great technological advances it may make possible.

The proliferation of nuclear power plants offers an example of just such a possibility. Our country and others place great demands on energy sources and resources. To say we are a power-hungry nation would not be overstating the case. Our need for electric power is doubling every ten years, and until we decide, as a nation, to reduce or limit our requirements, we will need new and clean sources from which to produce it. The nucleus of the atom is one such source.

Few, if any, would dispute the fact that the atom is a tremendous source of energy. But sizable segments of our population are afraid to employ atomic fuel on the wide scale proposed. Four fears appear to concern these people. To many, nuclear power plants are seen as nothing but large nuclear bombs that could "go up" at any time. To others, these power plants represent sources of dangerous airborne radioactivity. Some people are worried lest the disposal of spent fuels become a major hazard. A number of others are primarily concerned about water pollution, specifically in the form of waste heat. They fear rises in water temperature to the detriment of aquatic flora and fauna.

There is little doubt that these are real fears. But are they supported by available evidence?

In a conventional coal- or oil-fired steam generating plant, the firebox serves as the source of heat (and smoke) for converting water to steam. The steam is then directed upon turbine blades, which are connected by driveshaft to a generator. The steam, driving against the turbine blades, rotates them at high speed, enabling the generators to produce electrical energy. A nuclear power plant is much the same, but for the means of heating water to steam.

In place of a firebox (thereby eliminating smoke and with it a source of air pollution) there is a radioactive core. This core is fueled with uranium oxide, which produces great heat as a consequence of a controlled chemico-physical reaction.

All this appears innocuous enough. But what of the fuel? Uranium oxide—U_3O_8—is obtained from the ore, uraninite or pitchblende. As mined, uranium exists as a mixture of ^{235}U and ^{238}U, and it has been estimated that the earth's crust contains 10^{-5} percent (1/100,000th of 1 percent) of uranium of which 0.71 percent is ^{235}U. This isotope is the stuff of which bombs are made.

For energy production, the mixed isotope fuel is satisfactory. But for a bomb, pure ^{235}U is needed—and in critical amounts. Early in the "atomic" years it was learned that ^{238}U tends to capture and thus remove neutrons from circulation. And one of the principles learned at the Los Alamos test site was that samples of ^{235}U less massive than the critical mass would not detonate. From the foregoing, it is reasonable to state that a nuclear power plant has the wrong material to be a bomb.

What of the fear that nuclear power plants will release dangerous radioactivity into the atmosphere? On what grounds is this fear bred and nurtured? Obviously, power plants are not designed to permit escape of radioactive particles. Radioactivity emanating from a power plant must be considered the result of accident. How well designed are these plants and what are the chances for accidental discharge?

A number of nuclear power plants are already operating; they are a familiar sight.* One of their common and most conspicuous features is the dome. Power plants run to a height of some 150 feet, with the dome making up perhaps a third of this height. It is reinforced concrete three to four feet thick with an underliner of vapor-proof steel. Recalling Figure 90, it is highly unlikely that radioactive particles could penetrate this. On the other hand, power plants are built upon and into concrete slabs eight to ten feet thick. Their walls are also reinforced concrete with a thickness similar to that of the dome. And the entire structure is designed to withstand such violent environmental traumas as hurricanes and earthquakes.

Of greatest concern to engineers charged with designing

* As of January 1972, 23 reactors were in operation. Fifty-four are in various stages of completion and another 49 are in the planning stage. Within the next ten years, 120 to 130 nuclear power plants should be an integral part of the landscape. It is the proliferation of these plants, with their number of unknown factors, that engenders anxiety in large numbers of people.

power plants is sudden loss of water used to cool the reactor. Should a water pipe rupture, the fuel rods would heat up precipitously. Although the chain reaction would stop, the uranium would continue to emit its heat—a sizable load. With the lack of cooling water, the fuel rods could melt. Not only is there evidence for this, but it once occurred in the Enrico Fermi reactor in Michigan in 1966. However, no release of radioactivity took place. With this experience as a guide the current generation of nuclear plants has been designed with the steel and concrete as additional safety features to prevent release of radioactive material in the event of a "melt" and subsequent bursting of the reactor core.

There is another source of radioactivity from a plant. This is the planned—not accidental—release of radioactive effluents into the air and water. But this release is based on standards set by the Atomic Energy Commission. It is here that doubt about safety and questions of hazard are most pertinent, because standards are always a source of difference of opinion. Here science must give way to public opinion, as science and scientists do not have the answers necessary to satisfy an anxious public.

At a recent United Nations Atoms for Peace Conference, Professor F. L. Parker of Vanderbilt University concluded that in the year 2000, after what will be a vast increase in nuclear-generated electricity, the total amount of radioactivity produced would still be only one percent of the natural radioactivity emitted by minerals in the soil and cosmic rays.

Disposal of radioactive waste is cause for alarm and anxiety for another segment of the population, which feels that present disposal methods are inadequate and create a hazard to health. Once a year, spent reactor fuel rods must be removed and discarded. The process is not a simple one. Although the rods are spent as fuel sources, they are still "hot" by any standard of radioactivity. Accordingly, they are placed in water to cool. As a consequence of this contact (five months is not unusual) the water becomes a radioactive waste and it too must be discarded. After water cooling, another cooling-off period of up to a year occurs. The rods are allowed to remain fallow in a fuel reprocessing plant. Then they are treated to recover any ^{235}U remaining. It is these operations that produce the waste requiring disposal. At present two procedures account for almost all waste disposal: burial in abandoned salt mines, and burial at sea.

Recently a National Research Council panel concluded after careful study that radioactive materials put into the sea offer little or no hazard to man. The panel, headed by Dr. Allyn H. Seymour of the Laboratory of Radiation Ecology, College of Fisheries, University of Washington, found that although constant monitoring is needed and although safety guidelines are always subject to revision, an extraordinary awareness of radiation hazards has kept radiation levels in the sea well below hazardous levels.

Burial of waste in salt mines a thousand feet below the surface is still in an embryonic stage of development, and as such requires time for monitoring and evaluation. Essentially, it consists of placing the containers in holes or burial pits in the mine floors. These holes are then filled with salt, which, on contact with the heat of the waste, fuses into a solid plug. Leakage from these deep burial grounds is expected to be minimal.*

A question often raised is the effect of waste heat from nuclear reactors on aquatic life in streams receiving water used for cooling. In this instance the dislocation is called thermal pollution. While there is no doubt that nuclear-fired power plants discharge more waste heat than conventional power plants, plans and standards do not allow the heated water to be discharged directly into a watercourse. Heated water has its heat removed by circulation through air-cooled coils, a type of heat exchanger. At present individual states have moved or are moving to establish strict standards to limit the number of degrees a body of water can be elevated by thermal discharge. While this is a move in the right direction, it remains to be seen what technical skills can achieve and what enforcement can attain. Let us hope the two will be compatible.

An ironic twist occurred in the vicinity of the Oyster Creek, New Jersey Nuclear Power Plant. Prior to February 1, 1972,

---

* Plans to bury radioactive waste in the Lyons, Kansas salt mines have now been abandoned. In May 1972, the AEC decided against salt mine burial. It will now dispose of waste in above-ground concrete bunkers. The location has not been specified.

'Well, do you or don't you want me ?'

Figure 95. (*Courtesy Borgstedt, from the Philadelphia* Evening Bulletin.)

the water temperature near the plant was in the fifties. With the closing of the plant for repairs, water temperature dropped to the thirties, killing thousands of white perch, bluegill, and mossbunkers. Normally, these are warm water species that generally swim farther south in the early fall. Apparently nuclear power plants can affect temperature changes up as well as down.

As we survey the nuclear power plant scene, particularly as it is expected to grow in the next ten years, it is obvious that we are dealing with powerful forces and potential dangers. But this does not mean society must or should back away from this new source of power. It does mean that constant vigilance will be required. But that is hardly too great a price to pay for the anticipated benefits.

Figure 95, a political cartoon, exemplifies a widespread attitude that needs to change.

References

1. J. W. Hollingsworth et al., *Medical Findings and Methodology of Studies by the ABCC on Atomic Bomb Survivors in Hiroshima and Nagasaki, in the Use of Vital and Health Statistics for Genetic and Radiation Studies* (New York: United Nations, 1962), pp. 75, 99.

2. Abdul A. Al-Saadi and William H. Beierwalter, "Chromosomal Changes in Rat Thyroid Cells During Iodine Depletion and Repletion," *Cancer Research* 26 (1966): 676.

3. A. D. Bloom et al., "Chromosome Aberrations in Leucocytes of Older Survivors of the Atomic Bombings of Hiroshima and Nagasaki," *The Lancet* 2 (1967): 802.

4. L. Ehrenburg, G. V. Ehrenstein, and A. Hedgran, "Gonadal Temperature and Spontaneous Mutation Rates in Man," *Nature* 180 (1957): 1433.

5. D. Robinson, J. Rock, and M. F. Menkin, "Control of Human Spermatogenesis by Induced Changes in Intrascrotal Temperature," *Journal of the American Medical Association* 204 (1968): 290.

6. J. Clemmesen, "A Doubling of Morbidity from Testis Carcinoma in Copenhagen, 1943–1962," *Acta Pathologica et Microbiologica Scandinavica* 72 (1968): 348.

7. E. S. Weiss et al., "Thyroid Nodularity in Southwestern Utah School Children Exposed to Fallout Radiation," *American Journal of Public Health* 61 (1971): 241.

8. E. L. Green, "Genetic Effects of Radiation on Mammalian Populations," *Annual Review of Genetics* 2 (1968): 87.

9. Alvin M. Weinberg, "Technology and the Life Sciences," *Bioscience* 21 (1971): 1055.

10. *Food Irradiation: Proceedings of a Symposium, Karlsruhe, June 6–10, 1966* (Vienna: International Atomic Energy Agency, 1966). (Publication no. 127.)

Suggested Reading

Basic Radiation Protection Criteria. Report no. 39. Washington: National Council on Radiation Protection and Measurements, 1971.

Coggle, J. E. *Biological Effects of Radiation.* London: Wykeham Publications (The Wykeham Science Series), 1971.

Sterile-Male Technique for Eradication or Control of Harmful Insects. Proceedings of a Panel, Vienna, May 27–31, 1968. Vienna: International Atomic Energy Agency, 1969.

Engineering for Resolution of the Energy-Environment Dilemma: A Summary. Washington: National Academy of Engineering, 1971.

Rhoads, W. A., and Platt, R. B. "Beta Radiation Damage to Vegetation from Close-in Fallout from Two Nuclear Detonations." *Bioscience* 21 (1971): 1121.

Pellerin, P. "Nuclear Power Stations: Environmental Surveillance of Radioactivity." *Bulletin of the International Atomic Energy Agency* 14 (1972): 21.

POPULATION AND PROGRESS

The world is deluged with panaceas, formulas, proposed laws, machineries, ways out, and myriads of solutions. It is significant that every one of these . . . deals with . . . the structure of society, but none concerns the substance itself —the people. This despite the eternal truth of the democratic faith that the solution always lies with the people.

Saul D. Alinsky

With little warning, a cyclone struck the low-lying coastal plain of West Pakistan in November 1970. The fearsome wall of water moved inland and exacted an enormous toll in lives. Estimates of the dead ranged from 300,000 to 500,000. Few could recall a greater catastrophe. Yet by January 1971, the population had rebuilt itself. The fecundity of the people, combined with their disdain for contraceptive measures, rapidly restored their numbers.

At the height of the famine in Ireland during the eighteenth century, the population trebled. Even after the decimation of Europe's population by bubonic plague in the fourteenth century (estimates vary up to 25 million, a quarter of Europe's total population), the population rebounded in twenty years. Famine and pestilence, two of the apocalyptic horsemen, are credited with great destructive potential, yet they are not so great a force as man's ability to procreate.

People have been trying to control or regulate conception ever since the period we call prehistoric. An ancient French cave painting in the Dordogne has been interpreted as showing a man's penis covered by a sheath during coitus. The earliest accepted record of contraceptive efforts is contained in an Egyptian papyrus of the XII dynasty, dating from 1900–1780 B.C., the period of the Middle Kingdom. This scroll contains a prescription for a pessary * made of crocodile dung.

The fact is that until quite recently, nothing has been effective. Not crocodile dung, not honey (to catch sperm), ox gall, pitch, roasted walnuts placed in the bosom, not even swallowing live tadpoles. World population, under the most unfavorable conditions, has continued to increase at phenomenal rates. We have now, however, reached a point where our knowledge of reproductive physiology can turn the tide—if society and national policy deem it expedient or appropriate to do so.

In India, yearly population increases have all but wiped out gains in food production and continue to undermine economic growth. President Indira Gandhi's government will try a new approach to population control. Lottery tickets will be used to attract Indians to operating tables at a new mass sterilization camp in Cochin. A government team of fifty physicians plans on performing 20,000 vasectomies and tubal ligations ** on a regular bi-monthly basis. Every individual sterilized will be paid the equivalent of $13 and will also be given a free ticket for a lottery whose prizes range from $13 to $1300.

As Figure 96 shows, India has the world's second largest population. It is fourth in population density (Figure 97), and second in annual rate of growth (Figure 98). However, uncon-

* A diaphragm for insertion into the vagina as an occlusive contraceptive.

** This will also include excision of a portion of the fallopian tube (tubectomy) as well as ligation, the tying off of a portion of the fallopian tube.

trolled population growth, with its many undesirable by-products, is not limited to India. Within the next 25 years, England will have a population of seventy million. There, government committees are trying to define a population policy by asking what social mechanisms will be needed to meet the pressures on raw materials, the countryside, the transport system, and the environment in general.

In China, with a population density of 204 per square mile as compared to 54 for the rest of the world, the Communist Party has ruled that marriage must wait: the needs of the country come first. Translated, this means the Party intends to stabilize population. For some years, Chou En-lai has been aiming for an annual birth rate of 2 percent or less. Marriage before the age of 28 for men and 25 for women is officially discouraged. Marriage before the ages of 20 and 18, respectively, is illegal. As out-of-wedlock offspring are taboo in China, and as life generally is regulated by the Party, such legal acts can be an effective policy. To drain off sexual energy, long hours of hard work are the rule and

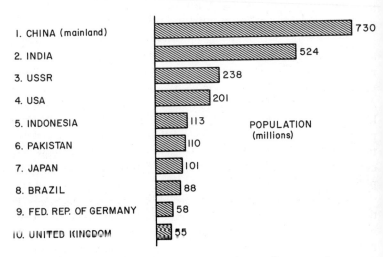

I. CHINA (mainland)	730
2. INDIA	524
3. USSR	238
4. USA	201
5. INDONESIA	113
6. PAKISTAN	110
7. JAPAN	101
8. BRAZIL	88
9. FED. REP. OF GERMANY	58
10. UNITED KINGDOM	55

POPULATION
(millions)

Figure 96. Population figures for the ten largest nations.

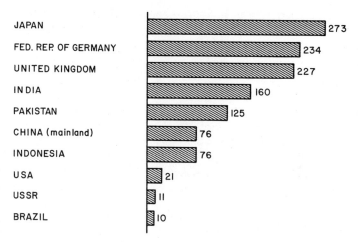

Figure 97. Population density as of 1968 (persons per square kilometer).

to aid in instilling self-control, Chairman Mao's Little Red Book offers abundant advice.

In Java, where the rate of population increase is between 2.8 and 3.0 percent per year, planning such as England is doing is not in sight; culturally, the Indonesians are not equipped to accept and use population controls. You may rightly ask, are we Americans any different? With our high literacy and technical level, why do we appear to be unable to move in the direction of population control, reduction, or limitation? At this point, additional questions must be put: Is such movement necessary or even advisable? Is population directly related to environmental pollution?

In two recent articles in *Literaturnaya Gazeta,* bachelors in the Soviet Union were scolded as traitors to Soviet society, while mothers of ten or more children, the author wrote, should continue to be praised and awarded the mother-heroine award. In Poland, a sharp decline in birth rate has forced officials to under-

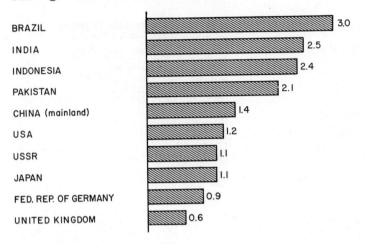

BRAZIL 3.0

INDIA 2.5

INDONESIA 2.4

PAKISTAN 2.1

CHINA (mainland) 1.4

USA 1.2

USSR 1.1

JAPAN 1.1

FED. REP. OF GERMANY 0.9

UNITED KINGDOM 0.6

Figure 98. Annual percent growth (1963–1968).

take an extensive press campaign to attempt to reverse the trend. The work force and the military are in jeopardy. Obviously, more than pollution directs national population policies.

Death rates have been falling rapidly all over the world, but birth rates have barely decreased—in spite of all manner of privation. It is obvious that if the same number of children are born, but fewer die, there must be an "explosion."

Concurrent with the rise in population in Europe and the United States was a development that affected the lives of all of us: the Industrial Revolution. This bloodless revolution not only changed the landscape for all time, substituting a manufacturing for a pastoral society; it also gave more people greater purchasing power. This fact is uniquely important to an understanding of today's problems.

Doubling of population, as Figure 99 indicates, keeps happening faster and faster. It at least doubles the need for food, housing, fuel, sanitary installations (sewage and water treatment plants), schools, hospitals, and the many other things that make for a decent life. These cost great sums of money. The countries

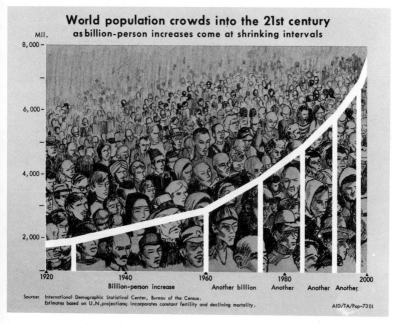

World population crowds into the 21st century
as billion-person increases come at shrinking intervals

1920   1940   1960   1980   2000
              Billion-person increase   Another billion   Another   Another   Another

Source: International Demographic Statistical Center, Bureau of the Census.
Estimates based on U.N.projections; incorporates constant fertility and declining mortality.

AID/TA/Pop-7301

*Figure 99. The ever-steeper population curve. (Courtesy
Agency for International Development.)*

of the West had major population increases during the Industrial
Revolution; and with it they also acquired buying power. Industrialization generated capital and stimulated productivity. As
population increased, its needs could be satisfied. The countries
prospered.

In the underdeveloped countries, population increased without the benefit of industry and its generation of capital. The
general rise in the standard of living that can support increased
population has not occurred in the Middle East, Africa, Central
and South America. A conception of this can be seen in Figure
100. Inadequate food, shelter and clothing—in short, poverty—
are the lot of many of these people.

Only a few years ago, President Lyndon B. Johnson said,
"All the combined production, on all the acres, of all the agriculturally productive nations, will not meet the food needs of the

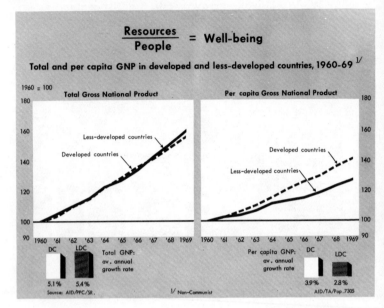

Figure 100. Population growth vs. standard of living. (*Courtesy Agency for International Development.*)

developing nations by 1985." When President Johnson made this statement, he may have had one stark fact in mind: by 1985, the world will have an additional billion people to feed. Two-thirds of that billion will be in the non-industrialized countries! All countries are not experiencing equal rates of population increase. Most of the increase is occurring in the economically depressed countries where the death rate has remained high in spite of the many public health measures seeking to reduce it.

To say that population is increasing while the death rate remains high is not as contradictory as it seems. High death rates are accompanied by even higher birth rates. For the most part, the high death rate occurs among children under five, especially babies less than a year old. These are the periods of greatest vulnerability to infection. The many children who do survive are able to reproduce and add additional numbers to an already bulging population. As a result, when plotted graphically as a trend line, the population shows an almost perpendicular ascent —the so-called population "explosion."

The control of a number of major communicable diseases, such as malaria, yellow fever, sleeping sickness, and typhus, has resulted in a sharp decrease in the deaths of children up to ten years of age. As a consequence, the structure of the population in the underdeveloped countries shows a preponderance of young people. An increasing number of children of school age increases the country's total financial burden. Children are nonproductive members of society; others must work to provide for their needs. More money must be spent on clothing and education and less on food. By comparison, the population structure of a highly industrialized nation reflects the large number of older people. Less than 25 percent of the population is under 30, while some 15 percent is 45 or over. In some underdeveloped countries half the population is under 18.

In the United States today, 97 percent of white females born live to age 20; more than 90 percent live to age 50. It is quite evident that almost no woman dies before she has an opportunity to have children. A similar set of circumstances is building up in many of the economically depressed areas. The reproductive potential is overwhelming. Along with this we must consider the drive of most countries to further reduce their infant mortality rates.

During the 1960s, most writers on the subject of population predicted worldwide famine by 1975.* The available food supply and the rising population were, it was often said, on a collision course and would meet head on by then. President Johnson's remarks were based on such predictions. In the past few years, all that appears to have changed. The green revolution with its "miracle" yields of rice and wheat has been producing bumper

---

* For the past two hundred years, we have been disproving the Reverend Thomas Robert Malthus. Since he wrote *An Essay on the Principles of Population,* the earth's population has increased from 1 billion to approximately 4 billion. The ingenuity of people has undermined Malthus' thesis that limitations on food supply would act as a check on population growth. Scientific and technological developments have enabled us to produce the food we require. But is that the end of the problem? As we now know, rather than increasing at an arithmetic rate, we do so geometrically—which of course is far more dangerous.

harvests in nearly all of the underdeveloped countries. It looks as though food may be available for the hordes of people that will be present in 1985. But what kind of life will these teeming masses lead? Do we want this in the United States or in the world?

By the year 2000, no longer very far away, the population of the United States will be at least 300 million. Figure 101 shows the estimates based on an average of one, two, three, or four children per family. Since this is an increase of 100 million over the current population, it is not idle to speculate on how additional food will be made available.

It is well known that the limits to our land area are fixed. It is also well known that large tracts of land are removed from agricultural use each year by the spreading cities. Greater productivity of land and animal resources must thus be the primary

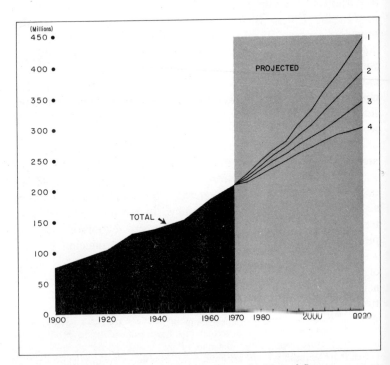

Figure 101. Population trends in the United States.

means of increasing food supply. Projections for the animal (meat) requirements by the year 2000 have been set forth in Table 28. These increases can only come from increased numbers of animals * and improvements in yield per animal. To increase the numbers of animals means breeding for qualities well beyond present genetic capacity. Artificial insemination, after more than twenty years of research, has yet to reach its potential for widespread use of sperm from superior sires. This would go a long way toward achieving production goals by the year 2000.

Cattle normally produce one offspring as a result of each pregnancy. Working out ways to produce twins would be a fantastic biological advance as well as a great support to the level of productivity. Current research suggests that this is a reasonable possibility. But scientists are only on the threshold of this venture. Multiple births would also aid lamb and sheep production. Pigs already produce eight to ten piglets per litter; if this could be increased to 12 or 14, the 33 percent increase would be a remarkable gain.

In addition to meat, a 50 percent increase in crop production will also be needed to feed the additional population. Can our dwindling number of farmers, farms, and acreage rise to this challenge? With crops as well as animals, new high-yielding varieties will be needed. The green revolution that appears to have worked so well for underdeveloped countries will be required for our own. Given our technical capabilities, it seems reasonable to suppose that we will be able to feed the population predicted.

But what of the political, social, and environmental consequences of this population increase? What do we know of these, and what are we prepared to accept for ourselves and our posterity? Are we concerned only with feeding the masses of people? Do we care about the quality of life?

Pollution, poverty, and violence are often seen as the spawn of rapid growth and high population density. From the daily newspapers it appears obvious that New York, Philadelphia, Detroit, Chicago, London, Paris, Rome, New Delhi, Tokyo, and a number of other high density areas are made-to-order breeders of

---

* Increased numbers of animals will, of course, mean increased manure to be disposed of.

TABLE 28.

Projected animal requirements in the year 2000 for a population of 300 million people.*

Product	Probable per capita consumption (lbs.)	Number required	Percent increase or decrease over 1968
Beef	105	53.5 million to slaughter	+ 51
Veal	9	19 million to slaughter	+244
Lamb and mutton	6	36.5 million to slaughter	+301
Pork	75	131.5 million to slaughter	+ 52
Broiler meat	40	4.6 billion	+ 78
Turkey meat	9	180 million	+ 69
Eggs	30 (dozen)	394 million laying hens	+ 25
Milk	610	11 million milking cows	− 22

(* Adapted from *A Good Life for More People*, Yearbook of Agriculture, 1971, U.S. Govt. Printing Office, Washington, D.C.)

the ills of the day. While this may be so, it is far from established fact. In its publication, *Rapid Population Growth,* the National Academy of Sciences said:

> There is no evidence that population growth decreases the level of political stability or increases the probability of conflict and violence and aggressive behavior. . . . One reason for what may be myths about population and political pathology is that population change is ordinarily associated with socio-economic change, and change carries with it the high likelihood of at least some disruption. Some of the characteristic forms of behavior associated in the public mind with high population density may, in fact, be much more significantly related to the prevalence of poverty and discrimination.
>
> Another reason is the neglect of the subject by serious scholars. In the presence of ignorance, the intellectual gap has been filled by opinion. For example, there is a feeling, quite unsupported by evidence, that people in densely populated countries are more prepared to behave in irrational ways and to seek remedies by violence for internal and external problems, because they value human life less. This feeling is supported sometimes by crude biological analogy and over-simplification of the complexities of the interdependency of demographic and social change. . . . clearly, they say, the only antidote to unverified hypotheses applied as guides to public policy or as sources of propaganda is to increase the sophistication of tested knowledge.[1]

Given that the few studies on population density have not demonstrated a direct relationship with social pathology, impacts on loss of personal freedom are not so vague. Japan, with a population density of 250 per square mile, equal to that of China, has had over the centuries to work out an elaborate and rigid system of personal behavior—manners—to compensate for lack of space. Dr. Hale Cook, who spent many years in India as a medical missionary, points out that social conformity tends to increase as population density increases. Most of us in the United States "cling to the pioneer passion for privacy . . . we like to sleep by ourselves, perform bodily functions in privacy, and close out the rest of humanity when we cogitate or study. The Indian villager does not have the opportunity in his simple one- or two-bedroom hut to have much physical privacy. What the Indian does is to create his privacy in his mind: he simply does not 'see' what he knows since earliest childhood he is not supposed to 'see.' An Indian can bathe beside the village well, squat to urinate at the edge of the bus stand, or feed her baby on baby's demand, secure in the knowledge that others simply do not 'see' these things." [2]

It is also worth noting, though little hard data are available to support the observation, that Holland, with one of the highest population densities in Europe, and Hong Kong, a city that literally is swamped by its teeming population, are said to have exceptionally high levels of physical and mental health. There is no doubt that Holland has one of the lowest infant mortality rates of any country in the world. And in Great Britain, where the National Health Service maintains scrupulous health records, it is clear that levels of death and illness are about equal for both urban and rural areas. The question that seems unanswered is whether our problems are the effect of population density or rapid urbanization.

For some, the answer to environmental pollution is people: fewer people, less pollution. On the face of it, this is an appealing and satisfying dictum. Unfortunately, a little more than casual thought finds its very simplicity wanting.

We can point to Lake Erie, the Potomac, and Ohio's Cuyahoga River as clear examples of water pollution. Some would include New York's Hudson River. If our population remained at its current figure of some 210 million, these waters would still be polluted. It should be evident by now that in the Western world sheer numbers are not nearly as important in causing pollution as are the high levels of consumption and the by-products of a highly developed technological society. If the polluted lakes are to have their levels of oxygen increased, it will not come merely by limiting numbers of people. It will come because people want to do it. There is a difference.

At a recent meeting of the American Association for the Advancement of Science, four experts on environment and population were asked to comment on environmental deterioration, the rise in crime, and the increase in per capita cost of government, as consequences of population upsurge.

Dr. Paul Ehrlich, Professor of Biology at Stanford University, cited experiments at Stanford that showed that increased crowding made men more aggressive, although women were not. Thus, he said, crime and disorder can be expected to increase as the population increases. Dr. Barry Commoner, Director of the Center for the Biology of Natural Systems at Washington University, argued that with a properly designed technology the country could support a considerably larger population without damage to the environment. Dr. Garrett Hardin, Professor of Human Ecology at the University of California, Santa Barbara, argued that by the year 2005, when the population of the United States is expected to have doubled, the crime rate will be four times greater than it is today. "The bigger we are, the worse off we are," he said. "The bigger, the poorer."

Dr. Ansley Coale, Director of the Office of Population Research, Princeton University, challenged Dr. Hardin's statements, pointing out that crime rates are also up in states that have lost population. Dr. Coale also cited the San Diego experience. As the population of that community grew toward the million mark, its pollution filled the harbor with sludge, rendered its beaches unfit for swimmers, and drove fish from the bay. But now, with the population exceeding a million, the water is cleaner, the beaches are usable again, and the fish are coming back. The reason, he explained, is that a large sewage plant has reduced discharge of wastes into the bay. Thus, there seems to be economy in size. Large communities can build disposal facilities that result in less per capita pollution than small towns and villages.

Dr. Commoner, reaching for a final word, strongly urged that efforts be focused on technology, which is our hope for improvement. He believed that the population problem is "beyond the reach of scientists and in any case, will take care of itself."

The fact that these experts disagree should be counted a plus. It can be interpreted to mean that thought is being given to these problems. It also indicates that they are not simple problems with simple answers. Black or white will not suffice here. Nor should it be allowed to. Not being an expert, I can comment on the remarks of an expert without feeling great remorse. I cannot agree that population will "take care of itself." If it is to be controlled, checked, or otherwise kept from further "explosion," suitable methods will have to be developed. A number are already available. But none is universally applicable. The "best" is the one an individual or couple will use consistently and effectively. Table 29 shows the types of contraceptive procedures

TABLE 29.
Current available contraceptive procedures.

Method	Effectiveness	Advantages	Disadvantages	Medical risk
Diaphragm	High, particularly with spermicide (about 17.5% failures).	No coital involvement.	Initial medical instruction required; cannot be used by women with certain uterine variations; precoital interference.	None.
Oral contraceptive (progestine estrogen combination)	Extremely high (under 1% failures).	No equipment or coital involvement; improved menses.	Requires motivation and physical checkups; many side effects—major and minor.	Reports of statistical association with thromboembolic disorders; metabolic and liver changes; possible relation to cancer; side effects include depression, weight gain, nausea, vomiting, headaches.
IUD	Extremely high (2.7% failures).	No coital involvement; no continued motivation required.	Requires physician for insertion and checkups; sometimes expelled.	Pelvic inflammatory disease; perforation of uterus; bleeding; cramps; backache.
Vasectomy	100%.	No equipment or coital involvement; no continued motivation required; permanent.	Physician visit required; not always reversible.	None (occasional psychological reaction).

Method	Effectiveness	Advantages	Disadvantages	Risk
Tubal ligation	100%.	No equipment or coital involvement; no continued motivation required; permanent.	Hospital stay required; usually irreversible.	Small surgical risk (occasional psychological reaction).
Postcoital douche	Very low (over 30% failures).	No coital involvement.	Requires bathroom facilities & equipment.	None.
Intercourse during lactation	Very low; ovulation unpredictable.	No equipment or effort needed.	Unreliable.	None.
Coitus interruption	High if practiced correctly (over 18% failures).	No mechanical or chemical equipment required.	Timing essential for effectiveness; often psychologically unacceptable.	None (occasional psychological reactions).
Spermicidal vaginal foam	Low (over 28% failures).	No prescription required.	Messy; precoital involvement.	None.
Calendar rhythm	Fair if practiced correctly (over 24% failures).	Sanctioned by Roman Catholic Church; no prescription or equipment required.	Requires motivation, intelligence, and long periods of abstinence.	None.
Condom	High when used correctly (16% failures).	No prescription required; male's responsibility.	Requires strong motivation; occasional breakage or leakage of semen; some loss of sensation; precoital involvement.	None.

and their estimated efficiencies. Within the next five years a variety of new methods, the prostaglandins * for one, will become available whose efficiency will be as great or greater, and whose purported side effects will be minimal.

As it has been declared a medication rather than a device, the copper-impregnated IUD will require at least five years of testing before it can be released for general use.

"Morning after" pills have been widely written and spoken of. Unfortunately, no such pills are even in clinical trials in the United States. And the once-every-four-weeks injectable contraceptive is no longer considered a practical possibility.

We really need a method that does not require skilled professional management; a method that does not require the services of a physician or trained nurse. Thus far, no such simplified procedure has even been suggested. But one may be available; I hinted at it in Chapter 14. It is known that raising the temperature of the scrotal area just a few degrees can be spermicidal. In India, curiously enough, certain religious groups practice a form of Sitz bath that has a depressing effect on spermatogenesis. Such a simple method might be worth large-scale trials to ascertain its degree of effectiveness.

For the present, an answer to population limitation that avoids racial, ethnic, and religious protestations has been suggested by the demographic studies of Charles F. Westoff and Norman B. Ryder of the Office of Population Research, Princeton University. They found that the rate of population growth would be substantially reduced if unwanted pregnancies alone were eliminated. For the period 1960–1965, 20 percent of all births—4.7 million children—were unwanted. If, as has been calculated, an average of 2.2 children per family would balance births with deaths to achieve a static population, it would come strikingly close to achieving the desired population stabilization, without coercion, laws, licensing, or the drumbeat of the Zero Population Growth movement.

---

* Human seminal fluid is the richest source of prostaglandins as the name indicates, from the prostate glands. Chemically, these are C_{20} fatty acids and at least two currently being investigated, PGF_2 and PGE_2, interrupt gestation by causing uterine contractions following intravenous administration.

The idea of ZPG was first enunciated by Preston Cloud, Chairman of the Cloud Committee of the National Academy of Sciences, which in 1969 produced the report *Resources and Man*. In it, the Committee urged that "efforts to limit population increase in the nation and the world be intensified by whatever means are practicable, working toward a goal of zero rate of growth by the end of the century." It is more likely that ZPG will be achieved because it is inevitable, than by legislation or social revolution.

Dr. Frank Notestein described this "inevitability" most aptly when he wrote, "Anyone who knows how to use a table of logarithms must be aware that in the long run the average rate of population growth will approach zero as a limit. If, for example, the world's population had grown at its present rate since the beginning of the Christian era, the water content of the human race would fill a sphere having a radius more than 10 times that of the earth. Zero growth is, then, not simply a desirable goal, it is the only possibility in a finite world. One cannot object to people who favor the inevitable."[3]

If, again, 2.2 children per family can achieve stabilization, the single-child family, according to the Population Commission, would achieve national disaster.

With single-child families, our population would peak at about 220 million in A.D. 1990, then fall rapidly; 218 million in 2000, 195 million in 2020 and by 2050, 125 million; a population equal to that in 1930. By 2050, sixty-year-olds would outnumber one-year-olds by three to one, and our consumption-based economy would be in disarray. It is not a pretty picture to contemplate.

It is because I feel strongly that control of the population level in and of itself is not the sole answer to environmental deterioration (though there are many among us who contribute to the blight) that I have placed this chapter toward the close of the book rather than at the beginning, where it might be construed as being the primary explanation of our precarious habitat.

Two additional aspects may have a bearing on the handling of the population problem. One is disease control; the second is that rather elusive factor, quality of life.

At a recent meeting of the Association of Teachers of Preventive Medicine (Houston, Texas, October 1970), Professor

Peter Peacock of the University of Alabama's School of Medicine recounted a cautionary tale.

Before coming to the United States, Dr. Peacock lived and practiced in South Africa. Much of his work brought him into intimate contact with native tribes. Over a number of years, he had become a recognized and welcome friend. Before he left South Africa, the chief of one tribe held a celebration for him to thank him for the many good works accomplished for the tribe's health and well-being—sanitary waste disposal, potable drinking water, insect and pest control, decrease in infant mortality. Dr. Peacock left South Africa taking the warmth of their friendship with him.

Late in the 1960s, after an absence of some fifteen years, Dr. Peacock returned. The greeting he received from the chief and the people was less than enthusiastic. The people no longer believed the medical advances were in the tribe's best interest. As a direct result of beneficial environmental changes population had risen explosively; crime, never before a problem, was rampant. Juvenile delinquency, rape, thievery, alcoholism, were breaking up tribal life.

This tale has unnerving implications for medical scientists. For as long as their profession has existed, the underlying credo has been: save life. Today, unsettling new questions are being asked. Is it in society's best interests to terminate life? Are we creating intolerable community conditions by life-saving research?

As a consequence of biomedical and bio-engineering research we have achieved removal of infectious water, food, and airborne disease; pest control; improved nutrition; reduction of infant and maternal mortality rates. Are we to hold our scientists responsible for inadvertently contributing to the population problem? Is it legitimate to suggest, as some are actually doing, that investigations into cancer and diabetes control and prevention of coronary artery disease may be at odds with attempts at population stabilization? The thought is devastating. Medical and biological scientists are about to step into the realm of creation of life itself. Is this in society's best interests? Do these questions need popular discussion? I think they do, if only to clear the consciences of those who believe they work for the public good.

Quality of life, the second factor, while intimately related to this question, is not the same. Although the expression is heard on all sides, it is rarely defined or explained. Just what is meant by "quality of life"? I'm not even sure I can define it for my own personal needs, let alone the needs and desires of others. Will it require a consensus of national opinion to work toward an agreed goal?

The statement that we "need to be healthier," for example, means nothing. Healthier than what? How healthy do we want to be? As long as these questions are only asked, never answered—or, at least, struggled with—our definition of the quality of life desired will remain elusive. Unfortunately, fuzzy thinking and florid writing, however therapeutic, bring us no closer to much-needed answers. One thing is certain: quality of life in an over-populated * community can mean subsistence living conditions. Surely the ability to fill all the stomachs requiring nourishment is not the end of our desires. Subsistence or survival—living on the brink, if you will—appears to be what those opposed to any form of conception control see for us. It is said that the food supply can be made adequate to feed many additional millions; no doubt we have the technical capability to do this. No doubt, too, people can adapt. Hitler's concentration camps amply demonstrated that people can survive under the grimmest conditions. But is grim survival the quality of life we want for one another?

In 1972, results of MIT's Phase One Project on the Predicament of Mankind were reported. (See Chapter 1.) Although the project directors termed the study imperfect, they did indicate the investigation was based on "real world" data. The report contended that the "world cannot wait for perfect models and total understanding." By the year 2100, if current population and industrial growth continue at their present pace, society faces an uncontrollable and disastrous collapse.

Among the predictions they forecast were:

(1) With growing population, industrial capacity rises, along with its demand for oil, metals, and other resources.

* Another concept that badly needs definition.

(2) As wells and mines are exhausted, prices go up, leaving less money for reinvestment in future growth.

(3) Finally, when investment falls below depreciation of manufacturing facilities, the industrial base collapses, along with services and agriculture.

(4) Later, population plunges from lack of food and medical services.

True, these predictions are only the end-product of computer simulated manipulations of variables in the feedback loops, but they do represent as good data as have been presented by anyone thus far. They give us a good deal to ponder.

References

1. *Rapid Population Growth: Consequences and Policy Implications. Summary and Recommendations,* vol. 1 (Baltimore: Johns Hopkins Press, 1971).

2. H. H. Cook, "Impact on Personal Freedom," *Archives of Environmental Health* 19 (1969): 560.

3. F. Notestein, "Zero Population Growth: What Is It?" In *The American Population Debate,* edited by David Callahan (New York: Doubleday, 1971).

Suggested Reading

Blake, J. "Reproductive Motivation and Population Policy." *Bioscience* 21 (1971): 215.

The Food-People Balance. Washington: National Academy of Engineering, 1971.

Djerassi, C. "Fertility Control through Abortion: An Assessment of the Period 1950–1980." *Bulletin of the Atomic Scientists,* January 1972, p. 9.

Fisher, J. L., and Potter, N. *The Effects of Population Growth on Resource Adequacy and Quality,* vol. 2 of *Rapid Population Growth: Consequences and Policy Implications.* Baltimore: Johns Hopkins Press, 1971.

Hardin, G. "The Immorality of Being Softhearted." *The Relevant Scientist* 1 (1971): 7.

Ridker, R. G. "Population and Pollution in the United States." *Science* 176 (1972): 1085.

The clearest expression of the population controversy, as it engages amateurs and professionals alike, can be found in the following two references:

McCracken, S. "The Population Controllers." *Commentary,* May 1972, p. 45.

"Letters from Readers—Responses to Prof. McCracken." *Commentary,* September 1972, p. 10.

THE POLITICS OF POLLUTION

Given the present outlook, only the faithful who believe in miracles from heaven, the optimistic who anticipate super wonders from science, the parochial fortunate who think they can continue to exist on islands of affluence in a sea of world poverty, and the naive who anticipate nothing can look to the future with equanimity.

Philip M. Hauser

When Herman M. Biggs was appointed State Commissioner of Health for New York in 1914, he coined this motto for his department: "Public health is purchasable. Within natural limitations any community can determine its own death rate."

At the time, communicable disease was rampant and the present concepts of community and public health had hardly been thought of. Although his motto was unduly optimistic for its time, it did reflect a fundamental truth: a community or nation largely decides its own destiny.

Today, Biggs' motto would not be considered unrealistic: now people even assume that complete health is their right. Medicine and biology are on the threshold of discovering the essence of life. The classical plagues that regularly took so many lives are now textbook curiosities. And cost no longer makes control of infectious disease an unreachable goal: funds are generally available for almost any community project, no matter how remotely linked with health. Nevertheless, we must ask why urban communities have not attacked their many problems more vigorously? I suspect that there are several formidable impediments.

In the introduction of this book I suggested that prosperity and pollution were coincidental. To population and prosperity I should now like to add politicians and prices. Thus, several major factors that appear to be at the heart of our "troubled cities" are population, prosperity, politicians, and prices. In the discussion that follows, I propose to develop this theme and show the contribution each might make to a satisfying urban life, and how each has contributed to our present precarious habitat. To simplify matters further, I will use the term *pollution* to refer to any and all of the environmental problems covered in the previous chapters.

Pastoral America is a thing of the past. As soon as we swallow and digest this unpalatable idea, the better off we will be. Too many of us continue to think, talk, and act as if ours were an agricultural rather than a technological society. We must begin to act on the conviction that life in the urban setting can be a wholesome experience.

Solutions to problems can at best be only temporary and imperfect, as our communities are continuously evolving. Thus solutions serve for five, ten, or twenty years, by which time yet newer problems will have been perceived. For the most part, solving problems this way will always be hindered by lack of information that invariably requires additional time to acquire. This lack should not prevent decision-making; but those made should not be arbitrary.

It must be emphasized that by all standards we are a healthy people whatever some prefer to believe. As a result of new and improved medical practices the result of greater biological knowledge—fewer people become ill from infectious disease, fewer die at younger ages. More are living on to the biblical three score and ten. The cult of youth notwithstanding, we are well on our way to becoming a nation of older people. Table 30 shows the significant decline of a wide variety of infectious diseases over the past twenty years.

T A B L E 3 0 .
Decline in deaths from infectious disease: 1949–1968.

Disease	Percent decline
Polio	Nearly 100
Whooping cough	Nearly 100
Dysentery	Nearly 100
Syphilis	95
Tuberculosis	88
Hypertensive heart disease	78
Nephrosis and nephritis (kidney diseases)	76
Maternal mortality in childbirth	73
Appendicitis	72
Asthma	58
Acute rheumatic fever, chronic rheumatic heart disease	46
Meningitis	36
Infant mortality	31

(SOURCE: National Center for Health Statistics, U.S. Department of Health, Education and Welfare.)

As a nation, we are healthier than ever before in our history. Mortality rates and infant mortality rates are at their lowest points, while lifespan is increasing with each new generation. Infectious diseases transmitted by food, water, or the airborne route are at the lowest points in our history. Nevertheless, we have become more concerned about health. Health consciousness can mean awareness of the dangers of disease and willingness to protect ourselves against them by, for example, accepting vaccines as they become available, or by visiting a physician routinely. Carried too far, it can also mean an unreasonably morbid fear of the world, rather than comfort in the knowledge that the natural defenses of the body are not easily breached. It is upon these fears that those who would have us believe our communities are perniciously polluted and our survival in doubt, constantly play. While an aroused public may be useful to get things done, there is no justification for misleading scares.

After careful scrutiny of published material, H. E. Stokinger, Chief, Laboratory of Toxicology and Pathology, National Institute for Occupational Safety and Health, U.S. Department of Health, Education and Welfare, developed a list (Table 31) which he believes contains the spectrum of conditions for which there appears to be supportive evidence of an environmental relationship.[1] While these dozen ailments represented Dr. Stokinger's efforts at distilling known from unknown, these cannot be accepted as final and fixed. For example, the relationship between heart disease and "hard" water seems more tenuous each year. On the other hand, asbestosis, not on the list, appears to have a high index of relationship. Here again, the difficulty in pinning down any illness as environmentally related is clear. This should not be interpreted to mean that the relationships don't exist. On the contrary, it only means that the relationships, if they exist, have thus far eluded our best efforts at detection. This is another reason why prevention and control are so difficult.

The longer lifespan and general health of our population mean that many more of us can look forward to living to and beyond age 70. One of the consequences of advanced age is susceptibility to the diseases that manifest themselves in the fifth, sixth, and seventh decades: lung cancer, emphysema, bronchitis, heart disease, and atherosclerosis. Two questions immediately suggest themselves. Are these related to some feature of the environment? And as advances in public health practices and medical science enable more people to reach old age in relatively good mental and physical health, what kind of a life can they look forward to? A greater amount of leisure time than before will be available; in what kind of an environment will it be spent? A substantial part of the answer may depend on the taxpayer. How many of his hard-earned inflationary dollars will each taxpayer be prepared to contribute for control and prevention of environmental pollution?

TABLE 31
Disease states for which evidence points to environmental pollutants as either direct or contributing causes.

Disease	Geographic distribution		Relative incidence index*	Etiologic pollutants and associated conditions	Direct	Contributing
	General	Localized				
Accelerated aging	+		High	Ozone and oxidant air pollutants	+	
Allergic asthma		+	High	Airborne denatured grain protein and other	+	
Cardiovascular disease	+		High	"Hard" waters, hereditary tendency, Cr Chromium deficiency states, CO (?)		+
Atherosclerotic heart disease				Carbon monoxide		
Beryllosis		+	Very low	Airborne Be compounds (Beryllium)	+	
Bronchitis		+	High	Acid gases, particulates, respiratory infection, inclement climate		+

Cancer of the gastrointestinal tract	+	Medium	Carcinogens in food, water, air, and hereditary tendency		+
Cancer of the respiratory tract	+	Medium	Airborne carcinogens and hereditary tendency		+
Dental caries	+	Low	Selenium	+	
Emphysema	+	Medium	Airborne respiratory irritants and familial tendency	+	
Mesothelioma	+	Low	Asbestos and associated trace metals and carcinogens (air, water) (other fibers?)	+	
Methemoglobinemia infant death	+	Low	Water-borne nitrates and nitrites	+	
Renal hypertension	+	Low	Cd in water, food and beverage in As and Selenium areas(?)		+

* A composite index derived from an estimate of incidence, geographic extent and seriousness of effect. (Adapted from The American Industrial Hygiene Association Journal, May-June, 1969.)

The Opinion Research Corporation, Princeton, New Jersey, found that "when the public nationwide is asked what they would be willing to pay per year in added taxes for a substantial improvement in air and water pollution control, about two in three say—nothing."

In the thirty-three years since 1940, the cost of most items has increased three, four, five, and six times. How is the hot dog, which cost five cents in 1940 and is forty cents today, related to public apathy concerning environmental pollution? Similar questions can be asked about the penny postcard of 1940, which now costs six cents, or a Chevrolet sedan that in 1940 cost $730 and currently sells for upwards of $3,000. I suspect there is a real connection. For the most part, these increases have paralleled wage increases. Shortly after his election to a third term in 1941, President Roosevelt signed a new minimum wage law—thirty cents per hour! Now the minimum wage is $2.00 per hour—an increase of almost seven times.

Along with increased wages and costs have come increased taxes, which skim off a substantial portion of our higher wages. To appear affluent and achieve the things that are equated with the "good life"—a TV set or two, a refrigerator, a car or two, dishwashers, clothes washers, a home, and travel, for example—women have had to go to work to increase family incomes, and many men have two jobs. This has engendered a distaste for "giving away" hard-earned money for such intangible, impersonal things as sewage-treatment plants, water pollution control, and the like, when, "after all, I don't pollute the water; I don't pollute the air. Let those who pollute clean up and pay up." These sentiments, heard more and more often, are behind the public apathy concerning control and prevention of community environmental pollution problems. Pollution is not perceived as something individual citizens do; the military-industrial complex is a more convenient and easily identifiable culprit.

It is a fact of political and economic life that people do not want to pay taxes. It is another fact that if they must pay, and pay they must, it shall be as little as possible. As a consequence, little enthusiasm can be generated for community improvement. Dr. Lee E. Farr of the University of Texas, speaking at the annual meeting of the American Medical Association in 1967, said "In general, a citizen will support all measures to control atmospheric pollution until it is pointed out that these measures personally affect him [economically]."

Perhaps it is because of this lack of motivation that attempts are made to associate pollution, however tenuously, with dire consequences to health, in the hope that people will be frightened into action.

That the desire for financial security is of greater urgency than vague threats to health can be seen in most elections. Recently, overburdened taxpayers in Atlanta and Los Angeles, two dissimilar communities, soundly defeated rapid-transit bond issues. A portent of this result may have been visible some months earlier, when voters in Seattle defeated, by large majorities, bond issues for rapid transit and other civic improvements. Bear in mind that rapid transit and air pollution are intimately related.

Several precedents show that it can be beneficial to impose upon a community what is good for it, rather than wait until the community is ready to accept the change. Few people were ready for chlorination of water supplies in the early years of the twentieth century. Some of the older public health officials recall being run out of town by irate citizens who didn't want their water "tampered with." Today, chlorination is well established and is responsible for the precipitous reduction in waterborne disease.

Smallpox and poliomyelitis vaccination also met with much popular resistance. Even at this late date, when these vaccines have proved their value time and time again, many people who should know better refuse to be vaccinated.

It seems that each new advance is met by a refractory public. Fluoridation is a case in point. In community after community, more heat than light was generated by overemotional partisans. In another ten years fluoridation will be accepted as a boon. Similarly, another ten or fifteen years may be needed for taxpayers to grow accustomed to the idea of parting with a portion of their incomes for community pollution problems.

How much control will local politicians be willing to sacrifice, for the greater good of the community, to state and federal "interlopers"? Probably it would be little indeed. How much federal intervention will generally be tolerated? Since the federal government is one of the very few sources of the huge sums needed for carrying out many vital projects, I suspect a good deal of intervention will be grudgingly permitted.

Perhaps it would be useful to accept as much federal intervention as meets Abraham Lincoln's test: "For the legitimate object of government is to do for a community of people whatever they need to have done, but cannot do it all, or cannot so well do for themselves in their separate and individual capacities." The period in which we live no longer permits the kind of thinking that produced the statement, "That government governs best, that governs least." If the federal government has moved into the province of state and local government, these sectors have only themselves to blame. Time and again opportunities to restore their own communities have been allowed to slip by, with the result that pollution has steadily increased.

The report on *Alternatives in Water Management,* by the National Academy of Sciences–National Research Council, states that

> planning carried out in concert—if not always in harmony—among federal, state, local and private interests would not only provide a larger input of diverse views but would as well encourage responsibility for decision. The states, had they fully exercised their voices in development decisions and had they not allowed themselves to be bypassed by federal agencies, might have enlarged and upgraded the staffs and programs of their water agencies and improved their performance in regulation. Full participation by local governments, especially if cost-sharing reforms come to pass, might reduce the tendency to look for federal and state "hand-outs." Greater participation by the private sector could result in better planning and more responsible criticism of public projects.[2]

Whereas the elite of a community, such as business leaders, politicians, ministers, and newspaper editors, try to shape public opinion, it is not until popular impatience reaches a high point that decisions to move on an issue are usually made. For example, although few studies, if any, correlating the objective fact of air pollution with the subjective evaluation of it have been undertaken, I suspect that the two are far from the same. Current attempts to organize community attacks on air polluters are based on the objective fact rather than the subjective perception of it.

Precise measurements of suspended particles or gases mean little to the population at large, particularly when no epidemiological correlations or cause-effect relationships with existing human illness can be shown. An example of the meaninglessness of data on air pollution levels occurred in August 1967, when the U.S. Public Health Service released its findings on levels of pollutants over some of our major cities. A *New York Times* article of August 4 boldly headlined the "fact" that New York City had the highest pollution level in the U.S. Surely this article would reveal information of great personal import to all city dwellers. Not so. It steadily proceeded to dismantle the initial implication by noting that levels of air pollution had little meaning by themselves, that levels in various cities could not be effectively compared because the type of pollutant varied from place to place. Thus, the fact that New York was listed as number one meant nothing—except possibly to the naive reader. The article appeared pointless and hopelessly confusing to the citizen interested in abating pollution. After reading that New York was first, Philadelphia second, and so on, he found that it was of no consequence; pollution levels had no relation to health. Certainly, no one could say that New York was a less healthy city in which to live than Chicago, Detroit, or Los Angeles. On the same subject, it is interesting to consider that in the past ten years, Los Angeles, with photochemically induced smog at least 260 days a year and with one of the country's highest levels of pollution, has the largest population increase of any city in the U.S. Apparently, the existing air pollution is of little concern to the new arrivals: people are influenced more by their subjective perception of air pollution than by the statistics obtained by precisely measuring pollution levels.

While no one cares to live in a dirty community, little meaningful data has been provided to assist the community in improving matters. The fact is that confusion and subjective opinions bordering on personal prejudice have been the daily fare of most city dwellers. If society is to continue to make decisions serving our best interests, clearer, more reliable dissemination of honest information is essential.

Public health authorities in England have a far longer history of dealing with air pollution than our Department of Health, Education and Welfare. After twenty years of intensive study of the effects of sulfur dioxide (SO_2) on health, British authorities have concluded, as they testified to our Congress, that adverse effects to health are thus far unprovable. Yet our Public Health Service continues to push for strong anti-pollution legislation, which it would be empowered to enforce.

Recent legislation set limits on atmospheric SO_2 at 0.1 ppm. To achieve this level requires coal and oil of extremely low sulfur content. In fact, federal buildings in several cities have been ordered to burn coal with sulfur content no higher than 0.2 per cent and fuel oil with sulfur content no higher than 0.3 percent. When one considers that the available coal and oil supplies are 4 percent and 2 percent sulfur, respectively, the technical task of effecting a tenfold reduction is formidable indeed, to say nothing of the increased costs that will ultimately be borne by the consumer. If means were presently available to significantly reduce atmospheric sulfur by controlling stack gases, the zeal of the Department of Health, Education and Welfare in moving Congress to put this law through might have been more understandable. Thus far, however, while several companies scramble to design and produce units that might meet the standards of the law, none have thus far proved feasible. It seems strange that a government agency should attempt to establish standards—not merely guidelines—in areas where reliable evidence of harm does not exist and which existing technology cannot meet.

The New York City Council recently pushed through air pollution regulations barring the burning of solid waste in incinerators in multi-unit dwellings before alternative means were available for disposing of the waste. The Department of Sanitation could not possibly manage the staggering tonnages diverted to it, having some time before reached its peak capacity. When waste lumber was burned on barges off Staten Island, an act manifestly prohibited by law, the pall of smoke drifting over the city forced the harried mayor to comment weakly that allowances had to be made. Allowances must be made when the commissioners of air pollution and sanitation do not keep track of each other's decisions and when laws that cannot be enforced or reasonably complied with are summarily pushed through. While there is a need to regulate and control the amounts of by-products released into the air, standards should be based on a reasonable ability to comply.

CHAIRMAN GUISTO: I think we are all aware of the background of this Fallon Water Supply. As a result of a letter written by the previous health officer it became evident that the Fallon Water Supply had been approved, although its arsenic levels were in excess of the levels adopted by the Health Division.

In essence, in a sense the people of Fallon were drinking un- approved water, if we went by the previously adopted rules and regulations.

Now, since this has come up there has been a great deal of question brought up as to the whole effect of arsenic, whether it is poisonous at the levels that have been suggested or whether the statute should be revised, whether an investigation should be made down in Fallon.

And today's meeting, as I see it, is to see what we can do to bring about a real scientific basis, or some realistic figures as regards the arsenic supply in Fallon.

Now, I would like to have Dr. Carr—by the way, I would like to introduce Dr. Carr. Dr. .Carr, would you stand for a minute. Dr. Carr is now the Acting State Health Officer. As you know, Dr. Crippen has been fired, and Dr. Carr, who is the head of the Crippled Children's and Maternal Health Section, is the Acting State Health Officer, and I have asked Dr. Carr to develop this plan in regards to the Fallon Water Supply. Dr. Carr.

DR. CARR: The plan is basically to study certain people of Fallon—we have to bring into this statisticians and biochemists, sanitary engineers, a number of disciplines, to actually take samples from Fallon residents of all ages and of all water-drinking habits and durations of times that they were residents of this area being served by the community water supply.

It is known that arsenic is gathered by hair and nails, that it is excreted at certain rates in the urine, that it has a certain composition in the blood, and the idea really and simply is to take certain population samples and study the arsenic levels in these tissues and see whether or not the people are being actually affected.

In other words, this particular phase of the study doesn't

consider the standards at all, it considers the people that are there, and this would, of course, be of interest to the people at the Naval Air Station, in addition.

We are taking the position that while the arsenic levels in the water are by the adopted standards high, there are other standards that are even higher and which under long-term and chronic use have not been known to produce chronic arsenic intoxication or arsenosis. For instance, Russia uses a standard of .1 milligram per liter, and there are laws which permit a certain amount of lead arsenate on the surface of apples for spraying. One of these permits 0.4 to 0.6 milligrams of arsenic per apple. Well, an apple a day is supposed to keep the doctor away, and if you have eaten one of these apples you have just drunk yourselves four, five or six liters of Fallon water; so there are a number of things from the statistical point of view which are open to question.

So our idea is to study the patient, people of Fallon, and then, since there has never been any documented evidence of a person being affected, we don't propose to do anything about the existing laws now, we don't feel it is necessary, and this briefly is the situation.

CHAIRMAN GUISTO: Have you set up any program, John, for doing this, and does this require the approval of the people of Fallon, or what kind of cooperation are you—

With these opening remarks, the hearing held by the Nevada Board of Health, In The Matter of Fallon Water Supply, began on March 24, 1969. After 143 pages of testimony, including statements by university and government scientists, physicians, and local citizens, it was apparent that the issue of natural levels of arsenic in its supplies of drinking water was tearing apart the town of Fallon, Nevada.

As a consequence of mandatory standards set by the U.S. Public Health Service, water containing arsenic in excess of 0.05 ppm is considered unfit for drinking. Fallon's water supply varies in arsenic content with the season: levels of 0.05 to 0.22 have been obtained. The issue is whether federal standards are unnecessarily restrictive, given the state of health of the people who live in Fallon and drink its water—and who have done so for as long as Fallon has had people. This issue will be some time in resolving, and in the process many people, and a town, may be hurt. The question of standards and criteria is currently being raised with respect to federal, state, and local laws dealing with noise, water and air pollution, food additives, and a number of other environmental problems. How will they be established? Will the popular enthusiasm of the moment lead legislators and politicians to unrealistic ordinances? That need not be.

In a series of seven commandments, H. E. Stokinger has set out criteria to help any town or group set up reasonable, livable standards for public health.

> Commandment 1: Standards must be based on scientific facts, realistically derived, and not on political feasibility, expediency, emotion of the moment, or unsupported information.
> Commandment 2: All standards, guides, limits and so on, as well as the criteria on which they are based, must be completely documented.
> Commandment 3: Avoid the establishment of unnecessarily severe standards.
> Commandment 4: Determine realistic levels.
> Commandment 5: Interpret the Delaney clause with informed scientific judgment.
> Commandment 6: Determine trends, not pro tempore monitoring.
> Commandment 7: Delimit banning.[3]

Dr. Stokinger did not simply set out commandments. Each one is fully explained. They could go far toward preventing incidents such as occurred in Fallon, or the mercury in tuna fiasco.

It would also be well for standard setters to recall the words of the late Professor W. T. Sedgwick. In his well-known book, *Principles of Sanitary Science and Public Health,* he remarked, "Standards are often the guess of one worker, easily seized upon, quoted and requoted, until they assume the semblance of authority."

The cry for an instant end to pollution is as unreasonable as it is ill-conceived. As the NAS-NRC report *Alternatives in Water Management* pointed out, to end further pollution and control its magnitude in the future will require a great deal of knowledge that is not now available. The report goes on to say that responsible decisions will have to be made about alternative ways to handle a problem. Unilateral political decisions are no longer desirable. Regional preferences based on expediency or leverage or patchwork jobs should be stopped in their tracks by an aroused, indignant, but informed citizenry, who will be capable of weighing the alternatives. Furthermore, homegrown insularity or the inability to think in terms of regional or overall schemes is to be deplored. But this fault is not unique with current planners. Shortsighted men have been around for a long time. The report stated that "while major steps in land and water policy were clearly tied to economic growth and development, a host of laws and policies dealt with particular resources or with particular places, disregarding pleas by Federal Commissions as early as 1907 for integrated development." [4]

Additionally, an ecological approach to environmental health will be necessary if we are to avoid the patchwork solutions so characteristic of past actions. This implies that fragmentation in response to regional or local pressures will have to be avoided. Thus air pollution, water pollution, chemicals in foods, radioactive fallout, and a host of other problems must be considered together rather than as separate problems at separate times.

In this regard it may be well to mention the benefits obtained through regional thinking and planning in West Germany, through the combined efforts of municipal, rural, and industrial water users. In the Ruhr Valley, one of the most intensely industrialized areas of Europe, water-resources associations known as *Genossenschaften* (literally, societies or companies) manage the waters of the Ruhr River and several tributaries of the Rhine to serve industrial, domestic, and recreational needs effectively. The *Genossenschaften* are essentially associations of water users—municipal, rural, and private—that control the volume and quality of water resources. They have, in addition, the power to develop and enact regulations needed to establish and maintain this control. Projected regulations to control pollution or water use are brought before the members and given wide discussion; if accepted, they have the force of law.

Basically, users of Ruhr River water are required to return to the river water of the same quality as that originally removed. The overriding value of the *Genossenschaften* lies in their regional and ecological responsibility. Any activity that can pollute the river, directly or indirectly, comes under their jurisdiction. This includes the use of chemicals, such as pesticides, that can be washed from the land into the water. It also includes all sources of effluents that may be discharged into the water.

If our abused environment is to be delivered from further misuse and perhaps irreversible damage, regional organizations patterned after the *Genossenschaften* may be part of the solution. We would do well to study, and perhaps adopt, some of their methods. Unfortunately, a region has no political or financial base in this country. Without either, preferably both, little movement can be expected in this direction. Nevertheless, the concept requires exploration and wide discussion.

A striking example of the need for federal intervention or regional authority to prevent severe water pollution may be developing in sections of Wyoming, Utah, and Colorado that contain extensive outcroppings of Green River shale, where new sources of petroleum are being developed. Because of the high organic content, up to 65 percent, of these sedimentary rocks, it is anticipated that large quantities of oil can be extracted from them. Estimates of the available oil resources run as high as two thousand billion barrels—enough for five hundred years if demand remains at its current level.

To unlock the oil from the shale, heat treatments in the range of 500° to 550°C (932° to 1020°F) will be required. Simultaneously, there will be produced large quantities of alkaline waste, which if dumped into the Colorado, North Platte, or Green Rivers could catastrophically pollute them.

The shale deposits extend over sixteen thousand square miles of public lands. Because the potential oil resources are valued at literally trillions of dollars, private interests, euphemistically called "developers," are scrambling to get control of these lands from the federal government and stake out claims. Local governments are simply unable to deal with problems of this magnitude. The fact is that only the federal government or a strong non-political regional authority has sufficient power to prevent pollution of the rivers in this area. Unfortunately, history suggests that new oil resources will be developed and rivers will continue to be polluted. And local politics will have played its usual role, in the name of progress and prosperity.

Another melancholy example in this regard will be the neat maneuvers shaping up between the federal government, the state of Minnesota, and rights holders in the Boundary Waters Canoe Area (a million-acre federal wilderness preserve in northwestern Minnesota) as moves are made to exploit the minerals known to be available. Discovery of minerals of significant value will surely join the issue of whether an economic tour de force will have priority over wilderness preservation. If mining in these woods is to be prevented, it will fall to one of the governments, either state or federal, to buy up the privately held rights. Are recreational and wilderness areas high on any list of priorities?

As 1971 passed into history and 1972 appeared, a decision still had not been reached on a case pending in federal court contesting the rights of mineral ownership holders. The original suit was brought by the Izaak Walton League against the mineral-right holders, the U.S. Forest Service, and the Minnesota Department of Natural Resources to enjoin attempts at exploration and mining. The court's decision is eagerly awaited as an indication of how highly valued wilderness is.

On September 10, 1969, the state of Alaska sold to the highest bidders (and there were many) 450,850 acres—both on and off shore of what may well prove to be one of the world's richest oil fields. This 110-mile-wide area, lying between the Brooks Range and the Arctic Ocean, has gained dramatic prominence among oil speculators and the public as the site of a modern-day "black gold" rush.

Never ones to be left at the starting gate, large commercial interests are unabashedly vying for leases that will enable them to tap the five to ten billion or more barrels of oil estimated to lie below the surface. Although Alaska and Alaskans stand to profit handsomely from the purchase of leases—at least a billion dollars added to the state treasury—one can only wonder at the degree of environmental dislocation almost certain to be wrought on this habitat as a result of the various processes required to gain the "black gold."

I also wonder if in the heady and often frenetic atmosphere of speculation over leases for drilling rights, who at the local, state, or federal levels has thought about the potential and actual effects of water and other types of pollution sure to accrue.

Will this be another fatal example of men, money, and machines turning a pristine land to dross? It should be both interesting and instructive to see what attention, if any, is given to the protection of our last outposts.

On May 11, 1972, Secretary of the Interior Rogers C. B. Morton approved a right-of-way permit for the 48-inch, 800-mile-long trans-Alaska pipeline. BP, Arco, Humble, Mobil, Phillips, Union, and American Hess have combined as Alyeska Pipeline Service Company to bring out the oil. It will carry hot oil from Prudhoe Bay to the ice-free port of Valdez. Because little is known about the effect of possible oil spills as well as the hot pipe, additional litigation to overturn Secretary Morton's action is anticipated.

As we see these hands played out—Colorado, Minnesota, Alaska, and others—the Everglades, for example—we will learn in no uncertain terms whether the millions of us striving for a satisfying habitat and felicitous environment are simply talking to ourselves. It will be interesting to watch developments unfold and see whether times have changed sufficiently to prevent the repetition of past indulgences.

Several recent community air pollution experiences offer counsel. We can expect to see communities eager for additional revenues invite industrial corporations to set up operations, without any real concern for waste disposal. Only after the waters around the town or the air above it become intolerable will grumbling be heard. Committees will be formed and petitions circulated, and the long uphill struggle to control further abuses of local resources will begin. Although the lessons of history are writ large, few communities read them.

One of the most crucial aspects of pollution, and one given little thought generally, is the national lack of trained manpower to tackle a host of existing problems.

In his masterful book *Living Resources of the Sea*,[5] Lionel Walford concluded that the most important prerequisite for utilization of the ocean's resources was well-trained manpower. Lack of trained manpower may be the shoal upon which prevention and control of pollution could founder.

At the Solid Wastes Conference held in Chicago in 1963, one of the most trenchant conclusions arrived at after three days of discussing ways and means of solving the solid-waste problem was the need for trained manpower. The President's Science Advisory Committee's Report of the Environmental Pollution Panel (1965) stated that "in the long run improving both numbers and quality of highly trained manpower engaged in key actions from research to enforcement, will do the most for us and merits the highest priority." [6]

Unfortunately, the national attitude on pollution is sluggish. This sluggishness is manifested by businessmen, politicians, and even scientists. The problems of waste disposal, whether solid or liquid, do not excite the inquisitive, creative mind. Waste-disposal research and development is low in status. Thus, it fails to attract the talented people desperately needed. As a consequence, few innovations are brought into the area. The past fifty years have witnessed little change in waste-disposal practices, which is precisely what is desperately needed. Communities want to spend little, if anything, on their waste, particularly with so many other problems that demand a slice of the tax dollar.

Fortunately (or unfortunately, depending upon your point of view), we humans refuse to part with our money without a clear prospect of gain. Can we really say that the prospect of gain has been made clear to those who must eventually pay the bills?

In 1970, the Commission on Obscenity and Pornography attempted to elicit public attitudes on concern over erotic materials. In response to an open-ended question, a number of other problems were mentioned. Pollution turned up halfway down the list (Figure 102).

In 1972, Response Analysis obtained data from a sampling of the general population with respect to problems people believed needed attention (Table 32). Although the two surveys are not comparable as to design and execution, it would appear that concern for the environment has risen slightly, particularly among younger citizens. However, the responses do not call for jubilation or widespread rejoicing.

How many families encourage sons or daughters to pursue careers in sanitation, public health, or the environmental sciences? Few indeed. Yet these are far more immediate community concerns than such luxuries as a billion-volt electron generator.

Certainly few public-spirited citizens, philanthropists, or private foundations set funds aside or campaign for cleaner water;

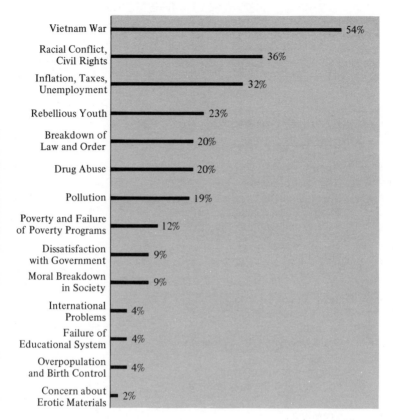

*Figure 102. Spontaneously mentioned national problems.
Question: "Would you please tell me what you think are
the two or three most serious problems facing the country
today?" (Source: Commission on Obscenity and Pornography, 1970.)*

after all, as Roger Starr pointed out recently in his essay "On the
Side of the Cities," "Who wants a sewage-treatment plant named
for him?" [4]

Not only have professional scientists withheld their irreplaceable skills from this area, they have given little thought to the
needs of their own communities. They have not attempted to

TABLE 32.

Local and national problems that need attention.

| | Need attention | |
	All adults	Age 18–25
	2405	741

Mentions in each problem area
  (Percents)

	All adults	Age 18–25
Economy		
High cost of living	21	20
Unemployment	18	18
Taxes	14	7
Poverty and welfare	10	15
International		
Vietnam	43	55
Drugs		
Drugs (nonspecific)	22	17
Availability	17	15
Crack down on sellers (users)	4	5
Problems of modern living		
Pollution and the environment	19	33
Transportation	12	11
Crowding	11	14
Climate of country		
Mistrust of government	12	12
General decline in morals	9	4
Lack of understanding/sympathy	6	6
Crime and law enforcement		
Threats to personal safety	17	14
Police cannot do their job	5	2
Race		
Race problems (general)	14	15
Busing	7	6
Too much discrimination	6	9

Youth
    Recreational facilities   6   9
    Decline of traditional values   5   2
    Criticism of behavior   4   2

Education
    Schools or education inadequate   12   12

(SOURCE: Response Analysis, Research Park, Princeton, N. J.
        1972.)

---

explain to laymen the dimensions, implications, and possible solutions to the varied environmental problems, nor have they attempted to explain *why* science and scientists do not deal in absolutes. Yes or no can never be the scientist's answer. He must be content with shades of gray. It is incumbent on the scientist to explain this and the non-scientist to understand and respect this. Peter Medawar, writing in the Literary Supplement (London *Times*) said it best.

> To what does science owe its power to arrive with certainty at the truth? Science has survived the latter-day realization that it has no such power. The only act which the scientist can execute with logical certainty is the repudiation of what is false. It is time laymen recognized for an embarrassing vulgarism the misleading and damaging belief that scientific inquiry is a cold dispassionate enterprise, bleached of imaginative qualities, and that a scientist is a man who turns the handle of a machine of discovery; for at every level of endeavor scientific research is a passionate undertaking, and the promotion of natural knowledge depends above all else upon a sortie into what can be imagined but is not yet known.[8]

In too many instances, scientists have only added to the din—demanding quick solutions to problems whose outlines were only dimly perceived. And our student body is not without blame. For many students, pollution seems to be something to rail against, but do little about. Many are convinced that the way to solve ecological dislocations is to enroll as sociology, political science, or law students. Few put themselves where it really counts—in chemistry, biology, physics, and engineering courses. It is interesting to speculate on how they believe the clean-up they demand will be accomplished. Who is going to find the answers to the environmental problems? Surely, Blackstone on Torts, the theory of government, or the principles of group dynamics will not determine the effects of DDT, noise, or air pollutants. This is not meant to disparage non-science studies; it does imply that the answers will come primarily through the sciences. But who is to find them if students prefer to argue the merits of this or that approach, rather than get in there and work. Professor Eugene Rabinowitch of The State University of New York at Albany put it squarely when he wrote:

> The only effective defense against knowledge is more knowledge. It is popular today to emphasize the need of counteracting the fear and despair created by exploding technology by restoring the emphasis on the humanities, on ethical value systems. They alone, it is said, could give people stability and strengthen their will to assert themselves against soulless technology. But man cannot return from the maturity of knowledge to the innocence of ignorance. Mankind needs a new sense of values, a new philosophy, perhaps even a new religion, but these must incorporate and not exclude scientific knowledge. We must make full use of and not throw away our technological capabilities. Humanism must learn to use mathematics, and not submerge it once again in a flood of qualitative, emotional responses.[9]

The classical reticence of scientists has, to an uncomfortable degree of late, been superseded by the desire to be heard. This has been painfully evident at a number of large professional scientific meetings. Reporting on the American Association for the Advancement of Science meeting held in Philadelphia in December 1971, the New York *Times* remarked: "All the verbiage is an active reflection of the tone of the meeting: more rhetoric than research." Is it any wonder that the halcyon days of bountiful resources are remembered with envy?

But there are signs that rhetoric, polemics, and simple-minded solutions to complex problems in the scientific community have almost run their course. *Bioscience,* the official journal of the American Institute of Biological Sciences (which includes some two dozen specialized organizations) has thought fit to publish editor John A. Behnke's straightforward reprimand of scientists who have shunned hard work, preferring "emotional flagellations" as a means of solving environmental problems. This seems to be evidence that we may be moving into a period devoted to quiet, hard work—a period dedicated to obtaining the data needed to substantiate claims, opinions, and beliefs given so freely and most often without basis over the past five years. Mr. Behnke evidently saw the malaise as demeaning. "Why," he asked, "must the pressure for scientists to be interested in society's problems lead to blindness to evidence, illogical thinking and irresponsible extrapolation." [10]

It is curious and embarrassing that scientists must be reminded of this. Perhaps this editorial will have a salutary effect. It is not alone in dealing with this theme. Dr. Philip Abelson, editor of *Science,* official journal of the American Association for the Advancement of Science (AAAS) made a remark that, again, one might have thought superfluous. Referring to the UN Conference on the Human Environment he said, "In part, disappointment would be in store because there are no magic wands or quick paths to clean environment, to proper resource management or to solutions of related complex social problems." His next sentence went to the heart of the issue. "One impediment to achieving a livable environment is that we do not really know in quantitative terms what we are trying to achieve." [11] We have already touched on this problem of definition (Chapter 15).

Perhaps we have shied away from some of these hard questions because they are more espoused than defined. But we must deal with these issues. Perhaps we are approaching that time.

Politicians, who presumably believe they have their fingers on the pulse of the community, claim that the meager funds available should be used for housing, welfare, schools, and clinics before they can be used for solid-waste disposal, control of water and air pollution, accident prevention, and noise abatement. These products of industrialization and swelling populations do not appear to have the same urgency as a decent dwelling, three meals a day, and drug abuse. Perhaps this is true.

Even idealists must accept the fact that politics and politicians are intimately involved in solutions to all community problems. An annoying example was recently reported in the *Wall Street Journal*. Although all parties are satisfied that the food additive sodium pyrophosphate (SAPP) is non-toxic, safe to use, it is very likely that it will not obtain USDA certification. Although Assistant Agriculture Secretary Richard Lyng declined to speculate on the fate of SAPP, he was quoted as saying, "Politics will be a factor in this, there isn't any question about that." One has but to recall that decisions so made are a two-edged sword and cut both ways. The consumer gets his way today, but "gets it" tomorrow.

Political maneuvering includes more than just politicians flexing their muscles. At 5 p.m. EST on November 6, 1971, the Atomic Energy Commission detonated its largest underground explosion on Amchitka Island, Alaska. Cannikin, the code name for this hydrogen bomb test (which registered 7.0 on the Richter Scale—equivalent to five million tons of TNT) was itself an "explosion" that reached all the way to the Supreme Court before the real bomb went off.

Opponents of the test forecast environmental calamity; a tsunami (tidal wave); an earthquake; radioactive contamination of the sea. Fortunately, none occurred. Unfortunately, mixed up in the environmental issues were opponents of military development, for the Cannikin test was to give data useful for the Spartan missile, a part of the Safeguard Antiballistic Missile System. Unfortunately too, the vigor of the opposition and the certainty with which predictions of dire consequences were intoned, clearly indicated that those who opposed the test were more eager to flex their muscles and show the political clout they could muster. It may well be that their rhetoric lost for them more than the Cannikin shot.

It is primarily in the more affluent segments of our communities that time and effort can be given to consideration of greenery, open space, pristine brooks, and air free of noxious odors. As is to be expected, all members of any community do not view all problems with equal intensity. Many do not even recognize a number of "problems" as problems. The ranks of those pressing for cleaner skies and water, less noise, lower accident rates, chemical-free foods, banning of pesticides, and the like are composed almost exclusively of the affluent—and that includes students. It is as a result of this skewed group of activists that a major controversy arises.

Among the affluent who have (and have long had) the many benefits of air conditioners, dish and clothes washing machines, TV and radio (2 and 3 units per home), as well as an assortment of devices listed in Chapter 10, there is an increasing demand to limit further growth in electric power generation. Varied reasons are put forth. However, little thought is given to the many people who do not have and have not had the benefits of cooling in the sweltering summer from air conditioners and refrigerators; who have yet to enjoy the benefits of a home clothes washer and dryer. People without them want them. Can they, in good conscience, be denied? I would think not. Before measures to limit electric power generation are accepted unquestioningly, the less than affluent members of our communities should be brought into the discussion.

Priorities are based on urgency. If the land available for waste disposal by New York City runs out by 1975, well, "that's so far away." Who can be bothered now, when so many other concerns demand immediate attention? Who can be seriously concerned with accidents, even though more than 55,000 people were killed on our highways and streets in 1971 and additional millions are maimed or disabled when there are riots in our cities? Besides, accidents are considered fortuitous events that "no one can do anything about anyway." The fact that this is patently false reasoning has no bearing on the matter. As long as such opinions are widely held, the purse strings will not be loosened. G. B. Shaw, not usually given to sparing the feelings of those he considered knaves, rogues, or hot-air artists, said, "There is no harder scientific fact in the world than the fact that belief can be produced in practically unlimited quantity and intensity, without observation or reasoning and even in defiance of both." [12]

In its summary, the Task Force on Environmental Health and Related Problems stated that "as the facts become clear, the public will be shocked at the price it is paying for its affluence." I doubt it; if past experience is any criterion, the bulk of the people will never learn the facts, because there is no mechanism

for bringing them to the public, and because too many othe
concerns are simultaneously demanding attention. And after th
steady pounding of the Cold War since World War II, I suspec
the public has been rendered shockproof.

Politicians who want to remain in public office seem to be
lieve they must go along with public opinion rather than shap
it. But just let state or federal officials attempt to remedy existin
problems and they will set up a hue and cry.

When in the history of man has the general communit
ever been in favor of attempts to upgrade the conditions of life
Advances have usually come through the efforts of a few bol
men who had to struggle against organized opposition and th
inertia of masses of people.

For years, dumping of high-oxygen-demand waste (see Chap
ters 7 and 8) directly from industrial processing plants into river
and streams was permitted by city administrators because c
the weekly payroll that the plant contributed to the financi
well-being of the area. The threat that the plant would mov
elsewhere hung over the mayor's head as he attempted to balanc
water pollution against full employment. Full employment, c
course, regularly won out. Similar conditions prevailed with re
spect to air-polluting industries. (This attitude is depicted in Figur
103.) Someday, we must hope this kind of threat will become
thing of the past. Owing to the efforts of bold men in communitie
throughout the country, fewer towns and cities will welcome pollut
ing industries. Plants will have to clean up their pollution or b
shut down.

Princeton and New Brunswick, New Jersey, for example, re
flect opposing views of what the primary needs of a state are
New Brunswick's mainly laboring population of middle-Europea
immigrants and their children is largely unconcerned with a
pollution, water pollution, noise, accidents, and the host of othe
environmental problems. Their world is the world of immediat
necessities: regular employment, fair wages and hours, housing
and education for their children.

In Princeton, on the other hand, the bulk of the populatio
consists of professionals: university professors, industrial scier
tists, business leaders, and others with time for consideration c
things other than their immediate jobs. For them, the beauty an

Figure 103. "You want business in this town or don't you?" [From The Herblock Gallery *(New York: Simon & Schuster, 1968).]*

charm of the community are of great importance. Air pollution for most Princetonians means "barn smell" from a nearby dairy farm. While air and water pollution have begun to occupy the minds of the governor and the citizens of Mercer County (Princeton), they are of less concern to the citizens of Middlesex, Hudson, and Essex Counties (New Brunswick, Jersey City, Newark), where job security is far more important. Princeton can afford to seek only non-polluting industries; New Brunswick, Jersey City and Newark cannot yet afford that luxury—or so they believe. Little thought is given to long-range concerns; immediate needs are too pressing.

This difference in attitude is not unique to the United States. Developing countries in Africa, Asia, and Latin America, viewing the extent of pollution in the United States, England, France, Germany, the Soviet Union, and Czechoslovakia, are rapidly moving in the same dirty direction, as though there were insufficient examples for them to profit by. Their need to become industrialized apparently permits no concern for the by-products of progress. The harbors and beaches of several of the new African states are already sewage-laden and oil-covered; many of the major cities are overpopulated and slum-ridden. Their credo appears to be, Let us first build; later there will be time for beauty. Will there be?

Although production and productivity are basic tenets of Marxist states, and pollution with environmental deterioration common, it is nevertheless frequently suggested that the way to solve our environmental problems is to substitute socialism for capitalism. State ownership of property, it is contended, should automatically effect a clean-up, since it is more concerned with the public interest. The observable facts, however, do not support the contention that private ownership is inherently more greedy and less capable of putting its house in order.

It is well known that in the Soviet Union managerial capability is judged primarily by ability to increase production. As Goldman so cogently pointed out, "State officials identify with the polluters, not the conservationists, because the polluters will increase economic growth and the prosperity of the region while the antipolluters want to divert resources away from increased pollution. . . . There is almost a political, as well as economic imperative to devour idle resources." On the contrary, he tells us, officials in State Planning, GOSPLAN, "do not have to face a voting constituency which might reflect the conservation point of view . . ."

Although private enterprise has nowhere near the power of a state, it often has greater flexibility and incentive to bend with public pressure. In a socialist state, it is the state that creates pressure and incentive. "If," as Goldman tells us, "the study of environmental disruption in the Soviet Union demonstrates anything, it shows that not private enterprise but industrialization is the primary cause of environmental disruption." [13]

Addressing the Third International Conference on Water Pollution Research held in Munich in 1966, Dr. August Rucker, former Bavarian minister of education and currently a professor at the Technical University, asked if life in the teeming cities of the world would, in the future, be worthwhile. Although Dr. Rucker did not answer his question directly, he discussed the idea of an urban landscape (*stadtlandschaft*), the future shape of the city based on ecological considerations. He predicted that

> the aim to let such an ecological consideration emerge out of the chaos of today will be realized during the period under consideration (2000 A.D.) neither in the advanced, highly industrialized countries, nor in the other ones, since there neither exists decisive legislation which would permit the planning to treat the entire area in an unrestricted way, nor is it to be expected that such legislation, while it has to come will still be passed in time. . . . the idea of the urban landscape is not yet clearly enough established, so as to have sufficiently convincing power for parliaments and governments.

Not a terribly encouraging prospect; nor does it compliment political leaders and planners the world over. Creativity and boldness have never been the genius of committees, but creative individuals can in the final analysis only suggest and advocate: action must come from communities.

At this point, some readers may be ready and waiting for grand solutions to the "urban crisis." Surely, after a discourse on the many problems currently afflicting our cities, a panacea should be offered.

I wish I could say that plans have been drawn and are so far along that, by 1975, we will have attractive cities, free of air and water pollution; that solid wastes will be disposed by methods so sophisticated that landfills will be obsolete; and that life in our central cities will be gratifying. Unfortunately, I cannot say this. There are no instant cures, no ready-made solutions, no panaceas. This does not mean that there is no hope for the future. On the contrary, there is a great deal; but it will take time, and money—lots of money—and a willingness on the part of all the people to see it through. It will also require that members of the community understand the problems they are called upon to consider. This book seeks to serve that need.

At regular intervals during the past several years, there have been predictions and speculation about disastrous environmental calamities as a consequence of continued technological advance with its ravenous use of natural resources as well as its by-products. To consider the evidence for such speculation as well as to plan a comprehensive research investigation of global proportions, a conference study of critical environmental problems was sponsored by MIT and held on the Williams College campus in July 1970. Among the findings and recommendations produced by the seventy participants were the following:

Although the burning of fossil fuels has produced an increase in atmospheric carbon dioxide, the possibility of climatic changes is believed small. They recommended continuous measurement of the carbon dioxide content of the atmosphere. As for the oxygen content of the atmosphere, recent measurements show that over the past sixty years, it has remained constant at 20.900 percent. The group noted, too, that if all of the world's supply of coal, oil, and gas were burned, the oxygen level would be reduced to 20.800 percent. This reduction presumably would have little or no ill effect on human or animal respiration.

Dealing with the issue of DDT's supposed effect on photosynthesis by ocean phytoplankton, the conference members did not expect any significant aberration in the ability of these microscopic plants to convert CO_2 to oxygen. They did go on record as requesting that measurements of DDT concentrations in the oceans be made.

While one should not expect or anticipate the end of speculation about environmental dislocations, it may be edifying to know that concerned scientists are alert to the problems and possibilities, and are beginning to deal with them.

In reviewing remarks made by participants in the conference on "Man and His Future" Professor Peter Medawar noted that "one of the lessons of history is that almost everything one can imagine possible will in fact be done, if it is thought desirable; what we cannot predict is what people are going to think desirable." Let us dwell for a moment on the word *people*. In this context *people* means many people, not simply a few vocal types. If pollution of one type or another is not removed, controlled, or prevented fast enough, it may be well to consider what is being done to motivate large numbers of people to attain the desired goal. I suspect that the referenda regularly voted down in communities around the country indicate that most people do not yet consider these measures desirable.

In his closing remarks Professor Medawar said:

> One thing we might agree upon is that all heroic solutions of social problems are thoroughly undesirable and that we should proceed in society as we do in science. In science we do not leap from hilltop to hilltop, from triumph to triumph, or from discovery to discovery; we proceed by a process of exploration from which we sometimes learn to do better, and this is what we ought to do in social affairs.[14]

Perhaps this statement will dampen the ardor of those seeking quick and easy solutions; I hope not. We need ardor, but along with it we should require sound knowledge; a well-informed, rational citizenry, not a hysterical, anxiety-ridden one, is needed to solve our problems.

In Chapter 10 I mentioned Dr. Goldsmith's critical essay, "Air Pollution Epidemiology." Although he wrote specifically about the need for more discriminating air pollution research to bridge the yawning gap between what are actually established facts and relationships and what is merely believed, his message is universal. The type of investigation and reasoning for which he petitions is directly applicable to any of our environmental problems, and more than likely with salubrious results.

The unpalatable fact is that too often more heat than light is generated by the plethora of unsubstantiated data impeding the resolution of our many problems.

A number of sure steps have been taken that will decidedly be good for the general environment. On the first day of January 1970, Public Law 91-190, the National Environmental Policy Act (NEPA), became law. Because the federal government itself initiates a number of programs throughout our fifty states, it can be a prime source of environmental dislocation. To prevent this, Congress specifically imposed a system of review by which all federal agencies are now required to consider possible environmental consequences of their programs and plans. Failure to observe these procedures places the offending agency in jeopardy of executive, legislative, and judicial challenge.

The Declaration of National Environmental Policy clearly states the intent of Congress.

> SEC. 101 (a) The Congress, recognizing the profound impact of man's activity on the interrelations of all components of the natural environment, particularly the profound influences of population growth, high-density urbanization, industrial expansion, resource exploitation, and new and expanding technological advances and recognizing further the critical importance of restoring and maintaining environmental quality to the overall welfare and development of man, declares that it is the continuing policy of the Federal Government, in cooperation with State and local governments, and other concerned public and private organizations, to use all practicable means and measures, including financial and technical assistance, in a manner calculated to foster and promote the general welfare, to create and maintain conditions under which man and nature can exist in productive harmony, and fulfill the social, economic, and other requirements of present and future generations of Americans.

To back up its intent, Section 102 was written. Here the full force of government can be applied.

> SEC. 102. The Congress authorizes and directs that, to the fullest extent possible: (1) the policies, regulations, and public laws of the United States shall be interpreted and administered in accordance with the policies set forth in this Act, and (2) all agencies of the Federal Government shall—
>
> (A) utilize a systematic, interdisciplinary approach which will insure the integrated use of the natural and social sciences and the environmental design arts in planning and in decision making which may have an impact on man's environment;
>
> (B) identify and develop methods and procedures, in consultation with the Council on Environmental Quality established by title II of this Act, which will insure that presently unquantified environmental amenities and values may be given appropriate consideration in decision making along with economic and technical considerations;
>
> (C) include in every recommendation or report on proposals for legislation and other major Federal actions significantly affecting the quality of the human environment, a detailed statement by the responsible official on—
>
> (i) the environmental impact of the proposed action,

(ii) any adverse environmental effects which cannot be avoided should the proposal be implemented,

(iii) alternatives to the proposed action,

(iv) the relationship between local short-term uses of man's environment and the maintenance and enhancement of long-term productivity, and

(v) any irreversible and irretrievable commitments of resources which would be involved in the proposed action should it be implemented.

PL-91-190 also created the Council on Environmental Quality and placed it in the Executive Office of the President to keep current Congress, the President, and the public on environmental issues.

Having capitulated to the idea that we are no longer a pastoral society, and believing it urgent to be adequately informed about matters scientific and technical, in order to reasonably evaluate programs it is asked to fund, an Office of Technology Assessment is about to be established. OTA will be the fact-finding arm of Congress. Individual technological assessments will be contracted out to ad hoc groups drawn from universities and other technically competent nonprofit organizations. If the OTA fulfills the expectations set for it, repetition of the SST fiasco will not be possible.

Realizing that the earth is finite and that deterioration at one point may have worldwide repercussions, the International Bank for Reconstruction and Development has developed guidelines to be used in appraising potential environmental impacts of economic development projects its funds.

It is now the practice of the World Bank to review each project submitted for funding for possible environmental dislocation as well as the health and well-being of the people in the area of the project. Before a loan is granted to a borrowing country, technically competent teams will evaluate the proposal as part of the loan negotiations.

From all the foregoing it must be clear that highly competent people will be in demand and that a great deal of sound research will be required in the coming years, if any of these policies and organizations are to work.

A book which seeks not specific answers but an overview,

cannot conclude without some attention to the phrase, "a hazard to health," that so often appears in speeches, discussions, lectures, and diatribes on environmental pollution.

To me, this phrase is meaningless, for it implies a desire for a germ-free, illness-free, danger- and risk-free world. Such an implication must be an absurdity. Is it necessary to flee from each environmental factor that may be perceived as a threat? Admittedly, our health and well-being have become much more precious now that lifespan and leisure have markedly increased. But truly, these bodies of ours are not so fragile. It becomes absurd, for example, to develop a "salmonella complex," to avoid the mere presence of salmonella bacteria (see Chapter 3) in dog lollies, chickenfeed, candy bars, and a hundred other products. Is sterility * to be our goal?

The presence of subclinical levels of microbes in food may in fact be a blessing. As with other microorganisms in air and water, subclinical levels may well be sufficiently antigenic to elicit antibody production that can protect us against clinical manifestations of disease.

As it is currently used, the word *contamination* is apparently supposed to conjure up visions of appallingly awful conditions. The fact is that the planet on which we have lived since Adam and Eve met in the Garden has never been biologically, chemically, or physically sterile; therefore, by definition it is contaminated. Populations of microbes are present in the surfaces of our skin; the linings of our mouth, ears, eyes, nose, and throat; the air we breathe; all the oceans, rivers, lakes and streams (which were contaminated long before man appeared on the scene); and all the food we eat—raw, canned, frozen, dehydrated, pickled, and smoked. These microbes are harmless and often beneficial. Surely we are not becoming so confused as to believe that bacteria are our mortal enemies. Every college freshman knows that life on earth would be impossible without the many beneficial activities of microbes.

Too many articles on the environment and its potential hazards to health depend for their effect on highly inflammatory

---

* Sterility is an absolute term. It means the complete absence of life. "Almost sterile" or "partially sterile" is a contradiction in terms.

words. Writers of such articles purposely avoid defining these terms, so that the reader will project his own psychological needs onto them. Some people are revolted by the words *filth* or *filthy,* others by *unclean,* yet others by *taint, dirty, rancid, moldy, odorous,* and, of course, *polluted* and *contaminated.* Although these words are not all synonyms, they are often used as though they were. As generally used, none of them really has anything to do with health or disease. For the most part they are concerned with aesthetics, which is a far different concept. "We live in a dirty

"And grant that I may take into my system only acceptable levels of mercury, cadmium, lead, and sulphur dioxide."

Figure 104. Drawing by Dana Fradon; © 1971 The New Yorker Magazine, Inc.

world" may be suitable as an advertising slogan aimed at our emotions; it is meaningless as far as health is concerned. Tirades composed of inflammatory words that quicken the emotions serve no useful end. They do not clarify; they do not educate; but they often do confuse and mislead.

In an incisive essay, Professor Eugene Rabinowitch commented on this attitude.

> Americans are continuously exposed to speculations about troubles which *could* [italics mine] befall them, of dangers lurking in the food they eat, the cigarettes they breathe; but they have not learned to evaluate such information critically—that means quantitatively—and to react accordingly. They are more scared by possible carcinogenic effects of artificial sweeteners, which threaten to make a few people among millions sick, than his forebears were by an approaching epidemic of plague, black death or cholera, which threatened to wipe out whole populations. . . . The threats of death, insanity, and—somehow, even more fearsome, cancer lurk in all we eat or touch.[16]

Is it any wonder people are worried? And is it any wonder that our humor reflects this anxiety? The cartoon in Figure 104 depicts the current attitude. Although we can smile at it, I'm sure we all offer our own little prayers. But this needn't be. It is neither right nor necessary that in addition to all their other problems, people should suspect and fear the world around them. And the solution to this problem is neither as esoteric nor elusive as might be thought. I heartily agree with Josh Billings: "It isn't ignorance that causes the greatest harm; it's knowin' so darned many things that aren't so."

References

1. H. E. Stokinger, "The Spectre of Today's Environmental Pollution —U.S.A. Brand: New Perspectives from an Old Scout." *Journal of the American Industrial Hygiene Association* 30 (1969): 195.

2. *Alternatives in Water Management* (Washington: NAS-NRC Research Council, 1966). (Publication no. 1408.)

3. H. E. Stokinger, "Sanity in Research and Evaluation of Environmental Health," *Science* 174 (1971): 662.

4. *Alternatives in Water Management.*

5. Lionel A. Walford, *Living Resources of the Sea* (New York: Ronald Press, 1958).

6. President's Science Advisory Committee, Environmental Pollution Panel, *Restoring the Quality of Our Environment* (Washington: Government Printing Office, 1965).

7. Roger Starr, "On the Side of the Cities", Horizon, Autumn 1966.

8. Peter Medawar, "Imagination and Hypothesis," *Times Literary Supplement* (London), October 25, 1963.

9. E. Rabinowitch, "Living Dangerously in the Age of Science," *Bulletin of the Atomic Scientists,* January 1972, p. 6.

10. J. Behnke, editorial in *Bioscience* 22 (1972): 73.

11. P. Abelson, editorial in *Science* 175: (1972).

12. G. B. Shaw, *The Doctor's Dilemma.* In *Representative Modern Plays,* edited by Robert Warnock (Glenview, Illinois: Scott, Forsman, 1964).

13. M. I. Goldman, "The Convergence of Environmental Disruption," *Science* 170 (1970): 37.

14. Peter Medawar, in *Man and His Future: A Ciba Symposium*, edited by Gordon Wolstenholme (London: Churchill, 1963).

15. Rabinowitch, "Living Dangerously."

Suggested Reading

Podhoretz, N. "Doomsday Fears and Modern Life." *Commentary,* October 1971, p. 4.

Wolman, A. "The Environment: Past, Present and Pluperfect." *Journal of the American Waterworks Association* 63 (1971): 651.

Lewin, R. A. "Pollution Is a Dirty Word." *Nature* 231 (1971): 65.

Fraenkel-Conrat, H. "What Threatens Man's Future?" *PHP,* October 1971, p. 26.

Passell, P.; Roberts, M.; Ross, L. Book reviews, "The Limits to Growth," "World Dynamics," "Urban Dynamics." *The New York Times,* April 2, 1972.

Steinfeld, J. L. "Technogenic Disease: The Price of Progress?" *Preventive Medicine* 1 (1972): 222.

Man's Impact on the Global Environment: Report of the Study of Critical Environmental Problems; Assessment and Recommendations for Action. Cambridge: MIT Press, 1971.

The Role of Engineers and Scientists in a National Policy for Technology. Report of the National Science Board. Washington: Government Printing Office, 1972.

INDEX

CAMROSE LUTHERAN COLLEGE
LIBRARY

TD
180
B 45 / 13,066